"This book is an eye-opener for anyone who works with trauma. Understanding, practice, and investigation are all integrated in a brilliant and needed complement to the existing literature."

Alfried Längle, MD, PhD, *professor of psychotherapy at the Sigmund Freud University, Vienna, and the University of Klagenfurt, Austria*

"The field of trauma studies often fails to consider relational and contextual aspects of trauma. *Psychological Growth After Trauma* seeks to correct that, exploring the experience of a variety of traumas, many of which frequently go under the radar. In all these contributions, the phenomenology of traumatic experience is foregrounded and should be a significant resource for therapists trying to avoid adhering too rigidly to the fashionable formulations du jour."

Martin Milton, *professor of counselling psychology and existential psychotherapist*

Psychological Growth After Trauma

Psychological Growth After Trauma is a guide to moving away from assumptions about trauma as a simple form of 'psychological damage.' Each chapter promotes an understanding of difficult experiences as learning opportunities that help us attune to the reality of existence and become more at ease with the truths that trigger our anxieties.

The book holds close to a phenomenological stance in which understanding emerges through experience and reflection. This is not a book that argues for a model that practitioners would be required to adopt and impose on their clients. Instead, *Psychological Growth After Trauma* brings insights and explorations together, allowing the reader to build their own framework for understanding.

Simon Wharne is a chartered counselling psychologist and existential psychotherapist who has experience in clinical practice, leadership, and education.

The Routledge Series in Posttraumatic Growth
Richard G. Tedeschi and Bret A. Moore
Series Editors

The Routledge Series in Posttraumatic Growth includes authored and edited texts that identify and distill the most relevant information for students, practitioners, researchers, organizational leaders, and policy makers in the areas of psychological health, wellness, and growth. Volumes in the series focus primarily on concepts that guide discovery, development, and implementation of interventions that increase psychological strength and flexibility, facilitate health and recovery, and support responses of individuals, communities, and institutions in times of adversity and trauma.

Psychological Growth After Trauma: Insights from Phenomenological Research
Edited by Simon Wharne

Posttraumatic Growth: Theory, Research, and Applications
Richard G. Tedeschi, Jane Shakespeare-Finch, Kanako Taku, and Bret A. Moore

Working with Bereaved Parents: A Practitioner's Guide
Louis A. Gamino

Trauma, Resilience, and Posttraumatic Growth in Frontline Personnel
Edited by Jane Shakespeare-Finch, Paul J. Scully, and Dagmar Bruenig

For more information about this series, please visit: https://www.routledge.com/The-Routledge-Series-in-Posttraumatic-Growth/book-series/TFSE00410

Psychological Growth After Trauma

Insights from Phenomenological Research

Edited by Simon Wharne

Routledge
Taylor & Francis Group

NEW YORK AND LONDON

Designed cover image: Getty Images

First published 2026
by Routledge
605 Third Avenue, New York, NY 10158

and by Routledge
4 Park Square, Milton Park, Abingdon, Oxon, OX14 4RN

Routledge is an imprint of the Taylor & Francis Group, an informa business

Library of Congress Cataloging-in-Publication Data
Names: Wharne, Simon editor
Title: Psychological growth after trauma: insights from phenomenological research / edited by Simon Wharne.
Description: New York, NY: Routledge, 2025. | Series: Routledge series in posttraumatic growth | Includes bibliographical references and index. |
Identifiers: LCCN 2025003579 (print) | LCCN 2025003580 (ebook) | ISBN 9781032791272 hardback | ISBN 9781032791234 paperback | ISBN 9781003493860 ebook
Subjects: LCSH: Psychic trauma | Psychic trauma--Treatment
Classification: LCC BF175.5.P75 P796 2025 (print) | LCC BF175.5.P75 (ebook) | DDC 155.9/3--dc23/eng/20250625
LC record available at https://lccn.loc.gov/2025003579
LC ebook record available at https://lccn.loc.gov/2025003580

ISBN: 9781032791272 (hbk)
ISBN: 9781032791234 (pbk)
ISBN: 9781003493860 (ebk)

DOI: 10.4324/9781003493860

Typeset in Optima
by Deanta Global Publishing Services, Chennai, India

Contents

Foreword

Emmy van Deurzen

An existential approach to trauma is deeply rooted in philosophical under-standing. From an existential perspective, pain and suffering are an inevi-table and inexorable part of human existence. Each of us will encounter trauma of some kind, as we weave our way from birth to death. Karl Jaspers (1951) showed that nobody is exempt from being exposed to the limit situ-ations of death, guilt, struggle, pain, loss, fear, and doubt, though many live in denial of that fact. Each of us will also experience pleasure, health, joy, confidence, creativity, and love, though their negatives always lurk in the shadows, under the surface. Viktor Frankl (1946/2004) spoke of the duty of taking responsibility for your own attitude towards your suffering, to learn to change tragedies into triumphs.

Not all of us are exposed to the intensity of deep emotional trauma that shatters every aspect of your existence and leaves you having to reconsider all you thought you knew or could take for granted. Existential philosophers and novelists have been experts at writing about such tragedies for centu-ries. Their genius has always been to demonstrate that such experiences, which are an attack on human integrity and equanimity, do not create victims, but anguished human beings who are confronted with the essence of the human condition in a very intense manner. When Gustave Flaubert (2014) writes about Madame Bovary's existential crisis, he describes her suffering in all its aspects, and he does not offer her any redemption. He paints the picture of someone who learns about the limits of life. Her husband is described as matured and mellowed by his suffering. Fedor Dostoyevsky, in his novel *Crime and Punishment* (2003), explores how a double murder not only destroys those whose lives have been taken, but also mortally injures the person who committed these crimes. Raskolnikov, the murderer, goes through a deeply traumatic time both before and after the killings, and he is forced to engage in intense reflection on his life and the impossible situation he finds himself in, eventually choosing to expiate his guilt and be punished. Tragic heroes and heroines learn from their traumatic experiences: that is the point of the narrative. Shakespeare's *Hamlet* (2015) is a very poignant example of such learning, as he discovers that weakness, manipulation, and ambition cannot lead to beneficial consequences and that being true to oneself is the only right way forward. Hamlet's final words as he is dying are particularly relevant, as he says: "the rest is silence," thus indicating that the saga has now been resolved and can cease. Tragedy and trauma bring a person to the limit of human existence, where it is all too easy to slide into the abyss, give up, or remain vengeful. The question is whether the protagonist will remain at the edge, crumbling and dissolving into a shadow of their former self, or whether they will be able to cross the frontier to change the narrative and discover new facts of life. This is not just about finding the courage and strength to surmount troubles; it is about achieving mastery over challenges, by understanding them and interpreting them in new and more intelligent ways.

When the body is exposed to extreme trauma, it naturally seeks to heal its wounds and is expert at doing so, especially if there is a safe place in which to rest for a while. Existential wounds are a challenge of a different kind, whether they are brought about by natural disasters, wars, or interpersonal relationships. Going through circumstances that cause an existential crisis, i.e. the collapse of many of the layers of a person's existence, physical, social, personal, and spiritual, is an emergency that calls on all your inner resources. Trauma brings an urgent surge of anxiety in the face of the disaster that you experience. You are called on to find a way to meet and transcend the situation that you find yourself in. Those who, for whatever reason, are unable to face up to the crisis may sink ever deeper into the experience of victimhood, feeling ever more disempowered. But those who pick up the gauntlet thrown down to them often gain more than they have lost in the process (van Deurzen, 2021). You will see in the following pages that there is much evidence that posttraumatic growth is a redemptive reality for many people and that they will later, as the critical period is behind them, point to the catastrophe or calamity they thought impossible to overcome as a turning point in their lives.

This is not to diminish the impact of such traumatic experiences, but rather to see them in a different light and to take them out of the embattled arena of perpetrators and victims and into the therapeutic space of healing, understanding, and resolution. As a bonus, this will lead to greater inner strength and existential resoluteness. When the emphasis shifts from the idea of loss and damage to the possibility of resilience, adaptability, and flexibility, a new moral strength and emotional plasticity are generated. This is not something that can be imposed on another person nor gifted to them, but it is possible for every human being to find this redemptive force for renewal inside, emerging naturally from their trials and tribulations.

At the New School of Psychotherapy and Counselling, existential princi-ples are not just treated as ideas; they are put into practice and are intensely scrutinised and researched. All the chapters in this timely volume, put together so carefully by Simon Wharne, a well-loved teacher supervisor and trainer at the New School, have been derived from doctoral work that students have completed around the theme of trauma. Many students at the New School, and on other programmes, are fascinated to research post-traumatic growth, approaching it from many different angles. In this pro-cess they engage in sensitive and intimate dialogues with those who have been through the mill of emotional ordeals, to gather more information about the manner in which they were able to overcome their plight.

The triangulation of philosophical explorations, clinical work, and research generates fresh understanding of this topic. This is what these papers highlight: that trauma is an intrinsic part of many people's lives and that to learn to live with it is only the beginning of the process. It will become clear too that many people are intuitively capable of transcending traumatic experiences, and that there is much practical wisdom to harvest from their stories. It illustrates that the process of overcoming is quite a lot like that of ecdysis, the emergence of a butterfly from its chrysalis, which it entered as a caterpillar. It is a painful and slow process, but in many ways a necessary and evolutionary one.

Not all those who have experienced emotional trauma will rise like a phoenix from the fire. Some people get stuck in old pain, which they keep reactivating and reviving. The trauma has become part of their identity as a victim, rather than having led to a revision of existence and a new begin-ning. Others who have been through deeply traumatic events will never speak about them as they have become frozen in horror, vanquished by the assault on their integrity. The dead are never able to argue with Nietzsche's famous motto that 'what does not kill me makes me stronger.' Some trauma is lethal and final. This must never be forgotten. There is a wide range in traumatic experiences, and not everyone will end up a hero or a heroine.

The common denominator of the various pieces of existential-phenom-enological research that formed the basis of the chapters of this book was that researchers defined their terms carefully. They were engaged in an intense and open dialogue with their participants to faithfully record their experiences of trauma and the ways they subsequently dealt with it. Putting all these pieces of research side by side, some clear patterns emerge, as summarised in the book's conclusion. We badly need such new insights into the human battle with adversity, as we struggle to find beacons of light in our troubled society.

There are various historical precedents for looking at adversity through the lens of courage and learning, including Hellenistic and Roman stoicism, Zen Buddhism, and Taoism. However, the pages that follow are not a search for an uncomplaining and enduring forbearance of fate. The existential-phenomenological search is not about finding ways to control destiny or foster emotional and mental toughness. It is a search for human truth and better understanding of how human beings overcome personal injuries and how they are altered and educated by their experience. We seek to go beyond the bio-medical approach that regards emotional human suffering as mental illness, by formulating a deeply philosophical and psychological understanding, based in the reality of people's capacity for facing and overcoming big existential challenges.

It will become self-evident as you read through this text that people who are curious to face, rather than avoid or simply react to, their disastrous experiences begin to see their misadventures in a different light. In this process they generate courage and hope in ways that cannot be forced or simply duplicated. It is a mental and emotional journey of transformation that is organic and different for each of them. There are many obstacles along the way, such as resentment, a desire for vengeance, the reality of losses, and the painful truth of life-altering experiences that can never be effaced. The objective is not simply to create scar tissue to repair personal wounds, and it certainly never is to linger in pain any longer than necessary. It is rather to derive new understanding and new ways of living by resolutely facing the treacherous nature of human existence.

What we are seeing is a total change in outlook and expectation. As soon as a person is able to reformulate their experience as an educational path and genuinely sees their life task as one of facing challenges, they begin to be able to take a different stance towards the traumatic times they have been through. It stops defining them as a hostage to fortune and instead creates a new mentality of authority, mastery, and virtuosity. People who are able to harvest the fruits of their bitter years to find that they taste far more sweetly than expected are people who do the work of overcoming and who see their participation in catastrophic events as that which opened their eyes and broke their shell, to expose an inner core far stronger than they ever knew was there. They are indeed the most refined of people in their character, because they went through the mill and were exposed to so much friction and danger that they were ground down very finely. They often remark that when they thought their life had become intolerable, they stopped their special pleading or their hoping against hope that things would ever be different. They sought to meet the reality of the situation and find the best possible response to it. This made them into truth finders and creative explorers for hidden opportunities. It also made them ultra-aware of the fragility of human existence and its preciousness. They stopped trying to sweeten what was sour and learnt to see their crisis as a transition towards something of greater value than they had when they were still living with illusions of continuous happiness. They learnt to tolerate anxiety and uncertainty and ever after were able to appreciate other people's difficulties with a sense of kinship and generosity. Often, they also discovered that a sense of humour allowed them to carry on when they thought they had come to the end of the line.

In short, there is much more to learn from those who have survived trauma than we ever thought. They are a source of information on resilience and human hardiness rather than the saddest cases of victimhood, misery, and affliction. You will find this book uplifting and inspirational and hopefully it will set you, too, on the track of a new kind of exploration, one that will benefit you as much as it will benefit your traumatised clients. For they are not patients, but agents, and authorities on their own fate. They are the unsung heroes and heroines who have gone to conquer previously unexplored areas and who have come back from their purgatory with nuggets of wisdom.

Emmy van Deurzen, Sussex, 2024.

References

Dostoyevsky, F. (2003). *Crime and Punishment* (trans. D. MacDuff). Penguin.

Flaubert, G. (2014). *Madame Bovary: Provincial Lives* (trans. E. Marx-Aveling). Penguin Classics.

Frankl, V. E. (2004). *Man's Search for Meaning*. Ebury (Original work published 1946).

Jaspers, K. (1951). *The Way to Wisdom* (trans. R. Marsheim). Yale University Press.

Shakespeare, W. (2015). *Hamlet*. Penguin.

van Deurzen, E. (2021). *Rising From Existential Crisis: Living Beyond Calamity*. PCCS Books.

Series Editors' Foreword

Richard Tedeschi and Bret A. Moore

The *Routledge Series in Posttraumatic Growth* is a collaboration with the Boulder Crest Institute for Posttraumatic Growth, and is broadly designed to bring together theory, research, and intervention approaches to trauma that use a posttraumatic growth-informed framework. Specifically, the Series includes authored and edited texts that identify and distil the most relevant information for students, practitioners, researchers, organisational leaders, and policy makers in the areas of psychological health, wellness, and growth. Moreover, concepts and topics relevant to the Series guide discovery, development, and implementation of interventions that increase psychological strength and flexibility, facilitate health and recovery, and support responses of individuals, communities, and institutions in times of adversity and trauma. In this volume, noted British psychologist Simon Wharne relies on his decades of clinical experience in the area of psychological trauma and shows us what we can learn about helping individuals recover and grow from adversity through the lenses of phenomenological research.

One of the features of this book that will be most rewarding is the richness of the experiences and understanding the various chapter authors bring to the volume. Even in the book's foreword by famed psychologist and philosopher Emmy van Deurzen, it is evident that the individuals selected to work on this book understand the deep connection between adversity and growth. As van Deurzen notes in her foreword, "pain and suffering are an inevitable and inexorable part of human existence. Each of us will encounter trauma of some kind, as we weave our way from birth to death." As researchers and practitioners in the field of trauma psychology and posttraumatic growth, we appreciate this truth and the real existential challenges individuals face during times of crisis. We also understand the profound psychological changes that occur as a result of one's struggles with these challenges.

Dr. Wharne has compiled a series of expertly written chapters that capture the essence of how humans face and deal with psychological trauma. In the volume's first chapter, Wharne rightly points out that trauma comes in various forms. However, whether trauma arises from natural disasters, illness, death, or the many faces of victimisation, people do not just suffer at the hands of adversity, but rather they find ways to resist, learn, and grow from their experiences. In subsequent chapters, Wharne takes us through key topics such as trauma during childhood and adolescence, interpersonal violence, bereavement, near-death experiences, psychosocial effects of war, and many others. However, the main focus is not on the pathological sequalae of these events, but rather the experiences of hope, strength, and psychological growth. The chapters bring our attention to the phenomenological and existential approach to understanding an individual's reactions to trauma.

The reader will find many, if not all, of this volume's chapters of considerable benefit. Unlike many edited books, this volume flows seamlessly and helps the reader develop in their understanding of the material. This seamlessness is a result of Dr. Wharne's careful selection of chapter authors and his own involvement in the writing of the book. He speaks to you as a colleague, clinical supervisor, and as an educator. The chapters are written as if you were sitting across from the authors and enjoying an expert discussion about their respective chapters.

We are convinced that *Psychological Growth After Trauma: Insights from Phenomenological Research* will be one of the lead textbooks in training future clinicians who work in the area of psychological trauma and who appreciate the capability of people to find meaning and purpose as a result of their struggle with trauma. It will also function as an excellent review for experienced practitioners looking for an easily digestible presentation of the latest science and thinking on the subject.

Richard Tedeschi, PhD and Bret A. Moore, PsyD, ABPP
Boulder Crest Institute for Posttraumatic Growth
Bluemont, Virginia, USA

About the Contributors

Claire Arnold-Baker is the principal of the New School of Psychotherapy and Counselling, a United Kingdom Council of Psychotherapy-registered existential psychotherapist, a Health and Care Professions Council-registered chartered counselling psychologist with the British Psychological Society, and a supervisor and trainer, publishing on existential psychotherapy and on her research into motherhood.

Marc Boaz is an existential psychotherapist and analyst, and a visiting Professor of Mental Health and Psychotherapy at the University of Northampton, UK. He teaches critical psychopathology at the New School of Psychotherapy and Counselling, UK, and is a former founding member of the UK Trauma Council, hosted by the UK charity Anna Freud.

Amy Bramley is an existential psychotherapist with a particular interest in childhood trauma. Her research looks at the lived experience of women who were sexually groomed as adolescents.

Tania D'Aloia is a Health and Care Professions Council-registered counselling psychologist with the British Psychological Society and an existential psychotherapist working with adults in public and private health, including trauma and bereavement services.

Armin Danesh is a United Kingdom Council of Psychotherapy-registered consultant psychotherapist, director of a human rights organisation, and chair of a mental health charity. He worked for over thirty years with refugee families who were traumatised or facing extreme crisis.

Emmy van Deurzen is an existential therapist who developed the existential-phenomenological approach. Emmy founded the New School of Psychotherapy and Counselling, the Society of Existential Analysis, and its *Journal of Existential Analysis* in the UK. Emmy has published widely on existential therapy, has been translated into over twenty-five languages and is president of the worldwide Existential Movement.

Natalie Fraser is a Health and Care Professions Council-registered counselling psychologist, specialising in trauma and sexual violence in research and clinical practice. Natalie founded Existential Offerings and The Global Existential Summits, offering free resources and events.

Susan Iacovou is a Health and Care Professionals Council-registered chartered counselling psychologist with the British Psychological Society and a supervisor, academic, and author. She has been a strategic leader in higher education in psychology/psychotherapy.

Polina Lukanova is a Health and Care Professionals Council-registered chartered counselling psychologist registered with the British Psychological Society, currently working in private practice, with adults who have single or complex trauma, relational difficulties, and ADHD.

April Mangion is a Health and Care Professions Council-registered Chartered Counselling Psychologist with the British Psychological Society. In clinical practice, she currently specialises in ADHD assessment and treatment.

Chloe Paidoussis-Mitchell is a Health and Care Professions Council-registered chartered counselling psychologist with the British Psychological Society and a supervisor and trainer. Chloe is an existential therapy, grief, and trauma specialist, author, coach, and mental health at work expert.

Niklas Serning is a Health and Care Professionals Council-registered chartered counselling psychologist with the British Psychological Society and a supervisor and trainer. He is also a United Kingdom Council of Psychotherapy-registered child and existential psychotherapist, and is a Captain in the British Army.

Jackie Sewell is a Health and Care Professionals Council-registered chartered counselling psychologist with the British Psychological Society, specialising in assessing and treating clients with symptoms of work-related or personal trauma and perfectionism. Previously a management consultant in industry, she is also a leadership coach.

Mary Spring is a psychotherapist and supervisor who has worked as a teacher and a special education needs coordinator. She is a teaching member of the International College for Personal and Professional Development. She has published regularly in Irish psychotherapy journals.

Chapter 1

Introduction: The Possibility of Posttraumatic Growth

Simon Wharne

Introduction

As a human possibility, psychological growth following trauma can be difficult to conceptualise. As a research topic, it is understood in several different theoretical frameworks. It is approached here as it emerges in phenomenological research studies. This means that it is not viewed as a kind of personality trait. There is no attempt to measure it with any form of psychometric scale. It is not reduced to a material thing or variable that we could capture or manipulate. The chapters in this book report on qualitative research studies which aim to reveal how participants experience their existence; when, that is, they endure difficult life circumstances. The reader will find that psychological growth shows up as a phenomenon that is forged through the challenge of coming through those traumas. It is a response to hardships, a way of living with difficult truths, a stance that is taken. When we examine this phenomenon, we do not see a fixed material thing. We see a person who chooses to live life, finding meaning in it, despite the difficulties that they have faced.

Traumas come in many forms. We can find ourselves caught up in natural disasters or accidents, overcome by sudden illness, injury, or bereavement. We might become a victim of crime, or made redundant from our job, become homeless, or subject to forced migration. Often, it is the random and unexpected nature of these events which troubles us the most. When we have become aware that these things can happen, it is difficult to put them behind us. They might happen again, maybe today, maybe tomorrow. Alternatively, we can find ourselves in a society where there are corrosive forms of abuse and discrimination. It is then inherently traumatic just to be born with a dis-preferred identity (Milton, 2017). We experience exclusion and violence and we suffer shame, just because of our ethnicity, religion, sexuality, gender, disability, age, neurodiversity, or other personal characteristic. Traumatic experiences become a part of our everyday existence. Yet somehow, people are not just enduring these traumas; they are

DOI: 10.4324/9781003493860-1

resisting, learning, and they report how they feel they are growing as a person.

This is the claim that we are making, that coming through traumas opens possibilities for learning, growth, and meaning. How, then, do we ensure the validity and reliability of the findings that we are setting out in these chapters? It would be a concern if we were to promote limited understandings, with the unexamined moral assumptions of a narrow cultural setting. One person's view on what psychological growth is can be quite different to that of another. Events that are highly traumatic for one person will be just the way things are for someone else. Academics usually try to overcome this kind of problem by starting with a definition. However, definitions are also built on a historical account of culturally located understandings. Different definitions will be found across societies where varying traditions maintain unexamined implicit beliefs.

If we are uncritical in accepting different accounts, there is a risk of falling into an unhelpful relativist position. It is unlikely that any salient meanings will emerge for us if we take the view that trauma and growth are whatever people say they are. The view taken here is that there is something that we all share in being human, when we face a specific life difficulty or challenge. Existential theory proposes that there are certain givens that everyone faces (Yalom, 1980). We are all encountering other people, making choices, trying to find meaning, and we are all bound within our limited mortality. Then, when we consider the deep impact that trauma can have at a physiological level, we are reminded that we all share a similar embodied biological state (Pitman et al., 2012).

Posttraumatic growth is a phenomenon that is found across cultural settings (Tedeschi et al., 2018; Weiss & Berger, 2010). Growth following trauma is not, however, just one simple thing. Cultural beliefs and different forms of trauma will push us in specific directions (Chen, 2021). Growth, or less favourable outcomes, will occur in complex ways. While the biological aspects of trauma responses can be conceptualised in the terms of evolutionary theory, different cultural norms will mediate the way these are made meaningful and managed (Zefferman & Mathew, 2020). It would not be helpful if we were to impose a 'one-size-fits-all' understanding, and sensitivity to specific cultural understandings is essential (Chen, 2021; Marsella, 2010).

The meaning of what we experience will be framed by our cultural beliefs, shaped by practices within our social group. A shared way of being in relation to historic traumas can be inherited within a cultural group, in cross-generational trauma (Johnson, 2022). However, because traumatic experiences are embedded in our individual biological processes (Pitman et al., 2012), meanings can also be highly personal. The functioning of our embodied state can be difficult to manage, sometimes conflicting with social expectations. This kind of difficulty is likely to be exacerbated by extreme trauma responses. Harmless situations which have a superficial similarity with a previous personal traumatic experience trigger our autonomic physiological systems. Our body goes into panic mode. While everyone else is calm and at ease, we are pulled out from the crowd and isolated in our irrational response.

Tedeschi et al. (2018) describe a model of posttraumatic growth. They identify various changes, expressed in the areas of personal strength, in relating to others, in new possibilities, in appreciation of life, and in personal spirituality. Growth in spirituality can inspire a new philosophic stance, a more engaged encounter with existence (Yalom & Lieberman, 1991). However, again, this is not just one phenomenon. The kind of growth that is experienced will depend on the nature of the trauma. It matters, for example, whether it is a bereavement, personal abuse, discrimination, or a tragic accident. These different traumas will lead to growth in different areas (Shakespeare-Finch & Armstrong, 2010). It is important to remember that many people do not experience any form of psychological growth. Many continue to struggle with the intrusive physiological responses that are associated with Posttraumatic Stress Syndrome and other mental health problems.

Psychological therapies can help, perhaps, to foster posttraumatic growth. However, therapeutic interventions are more often designed to reduce those intrusive physiological responses, conceptualised as 'symptoms.' Psychological growth and reduced symptomology can happen together, or separately (Shakespeare-Finch & Lurie-Beck, 2014). Tedeschi et al. (2018) observe that, for growth to occur, it is necessary for a person to recognise and explore the distressing reality of the trauma. When symptoms are resolved in a rapid return to functioning wellness, a person might miss the opportunity to consider the adverse and negative impact of their trauma. They can then fail to grow in response to that trauma (Shakespeare-Finch & de Dassel, 2009).

In phenomenological research approaches, we do not test models, but some patterns might emerge.

Tedeschi et al. (2018) review their model of posttraumatic growth, a model that was originally developed from phenomenological studies. They do not approach growth as if it were a fixed aspect of personality. They do however review tentative modelling, which links posttraumatic growth with the notion of resilience. This would be a kind of resilience in which we are more prepared for future traumas (Janoff-Bulman, 2004). There is some evidence to support this (Bensimon, 2012), where resilience is conceived of as a personality trait, and some that contradicts this (DeViva et al., 2016; Rodriguez-Rey et al., 2017). Tedeschi et al. (2018) also review the proposal that taking a positive psychological stance might be a maladaptive coping strategy, a form of denial, wishful thinking, or cognitive avoidance (Zoellner & Maercker, 2006). Tedeschi et al. (2018) suggest that, for growth to occur, a person will need to engage in some degree of effortful rumination, in which they remain aware of uncomfortable realities. Phenomenological research is aligned with existential philosophies, in which we are open to these deeper and more troubling truths.

Significant traumatic experiences are likely to bring existential concerns into sharp focus, concerns about issues such as the purpose of living, the inevitability of death, the meaning of each of our unique forms of existence, our situated freedoms, our place in relation to others, and the precarious vulnerability of our embodiment. Ruminating on these things might bring some wisdom (Walsh, 2015), while it is also possible that traumatic experiences are just accelerating a process of growth towards wisdom that we would ordinarily achieve as we mature (Weiss, 2014). If we experience a catastrophic change in our life, we can find that we can no longer sustain our previous beliefs and perspectives. This can be understood as an 'existential shattering' (Janoff-Bulman, 1992), a sense of no longer being anchored in a familiar world (Längle, 2007). We have been shifted into a new level of understanding, an understanding which no longer permits our old ways of being (Tedeschi et al., 2018). However, again it seems likely that a positive change will still require some purposeful rumination. Psychological growth will take time to emerge.

Tedeschi et al. (2018) do not limit their exploration of posttraumatic growth to the individual psychology of the traumatised person. They consider interpersonal dynamics, and this is an aspect of the phenomenon that will be picked up below in this introduction. The relationships between rumination and perceived social support are important (Choi et al., 2019), along with the stage that the person is at in their developing maturity (Xu et al., 2022). The social consequences of speaking up about an experience of trauma can be more distressing than the original event (Taylor, 2011). Traumatic abuse can be deeply embedded within cultural practices. People who survive traumatic abuse might continue to relate to others in a manner that is self-destructive. This would be an outcome of the way of being into which they have been socialised (Brown, 2015). To stand against the abuse can mean a loss of one's familiar way of being, and an alienation from one's family and friends. This is then not just a shattering of a person's world view, but also a dismantling of their social world.

It can be useful to understand trauma as a shattering of beliefs and a de-anchoring from an assumed safe world, but this is a limited conceptualisation. Where a person is a member of a minority group, and they suffer discrimination, it is unlikely that they will experience their world as safe.

Someone might grow up being told that they are inadequate. They might come to understand themselves as: too poor, too physically disabled, or their skin is the wrong colour, or they are the wrong gender, or they have an unacceptable sexuality. Their sense of safety is then already threatened (Gilfus, 1999; Wasco, 2003). These experiences can lead a person to conclude that there are unchangeable aspects of their being by which their exclusion and exposure to danger are justified; this is a form of 'insidious trauma' (Root, 1996).

There are again many complexities. Some people who are a member of a minority group do not experience significant discrimination in their upbringing. Then, when that discrimination occurs, this will be a shattering of their beliefs and a de-anchoring from their assumed safe world. Again, there are people who believe that actions such as excluding and threatening members of minority groups are justified, a familiar aspect of their world. Trauma will be a different experience if they find that they have become a member of one of those excluded groups; if they lose their health, grow old, become impoverished, and so on.

A phenomenological approach will conceptualise the transformational potential of trauma within its dynamics across physical, psychological, social, and spiritual domains. Meanwhile, studies which use quantitative research methods to establish relationships between variables often neglect more useful insights. In the interpretation of research findings, we do not need to treat the person as if they were a fixed thing, with a given nature that we might measure or test in our modelling. In the framework of existential philosophy, the person is responding to the world in which they find themselves; they are a free self-determining agent. We can understand psychological growth as a developing ability to face difficult truths, and to live an authentic life in response to those truths.

Aims

The main aim of this book is to deliver meaningful accounts of what it is like to be human. It is appropriate therefore that, as authors, we bring our own humanity. Each of us has been motivated to conduct research, driven by our own concerns and interests. A lot of work has been done, in the research processes, to identify and challenge assumptions, to overcome bias. However, without emotional investment, we would lack the motivation to work through those arduous research processes. It is appropriate that emotional awareness and related concerns are harnessed. Our findings are not presented as just plain facts. It is hoped instead that they have an impact on you as the reader, that they will stir you up, raise your awareness, and move you. It would be a positive outcome if you became more concerned about suffering in the world and were inspired to attend more to the meaning of psychological growth.

Most research in psychology employs an empirical science methodology, and it is likely that phenomenological research methodologies will be less familiar for many readers. This introduction aims to summarise and explain the philosophical principles behind phenomenological research. Unlike empirical science approaches, a phenomenological study would not edit the humanity of the researcher out of the account. The human condition is not approached as if it were being observed, perhaps, by a rational alien from some other time and place. The methodologies employed by researchers in this book are built on the principle that if you want to understand and find meaning in a person's human experience, you need to be human yourself. However, this does not rule out the possibility of empathetic emotional connection with other animal species, and with our shared planet (Abram, 1996).

I suggest that phenomena, such as trauma, and the possibility of psychological growth will prompt emotional and moral concerns. They cannot be rationalised or separated from systems of human value. They are embedded in our everyday orientation towards what it is that is important for us. They are expressed in varying ethical frameworks in which the meaning of what is happening is debated, disputed, or split between factions. The moral aspects of questions such as 'why do bad things happen?', or 'why have they happened to us?', and 'what should be done in response?' cannot be avoided. I will argue below that the problem for us is not just that a trauma happened. The greater difficulty is found in the task of giving a meaning to that disturbing event, a meaning that we can live with. It is my aim, in this introduction, to orientate the reader to the task of giving meaning. A form of meaning that will unfold for the reader in other chapters.

It is appropriate for psychological researchers to align themselves with emancipatory social movements. In the accounts given here, we approach symptoms of psychological trauma as an understandable and meaningful response to life's challenges. We are not assuming that a person is damaged or mentally ill. Instead, it can be argued that our responses to trauma are a part of our healthy embodied social functioning. When someone experiences hypervigilance, an exaggerated startle response, difficulty sleeping, fatigue, panic attacks, and so on, we can understand that it is evolutionary processes that have brought these responses to trauma into being. The way that we respond to trauma has come about because it has increased the likelihood that our social group will survive, that our children will prosper. The authors of this book are open to exploring this kind of understanding.

It can be argued that trauma responses are not the main problem. Problems develop when these responses are not attended to, not integrated adequately within our social groups. If a source of trauma exists, other people need to be made aware of this so that steps can be taken to reduce further traumatisation. As a society, we need to know that traumatic experiences have occurred, because those experiences are likely to occur for others. We all need to be aware and to do what we can to make changes and to look after each other. At first, a person might just want to go back to how they were before, to feel 'normal' again. It seems unlikely, however, that they can unlearn something which has been driven deeply into their embodied awareness. Yet that awareness has a social value. Problems will arise if an individual awareness is unheard or if an unhelpful interpretation is imposed on that person. As authors of this book, we aim to raise awareness so that we can deal more effectively, collectively, with the phenomenon of trauma in our societies.

The book is written mainly for people who work in the caring professions, although it will be of interest to anyone who has struggled with distressing life events, or those who care about others who struggle. In our contemporary Western societies, our psychological understandings are now informed by the development of Positive Psychology (Ickovics & Park, 1998; Seligman & Csikszentmihalyi, 2000). The notion of posttraumatic growth is popularised, and much is written about resilience (Joseph, 2012; Joseph & Linley, 2006, 2008; Tedeschi & Moore, 2020; Tedeschi et al., 1998, 2018; van Deurzen, 2021). In psychological therapies, the promotion of evidence-based practice has moved towards a compassionate stance in relation to trauma (Gilbert, 2009). The idea is promoted that caring services need to be 'trauma-informed' (Harris & Fallot, 2001; Sweeney et al., 2016). However, more recently, these developments have perhaps neglected to include humanistic and existential understandings (Calhoun & Tedeschi, 2008; Worth, 2022). These person-centred understandings are the foundations on which phenomenological research approaches are built. As authors, we aim to explore and develop these understandings, to bring them into a wider awareness.

Towards an existential understanding

Readers who want simple answers to the complexity of human existence are likely to be disappointed. This book will not be promoting the idea that psychological growth can be caused to come about through the application of standardised therapeutic interventions. In my experience, there are ways of working therapeutically which are more likely to foster this growth. However, people are complex, and the details of their unique ways of being matter. The understandings expressed in humanistic and existential practices include the notion of free will. Clients are free to choose how they respond to their experiences. We cannot claim, therefore, that our therapeutic interventions have caused a change in their disposition. Some therapeutic interventions are found to be generally more helpful than others, but the client can still choose how to respond to them.

There is a principle that, as individuals, people are free to take whatever stance they choose in relation to their suffering, and this is central to existential therapies (Frankl, 1946/2004). Interpersonal freedoms, however, are limited and people will need to accommodate the situated nature of their cultural, embodied, and social context (Merleau-Ponty, 1945/1962). While at the same time, it can be observed that everyone faces similar existential givens. As Irvin Yalom observes, we must all make choices, we are all embodied individually in relationship with others, we will all die, and meanwhile, we must all establish some meaning and purpose in our existence (Yalom, 1980).

The authors who contribute to this book take a phenomenological approach to understanding their topics. In these approaches, there is no attempt to step outside of the location in which the phenomenon presents. We are exploring the question of: 'how does the phenomenon turn up in this specific context?'. It is necessary, therefore, that as researchers, we are familiar with the cultural setting. Each contribution approaches the topic of psychological growth following trauma as it emerges in a certain contemporary setting. The question is extended, therefore, to ask: 'what is it like for this participant to experience that specific trauma, in this particular context?'.

Reflexivity is important in phenomenological research. Robert Stolorow, for example, is a psychotherapist who provides an account of his own response to the death of his wife, in an inspiring philosophical exploration (Stolorow, 2007). He observes how bereavement, as trauma, takes us out of our assumed and expected ways of being. An acute awareness, that someone you care about might cease to exist at any moment, is something that most people are not experiencing. Stolorow's work demonstrates the value of reflexivity, both in research and in clinical practice. Practitioners need to work continually to maintain self-awareness and to develop an understanding of their own motivations and limitations. Your own experiences of trauma will give you access to some understanding, but everyone is different and we cannot assume that we know what it is like for someone else, although there are some broad similarities that are brought about by those shared givens of our human condition (Yalom, 1980).

Stolorow explains that, while everyone else makes plans for how they will spend their time with their loved ones, a bereaved person is suddenly alone and outside of the ordinary flow of everyday life. This traumatised person might long to go back to a time before they became acutely aware of our human fragility and our potential for loss. They might feel a desperate need to take part again in the usual unthinking unawareness of everyday life. They find that it is difficult to envision a future in which they will join in and feel that they are a part of shared social activities. By bringing these things into awareness, Stolorow is helping to connect the bereaved with others who understand their experiences.

We need to challenge the assumption that traumas only happen to some people, along with the idea that psychological damage is an inevitable outcome. What are taken to be symptoms can be understood as an understandable and natural learning process, a response to challenging human realities (Bonanno, 2021). The situations that reveal these challenges can be viewed as learning opportunities, perhaps even a gift (Shiro, 2023).

Phenomenological approaches are employed in research and in existential therapies (van Deurzen, 2010). The authors in this book have conducted their phenomenological enquires while practising as psychological therapists; their research will be a part of their own professional and personal development. Often, the researcher will have chosen a topic related to trauma because they have been affected by that trauma themselves. Traumatic experiences can be isolating and stigmatising. Research is then a valuable means of finding personal meaning and connection. Phenomenological exploration can be healing both in the psychotherapy setting and in research practices.

The way that phenomenological research is conducted has a history, in its own cultural context, which I will introduce here. This account will help the reader to understand that no strong claim is being made about psychological growth following trauma as a universal or material variable. Each chapter is a tentative exploration. It is hoped that, brought together, these explorations enable a more complete picture to emerge. This offers some limited understanding of what psychological growth following trauma might be in a more general sense.

Philosophical underpinnings of phenomenological research

As contributing authors, we have employed research methods that are adapted to the specific topic that each of us addresses. These different phenomenological methods vary in the assumptions that are made, and the processes by which meaning is established in the analysis of data. All these approaches, however, originate in the work of Edmund Husserl. The way Husserl (2006) understood human existence was adapted and refined by his students. Subsequent explorations have refined approaches, at first by thinkers in France, the Netherlands, Canada, and the USA, and then across many other nations. This is the tradition that we inherit today.

Husserl's philosophy is built on the observation that human existence involves consciousness, consciousness that is always directed towards something in the world. This consciousness has intention; it attends to phenomena. It is important to note from the start, that Husserl was not writing about consciousness as a thing in the world that we might study. Neuropsychologists take that task on, but as Maurice Merleau-Ponty observed, conscious perception is not a thing out there in the world, <u>we are conscious perception</u>; it is only through our embodied and located conscious perception that we have access to the world (Merleau-Ponty, 1945/1962). While there are a lot of objective facts listed in scientific journals, for example, these understandings can only ever come into being for us while some person is thinking about them. Otherwise, they remain silent in the books on the shelf and in the datasets on the server. Existence, for us, is always in the present moment, a moment in which our attention is taken up. All the truths, all the awareness or understandings to which we can gain access must be grasped in this moment, before it slides into the next moment, and before it sinks back to become a moment in the past. Consciousness is not a thing; it is an event (Romano, 2009).

If we were able to live in the virtual world of objective data, we might line up all the phenomena in the world, to catalogue and define them. However, as explored in Husserl's later thinking, it is unhelpful to propose one world in this way, as if there is one totality that everyone encounters. He argued that everyone exists in their own 'lifeworld.' Due to our different life experiences, we each attend to different aspects of existence, in our own meaning-making frameworks. Husserl developed this principle from his observation that, when we attend to phenomena, those phenomena are brought into being for us, while, at the same time, we are brought into being in relation to them. We are formed and transformed by the phenomena we encounter in our existence. The impact that traumatic experiences have on us is clear evidence in support of this. Merleau-Ponty extended this observation, noting how we attach emotional value to phenomena. When we are moved by what we perceive, this is, as Merleau-Ponty explains, a literal move in our way of being (Merleau-Ponty, 1945/1962).

Existential thinkers have debated the question of whether consciousness is individual, or shared and intersubjective. Jean-Paul Sartre and Simone de Beauvoir often discussed the notion of the gaze. When we are alone, we might be seeing the world from our own point of view. However, whenever someone else is present, we sense that the world is being observed also from their point of view. We are aware that we are seen by them, as an aspect of their world. For Sartre, this meant that people can only ever alternate between a state of being an object in the eyes of someone else, or as the observer who is making that other person an object under their own gaze (Sartre, 1943/1958). The debate was based in philosophical questions inherited from Georg Wilhelm Fredrich Hegel, concerning power dynamics in relationships. It is also expressed in the notion of 'theory of mind,' related to a question posed in analytic philosophy, as to how we can know what is in the mind of another person (Gallagher, 2009).

When Husserl placed the 'consciousness of something' at the centre of his thinking, he was working to overcome the philosophical problem of duality between mind and body. This problem is encountered when we assume that there is one world with different kinds of people in it. We are imagining that we can see this world from a universal disembodied position. We imagine that there is a form of normality, from which different people deviate. In contrast to this, Merleau-Ponty developed Husserl's thinking to observe how consciousness is embodied, and intersubjective (Merleau-Ponty, 1945/1962). For Merleau-Ponty, it is in our shared intersubjective encounters with phenomena that meanings and values emerge for us. For example, with our modern technology we can calculate the exact value of a currency at any point in time. It is easy to forget that money is an abstract cultural construction. A monetary token only has a given value for us within the emotional volatility of our collective everyday human responses. This is demonstrated in the reoccurrence of international financial crises.

The idea of an embodied and intersubjective consciousness is useful for addressing questions of value and moral concerns. There are many moral concerns raised by the accounts given in the following chapters. Traumatic experiences are described, revealing the dilemmas participants face, when they must take a stance towards what has happened. Our understanding of these situations can be informed by considering several aspects of existential philosophy. It is likely that traumatic experiences will constitute 'boundary situations,' as described by Carl Jaspers (Jaspers, 1970). When we are in a traumatic situation, our options are constrained by what is happening. We are brought up against the nature of our world, becoming more aware of the limitations of our existence. We might long to be free of these constraints. However, 'situated freedom' is a key concept here. Freedom is only experienced in situations where specific choices are opened for us, and others are closed.

In our social relationships, it is only because we are free that we can be held to account for what we decide to do. While also, we can only have choices when we are in situations, which, of course, we always are. If we do manage to get out of an intolerable situation, we will find ourselves in a new situation, which might be just as difficult. We attach value to people, to events, to phenomena, and this is revealed in situations when we make choices about what it is that is important to us. When we feel envy, desire, and resentment, for example, this reveals the value of things that we do not possess. In an experience of posttraumatic growth, however, we will have adopted a different set of values. When that occurs, we feel grateful and closer to others, living a simpler life and being more present in the moment (Linley & Joseph, 2007; Tedeschi et al., 2018).

We experience a brush with death, an injury, a serious illness, a loss of social role, a loss of security, or a loss of meaning. We are suddenly adrift and acutely aware of the finite limits of our existence, our fragility, and our powerlessness; we are de-anchored (Längle, 2007). This can be understood as an existential shattering (Greening, 1992; Hoffman & Vallejos, 2019). Our values and our concerns can be transformed by these traumas (Jacobsen, 2006; Janoff-Bulman, 1992). Even when the trauma confirms our expectations in terms of discrimination and exclusion, this is still a challenging experience (Helms et al., 2012). We can experience the state and its institutions as complicit in the trauma that we have experienced, and we might resist the imposed interpretation that we are now a victim, subject to irresistible oppression (Burstow, 2003). From this perspective, understanding our responses to trauma as a kind of 'psychological deficit' can be unhelpful. It might be experienced instead as an inspiration, something which sparks a social or political movement. Meanwhile, all this takes place in relationships with others, prompting questions about moral responsibility, social status, as well as our sense of personal value (Boaz, 2022; Du Toit, 2017; Everly & Lating, 2004). It is important, therefore, that psychological therapists are open to exploring concerns that are prompted by trauma and social crisis (Hoffman, 2021).

Western philosophy has sought universal moral laws by which to define and judge people. A different form of ethics can be drawn from the empathetic emotional connectivity that is experienced in intersubjective consciousness (Daly, 2016; de Beauvoir, 1949/2015). In the notion of intersubjectivity, as developed by Edith Stein and Maurice Merleau-Ponty, consciousness is already shared. To some degree, we already have a direct awareness of the emotional disposition and ways of being of others (Gallagher, 2009). Edith Stein (1921/1989) explains how it is that we are together with others always and only in the present moment. It is only through imagination that we recall what has happened in the past and orientate to what might happen in the future.

While the individual nature of our being is evident to us in the present, imagined past and present selves are a matter of conjecture and interpretation. We talk together about who we might have been, who we might become. When events require that one of us steps forward, initially we all feel pulled towards a shared commitment and invested in it. In traumatic events such as accidents, wars, natural disasters, and forced migration, everyone's future self is in question. Will we be the hero who helps others, the martyr perhaps, or will we survive thanks to our selfishness? No one knows who they will become. For Stein, our possible past and future selves are just that, just possibilities (Stein, 1921/1989).

Empathy, as explored by Stein and Merleau-Ponty, includes a flow of emotionality. For Stein, there are levels of empathetic connection. The problem is not just that we might fail to understand the thoughts and feelings of the other person. There is also the risk that we might fail to maintain a distinction between their thoughts and feelings and our own. We might be taken up by an emotional connection to the degree that we will act unreflectively in the other person's interests, at the expense of our own (Stein, 1921/1989). The research presented in this book has been conducted with emotional awareness. Great care is taken to ensure, as much as possible, that it is the research participant's experience that is brought into awareness. The researcher and their participant are likely to be changed, transformed to some degree by the encounter, as understandings are developed. It is hoped that, by reading these accounts, you as the reader will also be transformed. Again, it is important to note that we are not measuring people as fixed objects; we are working with the transformational nature of empathetic understanding. The research findings that are revealed for you are brought into awareness through the researcher's capacity for empathetic connection with their participant's experiences.

Phenomenological research approaches usually attend to transcripts taken from interviews. To some degree, the data that are analysed include the original experiences that participants have described in the interviews. Some approaches stay with a close description of those experiences (Giorgi, 2009). Other approaches place more emphasis on the encounter between the researcher and the participant (van Manen, 1990). Some attend to the way that ideologies are imposed in the use of language (Langdridge, 2009). Some attend to embodied feelings, attempting to recover memories of the phenomena (Bitbol & Petitmengin, 2017). In these approaches, it is the transcribed record of what was said that is studied in detail, and an exploration can be conducted in a rigorous and systematic manner (Smith et al., 2022). The concern remains that we can never go back into the past; we cannot re-encounter events in the reality of how they happened. Researchers will therefore attend more to the construction of meaning (Ricoeur, 1981). The researcher will observe the way that the phenomenon emerges for us, in the descriptions that are reported in the transcripts (van Manen, 1990).

How to read the following chapters

My intention in setting out this brief and limited introduction to existential thinking and phenomenological research practices is to prepare you as the reader for the following chapters. At the time that these research method-ologies and related philosophies were becoming established, the Western academic world went through a crisis. There was a turn to linguistics, in structuralist thinking. This was deconstructed in a post-structural move, leading to our current post-modern attitudes. Paul Ricoeur explored devel-oping understandings of language, while maintaining a phenomenological stance (Ricoeur, 1981). He built on our phenomenological experience of time, observing how words that are written down become text. The author is no longer present to explain what they meant.

The understanding that Paul Ricoeur develops is that you as the reader must bring meaning to these words (Ricoeur, 1981). My world, and the worlds of the authors that I cite, are gone. If these words mean anything, that meaning will be taken from your world. It is in your world that you must make sense of what you are reading. I hope that you find meaning in the following chapters. I hope that this meaning enables you to live in your world with greater awareness and sensitivity. It is our intention that you take the accounts that we give here as a group of writers and make them your own. Do with them what you will, but please take some responsibility for the collective risk that we all face, that further traumatic experiences will come about.

References

Abram, D. (1996). *The Spell of the Sensuous: Perception and Language in a More-Than-Human World*. Vintage Books.

Bensimon, M. (2012). Elaboration on the association between trauma, PTSD and posttraumatic growth: The role of trait resilience. *Personality and Individual Differences, 52*(7), 782–787. https://doi.org/10.1016/j.paid.2012.01.011

Bitbol, M., & Petitmengin, C. (2017). Neurophenomenology and the micro-phenomenological interview. In S. Schneider & M. Velmans (Eds.), *The Blackwell Companion to Consciousness* (2nd ed., pp. 726–739). Wiley. https://doi.org/10.1002/9781119132363.ch51

Boaz, M. (2022). *An Existential Approach to Interpersonal Trauma: Modes of Existing and Confrontations with Reality*. Routledge. https://doi.org/10.4324/9781003181675

Bonanno, G. A., (2021). *The End of Trauma: How the New Science of Resilience is Changing How We Think About PTSD*. Basic Books.

Brown, L. (2015). *Not the Price of Admission: Healthy Relationships after Childhood Trauma*. Createspace Independent Publishing Platform.

Burstow, B. (2003). Toward a radical understanding of trauma and trauma work. *Violence Against Women, 9*(11), 1293–1317. https://doi.org/10.1177/1077801203255555

Calhoun, L. G., & Tedeschi, R. G. (2008). The paradox of struggling with trauma: Guidelines for practice and directions for research. In S. Joseph & P. A. Linley

(Eds.), *Trauma, Recovery, and Growth: Positive Psychological Perspectives on Posttraumatic Stress* (pp. 325–338). Wiley. https://doi.org/10.1002/9781118269718.ch16

Chen, J. C. (2021). The role of critical theory in the development of multicultural psychology and counseling. In I. Management Association (Ed.), *Research Anthology on Rehabilitation Practices and Therapy* (pp. 168–190). IGI Global. https://doi.org/10.4018/978-1-7998-3432-8.ch010

Choi, S., Lemberger-Truelove, M. E., & Cho, S. M. (2019). The influence of disruption of core beliefs, social support, and rumination on posttraumatic growth for Korean undergraduate students. *Journal of Humanistic Counseling, 58,* 223–232. https://doi.org/10.1002/johc.12121

Daly, A. (2016). *Merleau-Ponty and the Ethics of Intersubjectivity*. Palgrave Macmillan.

de Beauvoir, S. (2015). *The Ethics of Ambiguity*. Philosophical Library/Open Road (Original work published 1949).

DeViva, J. C., Sheerin, C. M., Southwick, S. M., Roy, A. M., Pietrzak, R. H., & Harpaz-Rotem, I. (2016). Correlates of VA mental health treatment utilization among OEF/OIF/OND veterans: Resilience, stigma, social support, personality, and beliefs about treatment. *Psychological Trauma: Theory, Research, Practice, and Policy, 8,* 310–318. https://psycnet.apa.org/doi/10.1037/tra0000075

Du Toit, K. (2017). Existential contributions to the problematization of trauma: An expression of the bewildering ambiguity of human existence. *Existential Analysis, 28*(1), 166–175.

Everly, G. S., Jr., & Lating, J. M. (2004). The defining moment of psychological trauma: What makes a traumatic event traumatic? In G. S. Everly, Jr. & J. M. Lating (Eds.), *Personality-Guided Therapy for Posttraumatic Stress Disorder* (pp. 33–51). American Psychological Association. https://doi.org/10.1037/10649-003

Frankl, V. E. (2004). *Man's Search for Meaning*. Ebury (Original work published 1946).

Gallagher, S. (2009). Two problems of intersubjectivity. *Journal of Consciousness Studies, 16,* 6–8.

Gilbert, P. (2009). Introducing compassion-focused therapy. *Advances in Psychiatric Treatment, 15*(3), 20, 199–208. https://doi.org/10.1192/apt.bp.107.005264

Gilfus, M. E. (1999). The price of the ticket: A survivor-centered appraisal of trauma theory. *Violence Against Women, 5*(11), 1238–1257. https://doi.org/10.1177/1077801299005011002

Giorgi, A. (2009). *The Descriptive Phenomenological Method in Psychology*. Duquesne University Press.

Greening, T. (1992). Existential challenges and responses. *The Humanistic Psychologist, 20,* 1–6. https://doi.org/10.1080/08873267.1992.9986784

Harris, M., & Fallot, R. D. (2001). Envisioning a trauma-informed service system: A vital paradigm shift. *New Directions for Mental Health Services, 89,* 3–22. https://doi.org/10.1002/yd.23320018903

Helms, J. E., Nicolas, G., & Green, C. E. (2012). Racism and ethnoviolence as trauma: Enhancing professional and research training. *Traumatology, 18*(1), 65–74. https://doi.org/10.1177/1534765610396728

Hoffman, L. (2021). Existential-Humanistic Therapy and disaster response: Lessons from the COVID-19 pandemic. *Journal of Humanistic Psychology, 61*(1), 33–54. https://doi.org/10.1177/0022167820931987

Hoffman, L., & Vallejos, L. (2019). Existential shattering. In D. Leeming (Ed.), *Encyclopaedia of Psychology and Religion* (pp. 1–4). Springer. https://doi.org/10 .1007/978-3-642-27771-9_200193-1

Husserl, E. (2006). *The Basic Problems of Phenomenology: From the Lectures, Winter Semester, 1910–1911* (trans. I. Farin & J. G. Hart). Springer (Original work published 1911).

Ickovics, J. R., & Park, C. L. (1998). Paradigm shift: Why a focus on health is important. *Journal of Social Issues, 54*(2), 237–244. https://doi.org/10.1111/j .1540-4560.1998.tb01216.x

Jacobsen, B. (2006). The life crisis in an existential perspective: Can trauma and crisis be seen as an aid to personal development? *Existential Analysis, 17*(1), 39–54.

Janoff-Bulman, R. (1992). *Shattered Assumptions: Towards a New Psychology of Trauma*. Free Press.

Janoff-Bulman, R. (2004). Posttraumatic growth: Three explanatory models. *Psychological Inquiry, 15*(1), 30–34. http://www.jstor.org/stable/20447198.

Jaspers, K. (1970). *Philosophy, Vol. 2: Existential Elucidation* (trans. E. B. Ashton). The University of Chicago Press.

Johnson, E. B. (2022). Intergenerational trauma and PTSD: Historic wounds necessitate treatment based on individual culture. *Journal of European Psychology Students, 13*(1), 7–17. https://doi.org/10.5334/jeps.570

Joseph, S. (2012). *What Doesn't Kill Us: The New Psychology of Posttraumatic Growth*. London: Piatkus Little Brown.

Joseph, S., & Linley, P. A. (2006). Growth following adversity: Theoretical perspectives and implications for clinical practice. *Clinical Psychology Review, 26*, 1041–1053. https://doi.org/10.1016/j.cpr.2005.12.006

Joseph, S., & Linley, P. A. (2008). Reflections on theory and practice in trauma, recovery, and growth: A paradigm shift for the field of trauma stress. In S. Joseph & P. A. Linley (Eds.), *Trauma, Recovery, and Growth: Positive Psychological Perspectives on Posttraumatic Stress* (pp. 339–356). Wiley. https://doi.org/10 .1002/9781118269718.ch17

Langdridge, D. (2009). Relating through difference: A critical narrative analysis. In L. Finlay & K. Evans (Eds.), *Relational Centred Research for Psychotherapists: Exploring Meanings and Experience* (pp. 213–226). Wiley-Blackwell.

Längle, A. (2007). Trauma und Existenz. *Psychotherapie Forum, 15*, 109–116. https://doi.org/10.1007/s00729-007-0200-7

Linley, P. A., & Joseph, S. (2007). Therapy work and therapists' positive and negative well-being. *Journal of Social and Clinical Psychology, 26*(3), 385–403.

Marsella, A. J. (2010). Ethnocultural aspects of PTSD: An overview of concepts, issues, and treatments. *Traumatology, 16*(4), 17–26. https://doi.org/10.1177/1534765610388062

Merleau-Ponty, M. (1962). *Phenomenology of Perception* (trans. C. Smith). Routledge (Original work published 1945).

Milton, M. (2017). *The Personal Is Political: Stories of Difference and Psychotherapy.* Bloomsbury Academic.

Pitman, R. K., Rasmusson, A. M., Koenen, K. C., Shin, L. M., Orr, S. P., Gilbertson, M. W., Milad, M. R., & Liberzon, I. (2012). Biological studies of post-traumatic stress disorder. *Nature Reviews Neuroscience, 13*(11), 769–87. https://doi.org/10.1038/nrn3339.

Ricoeur, P. (1981). *Hermeneutics and the Human Sciences* (ed. & trans. J. B. Thompson). Cambridge University Press.

Rodriguez-Rey, R. Palacios, A., Alonso-Tapia, J., Periz, E., Alvarez, E., Coca, A., & Belda, S. (2017). Posttraumatic growth in pediatric intensive care personnel: Dependence on resilience and coping strategies. *Psychological Trauma: Theory, Research, Practice and Policy, 9*, 407–415. https://psycnet.apa.org/doi/10.1037/tra0000211

Romano, C. (2009). *Event and World* (trans. S. Mackinlay). Fordham University Press.

Root, M. P. (1996). Women of colour and traumatic stress in "domestic captivity": Gender and disempowering statuses. In A. J. Marsella, M. J. Friedman, E. T. Gerrity, & R. M. Scurfield (Eds.), *Ethnocultural Aspects of Post-Traumatic Stress Disorder: Issues, Research and Clinical Applications* (pp. 363–388). American Psychological Association.

Sartre, J.-P. (1958). *Being and Nothingness* (trans. H. E. Barnes). Routledge (Original work published 1943).

Seligman, M. E. P., & Csikszentmihalyi, M. (2000). Positive psychology: An introduction. *American Psychologist, 55*, 5–14. https://doi.org/10.1037/0003-066X.55.1.5

Shakespeare-Finch, J., & Armstrong, D. (2010). Trauma type and post-traumatic outcomes: Differences between survivors of motor vehicle accidents, sexual assaults, and bereavement. *Journal of Loss and Trauma, 15*, 69–82.

Shakespeare-Finch, J., & de Dassel, T. (2009). The impact of child sexual abuse on victims/survivors. *Journal of Child Sexual Abuse, 18*, 623–640.

Shakespeare-Finch, J., & Lurie-Beck, J. (2014). A meta-analytic clarification of the relationship between posttraumatic growth and symptoms of posttraumatic distress disorder. *Journal of Anxiety Disorders, 28*, 223–229. https://doi.org/10.1016/j.janxdis.2013.10.005

Shiro, E. (2023). *The Unexpected Gift of Trauma: The Path to Posttraumatic Growth*. Harvest.

Smith, J. A., Flowers, P., & Larkin, M. (2022). *Interpretative Phenomenological Analysis: Theory, Method, and Research* (2nd ed.). Sage.

Stein, E. (1989). *On the Problem of Empathy* (trans. W. Stein). ICS Publications (Original work published 1921).

Stolorow, R. D. (2007). *Trauma and Human Existence: Autobiographical, Psychoanalytic and Philosophical Reflections*. The Analytic Press.

Sweeney, A., Clement, S., Filson, B., & Kennedy, S. (2016). Trauma-informed mental healthcare in the UK: What is it and how can we further its development? *Mental Health Review Journal, 21*(3), 174–192. https://doi.org/10.1108/MHRJ-01-2015-0006

Taylor, S. C. (2011). *Social Death and Sexual Violence*. Spinifex Press.

Tedeschi, R. G., & Moore, B. A. (2020). Posttraumatic growth as an integrative therapeutic philosophy. *Journal of Psychotherapy Integration, 31*(2), 180–194. https://doi.org/10.1037/int0000250

Tedeschi, R. G., Park, C. L., & Calhoun, L. G. (1998). *Posttraumatic Growth: Positive Transformations in the Aftermath of Crisis*. Lawrence Erlbaum.

Tedeschi, R. G., Shakespeare-Finch, J., Taku, K., & Calhoun, L. G. (2018). *Posttraumatic Growth: Theory, Research, and Applications*. Routledge. https://doi.org/10.4324/9781315527451

van Deurzen, E. (2010). *Everyday Mysteries: A Handbook of Existential Psychotherapy* (2nd ed.). Routledge. https://doi.org/10.4324/9780203864593

van Deurzen, E. (2021). *Rising From Existential Crisis: Live Beyond Calamity*. PCCS Books.

van Manen, M. (1990). *Researching Lived Experience: Human Science for an Action Sensitive Pedagogy*. The Althouse Press.

Walsh, F. (2015). What is wisdom? Cross-cultural and cross-disciplinary syntheses. *Review of General Psychology, 19*, 278–293. https://doi.org/10.1037/gpr0000045

Wasco, S. M. (2003). Conceptualizing the harm done by rape: Applications of trauma theory to experiences of sexual assault. *Trauma, Violence, & Abuse, 4*(4), 309–322. https://doi.org/10.1177/1524838003256560

Weiss, T. (2014). Personal transformation: Posttraumatic growth and gerotranscendence. *Journal of Humanistic Psychology, 54*, 203–226. https://doi.org/10.1177/0022167813492388

Weiss, T., & Berger, R. (2010). Posttraumatic growth around the world: Research findings and practice implications. In T. Weiss & R. Berger (Eds.), *Posttraumatic Growth and Culturally Competent Practice: Lessons From Around the Globe* (pp. 188–195). Wiley. https://doi.org/10.1002/9781118270028.ch14

Worth, P. (2022). *Positive Psychology Across the Lifespan: An Existential Perspective*. Routledge. https://doi.org/10.4324/9781003132530

Xu, W., Feng, C., Tang, W., & Yang, Y. (2022) Rumination, posttraumatic stress disorder symptoms, and posttraumatic growth among Wenchuan earthquake adult survivors: A developmental perspective. *Frontiers in Public Health, 9*. https://doi.org/10.3389/fpubh.2021.764127

Yalom, I. D. (1980). *Existential Psychotherapy*. Basic Books.

Yalom, I. D., & Lieberman, M. A. (1991). Bereavement and heightened existential awareness. *Psychiatry, 54*(4), 334–345.

Zefferman, M. R., & Mathew, S. (2020). An evolutionary theory of moral injury with insight from Turkana warriors. *Evolution and Human Behavior, 41*(5), 341–353. https://doi.org/10.1016/j.evolhumbehav.2020.07.003

Zoellner, T., & Maercker, A. (2006). Posttraumatic growth in clinical psychology: A critical review and introduction of a two component model. *Clinical Psychology Review, 26*, 626–653. https://doi.org/10.1016/j.cpr.2006.01.008

New Awareness in the Experience of Women

Birth Trauma and Existential Crisis: How Becoming a Mother Involves a Confrontation with Existence

Claire Arnold-Baker

Introduction

Becoming a mother is not normally thought to be traumatic; in fact, the opposite image is generally portrayed in society. Motherhood is often depicted as a time of joy, happiness, and fulfilment, and indeed it can be all of these as well as being difficult and challenging. Previously, when mothers experienced difficulties, these were generally thought of as 'the baby blues' and were grouped together as a form of postnatal depression. It was not until the early 2000s, when Ayers and colleagues (2001, 2004, 2016, 2018) and Beck (2004) began researching birth trauma, that medical and psychological professionals began to understand that women could experience a range of responses when becoming a mother. In some cases, birth trauma can lead to a diagnosis of PTSD (Posttraumatic Stress Disorder), and it has been suggested there are more mothers with PTSD in the UK than soldiers who had experienced traumatic experiences on the battlefield. It is estimated that about 30,000 women a year experience traumatic births (www.birthtraumaassociation.org.uk). As many of these mothers do not seek help, it has not been a widely recognised outcome of childbirth, creating a disconnect between the mothers' experiences and the societal discourse around motherhood. This makes it hard to realise that there is something wrong.

This chapter draws together my research into the experience of early motherhood (Arnold-Baker, 2015) – which maps Matrescence (mother-becoming) and concludes that motherhood is a confrontation with existence – with my later written work which demonstrates how this confrontation is experienced as an existential crisis (Arnold-Baker, 2020). The chapter will also draw on my clinical work with mothers, which predominately involves supporting those who have experienced birth trauma. It is through this clinical work that understanding has been gained into how women overcome their traumatic experiences and how this leads to changes not

DOI: 10.4324/9781003493860-3

just in the way they live their lives but how they think and feel about themselves and how this also impacts their sense of purpose and motivation for the future.

Literature review

There is a vast literature on motherhood, so for the purposes of this chapter a selective approach has been taken to give an overview and background to the research into the transition to motherhood and how that transition can be experienced as traumatic. Previous literature on the transition to motherhood has been broadly focused in three areas: changes to maternal identity, the emotional impact of motherhood, and social support. A fourth developing area is that of Matresence, which looks at how these different aspects come together during the transition to motherhood. Each of these areas will be explored below.

Maternal Identity

Changes in identity can be confusing and unsettling, especially when they coincide with other significant changes in a person's life. When it comes to the maternal identity, Stern and his wife, Nadia Bruschweiler-Stern, found that mothers not only have to give birth to their babies but also must give birth psychologically to a new sense of themselves as a mother (Stern & Bruschweiler-Stern, 1988: 3). They believed this identity transition enabled mothers to relinquish their previously held identity so that a new identity, that of mother, can develop. The idea that a previous sense of identity is lost by the mother was echoed in other research at the time (Price, 1988).

However, a maternal identity does not just appear at the moment of birth but develops gradually over time. A sense of self is a complex construct, and Miller (2005) argued that it is only through the 'mothering work' that mothers are able to begin to develop a conception of themselves as mothers. This was echoed by Stadlen (2005), who believed that it is through the relationship that is formed between mother and baby that mothers learn both about their babies and themselves and in this process get a sense of themselves as mothers. Therefore, rather than completely losing their old sense of identity, motherhood becomes a time when women renew the narratives they hold for themselves (Bailey, 1999; Laney et al., 2014). These new identities are creatively made in a dynamic process that is undertaken with others as well as through introspection. This is partly due to a shift of attention that occurs away from the public world to a more personal and private world (Smith, 1999), which enables mothers to begin to see themselves in new ways.

Research into how women create a maternal identity confirms an existential view of self, that individuals are not fixed in an object-like fashion but rather are a dynamic process of becoming (Arnold-Baker, 2015, 2019). Sartre (1943/1958) believed that a person's sense of who they are derives from their interactions with the world and with others. Indeed, Sartre's famous quote 'existence precedes essence' demands that we must live first and find out who we are later. Both Heidegger (1927/2010) and Sartre believed that people exist as possibility and projection and that our fundamental freedom means that we are able to create and recreate a sense of self for ourselves. Therefore, we can see maternal identity as an additional element which joins other elements which together make up a person's identity, all of which change and interact as a woman moves through her life.

Emotional Impact of Motherhood

There is no doubt that motherhood has an impact on a woman's emotions. Price, a psychiatrist and psychotherapist, noted that motherhood "can be the best or worst emotional experience of a woman's life" (1988: 16). Mothers often experience powerful emotions, namely anxiety and anger, which they are totally unprepared for. Maternal emotional responses are also often contradictory and paradoxical (Arnold-Baker, 2020). Stadlen (2005) described how nothing prepares a woman for the realities of life as a mother, which is echoed in my own research (Arnold-Baker, 2015) demonstrating how there is a gap between mothers' expectations and the realities they face in their day-to-day experiences. The greater the gap, the more difficulties a mother experiences emotionally. Motherhood is also confusing when mothers are faced with emotions such as anxiety, depression, anger, and worry when they expected to feel love, contentment, joy, and happiness. This gap in the societal discourse around mothers' emotionality has the effect of furthering the gap between expectations and realities. Mothers often say, 'I shouldn't be feeling this way.' Their explanation for this involves a turning inwards: 'there must be something wrong with me,' rather than looking outwardly and seeing that the problem lies in unrealistic images that abound in Western society of how a mother should be and act.

Price (1988) noted how depression is often missed by health visitors and GPs because it creeps up on a woman. Depression has also been shown to be connected to maternal identity. Donaghy (2020) highlighted the link between changes in maternal identity and emotional experience, where safety and meaning in life is linked to a stable sense of self. As already discussed, if mothers experience a loss or deconstruction of the self, this impacts greatly on their emotional experience, often resulting in postnatal depression.

Previously, anxiety was also missed by health professionals, as it was often assumed that postnatal anxiety was just motherly worry. However, recent research by Oakeley (2023) found that mothers were 'taken over' by anxious thoughts after the birth, which were frequently experienced as spiralling or racing and included other intense feelings of rage and fury or overwhelm. These intense emotions were often frightening for mothers. At the same time, Oakeley found that new mothers were faced with uncertainty, mirroring the theme of 'The Unknown' found in my research (Arnold-Baker, 2015) and the experience of 'Not Understanding' something significant, which was a finding of Simmons' (2020) research. This uncertainty also led to feelings of "confusion, guilt, frustration and despair" (Oakeley, 2023: 151).

However, the uncertainty that is highlighted in motherhood also contributes to a sense of unsafety. The world becomes a threatening place both externally but also internally. Mothers become very aware of the potential risks and dangers that surround them, and this leads to worry and in some cases fear. Price (1988) and Stern and Bruschweiler-Stern (1998) put this down to a primitive anxiety that mothers become attuned to, which means the response is often out of proportion in today's world. However, Stadlen argues that, on the contrary, mothers are just being careful and have not developed "enough experience to be able to assess risks accurately" (2005: 20).

A further emotional impact comes from the internalised ideal of the 'perfect mother,' which is a dominant discourse in the West. When mothers feel they are not measuring up to this idealised standard, they experience guilt (Liss et al., 2013). Mothers can also experience a fear of judgement from others for not meeting the expectations of being a good mother, and this also exacerbates feelings of guilt and shame.

Social Support

It is clear from the review of the literature thus far that motherhood is a challenging time for women. It is a time when they face changes to their identity and an integration of a new maternal identity which is just forming, as well as intense emotional responses to becoming a mother. Price noted how motherhood left women "psychologically vulnerable. Her physical resources are continuously drained with little time for respite and her psychological boundaries are breeched in a way that makes her vulnerable to any hint of criticism" (1988: 141). It is therefore understandable that at such a time of vulnerability, a mother's need for the support from others is essential.

However, despite the growing psychological literature and countless cross-cultural anthropological studies showing the importance of a social transition in motherhood and support for mothers in the postpartum period, this has become reduced in the West. Western practices have made mothering a more private experience mainly confined to the family home. Recognised societal support for partners is limited to two weeks directly after the birth, and support from midwives and health visitors is for the first six weeks. However, unlike other cultures there are no cultural practices in the West of structured familial help, although this sometimes takes place informally. This lack of organised cultural support can leave new parents feeling lost and out of their depth. New mothers are affectively left alone to work things out for themselves. Stern (1995) recognised how essential it was for new mothers to create a supportive network postpartum, which would attend to new mothers' physical needs as well as providing them with emotional support. Without this, Stern believed mothering would be challenging for new mothers.

A lack of social support does have a negative impact on the mother and can lead to a higher propensity for postnatal depression (Razurel et al., 2012; Webster et al., 2011). However, both familial and peer support have their own difficulties. For example, some women have complicated relationships with their own mothers, and peer support is only helpful if mothers are connected with like-minded mothers who are able to be open and honest about their own experience. Maushart's (1999) observations that mothers hide behind a 'mask of silence' is still present today. Often mothers feel unable to talk about their experiences if they go against the cultural discourse, which perpetuates this 'conspiracy of silence.' The recent advances in technology have made online support groups more convenient and reduced some of the barriers to in-person groups (Holtz et al., 2015). More individualised support by empathic health professionals would also be a benefit as well as postnatal education to help mothers navigate their expectations vs the realities of motherhood (De Sousa Machado et al., 2020).

Matrescene and Life Crisis

The term Matrescence has become increasingly used by researchers and authors working in the field of pregnancy and early motherhood. It was originally coined by Raphael (1975), a medical anthropologist who likened Matrescene to Adolescence as both represented life transitions or rites of passage, which involved biological, social, and identity changes. Raphael used Matresence to mean 'mother becoming.' This term was then reintroduced by Athen (2016) and reproductive psychiatrist Sacks (2017), who argued that we needed a term to enable mothers to talk about the tremendous shifts that occurred in their lives during this period.

There is now broad agreement that Matrescence is a life crisis event (Arnold-Baker, 2000, 2020; Donaghy, 2020; Garland, 2020). The anthropologist Kruckman (1992) noted that the experience of childbirth is "almost universally treated as a traumatic life crisis event" (Kruckman, 1992: 139). Other authors have concurred, with Smith (1994) describing becoming a mother as an extreme time of change; Stadlen observed how it involved a 'momentous inner shift' (2005); Prinds et al. (2013) concluded that it represented a 'significant life event'; and Miller (2005) noted that motherhood required an ontological shift, whereas Urwin's (2007) research showed how new mothers lose their bearings in life.

In 1995 Stern elucidated the concept of the Motherhood Constellation, a unique temporary Western construct, which highlights the subjective themes which occur for new mothers. The four themes which make up the constellation are *life growth*, which focuses on the mother's concerns about her baby's physical development; *primary relatedness*, which concerns the mother's relationship and connection with her baby; *supporting matrix*, which concerns the networks of support that are needed for the new mother to successfully raise her baby; and *identity reorganisation*, which involves a shift in the mother's focus which enables her to take on the responsibilities of a mothering role and the change she would need to make in her sense of self to incorporate this new motherhood identity.

It is little wonder that authors such as Stadlen (2005) have described becoming a mother as a 'shock.' Figes uses the term "nurture shock" (1988: 27) to sum up mothers' experience of the trauma of the birth and the subsequent chaotic nature of their new daily lives.

Birth Trauma

In recent years, there has been increased interest in how the birth has an impact on mothers postpartum. Even though the risk of mortality is relatively low these days due to improved health care, there can still be complications during or after the birth, which can be both life-threatening or perceived as life-threatening or result in life-changing injury. The DSM-5 defines trauma as "actual or threatened death, serious injury or sexual violence," and in many cases mothers are faced with the very real possibility of their own death or the death of their baby during childbirth (American Psychological Association, 2013). During the birth, "the birthing woman experiences intense fear, helplessness, loss of control, and horror" (Beck, 2004: 28).

It is important to remember that the experience of trauma is individual. Two similar births will not necessarily result in the same response, so it is not possible to determine from the outside whether a birth would have been experienced as traumatic or not by the mother. A mother's experience of trauma after a birth can also be impacted by previous experience; women are particularly affected if they have been previously subjected to sexual violence. But sometimes the distress a mother feels after the birth can be psychological and emotional.

It is easier to recognise physical events as being traumatic, but trauma can also be created by interactions with medical professionals and others, or previous experiences of trauma can be reactivated during the birth. Some examples of nonphysical traumatic situations can occur through a lack of information about what is happening, where no reassurance is given and the mother feels out of control and subject to insensitive comments and actions by medical professionals or partners either during or after the birth.

Birth trauma or distress can lead to heightened anxiety and fear that something bad will happen or something will go wrong, or there is a fear that the baby might die. Often mothers will have nightmares or flashbacks about the birth (Ayers, 2004). Mothers may find it hard to sleep or will wake up feeling frightened or anxious. In extreme cases mothers may experience dissociation, where they know that something bad has happened but are unable to remember what happened during the birth. Mothers who have experienced birth trauma may also find that they are unable to bond with their babies and may feel like they are going through the motions of mothering without feeling anything. Often mothers who have experienced birth trauma will find the time building up to their child's birthday difficult, and trauma may be re-experienced at this point (Beck et al., 2013).

An existential view of trauma sees it as an existential shattering, which is 'the sudden and unexpected dismantling, or shattering, of one's self-conception and worldview as a consequence of an event or process that the individual has experienced' (Hoffman & Vallejos, 2019). When applied to childbirth, it results in a permanently changed worldview for the mother (Shulman, 2020) as they grapple with the uncertainty and unsafety that have opened up in their lives, as well as being confronted by existential questions about their lives.

A gap in the literature

There is a vast literature on motherhood, both from a theoretical, personal experience, and a research perspective. As demonstrated in the literature review above, at the time my research was being conducted few studies had investigated motherhood through an existential lens, that is, apart from the scoping review conducted by Prinds et al. (2013). Subsequently, more research has been undertaken through this lens at the New School of Psychotherapy and Counselling (NSPC) (Garland, 2020; Ofori, 2020;

Shulman, 2020; Simmons, 2020), and NSPC has become a burgeoning maternal research centre in the UK. There was an obvious gap in the literature to gain an existential understanding of the experience of becoming a mother. The research question devised was general: 'What are the early experiences of motherhood for first-time mothers who have babies between 6–12 months?' At the time of the research, it was felt important to capture mothers' experiences as they experienced them but by taking a holistic, 360-degree view. This is an important element of existential practice, and van Deurzen's four-dimensional framework (2010) enables existential therapists to keep track of and gain a deeper understanding of a client's life by attending to the different dimensions in which they exist. Therefore, mothers were asked to talk about their experiences in as much detail as possible but were not guided to talk about trauma or difficulties in their experiences in particular. The focus was on what it was like to make the transition to motherhood and becoming a mother.

Methodology

In line with the researcher's position as an existential-phenomenological practitioner, a phenomenological research method was chosen which also enabled an existential analysis to be incorporated. Van Manen's lived experience method (1990) was chosen, and a further analysis using van Deurzen's Structural Existential Analysis (SEA) (2014; 2025) was undertaken. Participants were interviewed for about 60 minutes on their experience of becoming a mother. Prompt questions were used to ensure that participants were fully exploring their experiences. The interviews were then transcribed and analysed first using van Manen's method of analysis, which involved identifying themes within the dialogue for each participant before looking at overarching themes that were shared by all participants. A second layer of analysis involved reviewing the themes in terms of van Manen's lifeworld existentials, *lived space* (spatiality), *lived body* (corporeality), *lived time* (temporality), and *lived relations* (relationality or communality). During this process it was felt that applying van Manen's lifeworld existentials did not capture the personal elements around identity that were present in the findings. Therefore, van Deurzen's SEA four dimensions, physical, social, personal and spiritual, were used to draw out different elements.

Participants

Eight first-time mothers who had babies between the ages of 6–12 months were recruited for this research. The age of the baby was important as mothers whose babies were under 6 months would still be grappling with early motherhood and might not be able to have the distance to reflect on their experiences. Those mothers with babies over 12 months would also be in a different point in their experience with some mothers returning to work at this point, so keeping a tight age range of the baby ensured that the mothers interviewed had had recent experiences to talk about and reflect on. Participants were found through advertising in various baby groups and through a snowballing approach. This produced a sample of similar mothers who were White, heteronormative, and aged between 32 and 39. Whilst this gave a homogeneous sample, it was not diverse in terms of ethnicity or sexuality. Despite this lack of diversity within the sample, subsequent research into early motherhood in other ethnic groups has however shown similar findings to my own (Ofori, 2020).

Analysis and findings

Eight major themes were elucidated through the process of analysis, and they were *Being with Others, Developing a Relationship with the Baby, Living in Time, The Unknown, Life is Different, Challenging Expectations, Motherhood Identity,* and *Difficult Times*. Within the major themes, further subthemes were identified as detailed in Table 2.1.

The analysis and the resulting themes highlighted the multifaceted experience of becoming a mother. The theme *Being with Others* incorporated two aspects: first, the importance of the support of other people during the early changes of motherhood. This support helped the participants put their experience into perspective and helped them feel less isolated. Support offered both a distraction and a reassurance. The second aspect referred to the way in which the mothers became more understanding of others. Their relationship with other people changed, and they became more patient. This coincided with them relating to and trying to understand their babies. A new way of *Being with Others* and relating had opened up for the participants.

Developing a Relationship with the Baby was a major theme. Although the participants had chosen to have their babies and were ready for them, the reality was still quite different. The first couple of months were hard for the participants when they felt they did not get anything back from their babies. Reflecting back over their experience, they realised that the relationship changed gradually in a subtle way. The mothers realised that they were learning together with their babies and that, as the baby changed, the mother did too. Gradually, the mothers began to feel more confident, and when the babies were able to respond, the mothers found that very rewarding. All the mothers were motivated to develop a good relationship with their babies, which kept them going when it was hard in the beginning when they felt they didn't know what to do and the communication was limited.

Table 2.1 Themes and Subthemes

Major Theme	Subthemes	Lifeworld Existentials	SEA Existential Dimensions
Being with Others	The Importance of Support	Sociality (lived relationship with others)	Mitwelt (social dimension)
	Understanding Others		
Developing a Relationship with the Baby	Being Ready for a Baby	Sociality (lived relationship to others) And Corporeality (lived body)	Mitwelt (social dimension) And Eigenwelt (personal dimension)
	Learning Together		
	Gradually Changing		
	Building a Good Relationship		
	Getting Something Back		
Living in Time	All-Consuming	Temporality (lived time) And Spatiality (lived space)	Umwelt (physical dimension) And Eigenwelt (personal dimension
	Never-Ending		
	Living in the Present		
The Unknown	Not Knowing	Spatiality (lived space)	Uberwelt (spiritual dimension) And Eigenwelt (personal dimension)
	Searching for Answers		
	Responsibility		
	Worrying		
Life is Different	Nothing Prepares You	Spatiality (lived space) And Temporality (lived time)	Uberwelt (Spiritual dimension) And Eigenwelt (personal dimension)
	Life Before Doesn't Exist		
	Life is Different		
	Shock		
Challenging Expectations	Expecting Hard Work	Spatiality (lived space)	Uberwelt (spiritual dimension)
	The Surprise of Feeling Confident		
	Feeling out of Control		
	New Purpose in Life		
Motherhood Identity	Not Feeling Like a Mother		Eigenwelt (personal dimension)
	Adopting a Motherhood Identity		
	Not Feeling Different		
	Important Role		
Difficult Times (minor theme)	Overcoming Difficult Times		Eigenwelt (personal dimension)

The theme *Living in Time* had not been explicitly found previously in the literature and referred to the temporal aspect of motherhood. The experience of early motherhood was that it was all-consuming; there was no time or space for mothers to think or do anything else but focus on their babies. This made the mothers feel that they were constantly living in the present. The mothers had lost their sense of time and were living in an immediacy which made them feel that it would be never-ending.

The mothers were also living in *The Unknown*. They felt unskilled and unknowledgeable. They had to find their way with their babies, searching for answers and feeling the weight of the responsibility they had taken on. The mothers wanted to do the best for their babies but did not know what that was, and this made it an unsettling and worrying experience.

Life is Different was another major theme. The mothers reported how nothing can prepare you for having a baby, and as their expectations did not match their reality it made them feel forever vulnerable. Because they were living in the present, they felt that their lives before the babies did not exist, and their lives were now very different. The mothers felt that everything revolved around their babies, and they had entered a whole new world. Arriving in this new and unexpected world was a shock for the mothers.

The next theme, *Challenging Expectations*, led on from the previous theme. Motherhood was not what the mothers expected and was harder work than they had imagined it would be. Yet they were also surprised at moments when they did feel confident and were able to cope. They had a sense of being out of control, which eventually forced them to let go of their previous expectations. The experience of having a baby changed the mother's experience of life, and they reported finding a new sense of purpose.

The process of becoming a mother involved the participants developing a new identity. It was a confusing time for them as they did not feel like mothers, or what they thought a mother should be. At the same time the mothers reported not feeling different. Their lives were completely different, and their focus was purely on their babies, but it took a while for them to feel like a mother and add this aspect to their identity.

A minor theme, *Difficult Times*, concerned how some of the participants talked of how they overcame difficult times. They noted that it needed resilience and conscientiousness, whilst also focusing on the positives. Being able to find humour in their difficulties also helped.

Existential Analysis

The existential analysis of the data showed how mothers were facing challenges in all four dimensions of their existence. In the physical dimension, their experience of time (temporality) and space (spatiality) had changed. Life was being lived in the present, which made it feel urgent and active.

In the social dimension, the mothers' relationships changed and they were faced with forming a connection with their babies whom they did not know and who they felt they could not communicate with. This new way of communication and learning about the other took time and impacted how they related to other people too. In the personal dimension, the mothers' lives were different and how they thought about themselves was confusing and paradoxical. Living through this transition time was difficult because the reality was very different to their expectations, and it caused a lot of uncertainty and worry. The spiritual dimension saw the mothers enter a new unknown world, where they held responsibility for their babies but did not feel they had the skills needed to look after them well. Their change in focus meant that the mothers created a new sense of purpose as they had to shift their expectations when faced with the reality of their situation. This led to a change in their values and beliefs too. Their overall motivation remained to take care of their babies in the best way possible, and this kept them going through difficult times.

This research demonstrated how life-changing motherhood is for women. The existential analysis showed how mothers are changed and challenged in every dimension of their lives, and how this leads to mothers feeling unsettled and not at home in their lives at the exact point in which they are trying to create a sense of home for themselves and their babies.

Lifeworld Existentials Analysis

When analysing the data from van Manen's lifeworld existentials, the most prominent lifeworld was that of *Lived Space* or spatiality. This relates to the space in which the mother lives in and feels most at home in. The analysis shows how the themes of *Living in Time, The Unknown, Life is Different,* and *Challenging Expectations* demonstrate the momentous shift mothers must make in their lives to create space for their babies.

Discussion

The findings of this study confirm much of what had previously been found in the literature regarding support, the emotional impact of motherhood, and maternal identity. However, new elements were highlighted, such as the *Living in Time* and *The Unknown* themes, which had not been found previously. The existential analysis of the data did bring forth a new perspective on the experience. Taking a holistic perspective highlighted the tremendous shifts that are required of new mothers for them to create space for their babies in their lives.

A further exploration of the existential themes that were present for the participants showed how aware they were of their existence and how their freedom, choice, and responsibility were very evident. The most powerful element was the mothers' sense of responsibility for their babies. The mothers were conscious of being responsible for a vulnerable other and having to make choices for a baby who will bear the impact of those choices, which cannot be known in advance.

The participants were also aware of their own mortality and the vulnerability of their babies and their need to keep both themselves and their babies alive. As already elucidated, the mothers' time and temporality had also changed, and the participants experienced a sense of *thrownness* (Heidegger, 1927/2010) when they entered this new unknown world of their babies. Gradually, through their experiences of living in a new way, the mothers began to adopt a maternal identity.

The study found that a mother has much to grapple with when bringing a baby into the world. In addition to the care and mothering work that comes with looking after a newborn, the new mother is confronted by existence. She becomes aware of her existence as a whole and her place in it. The mother sees the realities of existence, such as life and death, freedom, choice, and responsibility and how her mothering role connects her and her baby to a wider community and society. This has the effect of the mother becoming tuned into life in a new way.

This experience can be seen as an existential crisis (Arnold-Baker, 2020). When the original Greek form of the word *Krisis* is used, its relevance to motherhood is clear as it means to choose or decide. When the participants talked about the all-consuming and never-ending nature of motherhood, they were referring to the number of choices they had to make on a continual basis. Many of these decisions revolved around the safety vs risk pole of existence which makes the decision making even more intense. However, an existential crisis also requires individuals to make decisions about their existence too. An existential crisis is experienced when a person becomes confronted with the unpredictability of life and comes up against the limits of existence. Childbirth is a good example of when this takes place. Mothers may try to plan and prepare, but the way the birth unfolds is unpredictable. Different possibilities suddenly open up which were not considered previously. The unpredictability of the birth and the experience of motherhood account for why these cause mothers difficulties and challenges. Mothers are not just making choices about their everyday lives, but they are making choices about how they are going to live too and realising that there are no certainties whatever choices they make. When new mothers are also faced with the experience of birth trauma, it is understandable that this could lead to distress or PTSD.

Overcoming Adversity

The participants in my research talked about how they overcame difficult times. Although these mothers had not suffered a traumatic birth, some of the same principles apply. Georgina summed up the resilience that is needed:

> *I think you need resilience to everything . . . as much as you can worry and panic and stress and what if the baby gets too hot, is it going to die?, what if it gets too cold, it's going to die – life has got a funny way, it doesn't matter how many things you plan for, what will happen will be off the radar.* (Arnold-Baker, 2015: 155)

Dani talked about how she held onto the fact that difficult times do not last forever:

> *That it isn't forever, everything is a phase, it will pass, you do get through it and you can talk to other people who've been there and done it and I does get better, I think for me, it was just drawing on the 'you will get through this' and there will be more better things to come and the good stuff definitely outweighs the difficult times.* (Arnold-Baker, 2015: 154)

It is not always possible for those who have experienced birth trauma to work this through for themselves, and there is a definite feel for those women that it will last forever. This is when therapeutic support is needed to help mothers heal and move to a place where they are not tethered to the past.

Conclusion – Existential rebirth

Birth transforms women. Often the more difficult the birth, the more trans-formational the process: "It is a transition in life, where existential con-siderations regarding the meaning of life are reinvigorated" (Prinds et al., 2013: 2). When mothers are faced with awareness of the ontological struc-tures of existence, they are called on to make a choice about how they live their lives. The shattering that occurs in the mothers' life after childbirth means that every aspect of their lives needs re-evaluating, and they have to respond to the existential challenge that is before them. This re-evaluation allows them to create a new, more authentic way of being. They develop a deep wisdom about life. They have been tested to their own limits and found a way to keep going. Therapists talk a lot about having strength. But this is often misunderstood, and clients might say, 'but I didn't feel strong' or 'well I can't be strong as I wasn't coping very well.' Strength comes from the ability to keep going despite not coping; it is about putting one foot in front of the other. There is a strength in keeping going even though it is incredibly difficult and painful. When mothers begin to make sense of and reframe their experiences, they recognise how they have risen to the challenges of life.

Existential courage is also needed; this is the courage that Tillich (1952/2014) describes that we all need to keep living and creating a life for ourselves in the face of non-being. Existential courage gives us the strength needed to overcome difficulties in life and find meaning in them. There is no way of going back to how a person was before, and the mothers found a new sense of purpose and priority through their difficulties. These experiences have allowed the mothers to grow and evolve, and whilst some may wish to go back to a more carefree way of living, they recognise that they now have more mastery of life and can see it as it really is. That, rather than avoiding uncertainty and the unknown, embracing it can actually be freeing. Once mothers begin to feel safe and have healed, they can become more flexible and adaptable. The mothers in my study realised that they had to let go of control and surrender themselves to the experience. They had to draw on their own reserves to find a way through. Reframing trauma in this way, in that traumatic events do not destroy a person but instead build a person, means that mothers find out what they are truly capable of. The confrontation with existence that mothers are faced with contributes to an existential rebirth that takes place as a result of the existential crisis of motherhood.

References

American Psychological Association. (2013). *Diagnostic and Statistical Manual of Mental Disorders* (5th ed.). APA.

Arnold-Baker, C. (2000). *Life crisis or crisis of the self? An existential view of motherhood* (Unpublished MA dissertation). NSPC and University of Sheffield.

Arnold-Baker, C. (2015). *How becoming a mother involves a confrontation with existence: An existential-phenomenological exploration of the experience of early motherhood* (Doctoral thesis). Middlesex University/NSPC. http://eprints.mdx.ac.uk/18278/

Arnold-Baker, C. (2019). The process of becoming: Maternal identity in the transition to motherhood. *Existential Analysis, 30*(2), 260–274.

Arnold-Baker, C. (2020). *The Existential Crisis of Motherhood*. Palgrave Macmillan. https://doi.org/10.1007/978-3-030-56499-5_11

Ayers, S. (2004). Delivery as a traumatic event: Prevalence, risk factors and treatment for postnatal posttraumatic stress disorder. *Clinical Obstetrics and Gynaecology, 47*(3), 552–567.

Ayers, S., Bond, R., Bertullies, S., & Wjma, K. (2016). The aetiology of posttraumatic stress following childbirth: A meta-analysis and theoretical framework. *Psychological Medicine, 46*(6), 1121–1134. https://doi.org/10.1017/S0033291715002706

Ayers, S., & Pickering, A. D. (2001). Do women get posttraumatic stress disorder as a result of childbirth? A prospective study of incidence. *Birth, 28*, 111–118. https://doi.org/10.1046/j.1523-536X.2001.00111.x

Ayers, S., Wright, D. B., & Thornton, A. (2018). Development of a measure of postpartum PTSD: The City Birth Trauma Scale. *Frontiers in Psychiatry, 9*(409), 427–430. https://doi.org/10.3389/fpsyt.2018.00409

Bailey, L. (1999). Refracted selves? A study of changes in self-identity in the transition to motherhood. *Sociology, 33*(2), 335–352. https://doi.org/10.1177/S0038038599000206

Beck, C. T. (2004). Posttraumatic stress disorder due to childbirth: The aftermath. *Nursing Research, 53*, 216–224.

Beck, C. T., Driscoll, J. W., & Watson, S. (2013). *Traumatic Childbirth*. Routledge. https://doi.org/10.4324/9780203766699

De Sousa Machado, T., Chur-Hansen, A., & Due, C. (2020). First-time mothers' perceptions of social support: Recommendations for best practice. *Health Psychology Open, 7*(1). https://doi.org/10.1177/2055102919898611

Donaghy, M. (2020). Postnatal depression: An existential crisis? In C. Arnold-Baker (Ed.), *The Existential Crisis of Motherhood* (pp. 133–154). Palgrave Macmillan. https://doi.org/10.1007/978-3-030-56499-5_8

Figes, K. (1988). *Life After Birth*. London: Penguin Books.

Garland, V. (2020). Existential responsibility of motherhood. In C. Arnold-Baker (Ed.), *The Existential Crisis of Motherhood* (pp. 57–76). Palgrave Macmillan. https://doi.org/10.1007/978-3-030-56499-5_4

Heidegger, M. (2010). *Being and Time* (trans. J. Stambaugh). State University of New York Press (Original work published 1927).

Hoffman, L., & Vallejos, L. (2019). Existential shattering. In D. Leeming (Ed.), *Encyclopaedia of Psychology and Religion* (pp. 1–4). Springer. https://doi.org/10.1007/978-3-642-27771-9_200193-1

Holtz, B., Smack, A., & Reyes-Gastelum, D. (2015). Connected motherhood: Social support for moms and moms-to-be on Facebook. *Telemedicine and e-Health, 21*(5), 415–421. https://doi.org/10.1089/tmj.2014.0118

Kruckman, L. D. (1992). Rituals and support: An anthropological view of postpartum depression. In J. A. Hamilton & P. N. Harberger (Eds.), *Postpartum Psychiatric Illness: A Picture Puzzle* (pp. 137–148). University of Pennsylvania. https://api.semanticscholar.org/CorpusID:151746057

Laney, E. K., Carruthers, L., Hall, M. E. L., & Anderson, T. (2014). Expanding the self: Motherhood and identity development in faculty women. *Journal of Family Issues, 35*(9), 1227–1251. https://doi.org/10.1177/0192513X13479573

Liss, M., Schiffrin, H. H., & Rizzo, K. M. (2013). Maternal guilt and shame: The role of self-discrepancy and fear of negative evaluation. *Journal of Child and Family Studies, 22*, 112–119. https://doi.org/10.1007/s10826-012-9673-2

Maushart, S. (1999). *The Mask of Motherhood*. Pandora.

Miller, T. (2005). *Making Sense of Motherhood: A Narrative Approach*. Cambridge University Press. https://doi.org/10.1017/CBO9780511489501

Oakeley, C. (2023). *Anxiety after birth: An existential phenomenological enquiry into others' lived experiences* (Doctoral thesis). Middlesex University/NSPC. https://repository.mdx.ac.uk/item/11499w

Ofori, J. (2020). Identity and mothering: The second generation of Ghanian migrants. In C. Arnold-Baker (Ed.), *The Existential Crisis of Motherhood* (pp. 177–198). Palgrave Macmillan. https://doi.org/10.1007/978-3-030-56499-5_10

Price, J. (1988). *Motherhood: What It Does to Your Mind*. Pandora.

Prinds, C., Hvidt, N. C., Mogensen, O., & Buus, N. (2013). Making existential meaning in transition to motherhood: A scoping review. *Midwifery, 30*(6), 733–741. http://dx.doi.org/10.1016/j.midw.2013.06.021

Raphael, D. (Ed.). (1975). *Being Female: Reproduction, Power and Change*. Mouton Publishers.

Razurel, C., Kaiser, B., Sellenet, C., & Epiney, M. (2012). Relation between perceived stress, social support and coping strategies and maternal well-being: A review of the literature. *Women & Health, 53*(1), 74–99. https://doi.org/10.1080/03630242.2012.732681

Sacks, A. (2017, May 8). The birth of a mother. *New York Times*.

Sartre, J.-P. (1958). *Being and Nothingness* (trans. H. E. Barnes). Routledge (Original work published 1943).

Shulman, R. (2020). Through the lens of trauma: The experience of mothering a very premature infant in the first year after hospital discharge. In C. Arnold-Baker (Ed.), *The Existential Crisis of Motherhood* (pp. 115–132). Palgrave Macmillan. https://doi.org/10.1007/978-3-030-56499-5_7

Simmons, E. (2020). Engaging with uncertainty and unresolved meanings during the transition to motherhood. In C. Arnold-Baker (Ed.), *The Existential Crisis of Motherhood* (pp. 93–111). Palgrave Macmillan. https://doi.org/10.1007/978-3-030-56499-5_6

Smith, J. A. (1994). Reconstructing selves: An analysis of discrepancies between women's contemporaneous and retrospective accounts of the transition to motherhood. *British Journal of Psychology, 85*(3), 371–392. https://doi.org/10.1111/j.2044-8295.1994.tb02530.x

Smith, J. A. (1999). Identity development during the transition to motherhood: An interpretative phenomenological analysis. *Journal of Reproductive and Infant Psychology, 17*(3), 215–235. https://doi.org/10.1080/02646839908404595

Stadlen, N. (2005). *What Mothers Do: Especially When It Looks Like Nothing*. Piatkus.

Stern, D. (1995). *The Motherhood Constellation: A Unified View of Parent-Infant Psychotherapy*. Karnac Books.

Stern, D., & Bruschweiler-Stern, N. (1988). *The Birth of a Mother*. Bloomsbury Publishing.

Tillich, P. (2014). *The Courage to Be* (3rd ed.). Yale University Press (Original work published 1952).

Urwin, C. (2007). Doing infant observation differently? Researching the formation of mothering identities in an inner London borough. *International Journal of Infant Observation and Its Applications, 10*, 239–252.

Urwin, C., Hauge, M.-I., Hollway, W., & Haavind, H. (2013). Becoming a mother through culture. *Qualitative Inquiry, 19,* 470–479. https://doi.org/10.1177/1077800413482101

van Deurzen, E. (2010). *Everyday Mysteries: A Handbook of Existential Psychotherapy* (2nd ed.). Routledge. https://doi.org/10.4324/9780203864593

van Deurzen, E. (2014). Structural Existential Analysis (SEA): A phenomenological research method for counselling psychology. *Counselling Psychology Review, 29*(2), 70–83. https://doi.org/10.1007/s10879-014-9282-z

van Manen, M. (1990). *Researching Lived Experience: Human Science for an Action Sensitive Pedagogy.* The Althouse Press.

van Deurzen, E. & Arnold-Baker, C. (2025). *Structural Existential Analysis: An Existential-Phenomenological Method for Researching Life.* Routledge.

Webster, J., Nicholas, C., Velacott, C., Cridland, N., & Fawcett, L. (2011). Quality of life and depression following childbirth: Impact of social support. *Midwifery, 27*(5), 745–749. https://doi.org/10.1016/j.midw.2010.05.014

Chapter 3

Experiences of Women Living Beyond Rape and Interpersonal Violence

Natalie Fraser

Introduction

Three years post-publication, this chapter begins by extending the authors' reflections of a study which set out to investigate the inner dialogue of rape survivors. As a survivor of sexual violence dedicated to working therapeutically with sexual violence, I took the clear and intuitive decision to devote my research to better understanding this experience. Bearing witness to the participants' stories as they generously invited me to walk back in time alongside them to their darkest moments was lifechanging: for the participants, for me, and for innumerable individuals around the world who have found healing and light as a direct result of the insights shared by these eight courageous women. This chapter is dedicated to all those who shared their voices, and to all those whose voices will never be heard.

For me as a researcher, therapist, and human, not a moment goes by without deep awareness of the interpersonal torment which haunts every corner of human history. Humans have oppressed, dehumanised, and silenced others since our species began. The encompassing phenomenon of colonisation takes many forms, from land to race to knowledge to bodies. To oppress another, they must be dehumanised, de-existentialised, objectified. No human is non-human, and no human deserves to be treated as so. I am dedicated to the silenced becoming unsilenced. Let this chapter shine light into the dark, and for each existential shattering offer a restoration of hope.

A literature review

A brief historical overview of sexual violence is hereby provided, before presenting summarised findings which emerged from applying a step-by-step method of Structural Existential Analysis (Fraser, 2023). The proceeding

DOI: 10.4324/9781003493860-4

discussion section highlights key concepts and implications for practitioners, abuse survivors, and the general public. The chapter closes by summarising several final reflections.

Sexual violence is a reality that innumerable people of all ages, genders, and backgrounds experience across the world today, and have done throughout human history. Sexual violence is an intentional act, perpetrated within all number of situations from spontaneous encounters to domestic and professional relationships, incestuous abuse, dedicated grooming, war crimes, and torture. Sexual violence has a long-lasting impact that manifests in a myriad of different physical, embodied, emotional, personal, and social ways. The abundance of 'rape myths' and inadequately limiting definitions within society distorts the reality of what rape really is, adding layers of additional disturbance, confusion, and invalidation for those who have been violated.

Different cultures and contexts propose numerous different definitions about what constitutes rape and sexual assault (Brown & Walklate, 2011). The British metropolitan police define rape as:

> – when a person intentionally penetrates another's vagina, anus or mouth with a penis, without the other person's consent. Assault by penetration is when a person penetrates another person's vagina or anus with any part of the body other than a penis, or by using an object, without the person's consent. (Met.police.uk, 2021)

'Consent' is generally considered the primary determining difference between sex and assault. Within legal settings the victim is burdened by the often-impossible responsibility of providing 'proof beyond reasonable doubt' that they did not consent, one of the many contributing factors to the horrifically limited number of cases which are successfully prosecuted. Since medieval times the experience of reporting rape was a long, traumatising, humiliating process for women, obliged to share their story with 'men of good repute' before being judged by authority figures. Over the evolution of rape, little has changed today (Vaughan, 2002).

A gap in the literature

The majority of rape research is quantitative rather than qualitative. This study speaks to the gap in literature and gives voice to silenced survivors. Central to this chapter is an emphasis on the lasting traumas of sexual violence – the unwanted responsibilities and burdens in 'life beyond rape.' These are presented to raise awareness, with implications for how practitioners and the general public may better support those who have been subjected to this crime. The terms 'psychological growth' 'posttraumatic growth,' and 'healing' are used interchangeably.

Methodology

The original study was conducted from an existential-phenomenological influence, initially drawing on van Deurzen's (2014) Structural Existential Analysis research method. While this method offered the opportunity for a dedicatedly existential approach to research, the methodology was found to lack clear guidance and structure and has been critiqued by experienced phenomenological researchers for having certain methodological short-comings (see Fraser, 2021: 43–44). For this reason, the author developed a clear step-by-step approach to Structured Existential Analysis from which the original study was conducted. This step-by-step approach to SEA has since been published as a method available for novice and expert research-ers (see Fraser, 2023). The eight steps are briefly outlined below:

Step 1: 'Immersion into philosophy' emphasises the importance of actively immersing oneself into global existential philosophies. Beyond the the-oretical enhancement of the researcher's perspective and worldview, deeply confronting existential themes opens passages of self-exploration and assists the invaluable development of self-awareness.

Step 2: 'Mindful Reflexivity' guides researchers to engage with ongo-ing reflectivity to develop awareness throughout the research process related to validity.

Step 3: 'Creative Formulation' supports researchers to confidently create a unique and reliable foundation from which to conduct their analy-sis. 'The Blueprint of Existential Dimensions' (Fraser, 2023: 9) draws on global existential philosophies to organise philosophical concepts in a more manageable overview and guide existentially orientated research-ers in the development of their project.

Step 4: 'Recruiting participants' guides researchers through the sampling process and rationale.

Step 5: 'Hermeneutic interview' guides researchers through the process of data collection through interpretive interviewing.

Step 6: 'Transcription' supports the process of transforming verbal data into written text.

Step 7: 'Application of heuristic models' guides researchers through the data analysis stage.

Step 8: 'Presenting the findings' supports researchers to present the insights gained from their analysis using a thematic overview appropriate to their unique piece of research.

Participants

The participants selected for the original study were eight women between the ages of 20 and 30 who had experienced at least 1 rape within the past 5 years. Interviews were conducted using semi-structured questions via video conferencing. Audio only was recorded using a voice recorder. Participants came from Europe, Asia, and across the Americas.

Analysis and findings

The original detailed findings, including excerpts from participant transcripts, can be found in Fraser (2021: 83–160). Catering for the scope of this chapter, the more relevant Part Two of the findings will hereby be briefly overviewed before elaborating on significant insights within the discussion section. Findings were deemed significant based on their originality and their implications for posttraumatic growth.

Table 3.1 provides an overview of the main themes and subthemes, according to the relevant 'existential dimension' (see 'The Blueprint of Existential Dimensions,' Fraser, 2023: 9).

Table 3.1 Themes and Subthemes

Theme	Subthemes	Existential Dimension
The Search for Meaning	The Burden of Self Creation	Personal
	Blame	
	Self-Esteem	
	Sex & Virginity	
The Myth of Sanctuary	Thrown into Danger	Physical
	Wolves in Sheep's Clothing	
	Suicide	
	Power	
Hell is Stigma	Therapy	Social
	Myths & Stigma	
	Intimacy & Isolation	
	A Labelled Life	
Thus Spoke the Survivors	Inner Advocate	Spiritual
	The Injustice System	
	Religion	
	New Depths of Evil	

Theme 1: The Search for Meaning

This theme name emerged in relation to the theme of meaning as articulated by the work of Frankl's *Man's Search for Meaning* (1946/2004). Unlike Freud, who spoke of a will to pleasure, and Nietzsche, who spoke of a will to power, Frankl suggests humans are driven by a will to meaning. The analysis revealed that a changed sense of self was experienced: their esteem was damaged, their sense of freedom was reduced, their self-creation now carried unwanted burdens, and their most intimate relationship with themselves had been violated by external forces and unwanted memories.

> *I used to have lots of vivid tactile flashbacks for a really long time. And now it's not that so much, but now it's more intrusive thoughts.* (Adriana)

Healing within the personal domain required a search for meaning related to re-creating their identity and rebuilding their intrapersonal relationship. All participants experienced an intense and ongoing struggle with vicious feelings of blaming themselves for the experience, which appeared to develop intuitively regardless of their awareness of rape myths and regardless of the context and nature of the rape. Healing was also experienced as a process of trying to rebuild their shattered sense of self-esteem. Complex for all participants was trying to make sense of their relationship with sex and the social concepts of 'consent' and 'virginity.'

Theme 2: The Myth of Sanctuary

This theme name emerged in relation to the theme of 'the absurd' as articulated by the work of Camus in *The Myth of Sisyphus* (1942). Camus suggests that life is ultimately 'absurd,' that human existence is an ongoing conflict between meaning and chaos, and that only by accepting life's absurdity is one able to live their life to the fullest. The analysis revealed that all participants were continually confronted by realities of trauma and chaos. The participants were required to try and reach a place of accepting the inevitable suffering which they had experienced during the traumatic event/s and which they continued to experience in life beyond rape.

> *Really the nature of it is that someone intentionally harmed you or that something happened to you that basically damaged you so much that it caused all these permanent changes to your brain, and the way you think, and the way you respond to things.* (Viola)

When acceptance was resisted or not possible, the horrors of facticity traumatised them, in some cases to the point of contemplating or attempting suicide.

Healing within the physical domain developed through grappling with a deeper understanding of the world no longer feeling safe, which included the following elements. Recognising that they did not choose to be raped but were 'Thrown into Danger.' Coming to terms with 'Abuser Resemblance Bias' and the awareness that rapists are 'Wolves in Sheep's Clothing,' everyday people who walk among the population without distinguishing features. Battling their inner dialogue in a fight for survival against suicidal ideation and attempts. And coming to terms with the physical, embodied, emotional, psychological, and social power which rapists have over their victims both during and following the experience of rape.

Theme 3: Hell is Stigma

This theme name emerged in relation to the theme of judgement, playing on the popular quote from Sartre in his play *No Exit* during which the protagonist concludes that "Hell is other people!" (1955: 47), observing that the 'gaze' of other people, the judgements of other people, perpetuate the experience of 'hell.' The author was uninformed of Sartre's personal involvement with paedophilia and grooming of students at the time of the original thesis, and the problematics of this are explored in the discussion section of this chapter.

Living in a world of other people and being unable to escape their influence is an inevitable part of being human and a central theme of many existential philosophies. In life after rape, the analysis revealed that this facet of interpersonal existence is shrouded with stigma and assumptions. Healing within the social domain emphasised the value of having access to therapy as an outlet to communicate their experience in a non-judgemental and informative environment. Rape myths and stigmatic assumptions were identified as having a powerful impact, invalidating and confusing the experience, damaging the healing process. Significantly, judgements related to rape myths and assumptions often came from close friends, family, and people in authority such as medical staff and law enforcement. Rape myths not only invalidated the participants' traumatic experience but often perpetuated a shameful and blameful sense of responsibility for their experience. Becoming aware of rape myths was found to aid validation and healing, yet the power of collective stigma and other people's judgements was found to override the validating impact of rape myth awareness, setting a troubling foundation for rebuilding their life beyond rape.

that opinion alone, from somebody that I looked at as my best friend that was supposed to have my back and support me. That brought me down to zero, when I didn't think that I was gonna get to zero. Because she put it out there like: 'you fucked up. You screwed up. You shouldn't have done that.' When really what I needed was, 'Okay. This is not okay. I'm gonna be here for you moving forward and it's gonna be okay.' I needed support, and I didn't get support. And I think she set the tone completely. (Silvia)

Belonging and isolation were significant themes in life beyond rape, which significantly shifted the participants' desire and ability to connect with others in the same way as before they were raped. Isolation was identified as a *relational* distance, as well as a physical distance. Intimacy was unanimously experienced as having been irreversibly changed. Some participants retreated from romantic encounters, whilst others experienced an overactive sex drive – both reactions driven by fear and a lack of control. Yet, a heightened sense of connection and compassion towards other survivors of abuse was expressed by all participants. Finally, life beyond rape was found to become a 'labelled life.' Words like 'survivor' and 'victim' and specific terminology such as 'sexual assault' and 'rape' now became interwoven with their identity – *without* their *choice, without* their *consent.* The meaning and function of these labels was experienced differently. Some participants felt more able to validate their experience and felt closer to others who'd undergone similar experiences. Others found these labels damaging, distressing, shameful, and stigmatising. Labels are not inherently meaningful; they take on the meaning which an individual or a society ascribes to them.

Theme 4: 'Thus Spoke the Survivors'

This theme name emerged in relation to the theme of collective values, as articulated by the work of Nietzsche. In *Thus Spoke Zarathustra* (1883/1976), Nietzsche suggests that humans create their values rather than God creating all values. 'The herd' refers to when most of society holds common values, assumptions, and beliefs. Healing within the spiritual domain involved participants being confronted with a new responsibility to question and re-evaluate the attitudes and actions of others. Unanimous was the discovery of an 'Inner Advocate' within themselves, finding meaning through engaging in various projects which supported and advocated for abuse survivors. This advocacy was identified as one of the most significant and important components of healing which manifested in various different creative and community endeavours. Despite no interview question mentioning the justice system, all participants referred to law enforcement in their interviews. Women from across the world took part in this study, and the overall analysis reveals that there is an international issue with how those in authority understand and respond to rape, and how rape cases are handled. The reporting procedures added new layers of trauma: re-traumatisation, invalidation, betrayal, and disappointment. All participants experienced feeling forced by societal expectations to report their experience whilst grappling with an awareness of how damaging the process of reporting can be.

> And the law is that it has to be – what is it like – proven guilty beyond unreasonable doubt. Like, it has to be 100% sure that the person did it. Which, the problem with rape is that it's generally like two people – alone. (dismayed short laugh) Like there's no witnesses. There's not – unless you're; unless there's dramatic force, which normally there's not. There's no like evidence. So, there's no way to ever prove anything. Which… (sigh). (Ely)

The analysis also unanimously found that experiencing rape had a transformative impact on their relationship with religion and/or spirituality. This shift manifested uniquely for each participant and was a fluctuating process involving investment of their time and emotional resources. For some participants, religion became a pivotal space to explore and understand their experiences. For others, their relationship with God was shattered irreversibly due to a sense of betrayal.

This section has provided a brief overview of the themes and subthemes which emerged from the analysis. The following section will elaborate on certain key themes and issues, making relevant evidence-based recommendations for practitioners and the general public.

Discussion

Rape Is Not Sex

Rape is to sex like a punch in the mouth is to a kiss. (Benedict, 1993: 14) This discussion will begin by emphasising that *rape is not a sexual experience… it is an unsolicited act of violence* (Benedict, 1993; Wright, 2019). Definitions of these forms of abuse are rooted in physical action and physical body parts: "penetration," "penis," "vagina" (Met.police.uk, 2021) related to sex and reproduction. This reality combined with the use of the word 'sex' in 'sexual abuse' perpetuates a misguided yet widespread affiliation with sexual behaviour. 'Consent' is considered the primary determining difference between sex and rape.

The terms *'sexual* violence, assault, abuse,' etc. have been used for decades and are deeply engrained within discourse. The reality of finding and popularising more appropriate terms seems unrealistic and hopeless at this point. Yet it is important to emphasise the reality that being violated is never a sexual experience for a non-consenting victim, and beyond this, in many cases the act is not always sexually driven for the perpetrator either. Relevant literature emphasises that this form of abuse commonly has less to do with a perpetrator's erotic or sexual desire as much as it has to do with power and control (Fuchs, 2004).

While the terminology is unlikely to change, this author recommends a reframing of how rape and related forms of violation are conceptualised: it is not bad or painful sex; rather, it is an act of violation across the existential dimensions.

Inappropriate Themes

The title themes 'Hell is Stigma' and 'Thus Spoke the Survivors' were inspired by the concepts of Sartre and Nietzsche respectively. The author was unaware until post-publication of Sartre's involvement with paedophilia and sexual grooming of students (Fraser, 2024; Lamblin, 1996) and Nietzsche's infamy of being misogynistic, chauvinistic, and sexist towards women (Oliver & Persall, 2010). It is undeniable that these philosophers have had immeasurable impact within the field of philosophy and beyond; however, this author considers the aforementioned title themes and inclusion of these philosophers' work fundamentally inappropriate within the context of a project aiming to provide deeper insights into oppression and sexual violence. Other relevant metaphors and concepts would have been selected had the author been made aware of these philosophers' actions at the time. This author advocates for honest and transparent education which may afford students and scholars the informed consent of whose work they choose to include.

To overcome this and prevent similar distress for future existential scholars who may be vicariously or personally impacted by sexual violence, the author has subsequently written and spoken publicly about this issue widely, calling for existential educators to uphold their responsibility for transparently disclosing the attitudes and behaviours of the thinkers behind these widely celebrated theories (see Fraser, 2024). This has led to changes in teaching policies within leading existential institutions.

Existential Shattering

Greening (1990) and Hoffman et al. (2013) significantly contributed to existential trauma literature offering the concept of 'existential shattering.' A distinction is made between PTSD which focuses on trauma and stress characterised by disruptive symptoms, and existential shattering which refers to experiences which annihilate one's sense of self and worldview. The focus is not on the event, but rather on the underlying impact of it over time. All participants experienced this annihilation of their sense of self and worldview, yet the nature of their existential shattering was found to drastically vary both between individuals and across time. Participants that experienced a lapse of time between the rape and their understanding and acceptance of being raped recognised that the 'shattering' – also expressed as 'breakdown' – occurred not during the rape but during the realisation. Much like the instantaneousness of a glass shattering upon contact with a hard surface, the sense of existential shattering was described as an instantaneous response to the personal acceptance and realisation of this profoundly traumatic truth.

Unlike common assumptions which focus on the traumatic event being the most traumatic element, referring also to many mainstream approaches to trauma treatment which promote the need for traumatic details to be explored for successful healing to occur (critiqued by Sanderson, 2013), the findings highlight that the ongoing aftermath of sexual violence is equally or more traumatic than the singular event itself. This may be due to the complex ongoing impact, and because many people being raped dissociate from the experience, often articulated as a numbness, a blackout, or leaving their body. Practitioners and society would do well to listen to the voices of survivors and put aside their preconceived assumptions of which aspect of the trauma is most traumatic. Therapeutic support should be guided by each individual and not presume a necessity to discuss the details of traumatic events. In many cases, it is more appropriate to explore the present lived challenges that are being experienced in the aftermath of trauma.

The notion that people should 'overcome' trauma, as if a 'completable' task, must be abolished and reframed. Psychologists must normalise and validate that everything we experience, including trauma, becomes embodied and existentially interwoven, inevitably altering our lives beyond the event in complex and ongoing ways. Developing awareness of this through continued self-inquiry and compassion is key to the ongoing process of healing and existing.

When considering healing and existential shattering, I draw on the Japanese art of Kintsugi. Kintsugi is an ancient Japanese practice of repairing broken ceramics using lacquer mixed with powdered gold. Kintsugi is not just an art, it is a philosophy recognising a process not just of restoration but that this rebuilding enhances the original entity. This is a powerful metaphor of hope in the context of existential shattering: trauma may shatter oneself into fragments, yet this creates a new foundation for individuals to re-create and restore their existence more meaningfully than ever before. Another fundamental feature of Kintsugi is the valuing of multiple people involved in the restoration process. Interpersonal violence may cause a sense of isolation, yet the positive support of others is fundamental for healing. Participants unanimously acknowledged the support of others, including therapists, as pivotal in their healing journey.

Rape Myths

Unlike other interpersonal crimes, victims of rape are uniquely vulnerable for being blamed and questioned for their assault. Research exploring victim blaming within the contexts of acquaintance and stranger rape has found significant experiential difference between the two, and widely highlight that rape is more commonly perpetrated by someone known to their victim (Gravelin et al., 2019). Stigma and rape myths are a central cause of victim blaming, especially within the context of acquaintance rape (Gravelin et al., 2019). Rape myths have been defined as false cultural beliefs that exist to shift the blame from perpetrators to victims (Burt, 1980), creating a hostile climate with significant implications for the underreporting of this crime (Rollero & Tartaglia, 2019). With such an expansive repertoire of rape myths embedded in different social contexts, it is impossible within the scope of this chapter to offer a detailed overview. Therefore, several common examples identified within literature and participant experience are hereby provided to give context to the phenomenon: 'women ask for it,' 'women cry rape when they're hiding something,' 'men can't be raped,' 'it's not rape if you know the person,' 'it's not rape if you're in a relationship,' 'it's only rape if it is violent,' etc. Social attitude is inundated with unrealistic and stigmatic assumptions of what 'counts' as rape and who is more likely to perpetrate rape. Practitioners and society would do well to abolish these harmful misconceptions.

Only one participant expressed undoubtingly 'knowing' that they were being raped at the time of rape, and all participants expressed questioning their experience after being raped. This chapter strives to not merely educate its readers into the presence and prevalence of rape myths, but also to illuminate the very real and profoundly damaging impact that they have on survivors of sexual violence. Central to this impact is the role rape myths play on preventing individuals to understand and subsequently accept the truth of what they have experienced. The understanding and acceptance of one's experience is central to the healing process. Practitioners and society would do well to become aware of rape myths and gently support individuals to identify the reality of their experience, reducing the confusion, shame, self-blame, and stigma surrounding these forms of abuse, and moving forward on their healing journey with self-compassion rather than self-judgement.

Abuser Resemblance Bias

As briefly outlined in the findings section above, life beyond rape includes coming to terms with the awareness that rapists are 'Wolves in Sheep's

Clothing,' everyday people who walk inconspicuously among the population.

> *They were normal, normal guys... like, I don't think they've ever done it to anyone else as far as I know. The other guy was a serial rapist, he was really violent. It was easy for me to see in hindsight that that's just the kind of person he is. The other two times it was difficult for me, because it felt like it had happened because of who I am instead of who they are. Which of course isn't true. But it just really starts messing with the way you see people.* (Adriana)

Despite stereotypical media depictions of shadowy figures hiding in parks and badly lit underpasses, in real life 'a rapist' has no distinguishing features. The rape myths section has already expanded on the unrealistic and stigmatic assumptions of who is more likely to perpetrate rape, abolishing the misconception that stranger rape is the most common and emphasising the reality that rape is more frequently perpetrated by someone known to their victim. This section will address the impact of this reality drawing on existential uncertainty and evolutionary bias development.

Unanimously experienced by all participants was a newfound involuntary embodied reaction towards people who resembled their abuser, predominantly manifesting as instinctive fear as well as disgust, hatred, mistrust, intimidation, shame, etc. This resulted in physical, embodied, emotional, social, and spiritual upheaval when encountering someone who resembled their abuser. In all cases, this developed unwantedly and intuitively. All the participants felt deeply guilty and shameful of these involuntary biased responses which began haunting their everyday lives in complex ways.

> *it was a police officer which [raped] me.... I'm the daughter of a police officer. My step-dad's a police officer. I come from a long line of police officers. And I was always raised to trust them. I was raised that in times of need always go to a police officer. And um... he used that badge and manipulated me with that badge. And it made me look at police officers completely differently. It made me look at my dad differently. It made me look at all my family members differently.* (Silvia)

Despite this phenomenon being described in detail by all participants during the original study and echoed frequently by clients in my clinical practice, surprisingly it remains unnamed in abuse literature with a shocking lack of specific inferences of this very important, very prevalent experience. Therefore, I am coining the term 'Abuser Resemblance Bias,' which this section will hereby discuss.

One example detailing this phenomenon is offered by the *Diagnostic and Statistical Manual of Mental Disorders* (DSM-IV)'s definition of PTSD which includes 'Fear of people who resemble the alleged abuser' as a primary symptom (American Psychological Association, 1994). Another example is offered by Sanderson (2013: 34), who recognises that people who resemble their abuser can act as a 'trigger' for victims of sexual abuse. Interestingly, this phenomenon is more commonly described outside academic literature such as on public blogs and forums which address the heartbreaking implications of this and call to the online community for help, such as when one's child or oneself begins to resemble one's abuser (e.g. Denby, 2021; [Grabba], 2019; [Tiny_Prancer_88], 2021).

As the term suggests, 'Abuser Resemblance Bias' refers to an innate development of biased feelings and attitudes towards someone that resembles the person/s that abused them. To discern between potential negative connotations of the word 'bias' and how bias is understood within the context of Abuser Resemblance Bias, it is important to understand its etymology. The word 'bias' derives from old 13th-century French *biais*, meaning "a slant, a slope, an oblique" (*Oxford English Dictionary*, 2021). It is thought to have entered into English language via the still-popular French game of boules in reference to balls made with a greater weight on one side, which caused the ball to curve obliquely. Over time, the word bias subsequently became used in reference to "a one-sided tendency of the mind" (*Oxford English Dictionary*, 2021).

It is widely accepted, for example in the context of phenomenological research, that to exist as a human is to exist with biases (Fraser, 2023). That is to say, from birth humans develop attitudes which slant towards or away from different phenomena as we come into contact with them either personally (learning through our own experience) or vicariously (learning through the experience or biases of others). Furthermore, having developed a bias of something directly impacts our feelings, attitudes, and behaviours towards it. A neutral example may be learning that fire burns us, developing the bias that fire is dangerous, and subsequently avoiding fire. A social example may be learning that certain people (e.g. parents, police, doctors, teachers, priests) are trustworthy, developing the bias that you should trust these people, and subsequently unquestioningly trusting them.

Humans have an organic threat detection system that is predisposed to bias attention towards dangerous stimuli as a means of basic existential survival. Existential and evolutionary psychology alike emphasise that the human world is one of uncertainty shrouded with abundant stimuli which humans must grapple with to make sense of. Evolutionary psychology research has identified that negative associations develop specifically to identify danger within a complex perceptual world, generating signals of threat, responses of fear, and behaviours of protection. Significantly to Abuser Resemblance Bias, once this negative association has been established, research clearly highlights that the fear response can be evoked by proximal (similar) and much briefer (less intense) presentations than the real/original reality (Öhman & Soares, 1993). Other people are arguably the greatest threat to life and greatest source of danger (Haselton & Nettle, 2005). Research into in-group/out-group dynamics explains the evolution of negative bias as a means of categorising unknown individuals into knowable entities, quickly discerning between the safe and the hostile, the kind and the violent.

It would be inauthentic to discuss this process without recognising arguably the most prolifically tragic manifestation of this: racial, ethnic, religious, sexual, and gender discrimination (Sidanius & Veniegas, 2000). While future publications intend to address this in more detail which the scope of this chapter does not permit, *choosing* to live and behave in a discriminatory way against certain racial, ethnic, religious, sexual, and gender groups must be understood as *fundamentally different* to the *involuntary intuitive* development of Abuser Resemblance Bias following interpersonal violence. Drawing on empirically supported evolutionary psychology perspectives aspires to psycho-educate helping professionals working with sexual violence and appease the guilt which many survivors of abuse become burdened with. The development of Abuser Resemblance Bias, such as involuntarily cognitive and embodied fear/disgust/mistrust responses when encountering someone who resembles their abuser, has nothing to do with the character, morality, or values of the person who has been violated and warrants no shame nor guilt nor self-hatred on their behalf. Rather, this experience is one connected with ancient inner wisdom and evolutionary survival instincts becoming 'overactive' in attempt to protect oneself from potential danger in an uncertain world.

The Myth of Virginity

The final theme discussed is virginity, another feature shockingly absent in relevant abuse literature. The meaning of the word 'virgin' has shifted over time (McArthur, 2022). Deriving from the Greek word 'virgo,' its early roots in ancient Greek mythology classified certain goddesses who were immune to the temptations of certain gods. It was a term meaning power. In medieval times the concept shifted, with virginity referring to a gift from the Christian God. It was a term meaning purity. Only the husband had the right to 'take' their wife's virginity through penetrative intercourse, and in this act she would 'become a woman.' Women were expected to remain 'chaste' or 'virgins' until marriage, dishonouring their family and often being punished if they were found not to be. Various humiliating and invasive mystical and medical tests were used to assess a woman's status, putting the woman on trial and causing suspicion of their character (Bennett et al., 2010). Central to this was checking that a woman's hymen was intact, a test later discredited as the fragile hymen can easily break with normal physical activities, and many women are born without one. In recent decades the term 'virgin' has become used in reference to people of all genders who have not experienced sexual intimacy, and the notions around what constitutes virginity are somewhat complicated and subjected to judgement within different cultures and sexual orientations. Virgin is now a term with different meanings, sometimes condescending (e.g. prude), sometimes in high regard (e.g. pure), sometimes a neutral fact.

In the context of rape and sexual assault, the findings of the original study highlight that the concept of virginity and the myth of what virgin status means about someone's character are highly problematic. Common social narratives around sex and sexuality are sexist and homophobic, with a medieval hangover overemphasising the power of men and the desired purity of women whilst paradoxically demanding women to be sexual. These outdated gender dynamics also impact males with cultural narratives using heterosexual sex to define 'becoming a man' with many reporting extreme pressure and social expectations to overcome this by having sex with a female during adolescence (Zajdel, 2020).

Underdiscussed is the deeply traumatic and confusing experience of rape being one's first 'sexual' encounter. Participants shared personal accounts of having 'lost their virginity' by rape, being penetrated against their will before intuitively feeling ready for sex, including *in all cases of childhood sexual assault*, and grappling with what this means in relation to constructs of virginity and purity.

> And this whole narrative of like, 'is she a virgin?' how that means that she's pure but then also it's like she's a prude. And there's something about her entire being changes the minute that she has sex. There's this insinuation… just seeing how harmful it is.
>
> And that view is incredibly homophobic. You know, gay experiences aren't taken into consideration when we talk about losing virginity and stuff.
>
> And also for sexual assault survivors and rape survivors. What does that mean about how they get to lose their virginity? This experience that they didn't want to happen or didn't ask to happen. Like does this have to be their defining experience where their whole being changes? Just seeing how that this social construct that we've been forced to accept. And now I kind of reject it.

It's something I speak out against. Definitely there are people who are struggling with it. Like, people who didn't want to lose it the way they did, or sexual assault survivors. And I tell them it's not a real thing.

And really when you look at it is really is just problematic. Especially the way that it's portrayed in western culture. (Viola)

If we consider the historical concept philosophically, virginity is paradoxically something that men can take from a woman but women are not rightfully able to give. The 'possession' of virginity belongs first to the father, then to the husband. In the context of rape, virginity is stolen by the rapist. Already emphasised is the intuitive blame and shame related to sexual violence. One participant disclosed being overtly told by family and community that she was now 'a whore; damaged goods,' having been raped before choosing to engage in sex – a sentiment echoed time and time again in my therapeutic work with victims of abuse. This is but one of many examples of the additional layers of long-lasting trauma which victims of abuse may experience.

Equally underdiscussed within literature is the impact that abuse can have on one's experience of their sexuality. Participants in the original study – both those who had no previous sexual experience and those who were sexually active prior to their rape – spoke of questioning their sexuality after being raped. Life beyond rape was haunted by unanswerable questions: Did being raped by a man impact my sexual orientation? What would my relationship with sex be if I'd never been violated? How is it possible to enjoy sex when such similar actions were violating and humiliating? Will I ever choose to have sex again? Am I choosing to have excessive sex in attempt to regain power of the experience? Am I choosing abusive partners to prevent the shock of being abused? This is not a discussion concerned with to-date understandings of sexuality; this is a discussion highlighting the lived experiences of rape victims questioning their sexuality when their relationship to their sexuality has been exploited and irreversibly impacted.

Conclusion

This chapter offered a glimpse into Fraser's (2021) original study concerning the lived experience of rape survivors. The discussion expanded on core themes. Despite being bound through definitions, the association between 'sex' and 'rape' is severely problematic. Indeed, "rape is to sex as a punch in the mouth is to a kiss." Rape creates a long-lasting 'Existential Shattering' of one's emotions, identity, relationships, and embodied world. Rape Myths invalidate and complicate reality, perpetuating blame and shame and preventing acceptance and healing. Abuser Resemblance Bias develops intuitively from ancient survival wisdom that evolves to protect us from danger and need not be a source of guilt. And The Myth of Virginity need be re-evaluated, liberating people of all ages, genders, sexualities, sexual experiences, and abuse from the dated and disempowering judgements by which this concept currently holds people captive. In a world where people are dehumanised, as practitioners and human beings we are responsible for confronting this reality and creating light for those whose paths have become shrouded in darkness.

References

American Psychological Association. (1994). *Diagnostic and Statistical Manual of Mental Disorders* (4th ed.). APA.

Benedict, H. (1993). *Virgin or Vamp: How the Press Covers Sex Crimes*. Oxford University Press on Demand.

Bennett, T. W., Mills, C., & Munnick, G. (2010). Virginity testing: A crime, a delict or a genuine cultural tradition? *Journal of South African Law/Tydskrif vir die Suid-Afrikaanse Reg, 2*, 254–270. https://hdl.handle.net/10520/EJC55312

Brown, J. M., & Walklate, S. L. (Eds.). (2011). *Handbook on Sexual Violence*. Routledge. https://doi.org/10.4324/9780203802434

Burt, M. R. (1980). Cultural myths and supports for rape. *Journal of Personality and Social Psychology, 38*(2), 217–230. https://doi.org/10.1037/0022-3514.38.2.217

Camus, A. (1942). *The Myth of Sisyphus*. Gallimard.

Denby, O. (2021, June 10). How can I love myself when I look like my abuser? *Medium.* https://medium.com/invisible-illness/how-can-i-love-myself-when-i-look-like-my-abuser-40089c304f66

Frankl, V. E. (2004). *Man's Search for Meaning*. Ebury (Original work published 1946).

Fraser, N. (2021). *You are not alone: An existential-phenomenological exploration of how inner dialogue is experienced by rape survivors* (Doctoral dissertation). Middlesex University/New School of Psychotherapy and Counselling (NSPC). https://repository.mdx.ac.uk/item/8q251

Fraser, N. (2023). Structural Existential Analysis (SEA) – A step-by-step guide for application to research. *Counselling Psychology Review, 38*(2), 4–19. https://doi.org/10.53841/bpscpr.2023.38.2.4

Fraser, N. (2024) Decolonising existential philosophy: Considering disciplinary decadence within Western existential thought. *Existential Analysis, 35*(1), 46–64.

Fuchs, S. F. (2004). Male sexual assault: Issues of arousal and consent. *Cleveland State Law Review, 51*(1), 93–121.

[Grabba]. (2012, March 19). My son looks like my abuser. *Mumsnet.* https://www.mumsnet.com/talk/am_i_being_unreasonable/3536942-my-son-looks-like-my-abuser

Gravelin, C. R., Biernat, M., & Bucher, C. E. (2019). Blaming the victim of acquaintance rape: Individual, situational, and sociocultural factors. *Frontiers in Psychology, 9*, 2422. https://doi.org/10.3389/fpsyg.2018.02422

Greening, T. (1990). PTSD from the perspective of existential-humanistic psychology. *Journal of Traumatic Stress, 3*(2), 323–326. https://doi.org/10.1002/jts.2490030213

Haselton, M. G., & Nettle, D. (2005). The paranoid optimist: An integrative evolutionary model of cognitive biases. *Personality and Social Psychology Review, 10*(1), 47–66. https://doi.org/10.1207/s15327957pspr1001_3

Hoffman, L., Hoffman, H., & Vallejos, L. (2013, March). *Existential issues in trauma: Implications for assessment and treatment* [Paper presentation]. 121st Annual Convention of the American Psychological Association, Honolulu, HI.

Lamblin, B. (1996). *Disgraceful Affair*. Northeastern University Press.

McArthur, N. (2022). The concept and significance of virginity. In B. D. Earp, C. Chambers, & L. Watson (Eds.), *The Routledge Handbook of Philosophy of Sex and Sexuality* (pp. 65–77). Routledge.

Met.police.uk. (2021). What is rape and sexual assault? *The Met.* https://www.met.police.uk/advice/advice-and-information/rsa/rape-and-sexual-assault/what-is-rape-and-sexual-assault/

Nietzsche, N. (1976) *Thus Spoke Zarathustra*. Penguin (Original work published 1883).

Öhman, A., & Soares, J. J. (1993). On the automatic nature of phobic fear: Conditioned electrodermal responses to masked fear-relevant stimuli. *Journal of Abnormal Psychology, 102*(1), 121–132. https://doi.org/10.1037/0021-843X.102.1.121

Oliver, K. A., & Pearsall, M. (Eds.). (2010). *Feminist Interpretations of Friedrich Nietzsche*. Penn State Press.

Oxford English Dictionary. (2021). https://www.oed.com/

Rollero, C., & Tartaglia, S. (2019). The effect of sexism and rape myths on victim blame. *Sexuality & Culture, 23*(1), 209–219. https://doi.org/10.1007/s12119-018-9549-8

Sanderson, C. (2013). *Counselling Skills for Working With Trauma: Healing From Child Sexual Abuse, Sexual Violence and Domestic Abuse*. Jessica Kingsley Publishers. https://doi.org/10.1002/car.2352

Sartre, J.-P. (1955). *No Exit and Three Other Plays*. Knopf Doubleday Publishing Group.

Sidanius, J., & Veniegas, R. C. (2000). Gender and race discrimination: The interactive nature of disadvantage. In S. Oskamp (Ed.), *Reducing Prejudice and Discrimination: The Claremont Symposium on Applied Social Psychology* (pp. 47–69). Lawrence Erlbaum Associates, Inc.

[Tiny_Prancer_88]. (2021). I look like my abuser. *r/CPTSD* [Online forum post]. *Reddit.* https://www.reddit.com/r/CPTSD/comments/nnrd2x/i_look_like_my_abuser/

van Deurzen, E. (2014). Structural Existential Analysis (SEA): A phenomenological research method for counselling psychology. *Counselling Psychology Review, 29*(2), 70–83. https://doi.org/10.1007/s10879-014-9282-z

Vaughan, A. E. (2002). *An evolutionary perspective of human female rape* (Doctoral dissertation). University of Central Lancashire.

Wright, E. Q. (2019). Rape trauma. In *The Encyclopedia of Women and Crime*. Wiley Online Library. https://doi.org/10.1002/9781118929803.ewac0431

Zajdel, A. A. (2020). *Stigmatized virginity and masculinity: Exploring in non-virgin cisgender heterosexual men* (Doctoral dissertation). The University of Nebraska-Lincoln.

Developing a Self Through Early Life Trauma

Chapter 4

Emerging from Adolescent Sexual Grooming: The Need for Truth

Amy Bramley

Grooming: "The process by which sex offenders carefully initiate and maintain sexually abusive relationships with children. Grooming is a conscious, deliberate, and carefully orchestrated approach used by the offender. The goal of grooming is to permit a sexual encounter and keep it a secret." (Knoll, 2010: 374)

Introduction

The need of truth is more sacred than any other need. Yet it is never mentioned. (Weil, 1949/2002: 36)

This study, conducted from 2020 to 2024, coincided with heightened awareness of adolescent sexual grooming as a phenomenon. In 2020, the most comprehensive report ever conducted on the safety of adolescents in the United Kingdom found adolescents six times more likely to be sexually abused, and nine times more likely to be groomed online than younger children (National Society for the Prevention of Cruelty to Children [NSPCC], 2020). Two years later, grooming had increased by 80% over four years, with four out of five victims being girls aged 12 to 15 (NSPCC, 2022). In January 2024, at the time of writing this chapter in France, 51-year-old French actress Judith Godrèche lodged a complaint for 'rape with violence on a minor' committed against her aged 14 by a director 25 years her senior (Foucher & Lefilliâtre, 2024). Her testimony fed into an ongoing reckoning with French society's tendency to ignore the sexual abuse of teenaged girls by older men that began with Vanessa Springora's (2019) memoir of her adolescent grooming at the hands of writer and paedophile Gabriel Matzneff.

DOI: 10.4324/9781003493860-6

My own interest in this subject stems from my experience of being sexually groomed, aged 13, by a man 16 years my senior. I did not go through a process of self-disclosure until my early forties, meaning that for many years I lived silently in the shadow of my abuse. Echoing this experience, participants in my doctoral study took an average of 15.9 years to wake up to the truth of their grooming, with 12.4 years being the average age at which their abuse began. Permissive societal attitudes heightened their sense of culpability for their abuse, preventing them from disclosing. Eventual disclosure to a supportive other emerged as an important milestone in their healing.

In this chapter, I provide a selective literature review that explores what makes an adolescent vulnerable to grooming, and why survivors frequently struggle to wake up to and disclose the truth of their experience. I also present literature on how disclosure and the context of disclosure relates to healing from interpersonal trauma. In my exploration of how sexual grooming in the adolescent years might impact the individual, I draw on contemporary psychological research as well as existential thought.

In conducting my interviews, the indifference of parents and other adults prior to, during, and after the grooming experience was striking. The idea that grooming is a social abuse and trauma, not merely a sexual and personal-relational one, emerged both in accounts of how grooming had been allowed to happen, and what healing might look like. Victims had felt unsafe, unheard, and unloved in their family home, making them vulnerable to attention from elsewhere, and incapable of seeking help when they were groomed. I explore this in my first theme: **the search for sanctuary**. Feeling culpable for their abuse, aware that bystanders had done nothing to intervene, they later struggled to speak up, becoming trapped in cycles of revictimisation and psychological struggle, as reflected in the second theme: **living the wounds of grooming**. Lastly, I consider what moving **towards a new way of being** might look like, emphasising the need for truth and validation, as well as the existential themes of finding meaning and living in ethical intersubjectivity with others.

Literature review

Defining Adolescent Sexual Grooming

Research in the area of sexual grooming is complicated by the fact that grooming is difficult to define (Winters et al., 2020). In academia, researchers complain that past definitions frequently fall short of incorporating all possible grooming behaviours, excluding tactics such as victim selection and post-abuse maintenance (as in Brackenridge & Fasting, 2005; DiLillo et al., 2010). Here, I summarise the definition of grooming provided within

Winters et al.'s Sexual Grooming Model (SGM, 2020: 860), see Table 4.1, which draws on "the commonalities identified in several previously proposed models, as well as identifying gaps of missing information" (Winters et al., 2020: 860).

Table 4.1 The Sexual Grooming Model: The Five Stages of Sexual Grooming (Winters et al., 2020: 860)

	The Five Stages of Sexual Grooming
1	The selection of a vulnerable victim
2	Gaining access to and isolating said victim
3	Developing trust with the victim
4	Desensitising the victim to sexual content & physical contact
5	A post-abuse maintenance stage

What Makes an Adolescent Girl Vulnerable?

Groomers are known to have clear strategies for victim selection, and emotionally vulnerable individuals are easier targets (Craven et al., 2006; Williams, 2015; Winters et al., 2020). There is comparatively little research examining societal and familial factors that increase vulnerability in adolescence. Adolescents might be attractive to groomers because they are more open to experimentation and less restricted by parents than other children (Williams, 2015), but what is it that makes some more vulnerable than others? Home environments with significantly higher levels of abuse (physical, psychological, and sexual) appear to be a factor (Jonsson et al., 2019). Family instability, such as single parenthood, which results in a lack of parental supervision of internet use, also increases vulnerability (Whittle et al., 2014).

One explanation for why maltreatment in childhood increases revictimisation in general is that it leads to difficulties in regulating emotions (Burns et al., 2010), a drop in self-esteem, and an increase in psychological struggles (Whittle et al., 2014). Emotion regulation incorporates "the awareness, understanding and acceptance of emotions"; "the ability to control behaviours when experiencing distress"; and "to use contextually appropriate emotion regulation strategies" (Gratz & Roemer, 2004, in Charak et al., 2018, para. 5). From an attachment theory perspective (Ainsworth, 1978; Bowlby, 1991), abusive and/or neglectful parenting creates an insecure attachment style in the child, feeding an internal working model that becomes a guidance system for future behaviour in relationships (Bowlby, 1991). Insecure attachment has been found to mediate between experiences of childhood maltreatment and the risk of sexual revictimisation

(Atmaca & Gençöz, 2016; Humphrey & White, 2000; Miron & Orcutt, 2014; Orcutt et al., 2005).

The Effects of Adolescent Sexual Grooming

Trauma symptoms in survivors of adolescent sexual grooming include re-experiencing, avoidance, and hyper-arousal (Leahy, 2010, 2011; Wolf & Pruitt, 2019). In one study, adolescents sexually groomed online presented more depression and anxiety symptoms than a control group (Gámez-Guadix et al., 2023). Meanwhile, high rates of suicidal ideation have been identified in adolescent girls who experience childhood sexual abuse (CSA) (Girard et al., 2021; Miller & Esposito-Smythers, 2013). Gomez (2019) explored the differential impacts of sexual abuse across the lifespan (child, adolescent, adult), finding that adolescent sexual abuse (between ages 13 and 18) was linked with non-suicidal self-injury, while earlier child sexual abuse was not.

In *Truth and Repair* (2023), Judith Herman argues that protracted relational abuse deforms the victim's personality, particularly when it occurs in childhood and adolescence. It results in "a broken identity" (Herman, 2023: 57–58), leaving the victim struggling to form relationships, to trust, to experience intimacy and mutuality (59).

Existential philosophy provides rich conceptual language to make sense of the struggle Herman (2023) describes. For Merleau-Ponty (1945/2011) and de Beauvoir (1949/2011), relational power battles are inherent to intersubjectivity. Both writers draw on Hegel's (1807/1977) concept of the emergence of self-consciousness and the master and slave dialectic. Merleau-Ponty (1945/2011) emphasises the inherent conflict of mastery within any human relationship. "To say that I have a body is thus a way of saying that I can be seen as an object and that I seek to be seen as a subject, that another person can be my master or my slave" (Merleau-Ponty, 1945/2011: 170). De Beauvoir (1949/2011) argues that woman can only ever be "Other" to man's existential subject (Butler, 1990: 49). "Humanity is male, and man defines woman, not in herself, but in relation to himself; she is not considered an autonomous being" (de Beauvoir, 1949/2011: 5).

Meanwhile, Levinas (1961), Weil (1949/2002), and de Beauvoir (1949/2015) assert the inherently ethical nature of relationships. These authors' attempts at an ethics of existentialism came out of their confrontations with the cruelty and atrocities of which man is capable – in particular, mass trauma in the form of the Spanish Civil War (Weil), World War II, and the Holocaust (all three). For de Beauvoir (1949/2015: 169), "the individual is defined only by his relationship to the world and to other individuals; he exists only by transcending himself, and his freedom can be achieved only through the freedom of others." Levinas (1961) arguably goes further, positing that ethics are innate within us, preverbal and pre-language: in the face-to-face encounter with another human being we feel an immediate ethical responsibility. Where responsibility to others is ignored and people commit acts of violence or abuse, such acts "do not consist so much in injuring and annihilating persons as in interrupting their continuity, making them play roles in which they no longer recognise themselves" (Levinas, 1961: 21).

Fisher (2005) writes that survivors of CSA are "living as exiles from our own homeland, the inner world of subjective experience" (Bugental, 1978: 124, as cited in Fisher, 2005: 37). Building on the imagery of forced migration, Fisher (2005: 37) adds scenes of war and tumult: the psyche is a "battleground," a place of "defensive storms," the voices of its exiled parts rising to a "cacophony." She quotes Yalom's (1980) four existential concerns of freedom, isolation, meaninglessness, and death, which are experienced "in an unusually stark and pervasive manner" (Fisher, 2005: 25) by CSA survivors.

Boaz (2022) encapsulates the desperation to find an anchor when confronted with reality via traumatic interpersonal experience in a physical metaphor: he describes a "state of spinning (…) seeking to find a form of meaning and set of values that will ground us and connect us to ourselves, others and the world around us" (Boaz, 2022: 103). While drawing on a philosopher who aligned himself with Nazism is, for Boaz, absurd in any exploration of interpersonal trauma, he nonetheless finds Heidegger's (1927/2010) concept of inauthenticity useful in describing the "turning away from our being" that occurs when we are overwhelmed by existential anxiety to the degree that we enter an ontic mode of forgetting (Boaz, 2022: 110).

When an experience is so fundamentally destabilising to our being, how do we proceed? Frankl (1946/2004) quotes Nietzsche: "He who has a why to live for can bear almost any how" (Frankl, 1946/2004: 84). It was thanks to Frankl's book that Eger, years after surviving the Holocaust herself (in 1966), was inspired to explore such questions as, "Why did I survive? What is the purpose of my life? What meaning can I make from my suffering?" (Eger, 2017: 162). She discovered she "had the power and opportunity – as well as the responsibility – to choose (her) own meaning, her own life" (162). Boaz (2022: 157) describes two positive modes to emerge from traumatic confrontations with reality: survivalism and survivorism. With survivalism, the survivor actively engages with "stressful environments and potentially threat-inducing relationships" to challenge and create change (157). Survivorism means "disclosing their experience of trauma" and using it as "a core explanatory mechanism to understand the experiences they have in the present" (157).

The Challenge of Disclosure

In stages two to five of Winters and colleagues' (2020) sexual grooming model, groomers isolate their victim, develop trust with her, habituate her to sexual content, and – post-abuse – maintain relations to prevent disclosure. These tactics partly explain why survivors often struggle for years to face the truth of their experience (Burgess & Hartman, 2018; Knoll, 2010; Lanning & Dietz, 2014; Winters & Jeglic, 2022). Meanwhile, in cases where parents or others were aware of the abuse, "the complicity and silence of bystanders feel like a profound betrayal"; survivors feel this "more deeply even than the direct harms inflicted by perpetrators" (Herman, 2023: 36–37). Familial and societal silence heightens shame and self-blame in the survivor (Gámez-Guadix et al., 2023; Gomez, 2019; Royal Commission into Institutional Responses to Child Sexual Abuse, 2017). "Out of necessity, the child turns her back on her experience of what is occurring and accepts the myth that nothing extraordinary is happening" (Fisher, 2005: 13).

In her (2020) novel about adolescent sexual grooming, *My Dark Vanessa*, Russell's eponymous heroine spends years framing her grooming by a teacher as a complex love story (Russell, 2020: 318), writing, "He never forced me, ok? He made sure I said yes to everything. (…) He was good. He loved me" (372). Russell (2020) calls grooming experiences "histories of abuse that look like love," encapsulating the confusion experienced by survivors, and recalling the concept of 'betrayal blindness' (Freyd, 1996), whereby incest victims struggle to accept that a relative who claimed to love them also abused them.

Meanwhile, Tedeschi and Calhoun (1995: 46) emphasise that how others respond at moments of disclosure is essential: "the combination of self-disclosure with accepting and supportive responses to the disclosure by members of primary reference groups" may reflect a form of posttraumatic growth. Wager (2015) agrees, underlining the importance of timely disclosure of CSA which is appropriately responded to, arguing that it may reduce the risk of revictimisation. For her book *Truth and Repair* (Herman, 2023), Herman interviewed thirty survivors of CSA, sexual assault, sex trafficking, sexual harassment, and/or domestic violence, finding that "the first precept of survivors' justice is the desire for community acknowledgement that a wrong has been done" (Herman, 2023: 77).

A gap in the literature

While a growing body of quantitative literature is emerging in the field, the voices of adolescent sexual grooming survivors in adulthood, particularly female, have barely been researched in a qualitative manner. Where survivor experiences have been explored, the focus has been on individual survivors, as in McElvaney's (2019) IPA study of one male survivor's adolescent grooming; and Owton and Sparkes' (2017) ethnographic study of one female teenaged athlete's grooming by her coach. No studies have taken an in-depth qualitative look at the experience of survivors into adulthood.

Methodology

Before recruiting participants, the study was approved by the ethics board of the New School of Psychotherapy and Counselling, a sub-committee of the ethics board of Middlesex University, London, whose code of practice for research and data protection guides the methods used. I conducted semi-structured interviews, using a list of prompts to ensure specific angles of experience were considered. I was less interested in the facts of being groomed, and more in the unfurling of thoughts, feelings, and perspectives survivors arrived at when asked to reflect, and the common themes that emerged across those reflections. I decided that the self-concealing nature of the grooming experience, and the ongoing need to make sense of it, meant a phenomenological-hermeneutic approach would be invaluable. "We are attempting to understand, both in the sense of 'trying to see what it is like for someone' and in the sense of 'analysing, illuminating'" (Smith et al., 2022: 30).

Following Smith et al. (2022), I conducted a six-stage process of IPA, firstly familiarising myself with the recordings and transcripts, and paying attention to use of language – repetitions, metaphor, contradiction, and so on. I extracted experiential statements from each transcript, and boiled these down to personal experiential themes (PET), gradually grouping these under higher general experiential themes (GET) across transcripts. I used regular reflexive journaling to articulate the prejudices and assumptions that came up for me in the process, a survivor myself. I was constantly aware of my own filter of subjectivity, meaning that no matter how much I tried to bracket my prejudices, a different researcher may have produced an entirely different list of themes and subthemes.

Participants

Participants are all cisgender women (aged 25 and over), groomed between 11 and 16 by a man aged 21 or older at the time. Alice, Daniela, and Laura are therapists. Jo works in prison management. Jenny, Alice, and Sandra work in the commercial world. Natasha is a music teacher. The age of grooming onset was between 11 and 13 years (average 12.4). It took an average of 15.9 years for participants to disclose the reality of their experience.

Analysis and findings

Searching for Sanctuary

The name for this theme came from Alice, who had *'never known sanc-tuary in (her) family'* and had *'always been looking for that.'* The word 'sanctuary' signifies here the emotional and physical protection that fam-ily should provide when it functions at its best: a relational place where the developing child feels protected and understood. All eight participants reflected that a lack of family sanctuary in adolescence was a major factor in their vulnerability to grooming. The combination of childhood maltreat-ment and sexual grooming had then left them struggling for years to build close friendships and choose appropriate partners, meaning they failed to find sanctuary with others.

Alice's mother's emotional abuse and neglect of her had pushed her to be *'out of the house a lot.'* Home was not a place Alice felt safe or wanted to return to, a sentiment shared by Laura, who commented that, *'On the way home from school every day, I'd literally be praying that Mum would be in a good mood and that I hadn't done something wrong. It was like a visceral fear.'* Jo, Clara, and Natasha described a similar experience with their fathers (stepdad in the case of Natasha). As Natasha said, *'I was hyper-vigilant of taking care of what was going on... wanting things to be okay and not blow up and not for my stepdad to go off on one. He would flair up out of nothing.'* Natasha's 'hypervigilance' reflects a trauma response: she lived in constant anticipation of conflict with an unpredictable individual. Meanwhile, Jo spoke of her experience of punishment by her dad. *'My dad used to hit me. He used to hit me with a belt, he used to hit me with his hands.'* In Jo's account, there was a sense that violence was a fact of her childhood, and the long-term emotional effects were still palpable.

Against this backdrop of childhood abuse, Jo experienced her groom-er's attention as comfort. She said, *'There was no relationship with my parents. There was no home life, which makes the predator, makes sense how he could get a grip of me, because there was nothing else around me.'* Similarly, Sandra reflected that, *'He was the only adult I could talk to, because my parents didn't have the time, energy, capacity to listen to me, because of everything that was going on.'* Meanwhile, Laura said her groomer would encourage her to write to him and not hide anything from him about her problems at home. *'He seemed to know everything about my mum's problems. He would coach me on how to deal with her mental health issues.'* Sandra described her groomer as a *'father figure,'* a poign-ant choice of words considering his arrival in her life coincided with her abandonment by her own father. Jenny described experiencing a sense of *'being special'* around her groomer that totally disarmed her, giving him complete power over her.

Living the Wounds of Grooming

Seven out of eight participants spoke of their grooming experience as 'trauma' – a word that comes from the Greek word for wound, in this case implying an impact to one's sense of self. While all eight participants used mental health terminology to describe their suffering around and following their grooming, they also used non-pathologising descriptions of difficulties experienced in the day-to-day of friendships and relationships, a battle with shame and with feeling confident in their own bodies, particularly in sex. They also reflected on how the power imbalance in the grooming relationship was something they repeated in later sexual and romantic relationships.

Shame was central in the way participants reflected on their grooming experience, and their own sense of being responsible. Daniela carried within her an awareness that her prematurely voluptuous body had invited her abuse. The result, for her, was a physical self-loathing. *'There is a heavy dislike for my body, because I wonder if it made a statement to him… to my groomer, and that's why the things that happened happened.'*

Jenny spoke of her sexual grooming as something she had been powerless to stop, and this was where the shame came from. *'I didn't know what to do, I didn't know how to let him know. I didn't know how to push his hand away. The shame of letting that happen.'* Later, she reflected that, *'No amount of bathing, no amount of water, can wash away the memory of it. You just feel really dirty,'* and *'shame and guilt are like a physical state of being for me.'* There was a visceral sense of the sexual experience having sullied Jenny. She articulated shame as a mark, redolent of Lady Macbeth's imaginary spot of murderous guilt – a mark she wished she could wash away.

Seven out of eight participants experienced repetition of the power abuse of grooming in subsequent relationships. Daniela was the exception here: she went on to have healthy sexual experiences in her twenties, eventually marrying a man she felt comfortable with physically. Alice referred to her tendency for revictimisation as *'the same people but different bodies,'* encapsulating the way her subsequent abusive experiences were all in the same vein. Jo commented that, *'the theme continued (…) I was fourteen (…) I ran away from home to another guy I met on the internet who was a lot older than me as well.'* Jenny described her sexual relations with men as transactional – a way to feel better about herself – linking this to her early grooming experience. She reflected that, *'I feel like maybe if none of that stuff happened I wouldn't view myself as just an object to be sexualised. And I wouldn't view my own value as transactional, because it really is just that.'*

Both Laura and Sandra experienced a repetition of their groomer's effects on them in their adult long-term relationships. In her late twenties, Sandra ended up leaving her long-term boyfriend, fourteen years her senior, because she *'realised that there was a lot of control, that the relationship was not very healthy in many ways.'* Laura described the effect her first husband had on her in the early days of their relationship as *'love-bombing... that feeling that this person is going to fundamentally change your life, like a saviour? It was so similar to how my groomer made me feel at the start. And then the way it evolved: he became abusive.'*

All eight participants struggled with their mental health. Clara had been diagnosed with borderline personality disorder. The overwhelming anger she frequently experienced would push her into self-harming behaviour. She reflected on this as *'internal rage that you don't know what to do with.'* Alice, who was diagnosed with bipolar disorder and experienced PTSD, reflected that, *'I still deal with the impact of being on edge (...) Being flooded with cortisol and adrenaline all the time.'*

Several participants used alcohol to numb themselves. Clara said, *'If I would be sleeping with someone, I had to be drunk, because (...) I didn't want to connect. (...) I found it difficult to be vulnerable.'* Sandra shared a similar need for alcohol, reflecting, *'I always wanted to connect with others, but how it would end up was it wouldn't happen until I was really drunk.'* Jenny said of her ongoing use of alcohol that it *'numbs, it just makes me feel good.'*

Towards a New Way of Being

While all the participants in this study experienced an ongoing sense of injustice and regret about their abuse as teenagers, they also reflected that waking up to the truth and feeling validated in that truth was crucial to their ability to heal. For several participants, this had only been possible thanks to some kind of external input: a documentary or news story about adolescent sexual grooming in the cases of Alice, Jo, and Sandra; a boyfriend expressing outrage, as in the case of Clara. For Sandra, seeing her story played out in the lives of other victims in grooming documentaries had been fundamental to her self-disclosure. She reflected that, *'I watched the Epstein documentary, and I was a little bit tipsy after having some wine, and I remember straight away thinking: wow. Like it became really clear to me.'* Jo spoke of a similar process of realising the truth through other victims' stories, commenting, *'you know you see and hear things – people talk about it – and you think gosh, actually, that makes sense, this isn't my fault, I didn't lead him on. I was a kid. I was 13, 14.'*

Daniela was the only participant who told her mother what was happening at the time and received an *'appropriate'* response. She was also the only one not to struggle in subsequent relationships. In stark contrast to Daniela's teenaged disclosure, Natasha experienced parental indifference when she disclosed: her mother told her groomer to stop what he was doing, but then turned a blind eye when the abuse continued. Natasha said, *'when Mum died, that was the opening, the start of being able to unpack and sort of go through that grieving process of: you failed me, but I know you didn't have, you weren't equipped.'* Meanwhile, Jo did tell her parents at the time, and was subsequently rejected by them and made homeless. Anger emerged as an important part of Jo's story: a right of passage she had to go through to reclaim her story. Referring to her mum in the second person, she said, *'I didn't ask you to be my mum, I didn't ask to be your child, and as my mum you have a duty to be there for me whatever I've been through.'*

Anger emerged in Alice's, Jenny's, Sandra's, and Clara's reflections, too. Alice said, *'When I look back on how it used to be, I feel so angry and disgusted. Why did nobody do something about this?'* Sandra expressed her outrage that grooming *'is a societal phenomenon,'* and *'society seems to be letting mainly men get away with these types of things.'* Clara said, *'I've been feeling really angry that that happened. (…) that kind of thing was so normalised, so normalised, and these men could so easily take advantage of someone, and I think that's made me angry.'*

Therapy played an important role for five out of eight of the participants in their healing journey. Laura reflected on this, saying, *'I went back to the beginning with her, told her the whole story, and she said to me: you were groomed, you know that, don't you? It was like seeing the light.'* Similarly, Sandra said, *'My therapist had an incredibly supportive reaction to my situation, which I think was really essential for me to be able both to discover this more and to start the process of understanding it better.'* For both Sandra and Laura, the therapist's validation of their experience as abusive was essential.

With or without therapy, ongoing self-reflection was important for all eight participants in their healing journey. Alice reflected on the work she had done on herself, saying, *'I want to learn, I want to grow, I want to know about myself.'* Natasha, meanwhile, spoke of having reached a point at which she was still very much aware of her experience of grooming and abuse, but had dealt with triggers and emotional reactions in a healthy way. She said, *'I don't feel I've done it with a therapeutic other person, in dynamic with another person. I've done it mostly myself, maybe to an extent with my partner.'*

The grooming experience had made participants far more aware of how they related to themselves and others. Alice reflected on how her relationships had fundamentally shifted as a result of her self-work. *'I set boundaries, I assert myself, whereas before I didn't feel I had the right.'* For Sandra, exploring other relationship forms, including polyamory, had enabled her to be *'really clear with (her) needs, and (her) boundaries.'* She reflected that, *'in a lot of traditional relationships people think the relationship will fix their problems; that being owned by, being controlled by someone, will solve things, but it doesn't.'* Similarly, Daniela reflected that experimenting with her sexuality in her twenties had allowed her to reclaim her sense of agency: *'I felt a sense of control I didn't feel with the situation with my groomer. Part of me thinks: that was quite freeing before marriage.'* While Daniela is now in a committed relationship, she emphasised her sense of agency in that relationship, too, saying, *'I've committed to giving my body to somebody now, somebody I can trust and who doesn't abuse it.'* Agency in the choice of whom to be with and how to be with them emerged as a fundamental.

Five participants (Daniela, Alice, Laura, Jo, and Natasha) entered caring professions as adults that they articulated as directly related to what had happened to them as teenagers. Alice is a trauma-focused therapist and trainer; she sees this as a way of using her grooming for the benefit of others. She said, *'I bring a lot of this trauma stuff into the teaching (…) I feel like I'm gaining a sense of power through actually teaching clinicians to look out for these things and to understand them.'* Laura expressed a similar sentiment in her work as a student counsellor, particularly when working with victims of CSA. *'I know to articulate the outrage. I know how to confront their sense of shame and self-blame. No counselling training could have taught me how to do that.'* Laura's emphasis on knowing points to a deep professional confidence that stems from her own experience of abuse. The distinction between training and lived experience is striking here: Laura feels accomplished because of what happened to her as a teenager. The same emphasis on lived experience emerged in Natasha's reflections on her work with disadvantaged teenagers. *'I have a lot of affinity for and love for teenagers. It's a kind of empathising. (…) I feel it. I really feel it.'*

Discussion

The findings presented in this chapter echo many of the studies mentioned in the literature review, particularly in terms of what might make an individual vulnerable to grooming in the adolescent years (Jonsson et al., 2019; Orcutt et al., 2005; Whittle et al., 2014; Williams, 2015); how grooming affects the individual (Gámez-Guadix et al., 2023; Girard et al., 2021; Gomez, 2019; Miller & Esposito-Smythers, 2013), and how difficult disclosure can be (Burgess & Hartman, 2018; Knoll, 2010; Lanning & Dietz, 2014; Winters & Jeglic, 2022). While initially exploring questions of vulnerability, effects on the individual, and the struggle to disclose in light of the literature, this section concludes with an existential exploration of participants' emergence from the shadow of their grooming into a new way of being.

In terms of their vulnerability to grooming, all eight participants reflected on negative, abusive, and distressing experiences with key caregivers in childhood. These experiences had created in them a certain way of relating and left them yearning for attention elsewhere. For example, in both her relationship with her stepfather and with her groomer, there was a powerful sense that Natasha had learnt to silence her feelings of discomfort. Meanwhile, the role reversal in Laura's relationship with her mother forced Laura into a relational position of self-sacrifice and emotional inhibition that was later evidenced in the way she talked about her groomer, too. Both Laura's and Natasha's experiences exemplify the attachment theory idea that children form "representational models of attachment figures, of themselves, and of themselves in relation to others based on their relationship history with their primary caregivers" (Bowlby, 1991, as cited in Crawford & O'Dougherty, 2007: 96).

The combination of childhood maltreatment and adolescent sexual grooming had a profoundly negative effect on participants' mental health and vulnerability to revictimisation. This supports research that finds adolescents who have had multiple experiences of abuse are more likely to experience mental health problems, difficulties coping, and revictimisation (Charak et al., 2018; Gratz, 2007; Messman-Moore et al., 2010; Negriff et al., 2015). Alice and Clara drew the connection between their emotional dysregulation, their respective diagnoses of bipolar disorder and borderline personality disorder, and their relational and sexual struggles in adulthood. Laura spoke of having battled for her entire adult life to deal with negative emotions, and of using alcohol to numb herself throughout her twenties, regularly having one-night stands that left her burdened with shame.

Jenny stood out as particularly prone to revictimisation, both in adolescence and adulthood: she was raped once in high school while still a teen, and then twice again in early adulthood. She also reflected on extreme emotional volatility, a tendency to experience fits of anger, and to walk away from friendships and relationships. Jenny's story is not unusual: those sexually abused in childhood are more likely to experience date rape or other sexual assault than non-abused control groups, with one explanation being that child sexual abuse impairs the ability to judge relationships or risky situations (Finkelhor & Browne, 1985).

Shame figured strongly in all participants' accounts of their grooming. This echoes studies that have found shame to be endemic to survivors of CSA (Browne & Finkelhor, 1986; Feiring et al., 2007; Herman, 1992, 2023; Wager, 2015). Sandra recalled the shame plaguing her in adolescence, causing her stomach aches at the time of her grooming *'because (she) knew it wasn't okay. It wasn't acceptable to society.'* Keeping the grooming to herself because she believed she had invited it, Sandra remained imprisoned by her own silence well into adulthood, indulging in self-harming behaviours. Sandra's experience also reflects Finkelhor and Browne's (1985) concept of stigmatisation in victims of CSA, which stems from the way society and/or loved ones ignore or judge victims of abusive behaviour: the victim loses confidence in herself, indulging in alcohol and drug abuse, and self-harm (Gámez-Guadix et al., 2023; Gomez, 2019; "The Sexual Abuse of Children," 2017).

Participants felt responsible for what had happened to them and, consequently, struggled to self-disclose. This finding supports multiple studies that find survivors have difficulties labelling their experience as abuse, because they feel they somehow invited it (Capone et al., 2021; Gámez-Guadix et al., 2023; Whittle et al., 2014). Jo reflected that, *'I just remember feeling for years that I can't put myself in that bracket of sexual abuse or rape or assault or any of those words, because I felt like it was consensual.'* Sandra's struggle to see her experience as abuse suggested the persistent effects of 'betrayal blindness' (Freyd, 1996). In her mid-twenties, when she first self-disclosed her abuse, Sandra was still very much in touch with her groomer. She reflected that seeing the truth of what he had done to her meant losing someone who had been both abuser and surrogate father to her. *'In betraying him, it felt like I was also betraying myself.'*

In the cases of Sandra and Laura, therapy helped free them of a sense of responsibility for their own grooming. Part of this was about gaining an understanding of grooming as a phenomenon: how it works, how society enables it. Krippner and colleagues' (2012) example of working therapeutically with a rape victim is of relevance here, as they address the cultural narrative of blaming the victim that remains so potent for survivors of sexual violence and abuse. An important part of the psychotherapist's role in working with such clients is, for Krippner and colleagues, to help them see the role in their rape of sexual permissiveness in certain cultures (2012, as cited in Boaz, 2022: 125).

In her memoir, grooming survivor Vanessa Springora (2019) emphasises the importance of expressing her "fury" to "reclaim this chapter" of her life. Likewise, the expression of anger emerged as an important part of self-disclosure for several participants in this study, in particular Clara, Sandra, Jo, Jenny, Alice, and Natasha. In underlining the value of anger in a disclosure of abuse and the subsequent rebuilding of one's sense of self, I reference Francophone Martinican psychiatrist and existentialist Frantz Fanon, who wrote of the oppressed rising up in his exploration of the dehumanising effects of colonisation. "When his rage boils over, he rediscovers his lost innocence and he comes to know himself in that he himself creates his self" (Sartre, 1963: 20).

This idea of 'creation' of the self was experienced by participants in this study in a decidedly relational way, echoing Merleau-Ponty's (1945/2011) emphasis on the intercorporeal nature of interpersonal trauma and healing. "Memory or voice are rediscovered when the body again opens to others or to the past, when it allows itself to be shot through by coexistence and when it again signifies (in the active sense) beyond itself" (Merleau-Ponty, 1945/2011: 168). For Sandra, this meant leaving her partner, a man 14 years her senior, living alone, and exploring new styles of relationship – polyamorous and bisexual – whereby needs were clearly articulated and respected. Laura, Natasha, Jo, and Alice each emphasised the importance of prioritising safety, listening to one's needs and setting firmer boundaries. For Daniela, her ability to trust her husband and protect her children gave her a crucial anchor.

Equally, embodying the idea that "He who has a why to live for can bear almost any how" (Frankl, 1946/2004: 84), participants redirected their sense of helplessness and injustice towards social ends. The idea that meaningful work can have therapeutic value, empowering people to push through and overcome suffering, has been widely recognised in contemporary trauma literature (Boaz, 2022; Eger, 2017; Herman, 1992, 2023). In the current study, Alice's choice to become a trainer of trauma therapists is an excellent example of this. Her drive was fuelled by her experience, and her work had instilled in her a 'sense of power.' Daniela made a similar use of a 'really negative experience in an ability to be with people who are feeling vulnerable and frightened.' Daniela articulated a dual benefit of her work: firstly, it made her feel of use to others who were suffering; secondly, it forced her to confront parts of herself and her traumatic memories that she might otherwise tend to bury.

Conclusion

In putting a traumatic experience to good use, participants in this study who had chosen to work with survivors of abuse were countering the stigmatisation that Browne and Finkelhor (1985) refer to as one of the key trauma-causing factors in CSA. Previously living in the shadow of their grooming, they had come to understand that they were uniquely equipped to help others make sense of and heal from abusive experience. They came across as emboldened, fighting off the shroud of shame and stigma, having seen the truth of the social and familial structures that had allowed their abuse to happen in the first place, and determined to empower others to do the same.

Meanwhile, in prioritising their own need for agency in relationships, participants had grown to believe again in the sanctuary that is possible in human connection. Becoming more mindful in their relational investments was an important part of this shift. There was a sense that they had returned to what Levinas describes as the preverbal, pre-language ethical responsibility we have to others (1961); and they had allowed themselves to "be shot through by coexistence" (Merleau-Ponty, 1945/2011: 168).

As a survivor myself, I can state that conducting this research has been a powerful motor of my own ability to find meaning in my grooming experience. Having spent twenty-five years telling no one of what happened to me from ages thirteen to seventeen, I can now talk about this experience without shame, as a significant part of my biography, and one that has informed my ability to work as a therapist with survivors of CSA. Having conducted this research, I am strongly motivated to help other practitioners, parents, educators, victims, and survivors understand how grooming works and how it affects the individual. I am driven by a belief that grooming is a social trauma, and one we must face together. In the words of Judith Herman (2023: 3), "if trauma is truly a social problem, and indeed it is, then recovery cannot be simply a private, individual matter."

References

Ainsworth, M. D. S. (1978). The Bowlby-Ainsworth attachment theory. *The Behavioral and Brain Sciences, 1*(3), 436–438. https://doi.org/10.1017/S0140525X00075828

Atmaca, S., & Gençöz, T. (2016). Exploring revictimization process among Turkish women: The role of early maladaptive schemas on the link between child abuse and partner violence. *Child Abuse & Neglect, 52*, 85–93. https://doi.org/10.1016/j.chiabu.2016.01.004

Boaz, M. (2022). *An Existential Approach to Interpersonal Trauma: Modes of Existing and Confrontations With Reality*. Routledge. https://doi.org/10.4324/9781003181675

Bowlby, J. (1991). *Attachment and Loss: Volume 1: Attachment* (2nd ed.). Penguin.

Brackenridge, C., & Fasting, K. (2005). The grooming process in sport: Narratives of sexual harassment and abuse. *Auto/biography, 13*(1), 33–52. https://doi.org/10.1191/0967550705ab016oa

Browne, A., & Finkelhor, D. (1986). Impact of child sexual abuse: A review of the research. *Psychological Bulletin, 99*(1), 66–77. https://doi.org/10.1037/0033-2909.99.1.66.

Burgess, A. W., & Hartman, C. R. (2018). On the origin of grooming. *Journal of Interpersonal Violence, 33*(1), 17–23. https://doi.org/10.1177/0886260517742048.

Burns, E. E., Jackson, J. L., & Harding, H. G. (2010). Child maltreatment, emotion regulation, and posttraumatic stress: The impact of emotional abuse. *Journal of Aggression, Maltreatment & Trauma, 19*(8), 801–819. https://doi.org/10.1080 /10926771.2010.522947.

Butler, J. (1990). *Gender Trouble*. Routledge.

Capone, C., et al. (2021). Trauma Informed Guilt Reduction (TrIGR) therapy for guilt, shame, and moral injury resulting from trauma: Rationale, design, and methodology of a two-site randomized controlled trial. *Contemporary Clinical Trials, 101*, 106251. https://doi.org/10.1016/j.cct.2020.106251

Charak, R., et al. (2018). Latent classes of lifetime sexual victimization characteristics in women in emerging adulthood: Differential relations with emotion dysregulation. *Psychology of Violence, 8*(5), 570–579. https://doi.org /10.1037/vio0000154.

Craven, S., Brown, S., & Gilchrist, E. (2006). Sexual grooming of children: Review of literature and theoretical considerations. *The Journal of Sexual Aggression, 12*(3), 287–299. https://doi.org/10.1080/13552600601069414.

de Beauvoir, S. (1997). *The Second Sex* (trans. H. M. Parshley). Vintage (Original work published 1949).

de Beauvoir, S. (2015). *The Ethics of Ambiguity*. Philosophical Library/Open Road (Original work published 1949).

DiLillo, D., Hayes-Skelton, S. A., Fortier, M. A., Perry, A. R., Evans, S. E., Messman Moore, T. L., Walsh, K., Nash, C., & Fauchier, A. (2010). Development and initial psychometric properties of the Computer Assisted Maltreatment Inventory (CAMI): A comprehensive self-report measure of child maltreatment history. *Child Abuse Neglect, 34*(5), 305–317. https://doi:10.1016/j.chiabu.2009.09.015

Eger, E. (2017). *The Choice: Even in Hell Hope Can Flower*. Rider.

Feiring, C., Simon, V. A., & Cleland, C. M. (2009). Childhood sexual abuse, stigmatization, internalizing symptoms, and the development of sexual difficulties and dating aggression. *Journal of Consulting and Clinical Psychology, 77*(1), 127–137. https://doi.org/10.1037/a0013475.

Finkelhor, D., & Browne, A. (1985). The traumatic impact of child sexual abuse: A conceptualization. *Am J Orthopsychiatry, 55*(4), 530–541. https://doi.org/10 .1111/j.1939-0025.1985.tb02703.x

Fisher, G. (2005). Existential psychotherapy with adult survivors of sexual abuse. *The Journal of Humanistic Psychology, 45*(1), 10–40. https://doi.org/10.1177 /0022167804269042

Foucher, L., & Lefilliâtre, J. (2024, February 8). Benoît Jacquot, un système de prédation sous couvert de cinéma. *Le Monde*. https://www.lemonde.fr/societe /article/2024/02/08/benoit-jacquot-un-systeme-de-predation-sous-couvert-de -cinema_6215357_3224.html

Frankl, V. E. (2004). *Man's Search for Meaning*. Ebury (Original work published 1946).

Freyd, J. J. (1996). *Betrayal Trauma*. Harvard University Press.

Gámez-Guadix, M., Mateos-Pérez, E., Alcázar, M. A., Martínez-Bacaicoa, J., & Wachs, S. (2023). Stability of the online grooming victimization of minors: Prevalence and association with shame, guilt, and mental health outcomes over one year. *Journal of Adolescence, 95*(8), 1715–1724. https://doi.org/10.1002/ jad.12240

Girard, M., et al. (2021). A longitudinal study of suicidal ideation in sexually abused adolescent
girls: Depressive symptoms and affect dysregulation as predictors. *Journal of Traumatic Stress, 34*(6), 1132–1138. https://doi.org/10.1002/jts.22608

Gómez, J. M. (2019). High betrayal adolescent sexual abuse and nonsuicidal self-injury: The role of depersonalization in emerging adults. *Journal of Child Sexual Abuse, 28*(3), 318–332. https://doi.org/10.1080/10538712.2018.1539425.

Gratz, K. L. (2007). Targeting emotion dysregulation in the treatment of self-injury. *Journal of Clinical Psychology, 63*(11), 1091–1103. https://doi.org/10.1002/jclp.20417

Hegel, G. W. F. (1977). *Phenomenology of Spirit.* Oxford University Press (Original work published 1807).

Heidegger, M. (2010). *Being and Time* (trans. J. Stambaugh). State University of New York Press (Original work published 1927).

Herman, J. (1992). *Trauma and Recovery.* Basic Books.

Herman, J. (2023). *Truth and Repair.* Basic Books.

Humphrey, J. A., & White, J. W. (2000). Women's vulnerability to sexual assault from adolescence to young adulthood. *Journal of Adolescent Health, 27*(6), 419–424. https://doi.org/10.1016/S1054-139X(00)00168-3

Jonsson, L. S., Fredlund, C., Priebe, G., Wadsby, M., & Svedin, C. G. (2019). Online sexual abuse of adolescents by a perpetrator met online: A cross-sectional study. *Child and Adolescent Psychiatry and Mental Health, 13*, 32. https://doi.org/10.1186/s13034-019-0292-1

Knoll, J. (2010). Teacher sexual misconduct: Grooming patterns and female offenders. *Journal of Child Sexual Abuse, 19*(4), 371–386. https://doi.org/10.1080/10538712.2010.495047

Krippner, S., Pitchford, D. B., & Davies, J. (2012). *Post-Traumatic Stress Disorder (Biographies of Disease).* Greenwood.

Lanning, K. V., & Dietz, P. (2014). Acquaintance molestation and youth-serving organizations. *Journal of Interpersonal Violence, 29*(15), 2815–2838. https://doi.org/10.1177/0886260514532360

Leahy, T. (2010). Working with adult athlete survivors of sexual abuse. In D. Tod & K. Hodge (Eds.), *Routledge Handbook of Applied Sport Psychology* (pp. 303–312). Routledge.
https://doi.org/10.4324/9780203851043

Leahy, T. (2011). Safeguarding child athletes from abuse in elite sport systems: The role of the sport psychologist. In D. Gilbourne & M. Andersen (Eds.), *Critical Essays in Applied Sport Psychology* (pp. 251–266). Human Kinetics.

Levinas, E. (1961). *Totality and Infinity: An Essay on Exteriority.* Kluwer.

McElvaney, R. (2019). Grooming: A case study. *Journal of Child Sexual Abuse, 28*(5), 608–627. https://doi.org/10.1080/10538712.2018.1554612

Merleau-Ponty, M. (2011). *Phenomenology of Perception* (trans. C. Smith). Routledge (Original work published 1945).

Messman-Moore T. L., Walsh K. L., & DiLillo, D. (2010). Emotion dysregulation and risky sexual behavior in revictimization. *Child Abuse Negl., 34*(12), 967–976. https://doi.org/10.1016/j.chiabu.2010.06.004

Miller, A. B., & Esposito-Smythers, C. (2013). How do cognitive distortions and substance related problems affect the relationship between child maltreatment and adolescent suicidal ideation? *Psychology of Violence, 3*(4), 340–353. https://doi.org/10.1037/a0031355

Miron, L. R., & Orcutt, H. K. (2014). Pathways from childhood abuse to prospective revictimization: Depression, sex to reduce negative affect, and forecasted sexual behavior. *Child Abuse & Neglect, 38*(11), 1848–1859. https://doi.org/10.1016/j.chiabu.2014.10.004

National Society for the Prevention of Cruelty to Children. (2020). *How safe are our children / Annual report.* NSPCC. https://thecpsu.org.uk/resource-library/research/how-safe-are-our-children-2020/#:~:text=This%20annual%20report%20from%20the%20NSPCC%20compiles%20and,safe%20are%20our%20children%3F%27%20from%20a%20different%20perspective

National Society for the Prevention of Cruelty to Children. (2022, December 7). *Online grooming crimes have risen by more than 80% in four years.* NSPCC. https://www.nspcc.org.uk/about-us/news-opinion/2022/online-grooming-crimes-rise/

Negriff, S., James, A., & Trickett, P. K. (2015). Characteristics of the social support networks of maltreated youth: Exploring the effects of maltreatment experience and foster placement. *Social Development, 24*(3), 483–500. https://doi.org/10.1111/sode.12102

Orcutt, H. K., Cooper, M. L., & Garcia, M. (2005). Use of sexual intercourse to reduce negative affect as a prospective mediator of sexual revictimization. *Journal of Traumatic Stress, 18*(6), 729–739. https://doi.org/10.1002/jts.20081

Owton, H., & Sparkes, A. C. (2017). Sexual abuse and the grooming process in sport: Learning from Bella's story. *Sport, Education and Society, 22*(6), 732–743. https://doi.org/10.1080/13573322.2015.1063484

Russell, K. E. (2023). *My Dark Vanessa.* Fourth Estate.

Royal Commission into Institutional Responses to Child Sexual Abuse. (2017). *Final report.* https://www.childabuseroyalcommission.gov.au/final-report

Sartre, J.-P. (1963). Preface. In F. Fanon, *The Wretched of the Earth* (pp. 7–34). Grove Weidenfeld.

Smith, J. A., Flowers, P., & Larkin, M. (2022). *Interpretative Phenomenological Analysis: Theory, Method and Research* (2nd ed.). Sage.

Springora, V. (2019). *Le Consentement.* Bernard Grasset.

Tedeschi, R. G., & Calhoun, L. G. (1995). *Trauma & Transformation: Growing in the Aftermath of Suffering.* Sage. https://doi.org/10.4135/9781483326931

Wager, N. M. (2015). Understanding children's non-disclosure of child sexual assault: Implications for assisting parents and teachers to become effective guardians. *Safer Communities, 14*(1), 16–26. https://doi.org/10.1108/SC-03-2015-0009

Weil, S. (2002). *The Need for Roots.* Routledge (Original work published 1949).

Whittle, H. C., Hamilton-Giachritsis, C. E., & Beech, A. R. (2014). In their own words: Young people's vulnerabilities to being groomed and sexually abused online. *Psychology (Irvine, Calif.), 5*(10), 1185–1196. https://doi.org/10.4236/psych.2014.510131

Williams, A. (2015). Child sexual victimisation: Ethnographic stories of stranger and acquaintance grooming. *The Journal of Sexual Aggression, 21*(1), 28–42. https://doi.org/10.1080/13552600.2014.948085

Winters, G. M., & Jeglic, E. L. (2022). *Sexual Grooming: Integrating Research, Practice, Prevention, and Policy.* Springer.

Winters, G. M., Jeglic, E. L., & Kaylor, L. E. (2020). Validation of the sexual grooming model of child sexual abusers. *Journal of Child Sexual Abuse, 29*(7), 855–875. https://doi.org/10.1080/10538712.2020.1801935

Wolf, M. R., & Pruitt, D. K. (2019). Grooming hurts too: The effects of types of perpetrator grooming on trauma symptoms in adult survivors of child sexual abuse. *Journal of Child Sexual Abuse, 28*(3), 345–359. https://doi.org/10.1080/10538712.2019.1579292

Yalom, I. D. (1980). *Existential Psychotherapy.* Basic Books.

Chapter 5

The Coexistence of Posttraumatic Stress and Posttraumatic Growth Related to Childhood Trauma

April Mangion

Introduction

Research suggests that 31.1% of the population in England and Wales experience trauma before 18 years of age, with the ensuing rates of psychopathology being high (Lewis et al., 2019). Despite the prevalence of childhood trauma and the vast amount of research exploring it, there remain many unanswered questions surrounding trauma responses. A predominant question is why some individuals experiencing trauma develop Posttraumatic Stress Syndrome (PTSS)/Posttraumatic Stress Disorder (PTSD), while others do not. An alternative but rarely addressed question is why some individuals experience posttraumatic growth following trauma, while others do not?

It is imperative to define the common trauma reactions relevant to this study. PTSD is the most commonly researched outcome of trauma. PTSD, as defined in the *Diagnostic and Statistical Manual for Mental Disorders,* 5th edition (American Psychological Association, 2013), is a prolonged response triggered by a trauma event. Symptoms include intrusive memories, nightmares, avoidance of reminders, negative alterations in mood and cognition, and heightened arousal.

PTSS, although not an official psychiatric disorder, is frequently used in clinical work and research. The term describes a posttrauma response that includes PTSD symptoms but does not meet the full PTSD diagnostic criteria. Participants in this study were not assessed for PTSD, therefore PTSS is used to summarise the presence of trauma symptoms without presuming they met the full PTSD diagnostic criteria.

Posttraumatic growth can be understood as a sense of growth following trauma. As Tedeschi and Calhoun (1995) stipulated, growth can include positive changes to personal strength, spirituality, appreciation for life, relationships with others, and the opening of new possibilities in life.

While PTSS and PTSD assume adverse outcomes, posttraumatic growth presumes positive effects. Often, PTSS/PTSD and PTG are considered

DOI: 10.4324/9781003493860-7

opposite entities, with only one or the other being possible, when they can, in fact, coexist (Tedeschi et al., 2018). The popular model of trauma, PTSS/PTSD, and posttraumatic growth is that trauma can lead to either PTSS/PTSD or posttraumatic growth, or PTSS/PTSD can lead to posttraumatic growth in a growth through suffering stance (Tedeschi et al., 2018). Figure 5.1 demonstrates such relationships.

However, taking into account the limited research on the coexistence of PTSS/PTSD and posttraumatic growth, an alternative relationship can be identified in which trauma may cause both positive and negative outcomes simultaneously (see Figure 5.2). According to recent research, PTSS and posttraumatic growth have a curvilinear relationship in which if one is high, the other is low (Weber & Schulenberg, 2023). For such a relationship to exist, both symptoms will be present at some point. Not only can PTSS/PTSD and posttraumatic growth coexist, but they can manifest in similar life domains; for example, there could be strengthened relationships with some and a lesser connection with others (Zięba et al., 2019). More research is needed to explore how PTSS/PTSD and posttraumatic growth co-occur.

Research into posttraumatic growth often finds that increasing posttraumatic growth decreases PTSS/PTSD (Wagner et al., 2016). However, alternative research has found that higher levels of posttraumatic growth are also related to higher levels of PTSD, with the two conditions co-occurring (Frazier et al., 2001). Yuan et al. (2021) further evidenced the coexistence of posttraumatic growth and PTSD when researching PTSD features, and posttraumatic growth participants disclosed distressing symptoms such as nightmares, flashbacks, and hypervigilance, alongside positive growth, including greater personal strength, new opportunities, and stronger religious faith. A further systematic review of posttraumatic stress and growth also found strong evidence of co-occurring PTSS and posttraumatic growth (Fletcher et al., 2023).

However, research into simultaneous posttraumatic growth and PTSS/PTSD remains limited and predominantly quantitative. Therefore, there is a

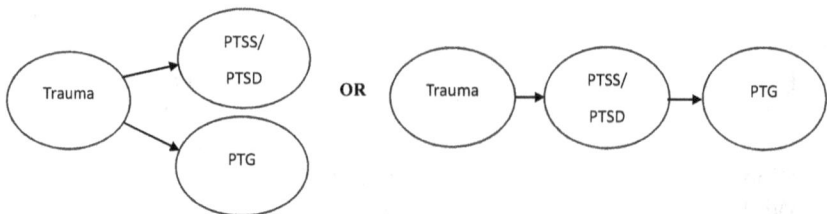

Figure 5.1 The trauma, PTSS/PTSD, and PTG relationship.

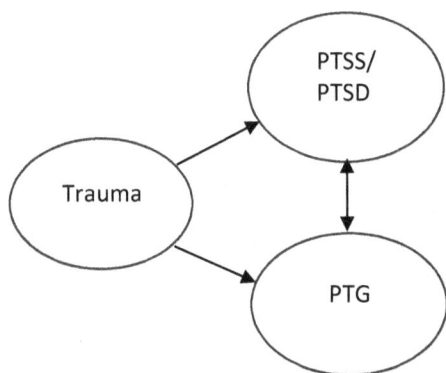

Figure 5.2 The coexistence model of trauma, PTSS/PTSD, and posttraumatic growth.

lack of understanding concerning the nature of coexisting PTSS/PTSD and PTG and how individuals experience it.

The primary study (Mangion, 2024), while exploring Event Centrality, discovered that research in this particular field of trauma was moving forward in identifying the intersection between PTSS/PTSD and posttraumatic growth. Bernsten and Rubin (2007) formalised Event Centrality upon observations that trauma events had developed into an overarching theme in some patients' lives. According to Bernsten and Rubin, "trauma becomes a reference point for other experiences, the world, and self-view" (Bernsten & Rubin, 2007: 418). Three critical elements of Event Centrality were proposed. Firstly, negative events can serve as a reference point to all other experiences and aspects of life. Secondly, adverse events become a turning point in life, changing previously held perceptions. Thirdly, the event can become central to a person's self-identity; their view of themselves.

As will be outlined in the following literature review, what Event Centrality has done is to uncover more understanding about the coexistence of PTSS/PTSD and posttraumatic growth. The current study both supported these findings, but with a dearth of quantitative research it also gives voice to the phenomenon in a way that the existing literature currently does not.

Literature review

A PRISMA systematic review of the literature on Event Centrality and trauma was conducted to identify research relevant to childhood trauma becoming central to self-identity. This section will cover aspects applicable to the coexistence of PTSS/PTSD and posttraumatic growth. Only eight papers focused directly on childhood trauma. Therefore, Event Centrality research based on adulthood is detailed where appropriate. Given that the study explored the effects of childhood trauma into adulthood, much of the general Event Centrality research remains highly relevant.

Research demonstrates that trauma in childhood correlates to Event Centrality, specifically in cases of natural disasters (Mordeno et al., 2018), traumatic loss (Kwon & You, 2021), medical trauma (Cook et al., 2021), maltreatment (Watts et al., 2021), and abuse (Robinaugh & McNally, 2011; Wang et al., 2020); meaning that children experiencing trauma often develop an identity centred on trauma, which impacts their view of themselves and the world.

Worryingly, Mordeno et al. (2018) evidenced higher rates of mental disorders in 9–17-year-olds with high Event Centrality, finding a link with heightened accessibility to trauma memories, with the impact likely to continue into adulthood. Ogle et al.'s (2013) research supports that Event Centrality from childhood trauma can impact adulthood. It shows links to higher Event Centrality in older populations who experienced trauma in childhood and adolescence rather than in adulthood. Moreover, those experiencing trauma younger were more likely to experience cumulative traumas throughout their life and at increased risk of adverse psychological outcomes.

Event Centrality research linked to childhood trauma finds correlations with PTSD or PTSS separately. In quantitative studies of Event Centrality and childhood trauma, higher Event Centrality scores correlate with trauma symptoms. In recent research, PTSS has been associated with the Event Centrality PTSD relationship, including ruminations (Watts et al., 2021), intrusive thoughts (Seyburn et al., 2020), negative self-talk (Ionio et al., 2018; Vagos et al., 2018), negative perception of trauma events (Cook et al., 2021; Robinaugh & McNally, 2011), and unwanted sensory memories or flashbacks (Mordeno et al., 2018).

Broader Event Centrality research focused on adults, some of whom having experienced childhood trauma, but not exclusively, also provides insights into the factors mediating the strong relationship between Event Centrality and PTSS/PTSD. Disruption to self-identity has been linked to higher Event Centrality and PTSS/PTSD (Meisels & Grysman, 2021), specifically where an individual lacks a coherent self (Saint Arnault & Sinko, 2019) and or has negative self-cognition (Clauss et al., 2021; Lancaster et al., 2011; Wamser-Nanney, 2019).

Further research on Event Centrality also locates common posttrauma responses including attachment issues (Ogle et al., 2015; 2016), trauma based rumination (Bishop et al., 2018; Brooks et al., 2017; Lancaster et al., 2015), and vivid intrusive memories or flashbacks (Blix et al., 2020;

Pociunaite & Zimprich, 2023) within the relationship between Event Centrality and PTSS/PTSD.

Alongside findings of Event Centrality correlating with PTSS and PTSD, posttraumatic growth was also found. Event Centrality often uses the term a 'double-edged sword' (Boals & Schuettler, 2011), meaning Event Centrality can be relational to both PTSD and posttraumatic growth. Multiple studies have found that high Event Centrality scores can predict both PTSD and posttraumatic growth (Barton et al., 2013; Bernard et al., 2015; Boals et al., 2010; Boals & Schuettler, 2011; Boelen, 2021; David et al., 2022; Eze et al., 2022; Glad et al., 2020; Groleau et al., 2013). Thus, assuming that an individual having an identity based on trauma is always indicative of a negative outcome would be incorrect.

Certain aspects of posttraumatic growth have been observed within Event Centrality research. For example, Steinberg et al. (2022) found components of posttraumatic growth linked to Event Centrality, such as an appreciation for life, changing priorities, closer relationships, stronger faith, resilience, a new path in life, valuing people, and feeling stronger. Further research also established the importance of resilience (Tranter et al., 2021), deliberate rumination (Seyburn et al., 2020), and disclosing trauma (David et al., 2022) in the relationship between Event Centrality and posttraumatic growth.

As Event Centrality predicts both PTSS/PTSD and posttraumatic growth, studies that examine both outcomes have often been conducted on the same sample set, indicating that a certain percentage of participants will demonstrate both positive and negative outcomes from the same event. Such a position is highlighted in the literature, with evidence that distress and growth can develop separately or simultaneously (Groleau et al., 2013). Moreover, some individuals may struggle between distress and growth (Schuettler & Boals, 2011).

Research conducted by Kuenemund et al. (2016) with stroke survivors illustrates the coexistence of PTSS and posttraumatic growth in Event Centrality research. Kuenemund et al.'s mixed quantitative and qualitative study found participants were likely to report growth in areas including spirituality, new possibilities, closer relationships, personal strength, and appreciation for life. The same participants also disclosed adverse effects, including disruption to or loss of self-identity and restrictions on life. As a result, a traumatic event can have both positive and negative effects simultaneously. Similar findings have been noted in additional research including that individuals with trauma Event Centrality can have both positive deliberate rumination and negative intrusive rumination (Allbaugh et al., 2016). Likewise, Bruce and Weaver (2021) observed PTSD in the form of anxiety, avoidance, a sense of not being in control, and intrusive rumination, co-occurring with growth.

Further evidence of the coexistence of PTSS/PTSD and posttraumatic growth emerges in Event Centrality literature when the reduction of PTSD and Event Centrality has been attempted. Interestingly, trauma distress was not found to decrease with the strengthening of posttraumatic growth (Boals et al., 2015), confirming that growth and distress can co-exist in spite of increased posttraumatic growth.

What an overview of the literature on Event Centrality's relationship to PTSS/PTSD and posttraumatic growth has then uncovered is a challenge to the idea that PTSS/PTSD and posttraumatic growth occur separately. Instead, the research evidences the simultaneous occurrence of PTSS/PTSD and posttraumatic growth in those with Event Centrality resulting from trauma.

Gaps in the literature

The systematic review highlighted multiple gaps in the existing literature. Most notable was the lack of qualitative research into Event Centrality. Only two papers contain a qualitative element, as part of mixed-methods studies (Kuenemund et al., 2016; Saint Arnault & Sinko, 2019); thus, there is a heavy bias towards quantitative data. There is a scarcity of research on Event Centrality relating to childhood trauma, and more so considering the coexistence of PTSS/PTSD and posttraumatic growth. Studies that identify the simultaneous presence of PTSS/PTSD do not provide insights into an individual's subjective experience of the phenomenon.

Methodology

Process

Following ethical approval, 8 participants were recruited. Participants completed the revised Adverse Childhood Events Scale (ACES) (Finkelhor et al., 2013), a self-reporting scale to measure adverse events occurrence before 18 years. The Centrality of Events Scale (CES) (Berntsen & Rubin, 2006) which measures the extent to which an event has become central to self-identity. A semi-structured interview was based on CES questions. The interviews were transcribed verbatim and analysed using Interpretive Phenological Analysis (Smith et al., 2022).

Participants

In accordance with the sample criteria, 8 participants lived in the UK, were female, had an average age of 34 years (26 > 44), were currently in therapy and had been for at least 6 months, experienced trauma before the age of

18, with a mean of 4.75 (2 > 7) traumas, and the self-identity was centred on a trauma experience with a mean CES score of 77.5 (68 > 82).

Findings

Three key factors emerged from the participants' data as they described their experience of living with Event Centrality resulting from childhood trauma. Firstly, the identification of PTSS with issues such as intrusive thoughts, nightmares, and hypervigilance. Secondly, the presence of post-traumatic growth in the form of understanding others, positive meaning, and spiritual growth. Lastly, the observation of both PTSS and posttraumatic growth co-existing. Below are the results of the study.

PTSS

Across all of the data there was a heavy leaning towards descriptions of PTSS symptoms. These included disruptions to self-identity, flashbacks, nightmares, intrusive thoughts, and issues relating to others.

Sense of Self

Collectively, participants struggled with their sense of self. In two cases, the disruption was extreme to the point of Marie feeling *'like I am dead'* and Zara not being *'anything.'* For many participants, lacking a sense of self meant taking on parts of other people's identities. Zara started noticing taking on bits of other people's personalities and emotions, further claiming she often didn't know where *'I start, and they begin.'* Charlotte spoke of ordering the same drink as others due to not knowing what she likes. Rose, Marie and Grace described how they had actively tried to become less enmeshed.

In addition, identity disruption was identified in the language used when referring to trauma as *'my trauma'* (Isla, Emily, Grace, Marie, Charlotte, and Zara). Participants internalised trauma and viewed it as their own. Trauma was not what happened to them but was a part of them.

Relationship Issues

All participants reported relationship difficulties. The primary issues appeared to be a lack of belonging and, thus, isolation. Isla spoke of being unable to *'find her people,'* while Zara claimed it left her feeling like *'an island.'* Charlotte declared, *'It can be a very lonely world.'* When participants spoke of loneliness, they did so with a deflated demeanour, as if resigned to such a position.

There was also a sense of rejection or exclusion. Charlotte noted that participating in conversations about childhood made her feel excluded because she could not contribute positively. Charlotte also believed others had an expectation that *'greatness'* must follow after trauma, and anything else was not wanting to be heard. For all the participants, a sense of not being understood was linked to a lack of belonging. Many of the accounts of lack of understanding had an air of helplessness. Emily's account notes: *'They would never understand.'* She believed the only people who understood were others who had similar experiences. Charlotte, who spoke extensively on the matter, mentioned that she could not show her genuine emotions or reveal her past.

Trust issues were common to seven of the participants. Marie claimed not to trust anyone, including herself. Charlotte spoke of constantly *'second guessing'* other people's motivations, often assuming these to be negative. Likewise, Isla bluntly states that she was *'hugely suspicious of others.'* Among the participants, only Grace expressed surprise at not being suspicious of others, given her childhood experiences.

Pushing away and withdrawing from others was mentioned in half of the descriptions. Zara, Anita, Isla, and Emily all described how they were fearful of letting others get close to them, had pushed away people who were good for them, and withdrew if they felt people were getting too close.

All of the participants noted at some point how they have or had times when they have put other people first to the detriment of themselves. Charlotte claimed that this was because other people were more *'important'* than her. In the case of Isla, Rose, Marie, and Grace, there was an overwhelming need to please others, to the point where Rose and Grace felt they needed to provide a *'service.'* Clearly, being with others often presented problems to the participants.

Involuntary Responses

A vast amount of the participants' interviews were taken up with talking about how childhood trauma still appeared in their adult lives, which was not by their choice. Grace, in describing trauma's ever-presence, stated it was *'the elephant in the room.'* Rose spoke of it as a *'CD constantly buzzing,'* and Anita like a *'whisper'* in the background. There was a unanimous sense of helplessness that trauma would always be there with no ability to prevent that. Charlotte, in particular, described trying not to let the trauma in but not being able to control this: *'The number of times I have woken up in the morning saying, that's it, I am not going to be affected by my past anymore. Then bam. Nope.'* She considered this as being *'haunted'* by trauma.

Participants reported different aspects of involuntary responses. Emily and Isla discussed anxiety, explaining how it impacted their daily lives and could build up into panic attacks when trauma memories were triggered. These two reports of anxiety suggested that anxiety could occur at any time. Isla further spoke about how this meant she had a body she could not trust. That the anxiety gave physical symptoms that caused distress and a distrust of how her body would react.

Zara called her involuntary responses 'leftovers,' referring to nightmares and flashbacks. She noted how her days were impacted by disrupted sleep and flashbacks. Marie spoke similarly about how exhausting life can be when dealing with flashbacks and intrusive thoughts linked to trauma experiences. That her brain would not allow her to forget or move on. Grace noted how she often felt forced to avoid social media due to the possibility of content triggering flashbacks and intrusive thoughts. When talking about triggers, flashbacks, nightmares, and intrusive thoughts, all of the participants commented on the distress this would cause them, mainly in terms of the constant reminder of events they would rather not think about but also on how it took them away from the present moment.

Posttraumatic Growth

The data showed a strong present of posttraumatic growth from all eight participants. Specific areas of growth emerging from participants' accounts were those of development of personal qualities, enhanced relationships with others, spiritual growth, and providing opportunities and a sense of purpose.

Personal Qualities

All eight participants described a direct positive impact of the trauma on the growth of personal qualities. Five of them considered how their experience of trauma had given them a sense of strength, with statements such as Anita's 'Going through that as a child has made me sort of stronger' being a typical sentiment that the trauma gave birth to a strength that may not exist without the trauma. Such a strength appeared to reassure some participants that they could handle future adversity: 'I can build myself back up from anything (…) if there's an earthquake tomorrow, I can handle it' (Emily).

Although considered a direct result of trauma, accounts in general, pointed to the felt sense of strength having taken time to develop, as shown in Emily's description of being strong: 'I consider myself a strong person now.' Further qualities that appeared special to individual participants were gentleness, acceptance (Rose), loving, honesty (Marie), wiser (Grace), and understanding (Isla).

The passage of time between trauma and the development of positive personal characteristics were further illustrated in discussions of resilience. Zara, for example, stated *'I am now seeing myself as a resilient type of person. That's more recent, like in the last three or four years. I used to think I was the complete opposite.'* From a slightly different perspective, Anita, when speaking of resilience, claimed to be *'more resilient,'* that although the trauma had not given her resilience, it had enhanced it beyond the level it might have been. Zara and Anita were certainly not alone in mentioning resilience as a positive outcome. All but one account claimed resilience as an integral factor in their experiences.

Relationships with Others

Each of the eight participants reported that trauma had a positive impact on their ability to relate to others. This manifested itself in different ways, such as being *'kinder to people'* (Marie), more accepting of differences (Rose), forgiving (Isla), more compassionate (Charlotte), able to advise and support others (Grace), and understanding (Zara). Rose spoke passionately on the subject, claiming experiences in childhood meant she had an increased ability to relate to others experiencing difficulties, being able to *'deep dive'* into painful conversations, which others without trauma could not do.

Further reflection on relating to others came from Marie, who spoke of an enhanced ability to be honest with people. That relationships could be based on complete honesty, which others cannot always achieve. For Grace, it meant she was more giving in relationships, that people saw her as *'giving or helpful or just wanting to please others,'* which enhanced her relationship with others.

Spirituality

Anita was the only participant claiming a link between religion and trauma, stating her childhood experiences *'brought me closer to religion.'* She did not affiliate with any specific denomination despite having *'tried'* many out. As a result of her religious growth, she began to feel that something was *'Something greater than us'* and that she had experiences that were *'useful.'*

Two further participants, Marie and Zara, spoke at length about how trauma had led them towards spirituality. Spirituality helped to make sense not only of their childhood experiences but the world in general. For Zara, spirituality was an aid to accepting *'what it puts in our path and work with that.'* Marie saw spirituality resources encompassing both mind and body to the point where she occasionally saw *'the world looks beautiful.'*

Aside from religion and spirituality, all of the participants described how trauma had come to make sense to them. For Grace, it made sense when thinking about the balance of good and bad, claiming this perspective helped her *'manage when things are frustrating or glum.'* Zara saw trauma from the viewpoint that everyone suffers at some point, and she has had her turn. Charlotte considered that there were reasons for events, and one day the *'whys will be revealed to me and my life will make sense.'*

Opportunities and Purpose

Emily forthrightly stated that trauma had led her to her current position in life. Had it not been for her experiences, she would not be in her current geographical location, would not be with her husband, have the children she has, or have a career. Whilst none of the remaining seven participants made such sweeping claims about the influence on their life situation, they did comment on how certain trauma had opened up specific parts of life and, for the most part, also provided them with a purpose to the trauma.

Anita, for example, identified a purpose in her trauma in the act of sharing her experiences with others, stating, *'sharing those experiences now and feeling that maybe they have some purposeful effect for someone out there at some point.'* For Anita, there was no real need to fully understand the nature of the purpose, but a belief that there is one was the important factor. Other participants, however, felt surer of what the purpose of the trauma was and how this had opened opportunities. Marie claimed that trauma had *'taught'* her how to connect with young people, specifically those *'that no one else sees,'* which had opened up an occupation working with young people. The interesting part of Marie's account was a sense of positivity from this; she claimed, *'There's been times where I've been, I've genuinely been so grateful and proud of the childhood.'*

Grace also conveyed a sense of trauma having laid a foundation for opportunities. For her, trauma had provided the possibility to help others and *'offer others advice'* on issues connected to her experience. For Grace, this had manifested in developing social media groups to support other trauma victims, something she believed would not be possible without her past experiences. Grace stated that trauma made her *'feel wiser.'*

Coexistence of PTSS and Posttraumatic Growth

Even without acknowledging the participants' awareness of the coexistence of PTSS and posttraumatic growth, it is easy to pinpoint it within the data. Observing the data on a case-by-case basis, we can see evidence of participants talking about PTSS and posttraumatic growth in all their accounts. In the above data alone, we can see that all eight participants spoke about at least one PTSS and one posttraumatic growth. Examples of this include Zara, who, in reference to PTSS, described problems with self-identity, relationships, and involuntary responses but also showed posttraumatic growth relating to personal qualities, relating to others, and spirituality. Taking the data set as a whole rather than observing only those reported in this findings section, a clear picture of individual participants having both PTSS and posttraumatic growth is presented.

As shown in the findings, participants might have PTSS in one area but growth in another. For example, Maire struggles with self-identity, but her spiritual awareness has grown as a direct result of her traumatic experiences. Similarly, Emily struggles in relationships but has found growth in personal qualities and finding purpose through trauma.

What is interesting is when we consider the categories the PTSS and posttraumatic growth fall into. Again, taking only the data presented in the above findings, we can see a distinct cross-over in distress and growth. All the participants in the study spoke about how trauma in childhood enhanced their understanding of others. Whilst on first observation, this might lead us to conclude that this growth would have a positive impact on their ability to be in relationships with others, it would appear from the participant descriptions of struggling in relationships that it does not.

Having observed the coexistence of PTSS and posttraumatic growth within the data, it was also helpful to see if the participants had any awareness of this phenomenon. Indeed, the data were rich in this regard. Anita recognised that sometimes there would be distress and other times growth. She spoke about how she felt resilient at times and weak on other occasions. For Anita, then, posttraumatic growth was not a fixed thing, but certainly, where resilience was concerned, it could fluctuate: '*I feel really, really resilient. But then, other times, I feel very low, fragile, and broken, the complete opposite.*'

Zara likewise spoke of such fluctuation, saying she was like '*Jekyll and Hyde,*' sometimes feeling confident and relaxed about the trauma and other days distressed to the point of hating herself. Isla also expressed a wealth of duality in her report, describing herself as a bundle of '*messiness, brokenness, and then strength,*' that she's never sure which one she's going to be at any given time.

The main area where PTSS and posttraumatic growth co-existed was in relating to others. All participants noted problems forming and maintaining relationships; however, they all also spoke of trauma providing benefits in terms of a better understanding of others and increased empathy. Charlotte mentioned that such an occurrence *'confused her.'* It meant that she was compassionate, which was positive, but that resulted in her being overly forgiving, which often caused issues in relationships. Rose also spoke of how she had an increased ability to be with others in times of pain for them, but was unable to turn to others when she needed them. Thus, the growth experienced by the participants was not always straightforward and frequently came with its own distress and dilemmas.

Discussion

The findings add to the literature that finds correlations between childhood trauma and Event Centrality (Cook et al., 2021; Kwon & You, 2021; Mordeno et al., 2018; Wang et al., 2020; Watts et al., 2021). All the participants in the study had experienced at least two traumas in childhood and had high Event Centrality scores which still presented into adulthood, which further aligns with research finding the impact of trauma in childhood and Event Centrality can continue throughout the lifespan (Mordeno et al., 2018; Ogle et al., 2013).

Furthermore, with participants describing PTSS symptoms, this supported existing research findings that intrusive thoughts and ruminations (Bishop et al., 2018; Brooks et al., 2017; Lancaster et al., 2015; Seyburn et al., 2020), and sensory memories, or flashbacks (Blix et al., 2020; Mordeno et al., 2018; Pociunaite & Zimprich, 2023) are integral to Event Centrality and trauma. The focal point of Event Centrality, that trauma can become central to an individual's self-identity, was noted. Participants actively described that the trauma had impacted their ability to retain a coherent sense of self, in line with numerous existing studies in the field (Bernsten & Rubin, 2007; Clauss et al., 2021; Lancaster et al., 2011; Meisels & Grysman, 2021; Saint Arnault & Sinko, 2019; Wamser-Nanney, 2019).

Likewise, the findings align with Boals and Schuettler's (2011) double-edged sword theory of Event Centrality by observing that Event Centrality could have positive or negative effects. Posttraumatic growth was shown in participant's descriptions of Event Centrality. As found by Steinberg et al. (2022), growth in relationships, providing opportunities, a sense of strength, and spiritual growth were also apparent in this study's findings, and so was the development of resilience, as located in Tranter et al.'s (2020) study.

However, the main focus of this chapter was to highlight the coexistence of PTSS/PTSD and posttraumatic growth to add to the existing literature in this field. The findings support the limited research that individuals can have co-occurring PTSS/PTSD and posttraumatic growth, such as that of Fletcher et al. (2023), Frazier et al. (2001), and Yuan et al. (2021). It also supports Event Centrality studies, specifically Kuenemund et al.'s (2016), by finding disclosures of distress in the form of identity issues and restriction in living and growth in areas such as relationships, personal strength, and spirituality.

It is worthy to consider at this point challenges to the concept of post-traumatic growth. Frazier et al. (2009) found that even when posttraumatic growth indicators are reported, overall psychological distress may not improve. Thus, posttraumatic growth does not always relate to a positive outcome. Indeed, the findings did not see posttraumatic growth lessen any distress within this sample.

Indeed, Boals (2023) argues that posttraumatic growth is very rare. Moreover, it can be somewhat Illusory, especially where there is a strong self-desire to be healed or where cultural expectations to experience growth from trauma exist. There was evidence of conforming to perceived expectations with the finding about masking emotions and not talking about trauma in line with what others would not want to hear or understand.

Boals (2023) further suggests that the prevalence of mistaking growth for coping mechanisms is possibly higher than current research on posttraumatic growth accounts for. This study somewhat supports Boals. Being better able to understand others as mentioned by several participants, whilst it could be a positive, could also be a heighted trauma reaction to help protect against future harm, a type of hypervigilance. Likewise, always being ready for more trauma, also common between the cases, whilst to the participants gave a perception of coping, is not necessarily a growth state and is more likely a trauma response given the observations of distress being caused in by preparedness for further adverse experiences.

Conclusion

This study's finding challenges the traditional trauma, PTSS/PTSD, and posttraumatic growth relationship. It demonstrates the coexistence of PTSS/PTSD and posttraumatic growth rather than one or the other being present or leading to the other. The findings supported Schuettler and Boals' (2011) position that individuals often grapple between the position of distress and growth. There is not a linear process between trauma, suffering, and growth; rather, participants in this study appeared to have frequent movement between PTSS and growth.

Limitations, relevance, and recommendations

The study has several limitations, including being reflective only of the sample. Replication of the study with more participants within the sample criteria and widening to other criteria would be useful, so that results could be generalised. This would also be achieved with similar studies on groups with differing genders, ages, and demography.

The main study's aim was to explore the lived experience of Event Centrality resulting from childhood trauma; thus, the coexistence of PTSS and posttraumatic growth, whilst emerging as an important feature of the participants' accounts, was not the main focus. Therefore, further research solely on the co-existence possible coexistence is recommended.

The study has clinical relevance for those working with childhood trauma clients. Assumptions should not be made that PTSS and posttraumatic growth present independently; time should be taken to observe possible coexistence. The presence of posttraumatic growth should be explored more fully to assess if for actual growth or trauma response appearing as growth. If working on developing growth, attention needs to be paid to whether this growth is genuine growth or a desire to meet societal expectations for growth, or a coping mechanism. Care should be taken when interventions are used to increase growth as these may not decrease distress.

References

Allbaugh, L. J., Wright, M. O., & Folger, S. F. (2016). The role of repetitive thought in determining posttraumatic growth and distress following interpersonal trauma. *Anxiety, Stress, & Coping, 29*(1), 21–37. https://doi.org/10.1080/10615806.2015.1015422

American Psychological Association. (2013). *Diagnostic and Statistical Manual of Mental Disorders* (5th ed.). https://doi.org/10.1176/appi.books.9780890425787

Barton, S., Boals, A., & Knowles, L. (2013). Thinking about trauma: The unique contributions of event centrality and posttraumatic cognitions in predicting PTSD and posttraumatic growth. *Journal of Traumatic Stress, 26*(6), 718–726. https://doi.org/10.1002/jts.21863

Bernard, J. D., Whittles, R. L., Kertz, S. J., & Burke, P. A. (2015). Trauma and Event Centrality: Valence and incorporation into identity influence well-being more than exposure. *Psychological Trauma: Theory, Research, Practice, and Policy, 7*(1), 11–17. https://doi.org/10.1037/a0037331

Berntsen, D., & Rubin, D. C. (2006). The Centrality of Event Scale: A measure of integrating a trauma into one's identity and its relation to post-traumatic stress disorder symptoms. *Behaviour Research and Therapy, 44*(2), 219–231. https://doi.org/10.1016/j.brat.2005.01.009

Berntsen, D., & Rubin, D. C. (2007). When a trauma becomes a key to Identity: Enhanced integration of trauma memories predicts Posttraumatic Stress Disorder symptoms. *Applied Cognitive Psychology, 431*, 417–431. https://doi.org/10.1002/acp.1290

Bishop, L. S., Ameral, V. E., & Palm Reed, K. M. (2018). The impact of experiential avoidance and event centrality in trauma-related rumination and posttraumatic stress. *Behavior Modification, 42*(6), 815–837. https://doi.org/10.1177/0145445517747287

Blix, I., Birkeland, M. S., & Thoresen, S. (2020). Vivid memories of distant trauma: Examining the characteristics of trauma memories and the relationship with the centrality of event and posttraumatic stress 26 years after trauma. *Applied Cognitive Psychology, 34*(3), 678–684. https://doi.org/10.1002/acp.3650

Boals, A. (2023). Illusory posttraumatic growth is common, but genuine posttraumatic growth is rare: A critical review and suggestions for a path forward. *Clinical Psychology Review, 103*, 102301. https://doi.org/10.1016/j.cpr.2023.102301

Boals, A., Murrell, A. R., Berntsen, D., Southard-Dobbs, S., & Agtarap, S. (2015). Experimentally reducing event centrality using a modified expressive writing intervention. *Journal of Contextual Behavioral Science, 4*(4), 269–276. https://doi.org/10.1016/j.jcbs.2015.10.001

Boals, A., & Schuettler, D. (2011). A double-edged sword: Event centrality, PTSD and Posttraumatic Growth. *Applied Cognitive Psychology, 25*(5), 817–822. https://doi.org/10.1002/acp.1753

Boals, A., Steward, J. M., & Schuettler, D. (2010). Advancing our understanding of Posttraumatic Growth by considering event centrality. *Journal of Loss and Trauma, 15*(6), 518–533. https://doi.org/10.1080/15325024.2010.519271

Boelen, P. A. (2021). The centrality of a loss-event: Patterns, correlates, and predictive value. *Anxiety, Stress, & Coping, 34*(3), 258–265. https://doi.org/10.1080/10615806.2021.1876226

Brooks, M., Graham-Kevan, N., Lowe, M., & Robinson, S. (2017). Rumination, event centrality, and perceived control as predictors of post-traumatic growth and distress: The Cognitive Growth and Stress model. *British Journal of Clinical Psychology, 56*(3), 286–302. https://doi.org/10.1111/bjc.12138

Bruce, M. J., & Weaver, T. L. (2021). Testing cognitive models to characterize trauma anniversary reactions marked by stress and growth. *OMEGA – Journal of Death and Dying, 88*(3), 1203–1217. https://doi.org/10.1177/00302228211066687

Clauss, K., Benfer, N., Thomas, K. N., & Bardeen, J. R. (2021). The interactive effect of event centrality and maladaptive metacognitive beliefs on posttraumatic stress symptoms and posttraumatic growth. *Psychological Trauma: Theory, Research, Practice, and Policy, 13*(5), 596–602. https://doi.org/10.1037/tra0001010

Cook, J. L., Russell, K., Long, A., & Phipps, S. (2021). Centrality of the childhood cancer experience and its relation to Post-Traumatic Stress and Growth. *Psycho-Oncology (Chichester, England), 30*(4), 564–570. https://doi.org/10.1002/pon.5603

David, G., Shakespeare-Finch, J., & Krosch, D. (2022). Testing theoretical predictors of posttraumatic growth and posttraumatic stress symptoms. *Psychological Trauma: Theory, Research, Practice, and Policy, 14*(3), 399–409. https://doi.org/10.1037/tra0000777

Eze, J. E., Ifeagwazi, C. M., & Chukwuorji, J. C. (2022). Locating event centrality in associations of emotion regulation with posttraumatic stress disorder symptoms and posttraumatic growth in emerging adults. *Journal of Migration and Health, 6*, 100139. https://doi.org/10.1016/j.jmh.2022.100139

Finkelhor, D., Shattuck, A., Turner, H., & Hamby, S. (2013). Improving the Adverse Childhood Experiences Study scale. *JAMA Pediatrics, 167*(1), 70–75. https://doi.org/10.1001/jamapediatrics.2013.420

Fletcher, S., Mitchell, S., Curran, D., Armour, C., & Hanna, D. (2023). Empirically derived patterns of posttraumatic stress and growth: A systematic review. *Trauma, Violence, & Abuse, 24*(5), 3132–3150. https://doi.org/10.1177/15248380221129580

Frazier, P., Conlon, A., & Glaser, T. (2001). Positive and negative life changes following sexual assault. *Journal of Consulting and Clinical Psychology, 69*(6), 1048–1055. https://doi.org/10.1037/0022-006X.69.6.1048

Frazier, P., Tennen, H., Gavian, M., Park, C., Tomich, P., & Tashiro, T. (2009). Does self-reported posttraumatic growth reflect genuine positive change? *Psychological Science, 20*(7), 912–919. https://doi.org/10.1111/j.1467-9280.2009.02381.x

Glad, K. A., Czajkowski, N. O., Dyb, G., & Hafstad, G. S. (2020). Does event centrality mediate the effect of peritraumatic reactions on post-traumatic growth in survivors of a terrorist attack? *European Journal of Psychotraumatology, 11*(1), 1766276. https://doi.org/10.1080/20008198.2020.1766276

Groleau, J. M., Calhoun, L. G., Cann, A., & Tedeschi, R. G. (2013). The role of centrality of events in posttraumatic distress and posttraumatic growth. *Psychological Trauma: Theory, Research, Practice, and Policy, 5*(5), 477–483. https://doi.org/10.1037/a0028809

Ionio, C., Mascheroni, E., & Di Blasio, P. (2018). The Centrality of Events Scale for Italian adolescents: Integrating traumatic experience into one's identity and Its relation to posttraumatic stress disorder symptomatology. *Europe's Journal of Psychology, 14*(2), 359–372. https://doi.org/10.5964/ejop.v14i2.1465

Kuenemund, A., Zwick, S., Rief, W., & Exner, C. (2016). (Re-)defining the self – Enhanced posttraumatic growth and event centrality in stroke survivors: A mixed-method approach and control comparison study. *Journal of Health Psychology, 21*(5), 679–689. https://doi.org/10.1177/1359105314535457

Kwon, J., & You, S. (2021). The effects of Event Centrality on complicated grief and Posttraumatic Growth among young adults with parental bereavement during adolescence: The mediating effect of traumatized self-system and meaning reconstruction. *Korean Journal of Clinical Psychology, 40*(2), 156–166. https://doi.org/10.15842/kjcp.2021.40.2.004

Lancaster, S. L., Klein, K. R., Nadia, C., Szabo, L., & Mogerman, B. (2015). An integrated model of posttraumatic stress and growth. *Journal of Trauma & Dissociation, 16*(4), 399–418. https://doi.org/10.1080/15299732.2015.1009225

Lancaster, S. L., Rodriguez, B. F., & Weston, R. (2011). Path analytic examination of a cognitive model of PTSD. *Behaviour Research and Therapy, 49*(3), 194–201. https://doi.org/10.1016/j.brat.2011.01.002

Lewis, S. J., Arseneault, L., Caspi, A., Fisher, H. L., Matthews, T., Moffitt, T. E., Odgers, C. L., Stahl, D., Teng, J. Y., & Danese, A. (2019). The epidemiology of trauma and post-traumatic stress disorder in a representative cohort of young people in England and Wales. *The Lancet Psychiatry, 6*(3), 247–256. https://doi.org/10.1016/S2215-0366(19)30031-8

Mangion. A (2024). An exploration of women's lived experiences of event centrality resulting from childhood trauma – an existential perspective. [Unpublished doctoral dissertation]. Middlesex University.

Meisels, H. B., & Grysman, A. (2021). Confronting self-discrepant events: Meaning-making and well-being in personal and political narratives. *Self and Identity, 20*(3), 323–338. https://doi.org/10.1080/15298868.2020.1714712

Mordeno, I. G., Galela, D. S., Nalipay, M. J. N., & Cue, M. P. (2018). Centrality of Event and mental health outcomes in child and adolescent natural disaster survivors. *The Spanish Journal of Psychology, 21*, E61. https://doi.org/doi:10.1017/sjp.2018.58

Ogle, C. M., Rubin, D. C., Berntsen, D., & Siegler, I. C. (2013). The frequency and impact of exposure to potentially traumatic events over the life course. *Clinical Psychological Science, 1*(4), 426–434. https://psycnet.apa.org/doi/10.1177/2167702613485076

Ogle, C. M., Rubin, D. C., & Siegler, I. C. (2015). The relation between insecure attachment and posttraumatic stress: Early life versus adulthood traumas. *Psychological Trauma: Theory, Research, Practice, and Policy, 7*(4), 324–332. https://psycnet.apa.org/doi/10.1037/tra0000015

Ogle, C. M., Rubin, D. C., & Siegler, I. C. (2016). Maladaptive trauma appraisals mediate the relation between attachment anxiety and PTSD symptom severity. *Psychological Trauma: Theory, Research, Practice, and Policy, 8*(3), 301–309. https://hdl.handle.net/10161/12029

Pociunaite, J., & Zimprich, D. (2023). Characteristics of positive and negative autobiographical memories central to identity: Emotionality, vividness, rehearsal, rumination, and reflection. *Frontiers in Psychology, 14*, 1225068. https://doi.org/10.3389/fpsyg.2023.1225068

Robinaugh, D. J., & McNally, R. J. (2011). Trauma centrality and PTSD symptom severity in adult survivors of childhood sexual abuse. *Journal of Traumatic Stress, 24*(4), 483–486. https://doi.org/10.1002/jts.20656

Saint Arnault, D. M., & Sinko, L. M. (2019). Hope and fulfilment after complex trauma: Using mixed methods to understand healing. *Frontiers in Psychology, 10*, 2061. https://doi.org/10.3389/fpsyg.2019.02061

Schuettler, D., & Boals, A. (2011). The path to posttraumatic growth versus posttraumatic stress disorder: Contributions of event centrality and coping. *Journal of Loss and Trauma, 16*(2), 180–194. https://doi.org/10.1080/15325024.2010.519273

Seyburn, S. J., LaLonde, L., & Taku, K. (2020). A sense of growth among teenagers after hurting others: A potential application of posttraumatic growth theory. *Journal of Loss and Trauma, 25*(1), 22–33. https://doi.org/10.1080/15325024.2019.1645449

Smith, J. A., Flowers, P., & Larkin, M. (2022). *Interpretative Phenomenological Analysis: Theory, Method, and Research* (2nd ed.). Sage.

Steinberg, M. H., Bellet, B. W., McNally, R. J., & Boals, A. (2022). Resolving the paradox of posttraumatic growth and event centrality in trauma survivors. *Journal of Traumatic Stress, 35*(2), 434–445.

Tedeschi, R. G., & Calhoun, L. G. (1995). *Trauma & Transformation: Growing in the Aftermath of Suffering.* Sage. https://doi.org/10.4135/9781483326931

Tedeschi, R. G., Shakespeare-Finch, J., Taku, K., & Calhoun, L. G. (2018). *Posttraumatic Growth: Theory, Research, and Applications.* Routledge. https://doi.org/10.4324/9781315527451

Tranter, H., Brooks, M., & Khan, R. (2021). Emotional resilience and event centrality mediate posttraumatic growth following adverse childhood experiences. *Psychol Trauma, 13*(2), 165–173.

Vagos, P., Ribeiro da Silva, D., Brazão, N., & Rijo, D. (2018). The Centrality of Events Scale in Portuguese adolescents: Validity evidence based on internal structure and on relations to other variables. *Assessment (Odessa, Fla.), 25*(4), 527–538. https://doi.org/10.1177/1073191116651137

Wagner, A. C., Torbit, L., Jenzer, T., Landy, M. S., Pukay-Martin, N. D., Macdonald, A., Fredman, S. J., & Monson, C. M. (2016). The role of posttraumatic growth in a randomized controlled trial of cognitive-behavioral conjoint therapy for PTSD. *Journal of Traumatic Stress, 29*(4), 379–383. https://doi.org/10.1002/jts.22122

Wamser-Nanney, R. (2019). Event centrality: Factor structure and links to posttraumatic stress disorder symptom clusters. *Journal of Traumatic Stress, 32*(4), 516–525. https://doi.org/10.1002/jts.22413

Wang, N., Chung, M. C., & Wang, Y. (2020). The relationship between posttraumatic stress disorder, trauma centrality, posttraumatic growth and psychiatric co-morbidity among Chinese adolescents. *Asian Journal of Psychiatry, 49*, 101940. https://doi.org/10.1016/j.ajp.2020.101940

Watts, J., Leeman, M., O'Sullivan, D., Castleberry, J., & Baniya, G. (2021). Childhood emotional maltreatment and Post-Traumatic Stress Disorder in the context of Centrality of the Event and intrusive rumination. *Rehabilitation Counselling Bulletin, 64*(2), 108–117. https://doi.org/10.1177/0034355220925889

Weber, M. C., & Schulenberg, S. E. (2023). The curvilinear relationships between posttraumatic growth and posttraumatic stress, depression, and anxiety. *Traumatology, 29*(2), 249–260. https://doi.org/10.1037/trm0000398

Yuan, G., Park, C. L., Birkeland, S. R., Yip, P. S., & Hall, B. J. (2021). A network analysis of the associations between posttraumatic stress symptoms and posttraumatic growth among disaster-exposed Chinese young adults. *Journal of Traumatic Stress, 34*(4), 786–798. https://doi.org/10.1002/jts.22673

Zięba, M., Wiecheć, K., Biegańska-Banaś, J., & Mieleszczenko-Kowszewicz, W. (2019). Coexistence of post-traumatic growth and post-traumatic depreciation in the aftermath of trauma: Qualitative and quantitative narrative analysis. *Frontiers in Psychology, 10*, 687. https://doi.org/10.3389/fpsyg.2019.00687

Encountering Death

Chapter 6

Living with Traumatic Bereavement

Chloe Paidoussis-Mitchell

What is Traumatic Bereavement?

Existentially, Traumatic Bereavement is the experience of alienation, isolation, and distress at the profound loss of meaning in life. The shock of such a loss throws the bereaved into an 'existentially awake' state, dysregulated by the temporality of life and disoriented at the loss of meaning (Paidoussis-Mitchell, 2012). Robert Stolorow, the eminent Existential Analyst, described losing his wife suddenly in the middle of the night whilst they were both asleep, as an experience that meant he had to face death, to be in that state of being-towards-death (Heidegger, 1927/2010) and own up not only to his own finitude but to the finite nature of those he loved (Stolorow, 2022).

As an Existential Counselling Psychologist, I conducted my doctoral research into the phenomenology of traumatic bereavement, have supervised a number of doctoral candidates researching traumatic loss, and have worked therapeutically with hundreds of traumatically bereaved clients in my private practice, The Grief Clinic, in London. I have witnessed the human struggle of life after loss. A client recently described feeling *'lost in loss'* after the sudden death of his partner, and these words evoked in me the dark and desperate loneliness of traumatic bereavement. Clients from all over the world describe their longing to be reconnected with their loved ones, their despair at the *absurdity* of the temporality of life, and their profound distress at the absence of what once was. We love and 'can't bear' to lose, and it is human to find it very difficult to engage in 'normal life' after a traumatic bereavement. As an Existential Psychologist, I am firmly grounded in humanising the trauma of losing a loved one traumatically and normalising the lived experience of it. I see it as a meaningful signal of what it means to love and to care.

In my therapy rooms, the intense grief and emotional pain of such loss seem to grow rather than abate as time goes on, and it can feel impossibly painful to sit with the existential wake-up call of 'bad things happen

DOI: 10.4324/9781003493860-9

to good people.' Big questions come crashing up to the surface, such as 'Why has this happened? What now? What is the point of life? What am I supposed to do now? Who am I now? How can I go on as usual?' These profound questions so relatable, are deeply existential, and I believe the Existential approach is ideally placed to hold the space for such distress.

Traumatic Bereavement is, in my view, an understandable response to a distressing and frightening event. I have yet to meet a person who is comfortable with the sudden and traumatic loss of life. We are wired to value life, to formulate meaning and express our purpose in authentic connection and love, and we expect safety in the physical realm, even if we know it is not guaranteed. Traumatic loss reveals our Heidegerian 'forgetfulness' (Stolorow, 2011) and our alliance with the illusion of safety. '*I never thought this would happen to me; I never saw it coming; I can't believe this is my story*' repeat in my therapy room. Some seem more psychologically resourced than others, but all, I believe, suffer the pain of it.

Most of us, wake up every day assuming it will be a 'normal' day. As a recent client said, whilst we were exploring the sudden death of her mother: '*it happened on such a normal day. It was 4 pm on a Tuesday and that was that. It seems so inane…*' She described feeling '*a profound sense of absurdity at the ordinariness of such a catastrophic event.*' She raged at the nature of it… every day is normal until it is not and something devastating disrupts us. '*What? That's it? Gone on a Tuesday at 4 pm because somebody else made a stupid mistake?*' Holding the space for her traumatic pain felt the very least I could do.

Cruse Bereavement – the largest bereavement charity in the UK (Cruse, 2024) – defines Traumatic Bereavement as the grief that arises in response to a sudden and traumatic event, such as a road traffic accident. The UK Trauma Council states that: "Traumatic bereavement arises when the natural grieving process is disrupted as a result of the trauma of the death of a friend or family member, leading to a lasting negative impact on wellbeing and everyday functioning" (UK Trauma Council, 2024).

An Existential perspective on Traumatic Bereavement may define the phenomenon of such loss as a confrontation with the temporality of the human condition, characterised by the loss of meaning and relational self.

Is Traumatic Bereavement a mental illness?

Traumatic Bereavement is not a clinically diagnosable condition in its own right, and there is little agreement on what constitutes traumatic and non-traumatic bereavement (Rubin & Feeling, 2013). The DSM-V (American Psychological Association [APA], 2013) and its latest traumatic grief inclusions do, however, stipulate that four grief-related mental illnesses can occur in response to a traumatic death. Although, as an Existential Practitioner,

I don't advocate for diagnosis, I do appreciate that the wider clinical field does, and many clients will arrive in our therapy rooms with an expectation that we understand and respect their diagnosis. I have found it helpful to deepen my understanding of these conditions and offer therapeutic guidance in support of the challenges their specific symptoms bring, rather than to oppose their efficacy. Many clients report that the diagnosis, amidst the trauma of loss, is a reassurance that something recognisable is happening to them, and there is help at hand. The four conditions present in the DSM V (APA, 2013) are Prolonged Grief Disorder (PGD), Post-Traumatic Stress Disorder (PTSD), Persistent Complex Bereavement Disorder (PCBD), and grief-specific Major Depression Disorder (MDD).

Prolonged Grief Disorder (PGD) involves experiencing intense longing for the person who has died a year from death, or 6 months for children, and feeling disabled by persistent thoughts and preoccupations about the deceased. Further indicators of PGD include encountering at least 3 of the following symptoms nearly every day, for at least a month before diagnosis:

1. Feeling identity disruption, and as though a part of you has died
2. Struggling to believe the death has actually happened
3. Avoiding all reminders of the loss
4. Experiencing overwhelming and intense emotional pain (such as anger, bitterness, and sorrow) about the death
5. Struggling to engage in normal life and withdrawing from all friendships, not pursuing interests, and avoiding making future plans
6. Being numb and experiencing the absence of all emotions
7. Feeling like life is profoundly meaningless
8. Experiencing deep loneliness and feelings of detachment and disconnection
9. Being indifferent to the wellbeing of others.

Prolonged Grief Disorder is different to grief-specific Major Depression Disorder, as in PGD the feelings of depression centre on the deceased and are followed by a persistent desire to be with them. In Depression the feelings are free-floating, with persistent hopelessness and worthlessness and guilt about oneself and life in general (Paidoussis-Mitchell, 2024).

Persistent Complex Bereavement Disorder (APA, 2013) is diagnosed when at least one of these symptoms is reported, a year after bereavement for adults, and 6 months for children:

1. Persistent yearning for the deceased
2. Preoccupation with the deceased
3. Preoccupation with the circumstances of the death.

As well as at least six of the following symptoms, on more days than not, persisting for at least a year:

1. Marked difficulty accepting the death
2. Experiencing disbelief or emotional numbness over the death
3. Difficulty with positive reminiscing about the deceased
4. Bitterness or anger related to the loss
5. Intense self-blaming about the death
6. Excessive avoidance of reminders of the loss
7. A desire to die to be with the deceased
8. Difficulty trusting others since the death
9. Feeling alone and detached from others since the death
10. Feeling like life is meaningless or empty without the deceased or the belief that functioning is impossible without the deceased
11. Confusion about roles in life or diminished sense of identity
12. Difficulty or reluctance to pursue interests or plan for the future
13. Avoiding friendships and activities
14. Experiencing clinically significant distress or impairment in social, occupational, or other important areas of functioning as a result of the symptoms.

The differences between Prolonged Grief Disorder and Persistent Complex Bereavement Disorder are small, with more symptoms being required for PCBD. Wishing to die to be with the deceased is a feature of PCBD, whilst difficulties remembering the lost person are not included in PGD.

Post-Traumatic Stress Disorder (PTSD) may be diagnosed if the loss was accidental, violent, considered outside the range of human experience, and there are flashbacks and intrusive memories which disrupt the capacity to function (Bui, 2018).

The existential view is that people do not fit neatly into these clinical definitions of trauma. For example, a mother who lost her elderly parent to cancer would not fit the diagnostics for PTSD as the death was not accidental or violent but may still be experienced as deeply traumatic and distressing. In my experience, it is not helpful to be too strict about definitions of trauma. Psychological challenges of an existential nature befall those traumatically bereaved, no matter what the diagnosis.

Traumatic Bereavement is personal to each client and subjective in nature. The descriptions of it reveal the profound shake-up involved, where normal no longer is normal, and a rebuilding and reconstituting of what it means to be is required amidst distress, meaninglessness, and pain (Paidoussis-Mitchell, 2024). Questions of meaning, choice, purpose, and personal evolution emerge in almost every client who seeks therapy with me for traumatic loss.

We know that many factors shape our mental health – that subjective measure of wellbeing – such as our living conditions, existing stress levels, mental and physical health, history of trauma and loss, childhood adversity, and attitude to life and self-worth (Paidoussis-Mitchell, 2024).

As an Existential practitioner, I avoid pathologising Traumatic Bereavement – even if the dysregulation is severe. Distress and maladaptive behaviours, in the Existential frame, are evidence not of mental illness but rather of the distressing nature of the human condition, which demands that we create meaning out of a chaotic, unpredictable world. As Sartre stated, "existence precedes essence" (Sartre, 1958), and I believe it is helpful to humanise traumatic bereavement as a disturbance in the loss of meaning. I will offer you an explication of my approach, with a short case study to highlight how the existential ideas of meaning, freedom, isolation, and death can help you guide your distressed clients to mental health and wellbeing through the pain of traumatic loss.

An Existential therapeutic approach

My approach to Traumatic Bereavement is a suggestion, not an instruction. Take from it what you feel resonates with your therapy. Existentialism is a philosophical exploration of humanity and as such is open to being interpreted by each practitioner. I am not suggesting that this is the best or the only approach to helping those struggling with trauma and loss. It is not. It is, however, my approach, informed by many years of therapeutic practice, and I believe it is a helpful approach to therapising Traumatic Bereavement, because it allows for phenomenological exploration of the dilemmas involved in what it means to:

1. live beyond traumatic loss
2. to face death and mortality and the possibility of more loss
3. to calm the nervous system amidst an unpredictable and chaotic material world
4. to find value and hope in life no matter what
5. to rebuild authentic connections amidst alienation and isolation
6. to bear loss and the absence of what once was
7. to reconstruct meaning and purpose and move towards a new future
8. to grieve all that is lost (identity, connections, the expected future) and maintain ongoing bonds with the deceased.

I draw from Existential philosophy the assumption that Traumatic Bereavement reveals the existential dimensions of our humanity and 'being-ness' (i.e. how we be and what we do). The Existential school asserts that we exist relationally in four worlds: Personal, Social, Physical, and Spiritual (van Deurzen & Arnold-Baker, 2005), and these four worlds have helped me contextualise the impact of traumatic bereavement, both personally and professionally. These four dimensions provide a therapeutic scaffold to contextualise the psychological journey through loss and Traumatic Bereavement (Paidoussis-Mitchell, 2024).

My approach is not to fix Traumatic Bereavement but rather to meet it. To engage with the lived experience of it, to share in its impact, to hold empathy for the client's meaningful choices – no matter what – in support of their humanity, individuality, and choice. I don't see myself as the expert with all the answers, but rather as a skilled conversationalist who has engaged deeply in the many stories of loss that have been shared in my practice over the years, and I have observed what works and what doesn't. As my focus has been to help clients therapeutically move through traumatic loss, I have always assumed that this means finding hope, growth, and love. If a client resists this, I do not judge but I do challenge.

The aim of my therapy is to reflectively 'hold the space' for each traumatically bereaved client, in a non-judgemental heartfelt way, to own my engagement with their material, and to express a deeply humane stance so we can delve into their existential struggles. It is through our shared humanity and respect for the challenge that we can all engage with the intense nature of these struggles, and I see it as my role to find the inner resource to withstand and face the tension. If my clients must live through it, I have to find the resilience to show compassion, resilience, care, and respect for their human struggle – no matter what.

In my experience, good therapy works when the clients can authentically and empathically meet themselves and engage meaningfully with their dilemmas. It's not like there is a right answer for most dilemmas, but sharing in this and feeling validated and witnessed by a compassionate empathic other seem to alleviate distress and give momentum to the client to rebuild a life with hope, purpose, and meaning.

The Existential approach in Traumatic Bereavement sees the trauma of a sudden loss as an existential injury that may result in the loss of self and meaning (Thompson & Walsh, 2010). Posttraumatic growth is possible – I have seen it many times – if there is ample opportunity to face death and the temporality of life in the spirit of agency, and to create meaning beyond it. Often this meaning is altruistic but not only, and galvanises hope and growth. As Viktor Frankl – the father of logotherapy – has so beautifully explicated in *Man's Search for Meaning*, when people have a reason to live, they can survive anything (Frankl, 1946/2004). Meaning is at the heart of Traumatic Bereavement, and the loss of it depletes our mental health and wellbeing.

Although I would never wish to be too prescriptive in what is addressed in therapy, I have found framing the existential struggles into the four dimensions to be a helpful therapeutic guide that informs the aim of my therapeutic work. An example of therapeutic work using the four dimensions is set out in Table 6.1.

Case study

Maderu was 42 and came to therapy a year after losing his wife in a road traffic accident. He was self-referred on the recommendation of his GP, who had prescribed a low-dose anti-depressant to help with his reported depression and constant low mood. Maderu had been married to Lainey for 10 years and had enjoyed a happy marriage. He described their life as perfect. They were soulmates, had financial security, both enjoyed their careers, and had just bought their forever home, which they planned to renovate. He would not have ever wanted anyone else and felt the luckiest man alive on their wedding day. This had been a happy affair with both extended families joyous.

Maderu never imagined he would not have the future he 'signed up for' when marrying Lainey. He felt like life was absurd in its pointlessness, and he fantasised about following her into death. He had no plans to harm himself – he wanted to protect his family from the devastation of suicide, but he found daily life intensively difficult and was self-medicating with alcohol daily.

Maderu came to therapy not really believing it would help, but recognised that if he didn't take care of himself, his wife would be very disappointed in the harm her death had caused him.

Client History

His life had been a comfortable one. He grew up in a middle-class Indian family in the outskirts of London, had no childhood adversity that he felt was noteworthy, though he did experience some bullying at school. He worked hard to qualify as an accountant and enjoyed his career in a busy London office. He had some great friends, was physically healthy, and enjoyed playing football in the park.

His parents were still alive, his two brothers lived nearby with their families, and all were very supportive of him. They loved Lainey and kept trying to encourage him to find happiness in cherished memories of her. He found their suggestions difficult, as remembering their love broke his heart repeatedly. His grief was intense, and he felt it was leaking out uncontrollably now.

Table 6.1 The Four Dimensions of Traumatic Bereavement & Therapeutic Aims

Dimension	Existential Struggle	Psychological Manifestation	Therapeutic Aim
Physical Dimension	Death struggle and mortality	Difficulty accepting the death. Intrusive flashbacks or thoughts. Dysregulated nervous system, with anxiety and feelings of dread, panic, and fear. Avoiding all reminders of the loss. Anxiety about harm befalling others. Avoiding facing death and the transient nature of life.	Explore the client's death struggle. Recognise attitudes to health and death. Empathise (both client and therapist) with the lived experience of traumatic loss. Reveal what being towards death is like for the client and what attitudes this evokes in the client. Understanding how the trauma of loss impacts the client physically. Regulate the nervous system and calm the body's heightened anxiety. Acknowledge history of previous adversity and trauma and recognise repeating patterns. Share in the humanity of the death struggle – moving to acceptance, rather than avoidance. Explore what accepting death looks like for the client.
Personal Dimension	Burden of freedom & choice	Poor self-care routines. Catastrophising and imagining the universe has singled the client out for punishment. Experiencing anger, helplessness, fear, and despair.	Explore the client's attitude to life's unpredictability. Explore feelings of despair, anger, and the impact of catastrophic or negative beliefs to wellbeing and growth. Explore how the client may take responsibility for their wellbeing and identify what this look like in practice, in the context of their life. Help the client recognise their freedom to choose life. Explore how the client authors their life story and reflect on their next chapters. What does this reveal about their intention or lack of to embrace life meaningfully post-loss?

Dimension	Existential Struggle	Psychological Manifestation	Therapeutic Aim
Personal Dimension	Love & the struggle of severed bonds	Loss of identity and self. Prioritising and believing the strong inner critic. Low or absent self-worth. Poor self-esteem. Judging grief as weak or faulty.	Explore the client's loss of identity and depleted self-worth. Rebuild self-worth and self-acceptance. Help the client fortify a compassionate relationship with themselves. Explore how the client may maintain an ongoing bond with the deceased in a personally meaningful way. Encourage the client to embrace their potential for growth and love. Engage the client in an exploration of attitudes to love. Help the client recognise that their pain and grief are love.
Social Dimension	Isolation & alienation	Isolating. Withdrawing from friends and family. Feeling alien, othered, and lost. Diminished interest in the welfare of others. Withdrawing from wider social realm. Dropping out of work.	Explore the lived experience of alienation, otherness, loneliness, and isolation. Encourage the client to nurture the potential for authentic connections with significant others (if that feels meaningful to them).

(Continued)

Table 6.1 Continued

Dimension	Existential Struggle	Psychological Manifestation	Therapeutic Aim
Spiritual Dimension	Loss of meaning & absurdity	Loss of purpose and meaning. Suicidal ideation. Wanting to follow the deceased into death. Avoiding thoughts of the future. Experiencing absurdity and deep sense of meaninglessness.	Explore meaninglessness and its impact on the client's wellbeing. Help the client reconstruct meaning and personal purpose post-loss. Help the client safeguard mental wellbeing. Explore rituals the client can rely on to honour those missed and deceased. Explore how the client may find comfort and purpose in maintaining the legacy of the deceased and honour lessons learned from the deceased, or in loss. Explore what the client values in life. Explore how meaning may be generated through helping others, giving for the collective good. Encourage the client to value personal growth to embrace life meaningfully.

In his view, friends and family didn't understand the profound alienation and isolation he was experiencing as their bonds were secure, and he did not want to share his despair. Partly because he didn't want to be the person who always brought the mood down, but also because he felt they just felt worried about him and tried to 'fix' his grief, rather than just sit with it.

He reported feeling overwhelmed by intrusive thoughts of Lainey's accident. Although he hadn't been there when she died, his brain had conjugated graphic images of her last moments, and he was not able to control the intrusive nature of these. He vividly imagined her body, sprawled on the road, thrown about like a *'rag doll,'* and although he knew this is not what happened, he could not stop feeling distressed by the imagery of it.

Exploring the Death Struggle

During the early stages of Maderu's therapy, death was ever present in the room, as is often the case in such traumatic loss. He described his profound shock at the loss of his beloved wife. On the day she died, they had enjoyed a lovely breakfast together and discussed plans for a week away. When he heard the news, he went into the Acute Stress Response, a recognisable phase of traumatic loss (Feriante & Sharman, 2023) with vomiting, shaking, crying, disbelief, and shock. Over the next few weeks, he found that his body was dysregulated, experiencing digestive issues and sleep difficulties (his nightmares were terrifying and distressing); he lost his appetite and drank a lot to numb his feelings. He cried uncontrollably and withdrew from all social engagements, spending most of his days at home. He had no energy and struggled to eat, move, and sleep. Over the ensuing months he had managed to calm his body down, but still experienced anxiety, tension, was highly irritable, and suffered short-term memory loss and at times cognitive disorientation. He did not feel okay himself, and he drank a lot to numb his pain.

Humanising this – rather than pathologising it – and seeing his symptoms and behaviours as understandable human responses to devastating circumstances gave him a sense that help was at hand. Of course, his drinking was a concern, and his intrusive thoughts evidence of PTSD, but humanising it and finding a way to respond to it all, in a way that gave him greater agency and calm, was significantly helpful.

The neuroimaging work of Mary F. O'Connor on grief (O'Connor, 2023) explains how the brain grieves and why intrusive thoughts may occur. The brain creates a virtual map of the material world onto its intricate neural network, and relies on this to assume predictability. When a person dies suddenly, this virtual map no longer matches the material world, and a fight or flight survival response is activated. Trace neurons will activate which will make the bereaved search for the person deceased – logic is switched off – in an attempt to correct the absence. At the same time the brain ruminates on events to try and identify danger, and to reset the parameters for predictability. This leads to severe difficulties assimilating the loss and avoiding discussing death, as feelings of hypervigilant anxiety and overwhelm can paralyse the bereaved. In Maderu's case, although he logically knew that his wife had died and nothing would bring her back, he could not stop his brain from imagining the terrifying violence of the impact of the accident on her body.

We spent a lot of time exploring the symbolic nature of his intrusive images, and when asked what they were actually signifying for him, he described it as such:

> When I think of Lainey, I feel utterly helpless. All my love could not have protected her from such a devastating injury. I feel horror and am so worried that she was afraid.

It was important to hold the space for him to sit with the devastation of this, to validate the helplessness, and to recognise that facing limits like that is understandably distressing and requires empathy. We explored the value in replacing catastrophic images with a symbolic safe place, in his mind. I suggested he conjures this image up as often as he needs to, filling it with colourful and meaningful details, so that when he felt distressed, he could focus his attention on this and slow his breath down to find some internal regulation, thereby disrupting the continual activation of his fight or flight.

This 'tool' is not particularly Existential, but it sits well alongside the existential exploration of what it means to face death. When the body and mind are calmer, reflection is possible. This was very important for Maderu. He couldn't engage in reflection when he was in terror as the cognitive paralysis was quite pronounced, and it took many weeks before he regulated his nervous system. We had many discussions about eating in support of his grief and reducing his drinking to aid this. We also explored what it would be like to reduce time on devices (which he was also using to distract himself), and he found that switching off socials and online work in the evenings was better for his nerves. He found that, armed with his safe space meditation, he could go for walks, which he started doing every day.

All these adjustments helped him face death and his struggle with the sudden loss of his love. Discussions of meaning were central. He couldn't bring her back, but he could honour her by looking after himself. He could honour her values – she loved life and sport – and he imagined she would be pleased that he was developing a habit of brisk walking every morning. He also felt that facing death actually helped him face life, and although he was far from exploring the possibility of meeting someone new, he realised that a tragic death had happened to his beloved wife, but he wasn't going to let it be the defining feature of her life.

He wanted to remember her for who she was and how she loved and lived, rather than how she died. He wanted to honour her by valuing his life and not wasting it. He was very resilient, and although the sessions were painful, they also provided him with an opportunity to take responsibility for how he was going to move through this. I felt my role was to meet him at his pace and walk his chosen route.

Exploring the Freedom to Choose Life

Choosing to value his life was a turning point in the therapy. It didn't mean his grief was over, far from it, but it meant he felt like the agent of his life. He took responsibility for the choices he had made and the ones he was going to make. He had avoided focusing on the house renovations he had planned. As he couldn't afford to sell his house in the current economic climate, he was going to permit himself to go ahead with renovations. She would have wanted that, and it would mean his living conditions would improve. He had not liked the décor, and it depressed him every time he walked through the front door. He was so pained at the absence of his wife, and this choice galvanised his grieving. He wept and allowed his sadness to travel through him.

He found it difficult to forgive himself for not being there on the day she died. He would ordinarily travel to work with her, but on this day, he had decided to work from home and had planned to meet a friend instead for lunch. His feelings of guilt were real, and logic could form no part of his perspective here. He wished he could have changed timings and decisions, but we explored the misleading nature of 'magical' thinking like this. The more he focused on what ifs, the worse he would feel, and eventually he recognised that to move through this, he would need to show himself some kindness and accept that there was nothing he could have done differently to prevent events from unfolding. Increasingly, he recognised that she may have lived a short life – as dying at 32 felt so young – but that it was a full life. We spent many sessions talking about how full her life had been, and how meaningful. He was not okay with it, and his sadness would not abate, but he felt less responsible for events. Taking responsibility for unpredictable events is often what we do as it is in our nature to want to control the material world and protect our loved ones, but in this case Maderu had to show himself compassion and recognise that events that led to her death sat outside of his control.

His responsibility now lay in making meaningful choices that helped him adapt to life without his wife. He wasn't sure what that would actually look like, but he was comfortable at the prospect of owning his choices rather than avoiding them. A simple thing he decided to prioritise was to go on holiday with two good friends, to a new location. This was important to him, and he also signed up to join a choir. He loved singing and he used to do this in his younger years. Although he didn't go often, when he did he found it a meaningful outlet that allowed him to destress and enjoy the music, as well as the company of some of his fellow singers.

Some days were dark and difficult, and on those days he saw his grief as understandable. He would spend a lot of time at her grave and remind himself of special things she would say to him that felt meaningful.

Exploring Love and the Severed Bond with Lainey

Exploring what living with the absence of his wife was like was a huge part of the therapeutic process. How did he hold his love for her? What did he do to express it? What was it like for him to live with all the love and nobody to share it with? He found it very meaningful and helpful to visit her grave, to tend it with flowers, and to sit there talking to her about the details of his life. He had many days where he felt like his pain was so severe he wouldn't have minded being struck dead.

He noticed that his grief would build as tension in his heart and body, and if he tried to compartmentalise too much, it would cause him to feel anxious and depressed. On those days, he drank more. He struggled with his alcohol consumption and decided after six months of therapy to join an AA group. This was very helpful for him; although he didn't believe he was an alcoholic, his dependence on alcohol to numb his grief was problematic. He found it valuable to share his experience with others who resonated with such dependence.

He took it upon himself to make picture books of their best memories together, and printed his favourite picture of them and put it in a frame. These little acts were important as they showcased her and their happy years, and it meant a lot to him to pass by this picture every day and kiss it goodnight. He felt deeply lonely and sad but recognised this sadness as love and saw it as understandable.

On a couple of occasions he raged and felt like he had let her down. He hadn't really spent as much time telling her how much he loved her as he would have liked. He described himself as quite unemotional. I didn't see that in him at all, as his grief had 'cracked him open,' to use his words, and he regretted not telling her every day how much he adored her. He had no choice but to sit with the pain of loss. To feel the love and shed the tears.

His wife was a figure respected in her profession, and in her community. He found comfort in maintaining connections with her family and friends, and on the anniversary of her death they all got together. It was a simple gathering, with everyone sharing a special memory of her. It was sad but poignant and meaningful, and he used his therapy as a space to reveal his experience of this and to process the grief.

My role was to hold his pain with him. To be compassionate about it. To not judge it. Or rush it. Or instruct it. But to meet it as authentically as I could, and to encourage him to see it as human and important self-care to share it.

At times he worried that he was hard work for me. He really wasn't, but his fear was that expressing difficult emotions would be a burden on others, even his therapist. I valued the honesty and the trust in our therapeutic alliance to seek reassurance for this. I explained that the experience of meeting and relating to him was not tiresome or burdensome but rather inspiring and hopeful. It was my belief that in exploring his lived experience of his grief, he was finding his way and I could see how meaningful choices were emerging for him. What a gift to bear witness to the immense courage and strength of his human spirit!

Exploring Alienation and Isolation

Throughout the therapy, Maderu struggled with a deep sense of otherness. None of his friends had suffered a traumatic loss. On the one hand, he was pleased for them; on the other, he felt alone. He hadn't known what to do with it all. At first, he had withdrawn from all social engagement – turning down every invitation. As the therapy progressed, he realised that he needed his friends. That sharing his grief was not a burden to them. That was something he feared but he could choose not to believe this fear. He opened up to a few of his lifelong friends. They hadn't wanted to intrude and were waiting for his cues. Their relief when he let them in was reassuring for him.

The AA and the choir provided much comfort against the alienation. He didn't know how to tell new people in his life his story. He wasn't ready for that, and he decided to hide it from acquaintances. He didn't want their pity or their questions about what happened and how he was doing. He found it exhausting explaining it all to people, and he needed respite from this.

In the therapeutic process, it was clear that leaning into his social support networks was going to be a helpful thing for Maderu. He could ask for guidance, reassurance, and emotional support, but he could also engage in humour and fun activities – to distract himself sometimes from the devastation of his loss. It was all about being open to it and not withdrawing. His journey with this was ongoing and required a continual compass – a gentle dance between his internal weather, grief, and need for connection.

Exploring Meaning and Personal Purpose

For Maderu, the exploration of what would constitute purpose for him was an ongoing theme. We discussed it almost every time we met, one way or another. His meanings were simple. To look after his life. His health. To continue with the renovations so he could find comfort in his living environment. To keep going to work. To stay connected with good friends. To spend time with his family.

Meaning doesn't need to be on a grand scale. He didn't have the energy to organise a charity event in her name. He felt perhaps next year. He didn't want to run a marathon. For Maderu, simply finding the way to engage positively and calmly with everyday life was meaning enough.

He practised a daily ritual of lighting a candle for her and saying a little prayer for her soul. He wasn't sure what he believed about an afterlife. Some days he felt her presence. Other days he told himself as a pragmatist, and a numbers person, that it was unlikely her soul was floating around. He visited a medium and was given some meaningful messages, but he chose to focus on the memories he had of her, rather than on questions about the afterlife. My role was not to impose my perceptions and beliefs, but to reflect on his with him.

Finding Growth

He spent a year in therapy and never missed a session. I was so humbled by his commitment and determination to respect not only the therapeutic process but his love for his wife, and for life itself. Growth was evident in Maderu. He showed compassion for himself, he nurtured his wellbeing, and he used the therapeutic space reflectively to process grief and reflect on meaningful choices. In my experience, posttraumatic growth is possible when we permit ourselves choices that allow us to be the kind of person we want to be, that foster good connections, and that generate love and ongoing bonds with those alive and those departed.

References

Admon, R., Milad, M. R., & Hendler, T. (2013). A causal model of post-traumatic stress disorder: Disentangling predisposed from acquired neural abnormalities. *Trends in Cognitive Sciences, 17*(7), 337–347. https://doi.org/10.1016/j.tics.2013.05.005

American Psychological Association. (2013). *Diagnostic and Statistical Manual of Mental Disorders* (5th ed.). https://doi.org/10.1176/appi.books.9780890425787

Benjet, C., Bromet, E., Karam, E. G., Kessler, R. C., McLaughlin, K. A., Ruscio A. M., et al. (2016). The epidemiology of traumatic event exposure worldwide: Results from the World Mental Health Survey consortium. *Psychological Medicine, 46,* 327–343. https://psycnet.apa.org/doi/10.1017/S0033291715001981

Bryant, R. A., Kenny, L., Joscelyne, A., Rawson, N., Maccallum, F., & Hopwood, S. (2019). Predictors of treatment response for cognitive behaviour therapy for prolonged grief disorder. *European Journal of Psychotraumatology, 8*(sup6). https://doi.org/10.1080/20008198.2018.1556551

Bui, E. (Ed.). (2018). *The Clinical Handbook of Bereavement and Grief.* Humana Press. https://doi.org/10.1007/978-3-319-65241-2

Cotter, P., Meysner, L., & Lee, C. W. (2017). Participant experiences of eye movement desensitisation and reprocessing vs. cognitive behavioural therapy for grief: Similarities and differences. *European Journal of Psychotraumatology, 8*(sup6). https://doi.org/10.1080/20008198.2017.1375838

Cruse Bereavement Support. (n.d.). https://www.cruse.org.uk/understanding-grief/grief-experiences/traumatic-loss/traumatic-grief/

Feriante, J., & Sharma, N. P., (2023). *Acute and Chronic Mental Health Trauma.* StatPearls Publishing. https://www.ncbi.nlm.nih.gov/books/NBK594231/

Frankl, V. E. (2004). *Man's Search for Meaning.* Ebury (Original work published 1946).

Gerra, G., Monti, D., Panerai, A., et al. (2003). Long-term immune-endocrine effects of bereavement: Relationships with anxiety levels and mood. *Psychiatry Res., 121,* 145–158. https://doi.org/10.1016/S0165-1781(03)00255-5

Heidegger, M. (2010). *Being and Time* (trans. J. Stambaugh). State University of New York Press (Original work published 1927).

Mazloom, M., Yaghubi, H., & Mohammadkhani, S. (2016). Post-traumatic stress symptom, metacognition, emotional schema and emotion regulation: A structural equation model. *Personality and Individual Differences, 88,* 94–98. https://doi.org/10.1016/J.PAID.2015.08.053

Milman, E., Neimeyer, R. A., Fitzpatrick, M., MacKinnon, C. J., Muis, K. R., & Cohen, S. R. (2018). Prolonged grief symptomatology following violent loss: The mediating role of meaning. *European Journal of Psychotraumatology, 8*(sup6). https://doi.org/10.1080/20008198.2018.1503522

O'Connor, M. F. (2023). *The Grieving Brain: The Surprising Science of How We Learn From Love and Loss.* Harper Collins.

Paidoussis-Mitchell, C. (2012). Traumatic bereavement: A phenomenological study. *Existential Analysis, 23*(1), 32–45.

Paidoussis-Mitchell, C. (2024). *The Loss Prescription: A Practical Roadmap to Grief Recovery.* Harper Collins.

Rubin, D. C., & Feeling, N. (2013). Measuring the severity of negative and traumatic events. *Clinical Psychological Science, 1*(4), 375–389. https://doi.org/10.1177/2167702613483112

Sartre, J.-P. (1958). *Being and Nothingness* (trans. H. E. Barnes). Routledge (Original work published 1943).

Stolorow, R. D. (2011). *World, Affectivity, Trauma: Heidegger and Post-Cartesian Psychoanalysis.* Routledge. https://doi.org/10.4324/9780203815816

Stolorow, R. D. (2022). Faces of finitude: Death, loss, and trauma. *Psychoanalytic Inquiry, 42*(2), 135–140. https://doi.org/10.1080/07351690.2021.1953834

Thompson, N., & Walsh, M. (2010). The existential basis of trauma. *Journal of Social Work Practice, 24*(4), 377–389. https://doi.org/10.1080/02650531003638163

UK Trauma Council. (2024). *Traumatic bereavement*. UK Trauma Council. https://uktraumacouncil.link/documents/Traumatic-Bereavement-Schools-Guide-v02-UKTC.pdf

van Deurzen, E., & Arnold-Baker, C. (2005). *Existential Perspectives on Human Issues*. Palgrave.

Chapter 7

Surviving Near Death Following Cardiac Arrest

Tania D'Aloia

Introduction

When an individual goes into a state of sudden cardiac arrest, the heart has stopped, causing their body and brain to be without oxygen. As the heart, lungs, and brain cease functioning (Parnia & Lunea, 2013), the beginnings of the biological process of death occur. Sudden cardiac arrest (SCA) is a medical term, meaning clinical death. Individuals lose consciousness quickly and will die if not treated quickly. Timely resuscitation and defibrillation are both needed, in which an electric current shocks the heart, so that a normal rhythm can resume. This can be in the form of an automated external defibrillator or implantable cardioverter defibrillator (ICD). This treatment attempts to reverse the effects of SCA.

The aim of this study was to explore and understand how adults experience life after surviving this trauma. This is the closest one can come to death and yet still survive. The study concerned itself with the outlook and emotional wellbeing of survivors who had no awareness of pre-morbidity. The emotional experience of survivors has not been widely captured in research. This phenomenological inquiry examined the nature of the experience of SCA and being close to death.

In the UK, there are an estimated sixty thousand SCAs per year outside the hospital context, and survival rates are poor, varying from 2 to 12% (Malhotra & Rakhit, 2013). However, with advanced medical interventions and community access to defibrillators, the number of people surviving SCA is increasing (Wilson et al., 2014). As survival rates in the UK and elsewhere in the world have been increasing over the past ten years, this decrease in mortality has led to an increased focus on morbidity in survivors of SCA (O'Reilly et al., 2003). Those affected have often intertwined issues around physical and cognitive impairment, and social and psychological maladjustment.

DOI: 10.4324/9781003493860-10

Personal Background

I grew up in Australia in the 1970s, in a small close family unit with traditional Italian values and culture. My father suffered a cardiac arrest because of an incorrect intubation in hospital, prior to a minor kidney operation. He survived but remained in a semi-vegetative state before dying two and half years later. Being a toddler at the time, I do not have a living memory of this, although growing up there was always a sense of deep loss and tragedy in the family. I remain naturally drawn to seeking an understanding of life and existence through the lens of loss, death, and meaning. This includes how life is lived after a sudden close brush with death.

Professionally, I started my clinical placement training in 2010 by working with adults in a bereavement service. For three years, I counselled individuals who had suffered untimely and often tragic losses of loved ones. The existential themes around loss and isolation, meaning making, inherent values, and needing to gain a different perspective on life were quite often evident. I found myself wondering what existential themes may emerge for survivors of SCA. This study hopes to fill a gap in SCA research, particularly in qualitative work. I have chosen to research this topic as this important phenomenon affects a growing number of people and can present without any prior illness or symptoms.

My belief has been that many people will view life differently after SCA and that outlook and emotional wellbeing are renegotiated. I have aimed to be constantly aware of this bias when conducting interviews as well as when analysing participant data to separate researcher subjectivity from the findings. In interviews, exploring lived experience through rich descriptions and detailed open narratives has provided space for the individual to tell their personal story. My attitude has been one of moving dialectically from an awareness of my own preconceptions to being open to participant experiences (Finlay, 2009). This is in keeping with hermeneutic phenomenology in which bracketing subjectivity is not attempted, as a person is not seen as a 'blank slate' or neutral contributor, but rather holds their preconceptions at the forefront for further reflection. This study of survivors' lived experience will, I hope, provide further understanding and awareness of this phenomenon to a wider group of counselling and psychology health professionals.

Literature review

I have chosen literature of relevance to my study, including work on the emotional or psychological aspects of the wellbeing of survivors of SCA. Most quantitative studies have attempted to capture wellbeing under the umbrella term 'quality of life.' This is determined by measuring the biological, psychological, and social functioning of an individual. A few studies have focused on psychological symptomologies only, measuring increases in anxiety, depression, and posttraumatic stress. These studies have all used several validated psychometric assessments in individual self-reporting. These studies have been omitted in this chapter to focus more on qualitative research with more relevance.

There is a smaller amount of qualitative research which refers to meaning making using varied approaches, including phenomenological methodologies. This will be discussed as 'qualitative research on making meaning out of the experience of SCA.' Firstly, I will discuss a theoretical perspective and ideas on emotion and wellbeing, in the context of this population group. This includes an existential lens on trauma from a phenomenological perspective.

Existential View

Personal outlook derives from circumstances that have constituted the life of a person. This is a combination of biological or innate characteristics, parental/caregiver care, early learning, and continual life experience. The culture and beliefs one is born into remain embedded in one's history. This sets the scene as to how one should view and forecast one's life within a social, political, and cultural context. In existential terms, these aspects are not seen in isolation from one another, but rather encompass and give context to an individual's entire way of being and existing in a relational world. This means SCA survivors will experience their outlook in ways that are unique to them and that make sense to them in their lives.

The way this experience translates and how one can make sense of it will reflect emotionality. The emotional aspect of wellbeing expresses what is valued (van Deurzen, 2012), showing what is felt between one's own perspective and the situation encountered. Survivors' feelings and emotions may indicate a particular stance on what they value and what they fear or avoid. The values, purpose, and meaning sought through the conflicts of an individual's life are an existential exploration of wellbeing.

The existential focus is one in which a balanced interaction of possibilities and limitations of life is sought (van Deurzen & Young, 2009). Arguably, one could say it has relevance for survivors of SCA who have first-hand experience of the ultimate dichotomy of life and death. How do they acknowledge and balance uncertainties, difficulties, and challenges? Do they deny them in search of all that is happy and positive? Happiness throughout periods of life is certainly possible but is not at the core of wellbeing in existential terms. It is authenticity and an openness to strive for what is important to an individual at a deeper level that sits at the heart of the experience of wellbeing. For survivors, finding meaning and purpose in life can clarify and increase an awareness of their choices. These possibilities may enable greater freedom and a sense of autonomy in grappling with their own lived sense of reality.

When one's wellbeing is disturbed, it can affect all aspects of oneself, giving a more heightened sense of one's own physicality. The body at the centre of each person's existence is also the seat of activities and emotions (Merleau-Ponty, 1945/1962). When one has faced the possibility of death unexpectedly, without a known cause, and survived, this may change the perception of how one views reality and one's relationship with mortality. As we are always getting closer towards death, Heidegger (1927/2010) argued that by actualising it as a possibility, we free ourselves from death rather than losing ourselves. SCA survivors have faced death as more than a theoretical possibility, confronting the reality of both human existence and its end.

Through a major life event or trauma, many survivors come face to face with the paradoxes in life. For instance, given the unexpected nature of SCA, management of a new diagnosis, and the uncertainty of recurrence, the unpredictability, transience, and nonsensical nature of life are highlighted. They then need to accommodate and make sense of this moving forward. In a sense, SCA has the potential to put a timeframe on one's life. Sartre (1943/1958) argues that by acknowledging the absurdity and meaninglessness of life, one can live better. Through lived experience, a sense of self or a previous version of oneself becomes altered and recreated. The idea here is that with all experience there is an element of learning and transforming oneself via the attitude one takes (Frankl, 1988).

However, engaging in meaningful existential exploration may be difficult for some survivors who are particularly focused on fear of their life ending, self-protection, and safety (Maslow, 1962). This may have more relevance at different points in their recovery.

Qualitative Research on Making Meaning out of the Experience of SCA

These studies are important as they focus on individuals' subjective experience and the phenomenon of SCA using qualitative methodology. Significantly, they explore how people interpret their lives and the importance and meaning placed on life events. One can argue that meanings help shape future goals and affect one's outlook (Park & Gutierrez, 2013). I will discuss some relevant studies that capture an individual's story and elucidate 'meaning making' in particular. A few recent studies conducted after my research and during the last five years will also be included.

Forslund et al. (2013) conducted a mixed design study that looked at psychosocial risk factors in people who suffered Myocardial Infarction

(MI), which led to SCA. Sixty per cent had no previous knowledge or earlier diagnosis of a heart condition. The factors studied were socioeconomic status, anxiety, depression, and work overload. The qualitative section gave questionnaires to thirty-two people, of whom fifteen were interviewed. The interviewees had a mean age of 68 and post-arrest time of eight years. The questions asked were what lifestyle meant to them and what was important to make them feel good. The main themes found were 'significance of lifestyle' (meaningful relationships); 'modifying current to new life situation' (finding reasons why it happened); and 'making changes and a changed view on life' (feeling grateful for a second chance).

These themes reveal how personal and social influences come together in terms of one's outlook on life. All participants believed negative work stress had contributed to their SCA. It revealed what meaning participants placed on their experience. Importantly, this was then reflected in how they envisioned their life moving forward in terms of self-management, life choices, and positive outlook. Paradoxically, they found that although many knew the risk factors and benefits of treatment, including behavioural changes, some chose to ignore this information, preferring to live a 'good life.' This suggests that some of these participants were exerting their choice and autonomy pre- and post-SCA, making a deliberate decision about how they wished to live.

Bremer et al. (2009) did a phenomenological study and found that well-being became discoverable through a sense of coherence and making meaning in life. The individual, upon awakening from SCA with memory loss and little sense of time or coherence, may experience a feeling of threat, needing to piece together and make sense of what happened. This study focused on the subjective experience of out-of-hospital cardiac arrest as well as the SCA phenomenon itself. This includes how individuals made sense of their experience using lifeworld phenomenology and reflective analysis (Todres et al., 2007) through being body subjects or embodied individuals. This entailing a descriptive (rather than interpretive) look at the indivisible interaction between individual personality and how it encounters the social world.

They conducted semi-structured interviews with nine survivors aged 44 to 70 years, most of whom had their SCA within three years. Interviews were analysed for meaning through the description of experience and focused on 'coherence' and 'memory gap.' This reflected an altered sense of time, and how significant memories were linked to the present. The 'elusive life-threat' becomes comprehensible through an increased understanding of its occurrence, enabling existential security and wellbeing (Bremer et al., 2009). Arguably, their future vision or outlook is only imaginable through being able to make meaning and seek coherence, particularly after a major life event. Thus, a more coherent awareness is formed where the gap in memory symbolises the cardiac arrest itself.

This follows a similar study by Ketilsdottir et al. (2013) focusing on the experience of the cardiac arrest itself, as opposed to other factors resulting from this experience, such as underlying disease, ICD implantation, and quality of life. Using interpretive phenomenology, the analysis drew on the five sources of commonalities in lived experience: situation, embodiment, temporality, concerns, and common meanings, until themes without contradictions were developed. Seven survivors up to two years post-arrest answered questions describing their experience and what effect it had on them in two semi-structured interviews.

The results revealed themes including 'feelings of insecurity; the need for support; striving to regain a former life; emotional challenges; responding to symptoms and a new view on life.' Cognitive limitations, anxiety, lack of security, and uncertainty regarding the future were participants' main concerns. Conducting two interviews to discuss further interpretations may have allowed additional insights and reflection. These concerns are like those found in the above studies and highlight individual worries around emotional support and a need to re-establish a somewhat different outlook. This study importantly addresses the historical, social, and cultural elements of an individual when looking at the phenomenon of SCA, suggesting a deeper exploration of lived experience.

Some recent studies include that of Forslund et al. (2017), which looked at the meaning made of lived experience and changes in everyday life. They researched eleven people over a six- and twelve-month period in Northern Sweden. Using a phenomenological hermeneutic interpretation with structural analysis as the method, they uncovered two main themes. The first after six months was 'striving to regain one's usual self,' and the other after twelve months was 'a second chance at life.' The latter adhered to more acceptance around a newer self, being grateful and establishing meaning.

Haydon et al. (2019) explored seven survivors aged between 48 and 92 years and their adjustment over a period of five and twenty-six years after SCA. Their narrative inquiry resulted in several existential themes, including 'disbelief, surveillance of body, loss of control, wanting normality, gratefulness, spirituality and fragility of life.' They concluded that a new normality stemmed from a re-appraisal and acceptance of their life course.

Whitehead et al.'s study (2020), using an interpretive phenomenological analysis (IPA) method addressing a knowledge gap for survivors, showed several themes up to post-twelve months. These included 'a disrupted normality, uncertainty, physical and social restrictions and altered family roles. A focus on creating a new normal and acceptance of an altered reality.' They interviewed eight survivors between 41 and 79 years old and some of their partners over an average post-arrest time of six months. Their findings revealed a need to focus on 'a new normal' within their physical, social, and emotional life rather than making pre-SCA comparisons.

A gap in the literature

A gap in the literature exists, particularly for younger individuals who experience their SCA trauma without knowledge of prior illness. I have attempted to capture this age group in my study where six out of ten participants were 40 years old and under. The emotional experience of survivors has not been widely captured in research, although it is increasing and perhaps reflective of improving survival rates.

Methodology

Interpretive Phenomenological Analysis (IPA)

IPA was selected as a method to enable a rich, detailed description of participants' narrated lived experience. It draws from wider phenomenology, using hermeneutics to achieve a more complex understanding of experience. At its core is the exploration of phenomena and how one expresses what an event has been like and what it has meant to them. This includes unique perspectives and meanings, representing one's relationship with the world. How this experience between researcher and participant collects itself requires an open phenomenological attitude and carefully selected questions and criteria aimed at describing phenomena in detail. Therefore, the data collected is a co-construction between researcher and participant during the interview.

This study used semi-structured interviews with open-ended questions to focus on the quality of each participant's experience. As this study is concerned with personal outlook and emotional wellbeing, the questions focused on exploring beliefs, feelings, and values.

Participants

There were ten participants in this study, 6 males and 4 females aged between 30 and 60 and living in the UK. The age at SCA was between 17 and 57 years, with a median SCA age of 38. The post-arrest time is between 2 and 20 years. Six interviews were conducted in person, while four were conducted online via video. The interviews took place between 2014 and 2015, were 60 to 90 minutes in duration and were digitally recorded. The gender of participants, along with their age at interview and when the SCA occurred, can be found in Table 7.1.

Table 7.1 Participant Demographics

Participant	Gender	Age at Interview	Age at SCA
1	Male	42	33
2	Male	51	49
3	Female	48	44
4	Male	60	40
5	Female	60	53
6	Male	39	34
7	Male	44	36
8	Male	59	57
9	Female	31	28
10	Female	37	17

Analysis

After each interview, the recording was listened to and transcribed. I read it once and then listened to the recording again, correcting any words that were missed and noting particular expressions and emotive cues. I noted descriptive comments important to the participant and the particular grammar used, syntax, repetition of words, analogies, and emotive expressions. I made conceptual comments on the data, which went deeper than mere descriptions and were more interpretive and enquiring (Smith et al., 2009). Text that seemed important, repeated words, and amplifications were underlined.

The next step was the development of emerging themes by linking overarching themes that seemed clear. These reflected my own meanings and interpretations, which compared and linked to the data and participants' meanings. The themes were psychological abstracts, based on particular phrases used in the text as well as the overall meaning of the transcript. Further refinements and clustering were made and looking at how the themes corresponded across participants. When a theme was obvious in at least four participants, then it became a recurrent group theme. A thematic table was created for each participant, with 3 superordinate and 11 subthemes. IPA being idiographic, I wanted to show uniqueness amongst themes. Hence, a few were chosen where they were expressed by several participants, and thereby rendered important.

Findings

Three superordinate themes appeared. These are illustrated below with connecting subthemes, in figures 7.1, 7.2, and 7.3.

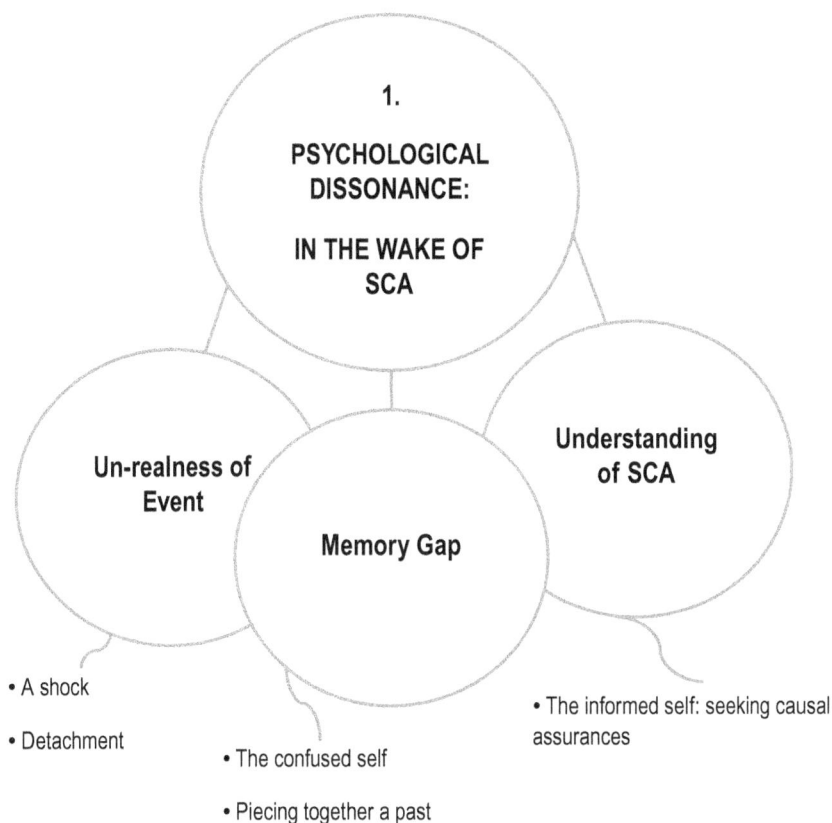

Figure 7.1 Theme one: Psychological Dissonance: In the Wake of SCA.

Table 7.2 shows recurrent themes present in the sample (please note original names have not been used).

Discussion

Psychological Dissonance: In the Wake of SCA

This was an overarching theme in which participants commented on their experience of awakening in hospital to the unexpected and sudden news that they had experienced an SCA. Most participants had no memory leading up to the event, and for some, this extended to days, weeks, and months. Some had fragments of memory linked to multiple arrests in hospital. Survivors now faced a new reality. Their responses include reflections

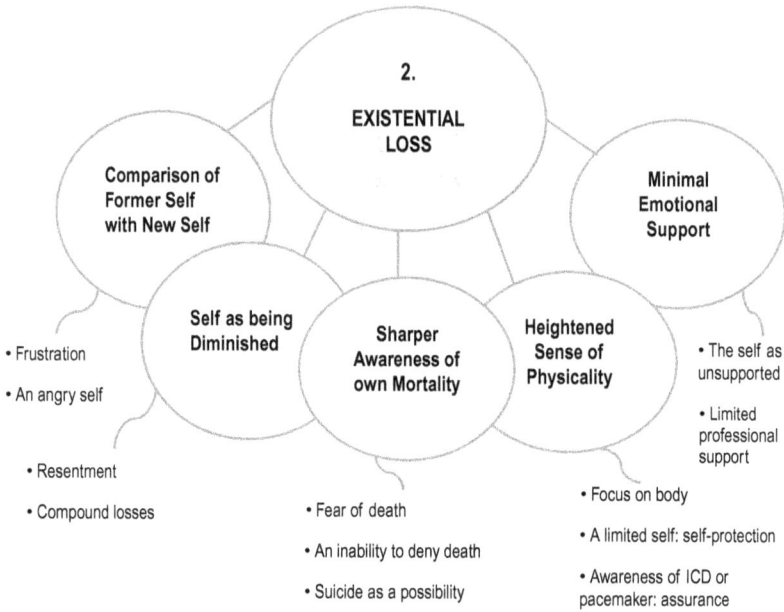

Figure 7.2 Theme two: Existential Loss.

Theme 2.

EXISTENTIAL LOSS

Comparison of Former Self with New Self

Minimal Emotional Support

Self as being Diminished

Sharper Awareness of own Mortality

Heightened Sense of Physicality

• Frustration

• An angry self

• The self as unsupported

• Limited professional support

• Resentment

• Compound losses

• Fear of death

• An inability to deny death

• Suicide as a possibility

• Focus on body

• A limited self: self-protection

• Awareness of ICD or pacemaker: assurance

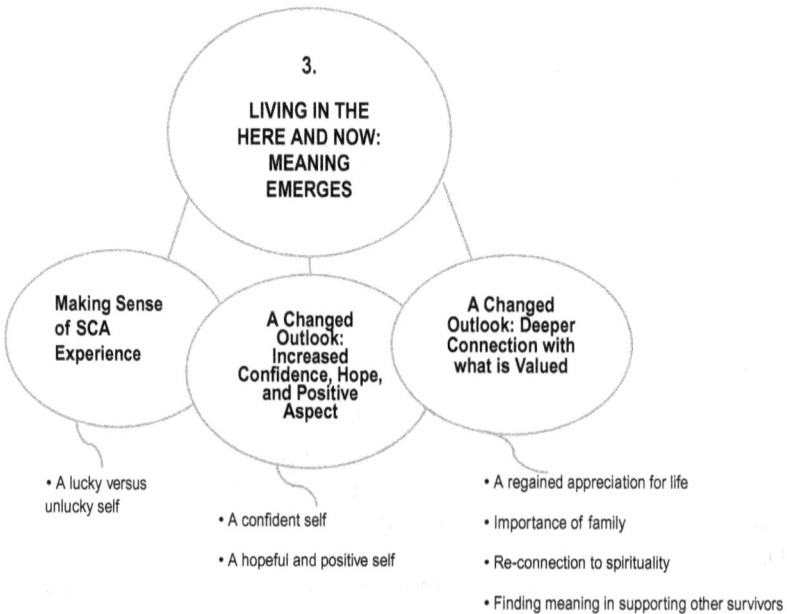

Figure 7.3 Theme three: Living in the Here and Now: Meaning Emerges.

Theme 3.

LIVING IN THE HERE AND NOW: MEANING EMERGES

Making Sense of SCA Experience

A Changed Outlook: Increased Confidence, Hope, and Positive Aspect

A Changed Outlook: Deeper Connection with what is Valued

• A lucky versus unlucky self

• A confident self

• A hopeful and positive self

• A regained appreciation for life

• Importance of family

• Re-connection to spirituality

• Finding meaning in supporting other survivors

Table 7.2 Themes and Subthemes

IDENTIFYING RECURRENT THEMES

Subthemes	Dave	Norman	Diane	Nick	Teresa	Bill	Harry	Steve	Wendy	Linda	Present in over half of sample?
SUPERORDINATE THEME ONE — PSYCHOLOGICAL DISSONANCE: IN THE WAKE OF SCA											
1A. Un-realness of Event	YES	YES	YES	NO	YES	NO	YES	NO	YES	NO	YES
1B. Memory Gap	NO	YES	YES	YES	NO	YES	NO	YES	YES	YES	YES
1C. Understanding of SCA	YES	NO	YES	YES	YES	YES	YES	NO	NO	NO	YES
SUPERORDINATE THEME TWO — EXISTENTIAL LOSS											
2A. Comparison of Former Self with New Self	YES	YES	YES	NO	YES	NO	YES	YES	NO	YES	YES
2B. Self as being Diminished	YES	YES	YES	YES	YES	NO	YES	YES	NO	YES	YES
2C. Sharper Awareness of own Mortality	YES	YES	YES	NO	YES	YES	YES	YES	YES	NO	YES
2D. Heightened Sense of Physicality	NO	NO	YES	YES	YES	NO	YES	NO	YES	YES	YES
2E. Minimal Emotional Support	NO	NO	YES	YES	YES	YES	NO	YES	YES	YES	YES
SUPERORDINATE THEME THREE — LIVING IN THE HERE AND NOW: MEANING EMERGES											
3A. Making Sense of SCA Experience	YES	NO	YES	NO	NO	YES	YES	YES	YES	NO	YES
3B. A Changed Outlook: increased confidence, hope, and positive aspect	NO	NO	NO	YES	YES	YES	YES	YES	YES	YES	YES
3C. A Changed Outlook: deeper connection with what is valued	YES	NO	YES	YES	YES	YES	YES	YES	YES	YES	YES

highlighted by the following subthemes: The '*Un-realness of the Event*,' which included a sense of shock and detachment, represented by six participants. '*It sort of hits then, like, you know, that something has happened. Something life changing has happened to you, but you're still here, um, which was just a big shock*' (Harry). Harry was shocked to find himself in hospital after being on the football field. '*I thought I must have banged heads with somebody and that's why I must have been knocked out. I thought that it must have been that; it couldn't have been anything else because I was probably the fittest person in our football team.*'

The '*Memory Gap*' was described by seven participants who had no memory of the event (up to months before). They spoke of confused feelings and a need to piece together information of events from loved ones in order to gain recollection of what happened to them. Often there is confusion as to which fragments of memory are remembered and a sense of disorientation at having to create a timeline that otherwise seems unreal. '*I had lots of things swimming around inside there [points to head] and lots of confusion about it all. It's not nothing to go to bed and then wake up in the hospital with people leaning over you telling you you've had a cardiac arrest*' (Steve). A few participants felt it was a positive thing not to have a memory of the event and construed it as a protective element whereby the brain shielded them from the traumatic experience.

An '*Understanding of SCA*' represented a need to gain further information and seek an explanation which was reported in six participants. Similar feelings of disbelief and bewilderment were expressed by participants in the studies by Bremer et al. (2009) and Forslund et al. (2017), in which survivors described an unknowing and disbelief upon being told of their experience. This awakening from SCA with loss of memory, time, and coherence, meant participants experienced a sense of threat, needing to piece it together. In my study, many participants did not have a direct causal link to their SCA, which created further uncertainty and fear. This meant they could not manage their lifestyle in a way that gave them some assurance over their lives and hence were susceptible to random recurrence. Many felt uninformed by medical staff, thereby having to gain further information and seek causal assurance from websites, support forums, and family members.

Existential Loss

This superordinate theme revealed what SCA has represented. The themes that stood out across participants were of personal loss. All participants recall some shift in how they viewed themselves and life after SCA, in that it stood for something to all. '*A Comparison of Former and New Self*' was present in seven participants. These changes are in the form of comparing a current and former self, for whom physical restrictions, memory loss, and/or emotional felt responses alter a sense of identity and reality. This awareness that, on some level, they are changed by the experience can be difficult for some who feel aspects of their 'normal self' have been taken away. This can also be seen as a loss of meaning (Sartre, 1943/1958), creating uncertainty and anxiety as to what an individual's place in the world is now. Participants reflect on changes or limitations to their physical health, which have restricted their work, social, and practical lives. Expressions of frustration, anger, and resentment when comparing selves often related to the fear of what they held tightly and valued, but now felt was removed, shifting their sense of 'normality.' This disruption (Bury, 1982) to their self-construct meant needing to re-examine their expectations and future.

After losing his coach licence and career, Norman felt his life lacked purpose and meaning, to the extent that he despaired. His career had meant a lot to his sense of duty and value as a person.

> *I get more frustrated about not being able to do stuff (…) not being able to work (…) my job was my life (…) I used to do 16, 20 hours a day (…) [long pause] it's gone (…) I used to love making people happy (…) when you take them away for a 10-day tour all around Italy, and you bring them back, and you see the smiles on their faces (…) you've done your job right (…) and that's gone!* (Norman)

The subtheme *'Self as being Diminished'* was represented in eight participants who experienced a diminished and limited self with compound losses. Those with post-morbidity meant their emotional recovery and adjustment was a longer journey at times. For some, this meant their sense of self diminished, such as for male participants who strongly identified with their gender role and felt aspects of their masculinity had been taken away. Those participants who had a traumatic exposure before SCA expressed compounded feelings of helplessness and fear.

A *'Sharper Awareness of own Mortality'* was represented in eight participants and meant feelings about one's own death, including fear, were confronted and continually negotiated. For many, this was the first time they had confronted this reality and considered their own deaths. This not only brought about a fear of death, but the awareness that it is not possible to avoid one's own death. This reminder changes the perception of life and reality. There is a need to manage the fear of death and another SCA whilst confronting the stark reality of an uncertain and limited life. 'It covers what is peculiar to the certainty of death, that it is possible at every moment' (Heidegger, 1927/2010). This can create tension and anxiety, with gratitude felt about surviving coupled with an increased concern about it reoccurring. In turn, these deep existential losses created feelings of helplessness, fear, anxiety, isolation, dislocation, and alienation. This had different interpretations where some felt more loss than others, which often resulted in a personal sense of self being diminished.

I mean (…) it makes you afraid of dying. I know that, and before, if you [had] asked me, I was never afraid of dying, never. If someone said (…) I'm not afraid of dying, it's fine, but when you come that close to it, um, I'm (…) I'm (…) I'm totally scared, because I know how quickly it can happen. (Diane)

A few considered suicide whilst undergoing difficult life changes in the first stages. There seems a contradiction between surviving near death on one hand and contemplating ending one's life on the other. This resonates with Altmaier's (2012) theory that in psychological and physical fear, an attempt made to protect oneself by escaping is, in a sense, gaining personal control. On a surface level, this suggests an ultimate expression of self, seeking meaning and fulfilment. These participants struggled to find meaning in their lives. Bremer et al. (2009) found the 'elusive life-threat' receded through gaining more understanding and finding meaning in their survival of SCA. Similarly, Ketilsdottir et al. (2013) found dominant themes of anxiety and lack of security and uncertainty in the future to be major concerns. A loss of control and wanting normality was also prevalent in long-term survivors studied by Haydon et al. (2019).

There was a *'Heightened Sense of Physicality'* and increased focus on the body present in six participants. There was an attempt to check physical wellbeing by limiting some of their activities and environments in order to avoid the risk of another event. A need to focus more on the body meant checking their heartbeats and any sensations or changes to functioning, which included managing their ICD.

I felt everything, every beat of my heart for a good six months afterwards… you're constantly looking, you become desensitised to that area because that's what's going to happen and it's about control. (Harry)

Van Manen (1988: 7) states that: "At the moment when our wellness is disturbed then we discover, as it were, our own body." Whitehead et al. (2020) also found that physical ramifications and awareness of fragility created an altered outlook, one which included restrictions and a new social identity. While SCA survivors do not have a cognitive memory of the event, their body knows the experience as central to their very existence. Merleau-Ponty (1945/1962: 192) states that: "The body expresses total existence because existence realises itself in the body."

This also created a sense of not having enough emotional support, as well feeling vulnerable and alone in their recoveries. *'Minimal Emotional Support'* was present in seven participants, in which they reflected on their experience of being let down and unsupported by family, friends, and/or professional staff. This led to changes in how they viewed some of these relationships. In essence, most participants experienced changes in how they related to people who had not met their expectations. A lack of emotional care in terms of no counselling support being offered was often mentioned. Many felt there should be ongoing emotional and financial support available, particularly because of their younger age, the sudden nature of SCA, long-term implications, managing a new diagnosis, treatment plan, and having an ICD. This often resulted in a sense of alienation where their struggle to be recognised and emotional fears were compounded. This is similar to Kellehear's (1996) theory in which a survivor's environment becomes threatening and unfamiliar, increasing the chances of alienation or isolation.

Living in the Here and Now: Meaning Emerges

This third superordinate theme brings together what it is like for participants to live in the here and now after their SCA. This is how they made sense of their experience and what meanings were created. This encompasses elements of a hopeful, positive, and confident self; regaining a new sense of normality through self-acceptance and moving on; and appreciating life and feeling grateful. On the social side, there is a deeper connection with relationships, particularly family, and helping others through similar situations. What is held dearly and valued is discussed through the importance of creating memories, closer attachment to others, and reconnection to faith.

A subtheme that stood out across participants was making sense of their experience. A 'Making Sense of SCA Experience' was represented in six participants. Most revealed that, although it was devastating living with the impact of SCA, they all experienced an urge to make the most of life and search for meaning in this second chance. A 'lucky versus unlucky self' symbolises this journey of progression, in which it was felt they were lucky to have survived the SCA, but also unlucky that it happened at all.

There seems to be a duality between being a minority in having experienced SCA and that of uncommonly surviving it. Integrating these thoughts into making meaning out of their experience allowed them to find the courage to live the life that one hopes for within the spectrum of uncertainty, anxiety, and uneasiness – which is always challenging. Participants' conflicting thoughts and emotions highlight patterns of how they are in the world where holding these tensions are commonplace. Similarly, Forslund et al. (2013) found a dominant theme of 'being grateful for a second chance.' This element of chance and feeling lucky reflects their outlook looking forward, in terms of integrating a more positive and hopeful self.

Martin and Kleiber's (2005) theory argued that, having faced death, individuals will have a tendency towards confidence, assertion, and enhanced appreciation for the ordinary things in life with less interest in material things. In my study, seven participants expressed 'A Changed Outlook: Increased Confidence, Hope and Positive Aspect' and were able to build strength from the experience. This outlook is positive and embraces a more authentic approach to life. There is also a lived sense of reality around mortality and acceptance of one's limitations, which highlights vulnerability, uncertainty, and fear. How each participant has made sense of and interpreted their experience enables them to create this balance between the possibilities and limitations of life. This confrontation with one's own death can cause individuals to reassess their plans and priorities (Yalom, 1980), and hence many participants expressed a changed perspective. There is a journey of self-discovery, having undergone the immediate impact and realisation of their SCA, recovery process, and post-experience years later.

An increased awareness of human fragility and facing death meant a sharper focus on life being limited. Therefore, needing to enjoy it by having fulfilling experiences and connecting with what is valued. Having faced the possibility of one's own death, living in the here and now affords a direct and more conscious focus on what value and importance are taken from life. A living truer to one's wishes and desires. Some expressed enjoying life more and having deeper, fuller conversations and experiences. Their attitude towards life had changed and felt more appreciative.

> I think I'm much more of a positive person, I really enjoy moments, yes! The change in me is that I'm more spontaneous because I used to be more careful. I'm sillier, I'm letting my silly side come out. (Teresa)

Amongst my participants, there was a deeper connection with what was valued and more awareness of what was important and meaningful to them. In essence, attuning to personal needs, appreciating close family and relationships, connecting to faith or beliefs, and helping others. Family bonds and the desire to protect loved ones were strengthened. Their sense of self, role, and purpose seemed shaped by acknowledgement of their values (Strasser, 1999). Arguably, there is an openness to existence, which is more authentic in following one's own values (Heidegger, 1927/2010). 'A Changed Outlook: Deeper Connection with what is Valued' was present in nine participants. Participants expressed what is of value to them through their gratitude for and importance to loved ones.

There is also meaning found in the social aspect of supporting other survivors. Using their own experience and sharing information enabled them to be part of a communal group. All participants in this study belonged to online support groups in which there is a clear recognition of the need for peer support amongst survivors. Helping others and raising awareness of SCA was important for many who wanted to give something back. There was also a focus on increasing knowledge and community awareness for defibrillators, enabling others to survive. In some, a reconnection with spirituality, expressed in terms of religious beliefs, provided comfort and helped support their meaning making. Bremer et al. (2009) and Ketilsdottir et al. (2013) all found that the main theme amongst participants was 'having a new view or outlook on life' after their SCA experience.

> I'm actually more confident now than I was before the arrest (…) I survived death, therefore, I'm actually quite positive about life now. I'm actually (…) more mentally confident in my own space. (Bill)
> It's inside that my attitude is altered and, um, I'm so grateful for where I am. (Nick)

This journey characterises an ontological awakening or discovery in which a renewed appreciation for living reflects gratitude at being given a second chance. This shift was in noticing and valuing the smaller and simpler things in life and not wanting to take things for granted. A sense of time and priority had shifted where life was limited and things that mattered took priority. Their outlook on life arguably has an altered sense of reality, which now encompasses their SCA experience and sharper attunement to their lives. Martin and Kleiber (2005) argue that individuals who have had a close brush with death emphasise personal values over culturally derived ones and focus on the present. Some of my participants felt this made them less patient with people who complained about smaller issues viewed as unimportant and time-wasting. Time in this sense had deep connotations: it felt precious, and there was value in simple moments.

> I'm very mindful that I'm here for a very limited amount of time and it's just up to me really to do what I want to do, and I can either do nothing and waste a gift or I can do something with it and try and achieve something on a personal level (…) so that's what I'm doing. I think my future is really positive, more positive than it was before, um, more positive than it was prior to the SCA. (Steve)

In terms of emotional wellbeing, participants in this study have shown remarkable change and a myriad of feelings and expressions during their reflective process and journey. Some of these are highlighted in existing studies, particularly in the qualitative research and perhaps indirectly in the quantitative research under the quality-of-life bracket. This reflects the varied results in emotionality often reported, not only due to the heterogeneity of methodology, but also suggests the uniqueness of the phenomenon of SCA.

Participants show a heightened focus on existential themes around life, death, survival (freedom), isolation, and meaninglessness. These are important to incorporate when working towards integration, acceptance, transition, and meaning in their post-recovery journeys. Focusing on individual outlook and emotional wellbeing provides a contextual setting in order to incorporate all these crucial sides of human development and experience.

Conclusion

Looking at the nature of trauma through the phenomenon of SCA whilst using an existential lens has revealed a journey that many take of transformation on many levels. This is not without enduring a difficult and turbulent journey at times. Exploring outlook has been important to tell us where a person is in regard to their attitudes, beliefs, and perception of life. The meaning and interpretation of life creates a certain worldview, which in turn affects health and wellbeing. SCA survivors are susceptible to further arrests and need to address their stressors to prevent negatively affecting arrhythmias and ICDs. Emotional wellbeing is an important aspect for many survivors who need to manage their recovery and long-term physical and emotional changes.

It is important for mental health professionals to gain more information about this phenomenon, which is affecting more people, particularly younger people and those without an earlier diagnosis. This also highlights the need for survivors to obtain emotional support throughout their recovery process as they regain their lives, and for the provision of added support to manage this experience. This is in terms of possible new diagnoses, ongoing treatment, and the effects on physical, personal, social, and spiritual health. The focus is on facilitating growth and autonomy by way of staying close to their values. This will offer clarity as to what is important to them and what makes life worth living, particularly what meanings they place on people, objects, and tensions that may exist. Enabling a person to be aware of, and able to incorporate, paradoxes in life allows more truthful living, as opposed to suppression. The aim here is to help guide a person through these life changes with more reflection on what is achievable, desired, attempted, lost, and unachievable.

Family and friends support many participants, but this can mean that individual struggles sometimes ensue where each person, protecting another, may not want to express that they are ill at ease. Younger participants are also managing careers, young children, and family life with the long-term prospect of managing a new diagnosis. This has clinical relevance to individual future health as well as the family unit. A therapist needs to be aware of this journey and facilitate concerns over loss and death with a reprioritisation of goals. The importance of finding value and meaning for survivors is entrenched in them being able to assimilate the experience and take something from it to support their future growth. This is an exploration of living incorporating a pre- and a post-SCA account of experience bound in one's individuality, culture, and historical period. This allows a person to gain a sense of perspective on their lives.

Moreover, SCA survivors may be without physical diagnosis and not need regular treatment, which means they go on with life on their own without any emotional support. This can be challenging for those who have to come to terms having had SCA alone. This is why more information on individual experience is needed. This is in line with others working with physical illnesses, SCA, and near-death situations, and psychosocial effects of fear, stress, and ambivalence versus hope and gratitude.

References

Altmaier, E. M. (2012). Through a glass darkly: Personal reflections on the role of meaning in response to trauma. *Counselling Psychology Quarterly, 26*(1), 106–113. https://doi.org/10.1080/09515070.2012.728760

Bremer, A., Dahlberg, K., & Sandman, L. (2009). To survive out-of-hospital cardiac arrest: A search for meaning and coherence. *Qualitative Health Research, 19*, 323–338. https://doi.org/10.1177/1049732309331866

Bury, M. (1982). Chronic illness as biographical disruption. *Sociology of Health & Illness, 4*(2), 167–182. https://doi.org/10.1111/1467-9566.ep11339939

Finlay, L. (2009). Debating phenomenological research methods. *Phenomenology & Practice, 3*(1), 6–25. https://doi.org/10.29173/pandpr19818

Forslund, A.-S., Jansson, J.-H., Lundblad, D., & Söderberg, S. (2017). A second chance at life: People's lived experiences of surviving out-of-hospital cardiac arrest. *Scandinavian Journal of Caring Sciences, 31*(4), 878–886. https://doi.org/10.1111/scs.12409

Forslund, A.-S., Lundblad, D., Jansson, J.-H., Zingmark, K., & Söderberg, S. (2013). Risk factors among people surviving out-of-hospital cardiac arrest and their thoughts about what lifestyle means to them: A mixed methods study. *BMC Cardiovascular Disorders, 13*(1), 62. https://doi.org/10.1186/1471-2261-13-62

Frankl, V. E. (1988). What is meant by meaning. In *The Will to Meaning: Foundations and Applications of Logotherapy* (pp. 50–82). Penguin.

Haydon, G., van der Riet, P., & Inder K. (2019). Long-term survivors of cardiac arrest: A narrative inquiry. *European Journal of Cardiovascular Nursing, 18*(6), 458–464. https://doi.org/10.1177/1474515119844717

Heidegger, M. (2010). *Being and Time* (trans. J. Stambaugh). State University of New York Press (Original work published 1927).

Kellehear, A. (1996). *Experiences Near Death*. Oxford University Press.

Ketilsdottir, A., Albertsdottir, H. R., Akadottir, S. H., Gunnarsdottir, T. J., & Jonsdottir, H. (2013). The experience of sudden cardiac arrest: Becoming reawakened to life. *European Journal of Cardiovascular Nursing, 13*(5), 429–435. https://doi.org/10.1177/1474515113504864

Malhotra, A., & Rakhit, R. (2013). Improving the UK's performance on survival after cardiac arrest. *British Medical Journal, 347*(f4800). https://doi.org/10.1136/bmj.f4800

Martin, L. L., & Kleiber, D. A. (2005). Letting go of the negative: Psychological growth from a close brush with death. *Traumatology, 11*(4), 221–232. https://doi.org/10. 1177/153476560501100403

Maslow, A. H. (1962). Some basic propositions of a growth and self-actualization psychology. In A. W. Combs (Ed.), *Perceiving, Behaving, Becoming: A New Focus for Education* (pp. 34–49). National Education Association, Association for Supervision and Curriculum Development.

Merleau-Ponty, M. (1962). *Phenomenology of Perception.* Routledge & Kegan Paul (Original work published 1945).

O'Reilly, S. M., Grubb, N. R., & O'Carroll, R. E. (2003). In-hospital cardiac arrest leads to chronic memory impairment. *Resuscitation, 58*(1), 73–79. https://doi .org/10.1016/S0300-9572(03)00114-X

Park, C., & Gutierrez, I. (2013). Global and situational meanings in the context of trauma: Relations with psychological well-being, *Counselling Psychology Quarterly, 26*(1), 37–41. https://psycnet.apa.org/doi/10.1080/09515070.2012 .727547

Parnia, S., & Lunea, K. (2013, April). *Why death isn't always permanent.* Macleans. http://www.macleans.ca/general/redefining-the-moment-of-death-why-its-not -permanent-for-a-while-and-who-to-bring-back/

Sartre, J.-P. (1958). *In Being and Nothingness* (trans. H. E. Barnes). Routledge (Original work published 1943).

Smith, J. A., Flowers, P., & Larkin, M. (2009). *Interpretive Phenomenological Analysis: Theory, Method and Research.* Sage Publications Ltd.

Strasser, F. (1999). *Emotions: Experiences in Existential Psychotherapy and Life.* Duckworth.

Todres, L., Galvin, K., & Dahlberg, K. (2007). Lifeworld-led healthcare: Revisiting a humanising philosophy that integrates emerging trends. *Med Health Care Philos, 10*(1), 53–63. https://doi.org/10.1007/s11019-006-9012-8

van Deurzen, E. (2012). *Existential Counselling & Psychotherapy in Practice* (3rd ed.). Sage.

van Deurzen, E., & Young, S. (2009). Setting the scene: Philosophical parameters of existential supervision. In E. van Deurzen & S. Young (Eds.), *Existential Perspectives on Supervision* (pp. 1–14). Palgrave Macmillan.

van Manen, M. (1998). Modalities of body experience in illness and health. *Qualitative Health Research: An International, Interdisciplinary Journal, 8*(1), 7–24. https://doi.org/10.1177/104973239800800102

Wilson, M., Staniforth, A., Till, R., das Nair, R., & Vesey, P. (2014). The psychosocial outcomes of anoxic brain injury following cardiac arrest. *Resuscitation, 85*(6), 6–11. http://dx.doi.org/10.1016/j.resuscitation.2014.02.008

Yalom, I. D. (1980). Life, death and anxiety. In *Existential Psychotherapy* (pp. 29–54). Yalom Family Trust.

Whitehead, L., Tierney, S., Biggerstaff, D., Perkins, G.D., & Haywood, K.L., (2020). Trapped in a disrupted normality: Survivors' and partners' experiences of life after a sudden cardiac arrest. *Resuscitation, 147*, 81–87. https://doi.org/10.1016 /j.resuscitation.2019.12.017

In the Aftermath of Colonialism, Political Conflict, and War

Chapter 8

Lived Experiences of Antiblack Racism: Is the Impact Always a Permanent Psychological Scar or Can There Be Growth?

Jackie Sewell

Introduction

Does the experience of antiblack racism result in psychological trauma? And if so, can this trauma be healed, and can there be psychological growth or is the impact permanent to the individual and group and possibly to future generations?

These are the main questions of concern in this chapter.

Gordon (1999) describes racism as: "The self-deceiving choice to believe that one's race is the only race qualified to be considered human or that one's race is superior to other races" (Gordon, 1999: 2). Gordon is referring to the experience of antiblack racism by white people against black people of African descent. What is interesting is how Gordon refers to racism as self-deceiving. The idea of white superiority is a lie that allows the antiblack racist to hide from the challenge of creating meaning from their existence; instead, their value and life purpose *precede* their existence just by virtue of them being white. Conversely, those who are not white have no value and must bear the angst of what Sartre (1943/1958) proposes is in fact a universal human challenge to create meaning from our existence.

The transatlantic slave trade was the first example of a systematic act of antiblack racism against groups of black African people. The abolition of slavery in America led to legal racial segregation between black and white. In the Caribbean, with the end of slavery, began a period of colonial rule by countries such as Britain. Segregation formally ended in America in 1964, while in the Caribbean, most of the English-speaking islands became independent during the 1960s. Islands such as Jamaica who never experienced segregation had, and still have, a majority black population. In America the black population was in a minority, often living alongside the white descendants of slave owners. The American context of a racialised society has a similar but also different history from other contexts such as in the Caribbean.

DOI: 10.4324/9781003493860-12

As a result of the racialised nature of America, it is perhaps not surprising that this has yielded a plethora of research into the impact of antiblack racism on the psychological functioning of the black subject, often concluding that the trauma is enduring. This has become the dominant global narrative. In this chapter, I will review the literature underpinning this narrative as well as alternative critical perspectives. As a challenge to the dominant narrative, I will also discuss my own research into the lived experiences of a non-American black group, black British people of Jamaican heritage, to illustrate the importance of context and cultural identity in the shaping of different responses (including examples of growth and healing) to the phenomenon of antiblack racism.

Literature review

When undertaking the review of the literature, what I wanted to specifically understand were perspectives on how the phenomenon of antiblack racism comes into being, the impact and immediate response to an act of antiblack racism, the trauma psychologically and or physically, and the long-term effects of the experience. To this end, the literature review will be divided into five separate but interrelated areas.

Firstly, I will examine key early psychosocial literature that emerged during the period of legal racial segregation in America following the abolition of slavery. Secondly, I will review literature focused on the events of the late 1960s and 1970s which saw the rise of black consciousness movements across America, the Caribbean, and Africa. There will then be an exploration of racial trauma literature post the 1970s that has now become somewhat dominant in the field of antiblack racism and its effects. This will be followed by a review of black existential phenomenological literature which offers an alternative perspective. Finally, there will be a review of the literature specifically related to the experience of one non-American black group, black British people of Jamaican heritage living in the UK.

Psychosocial Theories

Psychosocial studies by Clark and Clark (1947) sought to understand how racial attitudes and self-esteem emerged in children during the period of racial segregation in America. The Clark and Clark 'Doll Experiment' (1947) tested a group of black and white American children to assess their racial identification. The study found statistically significant evidence that black children favoured whiteness (the white doll) rather than the 'coloured' [sic] doll, used to represent them (Clark & Clark, 1947: 175). The conclusion from this study and others such as Kardiner and Ovesey (1951/2021) (who examined the psychological impact of racism on a group of black American adults) was that there was demonstrable psychological damage present in black American children and adults because of their experiences within a racially segregated America (Hughes et al., 2015). Furthermore, according to Kardiner and Ovesey, the 'mark of oppression' (internalised racial hatred) would endure for as long as discrimination remained (Kardiner & Ovesey, 1951/2021: xiii).

The 1970s Black Consciousness Movements – Self-Esteem Restored?

The rise of the black consciousness movements in the 1970s among black groups across the globe (America, Africa, and the Caribbean) heralded in era in which there was a "negro to black metamorphosis" (Cross, 1991: 90). Black people were no longer 'coloured' or 'negro,' they were no longer inferior – they were *black* and proud. As a result, research which previously focused on the link between antiblack racism and low self-worth among black people was replaced by research into black identity development (Adam, 1978: 48).

Cross (1971, 1991) developed a five-stage model of black identity development (Nigrescence). In his original model, he sought to demonstrate the progression of black identity from 'negro to black' in America rooted in the historical events in the 1970s. In an updated model he described how black people within the context of continuing antiblack racism are able to transform from negative self-identity (along stages of encounters and experiences of these encounters) to a positive self-identity which they are able to internalise as their new sense of self (Cross, 1991: 90). However, with the persistence of antiblack racism both at an institutional and personal level after the social revolution of the 1970s, we also begin to see a return to research concerned with the impact of this phenomenon on the negative psychological functioning of the black subject.

Racial Trauma and Internalised Racism

Carter (Carter, 2007; Carter & Pieterse, 2020) offers a critique of the *Diagnostic and Statistical Manual of Psychiatric Disorders* (DSM) for its failure to recognise racism against what he describes as "people of colour" as a specific type of trauma. Carter proposes specific racist encounters such as racial harassment, racial discrimination, and discriminatory harassment. He argues that using these criteria focuses the enquiry on how the victims of such encounters have experienced these specific trauma events either at an individual or institutional level, and what specific psychological and physical injury has occurred as a result (Carter, 2007: 89).

Speight (2007) supports Carter's thesis but argues that he "has over-looked a key piece of the puzzle necessary to fully assess the impact of racism. Carter has not accounted for the internalisation of racism by its victims" (Speight, 2007: 126). Speight does not regard racism as character-ised by distinct acts; rather, she feels that racism functions on an interper-sonal and institutional basis at the same time. Furthermore, she maintains that the impact is not just experienced immediately or individually; it can be long-lasting and lead to feelings of low self-worth and self-hatred that can be passed onto future generations and the wider racial group (Speight, 2007: 130).

As mentioned previously, there has been little research into the effects of racism on different black populations in different contexts such as Britain. Since the arrival of black people in significant numbers into the UK starting with the Windrush Generation from 1948, much of the research into the impact of racism on black British people has traditionally focused on the high prevalence of serious mental disorders such as schizophrenia among the black population (Qassem et al., 2015).

Based on a study conducted in 2009 among non-clinical black British subjects of African and Caribbean heritage, Maynard argued that even with individuals who are not mentally unwell, a level of dissociation can occur when confronted with a racist experience. In the perceived racist encounter, the black subject constructs a mental representation of the self and other with respect to the nature of the encounter. This goes beyond internalised racism per se and appears to be an 'in the moment' response to the encounter that the black subject perceives as racist. For example, a negative comment about an aspect of their (or indeed the black group's) physical appearance or behaviour may lead to a sense of discomfort with this aspect of their blackness which may be temporary or endure (Maynard, 2009: 43).

While Maynard's work provides an important contribution to research into the black British experience of antiblack racism, it still generalises black experience to some extent. There is no reference to the impact of his-torical and social context; for example, the participants were of a wide age range, and there was no exploration into the other factors contributing to self-esteem. The black existential perspective is an attempt to focus on the situated lived experience of black individuals and in doing so recognises the complex interplay between objective, universal, and individual factors in a context which contributes to the subjective experiences of individual black people.

Black Existential Philosophy

Black existential philosophy focuses on how existential concepts such as alienation, freedom, responsibility, choice, agency, meaning, 'throwness,' and temporality (Kierkegaard, 1843/2005); the meaning of 'being-in-the-world' and 'being-in-the-world with-others' (Heidegger, (1927/2010); 'being and nothingness' (Sartre, 1943/1958); and embodied experience and perception (Merleau-Ponty, 1945/1962) specifically relate to the existence of black people of African descent (Gordon, 1997). The philosophy is also influenced by post-colonial thinkers such as Du Bois (1903/1994), Cooper (1912), Garvey (2004), and Fanon (1952/1986). It is aligned with Husserl's emphasis on the importance of gaining meaning from an experience within a context (Husserl, 1911/2006) (and therefore the given context of anti-black racism). To this end, black existential philosophy is concerned with the situated lived experience of black people (Gordon, 1997).

Fanon (1952/1986) and Sartre (1943/1958, 1960/2004, 1964) both saw that the oppression of black people by white people was maintained by the 'othering' of black people, both at an individual and a group level. Gordon (1999) argues that the superiority of whiteness is in 'bad faith.' However, it serves a purpose as it allows the white subject to see themselves as perfect, and as 'something,' yet this position of false superiority can only be maintained by the black subject remaining inferior. This is bad faith as it challenges one of the universal principles of existentialism espoused by Sartre, that all humans are 'thrown' into this world as nothing and it is only through our experiences that we come into 'being' (Sartre, 1943/1958).

In *Existence in Black: An Anthology of Black Existential Philosophy* (Gordon, 1997), Gordon draws together authors presenting different experiences of situated black experience. In the chapter entitled "Rastafarianism and The Reality of Dread," Henry (1997) describes the impact of Rastafarianism on the Jamaican identity as a black nation emerging from colonialism in the 1960s. The early part of the 20th century saw the emergence of Rastafarianism as an ideology and spiritual movement among the poorer classes in Jamaica. It was inspired by the ideas of the Jamaican Marcus Garvey (2004), who encouraged black people in Jamaica and beyond to reject the European ideas of Africa and blackness as inferior.

As Jamaica and the Caribbean approached independence in the early 1960s, Rastafarianism emerged as a powerful ideology in Jamaica, the wider Caribbean, and the diaspora, allowing the framing of the development of a new black conscious identity (Henry, 1997). The impact of these events in Jamaica was to have a significant impact on the experiences of Caribbeans who had migrated to Britain (and their children who were born there) as part of the Windrush Generation, as they responded to the reality of antiblack racism in the UK.

The Windrush Generation and Their Children's Experience of Antiblack Racism

Jamaicans and other Caribbeans arrived at the invitation of the British from 1948 to 1962. Known as the Windrush Generation, these individuals were the descendants of slaves, and since the end of slavery, they had lived in the English-speaking Caribbean under British colonial rule. Although there had been black people in Britain for centuries (Olusoga, 2017), the numbers of Caribbeans arriving and settling in Britain at the same time can be regarded as the first significant black population in the UK (Hall, 1994).

Foner (1985) describes the experiences of Caribbeans arriving from countries where they as black people were in the majority and so had not previously experienced antiblack racism. She describes what many found shocking was the negative response from white people to their blackness (Foner, 1985: 4). The racial prejudice and open hostility towards the Caribbeans who were mainly from Jamaica reached a defining moment in 1958, with the first race riots in Britain in Notting Hill in London.

The riots revealed that black people had no protection under the law, and they felt rejected and unprotected by their experiences. However, for many this rejection resulted in them reasserting their 'Jamaican-ness' (Hall, 1994). This manifested itself in Jamaicans creating their own social communities including social clubs and credit unions known as the 'pardna' system. The pardna system is a powerful and interesting response to their specific experience of antiblack racism. Many Jamaicans (and other Caribbeans) were barred from private renting (because they were black), and so many saw their only option was to buy a property. However, unable to secure finance from the banks, the pardna system (in which individuals regularly saved money along with other members of their community) provided the means by which they could accumulate a deposit to purchase a home (Foner, 1985).

While seeking ways to adapt to their rejection, the hope among these Caribbeans was that their children born in Britain would have a more positive experience (Windrush, 1998). However, the reality was that the second generation faced their own challenges of overt antiblack racism, low educational achievement, and high unemployment (Foner, 1985). Both the Windrush Generation and their children lived not only in a period of overt antiblack racism in the 1960s, 1970s, and 1980s, but this period also saw the rise of black consciousness in Jamaica, America, and Africa.

According to Hall (1994), the 1970s was an historic time for Jamaicans both in Jamaica and the diaspora. For the first and second-generation Jamaicans in the UK, Jamaican independence, the rise of Rastafarianism, and the emergence of roots reggae music closely associated with the messages of Rastafari enabled this diaspora to become black in a very Jamaican way. For the second generation, in particular, they now had a distinct black identity that in many ways amplified their difference within the country of their birth but appeared to enable them to be something of value to themselves.

A gap in the literature

There is a gap in the psychological literature on the specific lived experience of the Windrush Generation and their children in the UK as the first significant black population in Britain living their lives in a context of overt racism during the 1960s, 1970s, and 1980s alongside the emergence of black consciousness movements in America and the Caribbean. Furthermore, there is a gap in the knowledge of how an emerging new black identity coupled with a Jamaican cultural identity helped many to develop a healthy sense of self in the face of antiblack racism.

The objective of this current research study

The research study itself was not primarily concerned with the impact of antiblack racism on the psychological functioning of its target group. The objective of the research was to enquire into the lived experience of a group of second-generation professional black British-born women of Jamaican heritage. The aim was to discover what their experiences meant to them, and how these shaped their relationship with work and achievement and their sense of identity. However, as these were black women, the phenomenon of antiblack racism framed their existence and their stories.

Methodology

To address my research questions: *What is the lived experience of second-generation professional black British women of Jamaican heritage? What did this experience mean to them and how did it shape their relationship with work and achievement?* I selected a qualitative approach to my study aligned with the existential phenomenological philosophical perspective. As I was seeking to understand the embodied relational nature of the black existence of my target group, the ideas of European existential thinkers such as Sartre (1943/1958, 1964) and Merleau-Ponty (1945/1962) and black existential thinkers such as Fanon (1952/1986), Du Bois (1903/1994), Garvey (2004), Hall (1994), Gordon (1997, 1999), and Henry (1997) were especially relevant.

The existential phenomenological perspective is consistent with my belief about the nature of how knowledge is produced through experience in the world. This epistemological position was informed by the work of Husserl (1911/2006), his concept of *intentionality* and his emphasis on 'experiencing' and meaning when we encounter a phenomenon; and the ideas of Gadamer (1960/2004) and his emphasis on the situated construction of knowledge. Gadamer's focus is on narratives created within an historical, social, and cultural context. This enables understanding of how an individual experiences the world as they interact with others in context. This was relevant to my enquiry. I also drew upon the ideas of Ricoeur (1981) and his focus on how narratives have *meaning* to the individual constructed within a context. These perspectives led me to my choice of method.

Method

Chosen Method — Critical Narrative Analysis (Langdridge, 2007)

Critical Narrative Analysis (CNA) is a method of narrative research enquiry devised by Langdridge (2007) and influenced by the ideas of Ricoeur's hermeneutic existential phenomenology (Ricoeur, 1981). As with other qualitative methods, it is concerned with accounts of subjective experience. As with narrative analysis, the key source of data are the stories that the individual recounts about their experiences. However, CNA applies critical theories such as existential themes, black existential philosophy, and post-colonial theories to further enquire into the narrative. This enables the researcher to apply a 'critical' lens to the narrative to uncover underlying meanings and propose an alternative explanation for the narrator's position and their experience of their experience.

The method is designed to interrogate the life story of an individual and recommends either using one participant or at least a very limited number. I opted for six participants because I wanted to tell some stories that haven't been told and to illustrate the diversity of black experience among those of Jamaican heritage in the UK.

Each narrative was interrogated across key **life stages: Formative, Adolescence/University, Early Career,** and **Present.** The narrative was then analysed using the five-stage CNA steps below.

Stage 1 – Critique of the illusions of subjectivity. The purpose of this stage was to reveal my own subjective position as the researcher by applying the hermeneutic of suspicion to key stages and experiences across my life.

Stage 2 – Identifying narratives, narrative tone, and rhetorical function. From this stage, the focus of enquiry was into the lived experiences of each participant. Although all the interviews were recorded, during the interviews I noted any moments when I detected a specific change of tone or physical reaction to my questions or the discussion. The transcripts were then analysed in accordance with traditional narrative analysis (Riessman, 2005).

Stage 3 – Identities and identity work. I was interested in how the individuals saw themselves, who they identified with and what were the most important identities to them across key life stages.

Stage 4 – Thematic priorities and relationships. I identified general themes occurring within the participant's narrative and across each life stage.

Stage 5 ––Destabilising the narrative. The hermeneutic of suspicion was applied. The narratives were analysed with specific reference to critical theories and specific social narratives arising out of the context of historical events to understand the impact they had on the participant's narrative and meaning making.

Stage 6 – Critical synthesis. This stage is designed to ensure that the coherence of the narrative is not lost in the process of dividing it into the different stages. To this end, I summarised each narrative focusing on how they related to existential themes such as 'being-in-the-world,' choice, freedom, responsibility, meaning, temporality, and isolation.

To complete the analysis, I undertook two additional steps, which involved firstly identifying common themes occurring across all participants' narratives and finally an analysis of the individual differences between the participants.

Data Collection Process

I conducted two semi-structured face-to-face interviews with each of the participants based around the questions in Table 8.1. The participant

Table 8.1 Interview Questions

1	What does the word identity mean to you?
2	What does being a black woman mean to you?
3	What does being of Jamaican heritage mean to you?
4	What does being British mean to you?
5	What does work mean to you?
6	How has being a black woman of Jamaican heritage influenced your choice of career and life choices?
7	What aspirations did/do you have with regard to work?
8	How has work affected you as an individual, both good and bad?
9	When you reflect on your experiences and influences, what have been the most positive and what the most negative?
10	What role has religion or spirituality played in your life?
11	Reflecting on being both black and a woman, how have you experienced sexism and racism?
12	What knowledge do you wish to pass on to the next generation?

Source: Sewell (2020: 94–95).

Rachel was used as a pilot to ensure that the interview questions captured the information that I was seeking. As a result of the pilot, I subsequently included an initial general question, inviting the participants to reflect on what identity meant to them. All the interviews were recorded and transcribed verbatim. The data from the pilot was collected and analysed in the same way as the data from all the other participants.

Research Context

The research was undertaken in London from 2017 to 2019 during the 70th anniversary of the arrival of the Empire Windrush in 1948. The research also coincided with the Windrush scandal (Gentleman, 2019).

Recruitment Process

The participants were sought using a flyer which was distributed via social media. Each respondent had a short pre-selection interview to assess their suitability in terms of meeting the criteria and to confirm that they were in good mental health. Six participants were eventually selected.

Profile of Participants

All participants were second-generation black women of Jamaican heritage, born in Britain to parents who had arrived in the UK as part of the Windrush Generation. The women were all professional, currently holding senior or executive positions in the workplace. The definition of 'professional' was that each participant had to be educated to at least degree level or the equivalent. See Table 8.2.

Table 8.2 Profile of the Participants

Pseudonym	Age	Current Profession
Rachel	50	Partner
Natasha	61	Chief Executive
Cynthia	51	Senior professional in the public sector
Georgina	50	Senior professional in the private sector
Melanie	52	Senior Civil Servant
Lorraine	62	Senior professional in the public sector

Source: Sewell (2020: 93).

All participants (except Lorraine) obtained a university degree, through the traditional route of 'O' and 'A' levels and then university. Lorraine obtained an equivalent professional qualification as a mature student. Rachel and Melanie attended Russell Group universities (equivalent to Ivy League institutions in America), with Melanie gaining a place at 'Oxbridge' (the exact university, Oxford or Cambridge, was not revealed in the study to protect Melanie's identity).

Analysis and findings

Summary of Findings

Table 8.3 shows a summary of reported experiences reported by each participant across key life stages.

The Participants' Narratives

Regarding the context of their early experiences at home, three of the participants (Lorraine, Cynthia, and Melanie) reported adverse childhood experiences which included neglect, parental mental illness, exposure to emotional and physical abuse in the home, abandonment, rejection, and attachment issues. Lorraine experienced periods of homelessness and attendance at different schools at a young age. Melanie reported being placed in foster care for a time because of her mother's mental illness. All three reported subsequent difficult relationships with their blackness and their relationships with black people which lasted across their life. Melanie reported that she had had psychotherapy as an adult and this had healed her relationship issues. Lorraine and Cynthia reported continued issues with their relationship with their blackness and other black people.

Rachel, Georgina, and Natasha reported being brought up in stable, loving 'black Jamaican' households. They reported that both parents worked and owned their homes. This contrasted with the experiences of Lorraine, Cynthia, and Melanie, who reported that they lived in social housing and that their parents struggled to find stable employment. Rachel and Georgina reported having positive experiences of their Jamaican culture, whereas Natasha reported receiving mixed messages about the value of being Jamaican and black.

Experiences of Racism and Self-Hatred

All participants, except Rachel, reported experiences of self-hatred that occurred when they first went to nursery or infant school. This was the first

Table 8.3 Participant Experiences

Experience	Formative	Adolescence/University*	Early Career	Present
Self-hatred	All **except** Rachel	Cynthia Lorraine Melanie Natasha	Cynthia Lorraine	Cynthia Lorraine
Being seen as different	Melanie Natasha Georgina	All	All	All
An experience of racism	Lorraine Melanie	Melanie Natasha Rachel	Lorraine	Georgina
Rejection/belonging	All	All	Not reported	All
Working hard/achieving	Rachel Cynthia	All	All	All
Being the only black person in the 'room'	Natasha Georgina	Natasha	All	All
The importance of a black identity	Not reported	All **except** Lorraine & Cynthia	All **except** Lorraine & Cynthia	All **except** Lorraine & Cynthia

*This includes young adulthood. It should be noted that Lorraine achieved her degree as a mature student in later life.

time that they had any meaningful contact with white children, and they reported experiencing racial insults or feelings of difference. Only Lorraine and Melanie reported actual experiences of racism in their formative years. Lorraine described some disturbing experiences, including an incident with a childminder.

> Lorraine: *I am wondering whether she got me my own cutlery set – because some parents didn't want their children to use the same cutlery that I did.*
> Jackie: *But you at the time – you took it to mean that somehow, she saw you as special?*
> Lorraine: *Yes, that's how she presented – and also, she would let me choose things that she didn't let others choose – so she would say – what do you want us to have?* (Source: Sewell, 2020: 170)

Natasha also described incidents of people making comments about her blackness (skin colour and hair); she reported that this, together with comments that her parents made about black hair not being 'good hair,' led to feelings of self-hatred:

> Natasha: *Confusing – just difficult, difficult. It led to me not having a sense of good, it led to me not being proud of my blackness. We didn't talk about black, in those days. It led to me, not having a sense of pride in who I was even though, my mother in particular had so many stories [about Jamaica].* (Source: Sewell, 2020: 131)

Identities

In their formative years, before attending nursery or school, the participants could not recall any real sense of being black. In the case of Lorraine, she reported feeling that she had more of a white identity. All participants except Lorraine and Cynthia reported that having a black identity was of significance to them especially during their adolescence (during the 1970s and early 1990s). Rachel, Natasha, Georgina, and Melanie all reported this as a key turning point for them in terms of how they began to hold their blackness with pride.

Natasha reported that until adolescence, she had lived a life of self-hatred, and this led her to her facing expulsion from school. As a result, her parents sent her to America to spend time with a relative who was active in the black conscious movement. Natasha reported that she came back to the UK transformed, eventually going on to university. She was now 'black' (Sewell, 2020: 134).

The Impact of the Historical Context on the Experience of Experience

All participants reflected on the context of 1970s and 1980s Britain, within an environment of overt racism characterised by regular National Front marches in southeast London and the race riots across major British cities. Lorraine expressed concern about how white people would view her as she was keen to be seen as different from the black rioters. All participants except Lorraine and Cynthia mentioned how the black conscious movement in America, and Rastafarianism and roots reggae music from Jamaica, impacted on their self-esteem. Georgina and Melanie were particularly impacted by the messages of Rastafarianism and the music. Georgina remarked that:

> Georgina: *It was – because my siblings were older, so they were listening to a lot of music – you know reggae music was coming out of Jamaica – which I think – reggae music coming out of Jamaica was amazing – because it's not – it tells a story – storytelling for me – it's not just music so a lot of classic music that was coming out of Jamaica at that time about – you know slavery, black history and Marcus Garvey.* (Source: Sewell, 2020: 204)

Common Themes Emerging from the Analysis

What became clear from analysing the findings was that there were three common themes across all participants' narratives (see Table 8.4). However, what may have been a common experience appeared to have a specific meaning.

Identity and Identification

The participants took different positions towards their black identity and who they identified with. Being 'black' for Lorraine appeared to mean being 'trapped' in her black body. She identified more with white people and wanted to be seen as different from other black people. For Georgina, 'being black' was more akin to having a fixed shared black identity. She felt most comfortable with black people who shared her idea of what it meant to be black. All participants except Lorraine, Cynthia, and Melanie spoke in vivid terms about their connection with their Jamaican heritage, viewing it as a strength and inextricably linked with their black identity.

Table 8.4 Three Common Themes

Common Themes	Subthemes	Number of Participants Reporting a Subtheme
Identify and identification	Being black	All
	Sameness and difference	All
	Rejection and belonging	All
	Being Jamaican	All (dominant Georgina)
	Being special	1 (Lorraine)
	Being adored	1 (Natasha)
Working hard and achievement	Being smart	1 (Melanie)
	Trying hard/achievement	1 (Lorraine)
	Limiting and being limited	1 (Rachel)
	Never good enough	All (dominant Cynthia)
	Working hard/achievement	All (except Lorraine
Responsible to and for all black people	Working hard/achievement	All (except Lorraine)
	Trying hard/achievement	1 (Lorraine)

Working Hard and Achievement

This theme relates to the messages that the participants received from their family and significant others and connected with the prevailing negative narrative at that time about the low potential for academic achievement among black Caribbean girls. There appeared to be a difference between 'working hard' and 'trying hard.' All except for Lorraine and Melanie received the former message, which they interpreted as setting their goals high and achieving because they *were* good enough and therefore deserved that level of achievement as much as their white counterparts. However, the reality of racism meant that they would have to do more to get what they deserved. Lorraine's use of the term 'trying hard' related to her subjective experiences. Of all the participants, only her narrative revealed a history of academic failure. It was not until adulthood that she achieved a professional qualification that had eluded her for many years.

Responsible to and for All Black People

All participants described feeling responsible to and for other black people. They regarded themselves as role models, and this contributed to a feeling that they should always function at a high level.

Discussion

Throughout this chapter I have been concerned with the questions posed in the Introduction:

Does the experience of antiblack racism result in psychological trauma? And if so, can this trauma be healed, and can there be psychological growth or is the impact permanent to the individual and group and possibly to future generations?

From the work of Carter (2007) and Speight (2007), the perspective is that antiblack racism not only results in specific types of psychological and physical trauma but leads to internalised racism at an individual and group level, which is maintained and passed down the generations. The work of Carter and Speight and others which focus on a black American existence has become the dominant perspective from which conclusions about the impact of antiblack racism are generalised irrespective of context.

The black existential perspective from the work of Gordon (1997) and Henry (1997) was important in this research into the lived experience of a group of black women. Applying universal existential themes (including agency, freedom, responsibility, choice, meaning, and relationship with self and others) to this target group enabled an exploration of the phenomenon (in relation to these themes) within the situated context of their black existence.

The purpose of the current research was to fill a gap in the literature about black experience which in the UK tended to focus on general black experiences with little reference to the impact of culture, historical context, and lived experiences. With respect to the focus of this chapter, the research provided a different lens through which to view the impact of antiblack racism from the dominant American perspective. However, one experience that appears to be universal to all black people is the encounter with the white 'other' in which there is an experience of the negation of blackness either towards the individual black subject or the black group. This is consistent with the work of Maynard (2009) and early ideas from Fanon (1952/1986) and Sartre (1960/2004).

In the research all the participants, except Rachel, recalled an early experience of antiblack racism. The immediate impact of the encounter as described by the participants resembled typical trauma responses such as disassociation, which led to discomfort with their black body – for example, Natasha's hatred of her hair. What appears to be the main contributor to whether the encounter resulted in a temporary or longer-term negative impact were other experiences within their early childhood.

The work by Carter and Speight abstracts antiblack racism from any other type of trauma. In doing so, the impact of the trauma is not considered in relation to other factors and context. The current research illustrated the extent to which adverse childhood experiences impact the relationship with the self and others in general. Merleau-Ponty (1945/1962) describes how, in our early experiences in a context, we take up positions in the world. It is from these positions that we perceive the world. Lorraine, Cynthia, and Melanie described very challenging experiences in their early home lives, all of which are well-known factors contributing to low self-esteem.

Lorraine and Cynthia appeared to have a lifelong struggle with self-hatred. For the other participants who were also being challenged within the historical context of the time, the impact of the 1970s social events had a positive impact on their black identity. This resonates with the work of Cross, who saw the 1970s as an historical moment in black history and an enabler for black people to restore value to their blackness. Additionally, the 1970s social and cultural events in Jamaica in particular were seen as a transformational moment in terms of how most participants and their parents saw themselves as black people.

Work and achievement had significant meaning to the participants. While there was a difference between 'working hard' and 'trying hard,' it appeared that for all of them extraordinary rather than ordinary achievement was a way of restoring value to their blackness. What also appears to have been important was a connection again to their Jamaican culture, where post-independence there was a growing sense among Jamaicans that anything was possible. It was during this period we began to see the emergence of what has now become a standard mantra in Jamaica: 'Wi likkle but we tallawah' (Knibb, 2016). Jamaicans knew they were a little island, but they believed they were strong (tallawah) and could achieve anything.

Conclusion

Antiblack racism is an objective reality and can have a devastating impact on some black individuals, but not all. Capturing different black experiences challenges the stereotype of a singular black experience and the belief that all black people are permanently damaged by antiblack racism regardless of context and experience. Such a narrative robs the black subject of their agency and their experience of their experience. Yet this stubbornly remains the dominant narrative. This perpetuates the stereotype of black people unable to reflect upon and grow from their experiences and create meaning in their lives. Perhaps it also maintains the position whereby the antiblack racist and the white saviour can continue to hide from their 'nothingness,' seeing themselves as 'something'; either as superior or privileged by virtue of their whiteness. Either way, yet again, black people are stereotyped; they are either inferior or victims. Some black researchers and thinkers are also complicit in perpetuating the dominant narrative. By taking a position that all black people are affected by anti-black racism in the same way dehumanises them by not recognising or valuing their subjectivity.

The research illustrated how some black individuals within a specific context and of a specific heritage were able to create a meaningful and healthy life within the context of an environment of overt antiblack racism. The research showed the importance for black people to have a healthy black identity and connection with their cultural heritage. The current black population in the UK is diverse, and those of Caribbean heritage are in the minority. The descendants of Windrush are now on the third or fourth generation, and what is not known is how similar or different are their experiences to those of their parents, grandparents, or great-grandparents. This requires further research.

References

Carter, R. T. (2007). Racism and psychological and emotional injury: Recognising and assessing race-based traumatic stress. *The Counseling Psychologist, 35*(1), 13–105. https://psycnet.apa.org/doi/10.1177/0011000006292033

Carter, R. T., & Pieterse, A. (2020). *Measuring the Effects of Racism: Guidelines for the Assessment and Treatment of Race-Based Traumatic Stress Injury*. Columbia University Press. https://psycnet.apa.org/doi/10.7312/cart19306

Clark, K. B., & Clark, M. P. (1947). Racial identification and preference in negro children. In T. M. Newcomb & E. L. Hartley (Eds.), *Readings in Social Psychology* (pp. 169–178). Holt Rinehart & Winston. https://doi.org/10.1177/004208598301800302

Cooper, F. (2012). Decolonization and citizenship: Africa between empires and a world of nations. In E. Bogaerts & R. Raben (Eds.), *Beyond Empire and Nation: The Decolonization of African and Asian Societies, 1930s–1970s* (pp. 39–68). Brill. http://www.jstor.org/stable/10.1163/j.ctt1w8h2zm.6

Cross, W. E., Jr. (1971). The negro to black conversion experience. *Black World, 20*(9), 13–27.

Cross, W. E., Jr. (1991). *Shades of Black: Diversity in African American Identity*. Temple University Press.

Du Bois, W. E. B. (1994). *The Souls of Black Folk*. Dover Publications (Original work published 1903).

Fanon, F. (1986). *Black Skin, White Masks*. Pluto Classics (Original work published 1952).

Foner, N. (1985). Race and color: Jamaican migrants in London and New York City. *The International Migration Review, 19*(4), 708–727. https://doi.org/10.1177/019791838501900403

Gadamer, H. G. (2004). *Truth and Method* (2nd ed.) (trans. J. Weinsheimer & D. G. Marshall). Continuum International (Original work published 1960).

Garvey, M. (2004). *Selected Writings and Speeches of Marcus Garvey*. Dover Publications.

Gentleman, A. (2019). *The Windrush Betrayal: Exposing the Hostile Environment*. Guardian Faber Publishing.

Gordon, L. (1997). Black existential philosophy. In L. Gordon, *Existence in Black: An Anthology of Black Existential Philosophy* (pp. 1–10). Routledge.

Gordon, L. (1999). *Bad Faith and Antiblack Racism*. Humanity Books.

Hall, S. (1994). Cultural identity and diaspora. In P. Williams & L. Chrisman (Eds.), *Colonial Discourse and Postcolonial Theory: A Reader* (pp. 227–237). Harvester.

Heidegger, M. (2010). *Being and Time* (trans. J. Stambaugh). State University of New York Press (Original work published 1927).

Henry, P. (1997). Rastafarianism and the reality of dread. In L. Gordon, *Existence in Black: An Anthology of Black Existential Philosophy* (pp. 157–164). Routledge.

Hughes, M., Kiecolt, K. J., Keith, V. M., & Demo, D. H. (2015). Racial identity and well-being among African Americans. *Social Psychology Quarterly, 78*(1), 25–48.

Husserl, E. (2006). *The Basic Problems of Phenomenology: From the Lectures, Winter Semester, 1910–1911* (trans. I. Farin & J. G. Hart). Springer (Original work published 1911).

Kardiner, A., & Ovesey, L. (2021). *The Mark of Oppression: Exploration in the Personality of the American Negro*. Lushena Books (Original work published 1951).

Kierkegaard, S. (2005). *Fear and Trembling*. Penguin (Original work published 1843).

Knibb, P. (2016). *Origin of Tallawah phrase*. The Gleaner. https://jamaica-gleaner.com/article/letters/20161107/origin-tallawah-phrase

Langdridge, D. (2007). *Phenomenological Psychology: Theory, Research and Method*. Pearson Education.

Merleau-Ponty, M. (1962). *Phenomenology of Perception* (trans. C. Smith). Routledge (Original work published 1945).

Olusoga, D. (2017). *Black and British: A Forgotten History*. Macmillan.

Qassem, T., Bebbington, P., Spiers, N., McManus, S., Jenkins, R., & Dein, S. (2015). Prevalence of psychosis in black ethnic minorities in Britain: Analysis based on three national surveys. *Soc Psychiatry Psychiatr Epidemiol, 50*(7), 1057–1064.

Ricoeur, P. (1981). *Hermeneutics and the Human Sciences* (ed. and trans. J. B. Thompson). Cambridge University Press.

Riessman, C. (2005). *Narrative Analysis*. http://eprints.hud.ac.uk/4920/2/Chapter_1_-_Catherine_Kohler_Riessman.pdf

Sartre, J.-P. (1958). *Being and Nothingness* (trans. H. E. Barnes). Routledge (Original work published 1943).

Sartre, J.-P. (1964). *Black Orpheus*. http://massreview.org/sites/default/files/Sartre.pdf

Sartre, J.-P. (2004). *Critique of Dialectical Reason, Vol. 1*. Verso (Original work published 1960).

Sewell, J. (2020). *What does work, achievement and identity mean to black British women? The lived experience of professional black British women of Jamaican heritage* (DCPsych thesis). Middlesex University/New School of Psychotherapy and Counselling (NSPC) Psychology. https://repository.mdx.ac.uk/item/89467

Speight, S. L. (2007). Internalized racism: One more piece of the puzzle. *The Counselling Psychologist, 35*(1), 126–134. https://doi.org/10.1177/0011000006295119

Windrush. (1998). BBC Four.

Chapter 9

Political Refugees: Rising Above Trauma

Armin Danesh

Introduction

> I have cherished the ideal of a democratic and free society in which all
> persons live together in harmony and with equal opportunities. It is an
> ideal which I hope to live for and to achieve. But if needs be, it is an
> ideal for which I am prepared to die. (Mandela, 2011: IX)

The discourse surrounding political refugees and their encounters with
trauma is a pivotal area of inquiry in academic circles. My doctoral thesis – an existential-phenomenological study exploring the experiences of
Iranian political refugees in the United Kingdom – laid the foundation for
a deeper inquiry into the subject. This culminated in the publication of a
book entitled *Political Refugees: A New Perspective* (Danesh & Assiter,
222). The forthcoming chapter represents a natural progression from my
previous research endeavours, with a more intensive focus on the intricate
dynamics of trauma. The evolving trajectory of my investigation led to its
original title being refined from "Political Refugees Rising from Trauma" to
"Political Refugees Rising Above Trauma." This revision reflects a nuanced
understanding cultivated through ongoing scholarly inquiry, highlighting
the resilience and transcendence demonstrated by political refugees in the
face of adversity. It must be emphasised that, while the insights gleaned
from this study are not intended as broad generalisations, my aspiration is
that this chapter will contribute to a deeper understanding of the complexities surrounding trauma within the context of political refugees.

Political refugees, within an existential framework, emerge as individuals driven by the pursuit of freedom to imbue life with meaning, exercise responsibility, and secure survival amidst major existential threats in
their home countries. While legal delineations of refugees often adhere to
the parameters outlined in the 1951 UN Convention on Refugees, existing scholarly discourse predominantly centres on the themes of loss, torture, trauma, homelessness, and heightened emotional distress and mental

DOI: 10.4324/9781003493860-13

disorders among this demographic (Ahearn, 2000; Alayarian, 2007; Bemak et al., 2003; Bhugra et al., 2010; Blackwell, 2011; Colin, 2011; Espin, 1999; Fiddian-Qasmiyeh et al., 2014; Papadopoulos, 2002; van der Veer, 1998). However, critical inquiry calls into question the ability of such perspectives to capture all the multifaceted realities of refugees' lived experiences (Danesh & Assiter, 2022). Existing literature lacks recognition of the psychological state of political refugees who belong to specific political movements, with regard to their group and political identity.

This chapter seeks to shed light on the subjective perceptions and articulations of Iranian political refugees' experiences. Participants in this study display a conscious commitment to resistance against injustices, manifested in opposition to inequalities, repression, and religious dictatorship in their countries of origin. On resettlement in the United Kingdom, these political refugees face the complex task of reconciling their values, philosophies, and political convictions with a new socio-cultural milieu. This requires them to explore avenues that will not only facilitate the continuity of their political endeavours but also capitalise on the host country's diverse array of opportunities and freedoms to advance their aspiration to effect regime change in Iran.

Trauma, as a central theme within this discourse, emerges as a complex and multifaceted phenomenon requiring a nuanced understanding that encompasses psychological, social, neurological, philosophical, economic, cultural, sociological, political, and spiritual dimensions. From this perspective, conventional therapeutic approaches display limitations in providing holistic and tailored solutions to address the diverse manifestations of trauma. This chapter advocates for an existential-phenomenological approach, transcending the confines of the medical model, to effectively explore the multifaceted nature of trauma within the context of political refuge.

The chapter begins with a critical review of existing literature on political refugees and trauma, aiming to highlight gaps and limitations in the current scholarly landscape. The subsequent sections unfold in a structured manner. The focus shifts to the traumatic experiences of political refugees. I immersed myself in their community environment, engaging with and observing their cultural behaviours and lifestyles to gain deeper insight. Later sections analyse and discuss findings derived from the data. Building on these findings, research outcomes are contextualised within broader theoretical frameworks and existing literature. The chapter concludes by synthesising key insights and proposing an approach for working with trauma among political refugees, aiming to inform scholarly discourse and practical interventions in this field. Through this comprehensive and structured approach, the chapter seeks to advance scholarly understanding and contribute to the development of effective interventions within the realm of political refuge and trauma.

Literature review

This segment critically evaluates extant literature relating to the experiences of Iranian political refugees in the UK. I began by probing the essence of a political refugee and the discourse surrounding refugees' encounters with trauma. Despite an extensive review, academic investigations into the lived experiences of Iranian political refugees in the UK proved elusive.

As a political refugee myself, I adopted an insider perspective for this study, centring on the subjective experiences of my participants. Notably, most existing research is conducted from an external standpoint.

Since the 1979 Revolution, which ended over five decades of the Pahlavi regime, some 4 million Iranians – mostly intellectuals, highly educated professionals, and human rights advocates – have had to seek refuge outside their homeland (Elik, 2012). This exodus continues to the present day and is meticulously chronicled within the socio-political milieu.

Iran's historical trajectory since the early 20th century underscores the pivotal role of Iranian women. The 'women's question' assumed prominence with the advent of the Khomeini regime in 1979/1980 and its initial onslaught on women's societal standing. Yet, scant scholarly attention has been devoted to the psychological ramifications of the clerical regime's punitive attitude to women (Danesh & Assiter, 2022).

One major lacuna in the existing literature is the failure to differentiate between various categories of migrants, with refugees often being conflated with emigrants (Aidani, 2007; Morrice, 2011). Existing literature overlooks the psychological wellbeing of political refugees who are affiliated with specific political movements, with respect to their group and political identities.

What propels such a huge exodus from Iran? Over the past four decades, hundreds of thousands of political and human rights activists and members of religious and ethnic minorities have endured imprisonment and torture. Their families have faced harassment, confiscation of assets, and cessation of pensions, rendering them destitute. Arbitrary imprisonment has become commonplace. Conservative estimates suggest that over 100,000 individuals have been executed for their political convictions. Barbaric practices such as public floggings, stoning, mutilation, and ocular gouging further punctuate the oppressive regime. Consequently, millions of Iranians have risked their lives to escape. Notably, there exists a dearth of scholarly exploration into the individual experiences of these victims.

In the extant literature, a distinct focus on political refugees is notably scarce. Most texts rely on the 1951 UN Refugee Convention for defining refugees (Bhugra et al., 2010; Frelick, 1988; Linesch, 2013; Papadopoulos, 2002; van der Veer, 1998), reflecting a primarily legal perspective. However, such definitions fail to capture the nuanced levels of distress and psychological exigencies amongst individuals (Hollifield et al., 2002).

The prevailing portrayal of refugees is as individuals traumatised by the ordeal of forced migration – helpless; socially isolated; and struggling to acclimatise owing to perceived 'cultural differences,' thus requiring comprehensive support (Papadopoulos, 2002). This generalised overview lacks a phenomenological perspective from the refugees' own vantage point.

Within the extensive literature, the predominant emphasis concerning refugees' psychological wellbeing revolves around trauma, with assertions that a significant majority of refugees endure such distress (Reyes & Jacobs, 2006). Since the 1990s, in numerous Western host nations the concept of 'trauma' has become synonymous with the refugee experience (Overland et al., 2014).

According to Sadavoy (1997), trauma heightens sensitivity to one's mortality, a perspective echoed by existential therapists who suggest that some individuals may utilise this crisis as an opportunity for profound self-definition and existential exploration (Frankl, 1946/2004; Jacobsen, 2006; Park et al., 1996; van Deurzen, 1997; Yalom, 1980). However, critics question the applicability of Western notions of traumatic stress to refugees from diverse cultural backgrounds (Eyber & Ager, 2002; Pupavac, 2004; Summerfield, 2008).

The indiscriminate use of the term 'trauma' is problematic insofar as it neglects collective and communal responses to adversity and the potential for adaptation (Summerfield, 1999; Wilson & Drozdek, 2004). Papadopoulos (2002), however, contends that the fundamental condition shared by all refugees and immigrants is the wrench from their home environment and the ensuing challenge of forging a new one. He argues that it is the loss of home rather than trauma that unites their experiences.

The multifaceted nature of trauma has evoked varied scholarly responses. For instance, Montgomery's (1998) extensive study of Middle Eastern refugee children underscores their predominantly trauma-induced distress stemming from violence in refugee camps. Meanwhile, the literature often emphasises posttraumatic stress disorder (PTSD) in the context of natural disasters and conflict, primarily focusing on individual experiences.

However, the cross-cultural applicability and universality of PTSD diagnoses have sparked considerable debate within psychosocial programming and related disciplines (Hinton & Lewis-Fernández, 2011). This debate intensified with the release of the DSM-V in May 2013, raising questions about the cultural relevance of psychiatric diagnoses, particularly PTSD.

Together with their focus on the individual, researchers have often given inadequate attention to the collective dimensions of refugees' experiences, along with their broader socio-political contexts. Further scrutiny is warranted concerning the benefits and drawbacks of existing classifications and their cross-cultural applicability.

Herman (1992) underscores that psychological trauma is characterised by disempowerment and disconnection from others, highlighting the indispensability of relational dynamics in the recovery process. Nevertheless, the legal definition of refugees overlooks the crucial aspect of self-identity, which holds significance in therapeutic processes.

Refugees' political stances and identities, as well as their cultural values and attitudes, inherently shape their experiences of trauma. Their psychological states may be influenced by the choices they make – to remain silent, to resist, or to flee. Furthermore, the focus on loss, experiences of torture, trauma, homelessness, and heightened emotional distress and mental disorders underscores the multifaceted nature of refugees' experiences.

Numerous scholarly works on the subject categorise refugees as individuals who have lost their home, livelihood, and social identity (Bhugra, 2010; Colin, 2011; Papadopoulos, 2002; van der Veer, 1998). However, such labelling inadequately describes their circumstances. Papadopoulos asserts that "being a refugee is not a pathological condition," yet acknowledges the intricate challenge of responding to their undeniable suffering without pathologising it (Papadopoulos, 2002: 36). Despite the prevalent focus on refugee suffering in the literature, there is a notable absence of discourse delineating the capabilities of political refugees.

Within the domain of trauma literature, instances abound of individuals whose resilience has facilitated a positive transformation of their traumatic experiences (Herman, 1992; Joseph & Linley, 2005; Papadopoulos, 2002; Splevins et al., 2010; Tedeschi & Calhoun, 2004). However, the literature fails to address the root of such resilience. Such transformations have bolstered interpersonal relationships and self-awareness, and have often engendered a shift in worldview, attitudes, philosophy of life, and political and community identity.

Remarkably scant attention has been paid in the literature to the crisis experienced by refugees who have been removed from the front lines of political conflict or experienced defeat. Psychotherapists generally acknowledge the relevance of cultural considerations when working with refugees (Ahearn, 2000; Colin, 2011; Dana, 2000; Espin, 1999; Sue, 2015; Vera, 2012), but this understanding is not much reflected in the existing literature. Several scholars point out that Western interpretations of mental illness and emotional distress differ significantly from those of other cultures (Ahearn, 2000; Burnett & Thompson, 2005; Gregg, 2005; Laungani,

2006; Li, 2012). However, a generalised comparison between cultures fails to encapsulate refugees' personal experiences within their cultural context, and insufficient phenomenological inquiry has been conducted in this regard.

The inner journeys of my participants are intricately entwined with their political environments. However, little scholarly attention has been paid to the interplay between psyche and politics, or the nexus between mind and power. Controversy often ensues when politics is intertwined with psychology – a sensitive juncture, particularly in endeavours to transcend labels. The question arises as to whether one's own ideological and political values can foster valid insight or engender bias and distortion.

Political psychologists, representing a relatively recent interdisciplinary approach, draw upon theories and methodologies from psychology, political science, anthropology, sociology, history, and philosophy (Jost & Sidanius, 2004). Andrew Samuels' work on the political psyche integrates Jungian, post-Jungian, and Freudian thought to bridge psychology and politics in clinical practice (Samuels, 2015). He underscores the potential reciprocal enrichment between these domains rather than reducing one to the other.

Existential perspectives, as explored by Langdridge (2012) and van Deurzen (2012), shed light on the role of politics and power within therapy and the existential dimensions of human existence. However, there remains a paucity of inquiry into political refugees' loss of psychological orientation amid political upheaval and the potential intertwining of subjective trauma with altruistic endeavours for the greater good.

In conclusion, further research is needed to explore the phenomenology of political refugees' experiences, prioritising an interior or first-person perspective over external analysis and considering their political and community identity. These will highlight the foundational role of resilience in the experience of political refugees.

The traumatic experiences of political refugees

> On the battlegrounds and on the cruel beds of torture, our nation's finest have wholeheartedly embraced the ideology of love for others. They have sacrificed life and limb to uphold their beliefs and principles. (Danesh, 2019: participant transcript)

This chapter continues my exploration of the lived experiences of nine Iranian political refugees who resettled in the United Kingdom. In my previous study, I discovered that my participants' perception of trauma is related to their ideological commitment and existential crisis (Danesh & Assiter, 2022).

I wanted to know how this group of political refugees encountered trauma. To this end, I engaged with them and their cultural milieu. My prime focus over four years was to observe and comprehend their actual way of life, and how they position themselves in the world. I set up informal interviews and in-depth conversations to comprehend the case of four political refugees whose trust I had gained. They were willing and open to explore their experiences and the changes they had made.

In June 2018 I attended the annual public gathering of tens of thousands of political refugees, along with more than six hundred distinguished Western leaders. Here I was able to contact them in their own environment. I subsequently participated in their diverse political activities, cultural events, and routine meetings. I cultivated a trusting relationship with them and gained access to their private spaces, which allowed me to observe their behaviours in private and in public.

What Did I Want to Find out?

How did this group of political refugees tackle persecution, imprisonment, and torture in their homeland, and the breakup of their families? What helped them to survive their losses and to adapt to extreme circumstances?

Who Were My Participants?

The participants in my study were ex-political prisoners whose family members and friends had been executed or severely tortured and who had devoted their entire lives to bringing freedom and democracy to their country of origin. For reasons of safety and confidentiality, I chose pseudonyms and disclosed no personal details.

Stories That Need to Be Told

Mother Mona

Mother Mona is a political refugee in her early eighties. She escaped from Iran about 20 years ago and now lives in London. When I met her amongst other political refugees on different occasions, I was impressed with her kindness to others. I first met her at the grand gathering of the Iranian opposition held in Paris in June 2018, attended by tens of thousands of Iranians in exile, together with hundreds of international dignitaries, senior former officials, lawmakers, and human rights activists. As I browsed the books on a large table I saw her, holding a bottle of water. She greeted me warmly, asking me where I was from. When I said London, she invited me to join her group. She said it was necessary to combat the Iranian regime's malign and terrorist activities outside the country as well as its human rights abuses at home. She gave me an informative analysis of the political and human rights situation in Iran. She asked about my work and my background, then introduced me to one of the senior members of the movement. This was my connection. On another occasion when I saw Mother Mona, she was encouraging other Iranians to be more active. I heard her tell the younger people:

> Look, you are studying here. Very good! But remember, Mother Mona is fighting to change the regime. My dream is to see all of you as my grandchildren in our homeland. I didn't come here to have a better life. In Iran, I couldn't be active. I couldn't bear the situation there. I wanted to be the voice of the people.

I stood nearby and listened to Mother Mona saying that she had come here not only to live but to fight for freedom. She told me, 'our people daily pay a huge price for their freedom. They have given over 100 thousands of their children.' Mother Mona's three sons were executed by the regime. She said, 'my children are our heroes, among the other martyrs.' She was willing to share her story and felt proud to be their mother:

> My children were politically active, they were university students. They were arrested for selling the movement's newspaper. They were tortured in prison. The regime didn't let me visit them. The religious guards attacked our house and took all the children's belongings. I tried to stop them – papers, books, everything. They hit me and threw me on the floor. I shouted, 'What's happened to my children?' They took me to the prison. I was there for a few months. I saw many young girls and boys arrested. Many of their parents were also arrested. The prison didn't have enough space, we were kept in a very small room, twenty people in a cell for four or five.
> After a few months, they released the parents and I came home. One night I heard something outside. When I went out, a car was leaving, and I saw the dead bodies of my three children. I knew this might happen. My children also knew the risk they took, and I didn't stop their activities. They were popular in our area. Their father died of a heart attack, and I brought them up. Neighbours supported me and we tried to bury them in the local cemetery, but the religious guards wouldn't allow it. We were not allowed to hold a funeral.

Mother Mona held out her hands firmly in front of her and said, 'I buried my three sons with my own hands at the end of my garden. I felt proud of them and relieved they are not being tortured anymore.'

When I apologised for reviving these memories, she said, *'No – everyone knows. I want everyone to know this is happening now. They are everyone's sons.'* She continued, *'We don't grieve for our martyrs, because they are alive. They are a source of inspiration. I am not alone. 120,000 of our children have been executed by this regime.'*

She was sharp and decisive: *'You must come and help us to change the regime. They are in a weak position.'*

When I asked Mother Mona whether she had nightmares or suffered, she replied, *'When I was in Iran I only wanted to come out and join the movement at liberty overseas, and carry on my activities. We don't have time to grieve over our martyrs. They are heroes. They sacrificed their lives for the freedom of their people.'*

When I mentioned trauma, she smiled, *'I will traumatise the supreme leader. Our main responsibility is to change the regime.'*

Mother Mona was full of life and vigour. *'You must come to our centre and eat our food. Sometimes I cook, I am a good cook.'* She smiled. She was also intellectually bright. It wasn't in her nature to complain.

Mother Mona is transforming the force of her grief into lifting her heart. She is living not from her ego, which would dramatise her trauma; she is living for the greater self of others, and for creating a better world.

She also told me, *'I had three children physically, but I feel I am the mother of thousands.'*

Mother Mona is a soldier on the battlefield. There is no time to dwell on one's personal wounds; one has to be alert and to act. She does not suppress her grief for her children. The strong emotion is there, but it is transmuted in quality; it sustains her purpose and her ideal. She does not feel alone but is carried along in a movement for freedom.

Through her commitment, Mother Mona gives birth to her children again. She sees her children amongst those who fight for freedom.

She was a farmer. She said, *'When you plant one healthy seed, you reap hundreds.'* Her children are planted in her garden.

Pooran

Pooran was a political prisoner, having been a student and become a political activist at the age of 17 when she joined a political movement. She is now a political refugee and writer on various topics related to the democratic version of Islam, the rights of women, and political prisoners. Her writing about political prisoners relates mainly to her experiences and observations during her twelve years in prison.

From my first meeting, I found her to be very serious in her commitment to freedom for her people. She was highly intellectual; she said that the purpose of her life was to work to change the current regime, and she was very optimistic.

She was tortured severely in prison, and because of that, she had difficulty walking. She said that from the first day of her imprisonment, she and her friends were resisting and they carried on their opposition towards the regime. They established a secret organisation in the prison and were able, via visiting relatives, to receive political information from outside and to pass information – such as the names of executed prisoners – to their political movement outside. She said that they kept busy, analysing the situation and finding ways of resistance collectively. They organised their time, using every opportunity to resist, to act collectively to find ways to escape and join the movement outside. She said that the Religious Guards in prison did everything to break them and separate them, but failed. Resistance was a common culture amongst political prisoners. She said that one of her best friends faced a death sentence. This friend wished to be executed in the town centre to be able to speak and encourage people to resist the regime. This she was able to do.

When I pointed out that she had written about other prisoners' resistance and bravery but less about herself, she said that she wasn't separate from them. She added that it was important for her to talk about their national heroes. When I asked what made her and others resist, she replied:

> When I decided to join the movement I was completely aware of the risk; it was a challenge for me to make my decision but I could not accept the violation in the name of Islam, the way women were treated. I made a conscious choice and I believed in what I was doing; I was ready to sacrifice my life. The situation in prison made us stronger; I carried our martyrs' wishes and their strength with me. I lived with their inspiration.

She said that when their situation changed, they had to make a fresh choice and most of them carried on their battle against the regime in prison.

One setback, she said, was that some prisoners betrayed them, recruited by the regime to report their activities to prison authorities. Despite all the challenges, however, after several months of planning, two of them were able to escape. This was a huge victory.

When I asked about her psychological state during her imprisonment, she looked into my eyes and stated firmly that it was difficult to hear or see her friends under torture:

> It was even more difficult to have to say a final goodbye to a friend who was going to be executed. But these things strengthened my

commitment. We used imprisonment as an opportunity to defeat the regime. I desired to keep my commitment until my last breath.

Pooran now is one of the senior members of the resistance movement.

Hassan

Hassan was a political prisoner for fifteen years. When the government turned hostile towards its political opponents and violated fundamental human rights, he and his wife supported the opposition movement. While not actively involved in opposing the new regime, they stood in solidarity with those who did.

Hassan lives in England as a political refugee and has authored a book detailing the history of the resistance movement following the 1979 revolution against the Iranian monarchy.

In Iran, he worked as a dentist, and just six months after their wedding, he and his wife were detained. Tragically, his wife was among the approximately 30,000 political prisoners executed in 1988 while they were still serving their sentences. Upon meeting him, I was struck by his kindness and serenity. These were his initial words:

I was not fortunate enough to be a martyr; rather, I see my duty as being the voice for political prisoners and martyrs whose courage and human dignity form integral parts of our nation's history, a history marked by resistance against Islamic Fundamentalism.

He expressed his sincere wish and life's purpose as attaining freedom for our people.

In prison, he became an active member of the secret resistance organisation. He described his time in prison as a *'University of Justice and Human Values.'* He explained how the prison environment deepened his comprehension of the regime and the values upheld by the resistance movement. He described how they were well organised and did everything in the prison collectively.

He said prisoners were systematically tortured. He himself was severely tortured for three days when prison guards found his drawing of two birds in flight.

He witnessed first-hand the resilience of his fellow countrymen enduring severe torture with bravery, sacrificing their lives for their beliefs and the love of their people. Reflecting on a pivotal moment, he recalled the decision he made: *'As long as there's blood in my veins, I will fight for the freedom of my people.'* He went on to explain that after that moment, he became a different person. All his fear, anxiety, and nightmares faded away, and he felt calm and relaxed. He said he was born again and realised he was no longer just for himself; he had a strong sense of having defeated the regime. Hassan devoted his entire life as an active member of the resistance movement to help his people to free Iran.

Ahmad

Ahmad is an electrical engineer. He was a political prisoner for seven days. He is a political refugee living in England. His wife and his sister were executed in 1988. His only daughter lives with her grandparents.

He was a well-known member of the resistance movement and was very popular in his hometown. He was arrested trying to escape from Iran, with a cyanide capsule in his cheek. He was severely tortured for seven days, at one of the Religious Guards bases in Tehran. The torturers were unable to secure any information from him and decided to send him to another Religious Guard centre. He was able to escape on the way there, though struggling to walk. He found a safe place to stay, and with the help of one of the resistance movement units he fled from Iran. He said that when he was surrounded by the Religious Guards, he had tried to use a cyanide capsule because he didn't want to be captured by them alive, but the capsule didn't work. He lost consciousness several times under torture.

Upon his arrest, he found himself perplexed as the cyanide capsule failed to function. As he recounted his experience, he detailed enduring severe torture from four torturers right from the beginning, likening it to being thrust onto a battlefield. Despite relentless efforts by the Religious Guards to break him, he steadfastly fought back, feeling as though he embodied the spirit of martyrs and the resistance movement, which served as his source of inspiration to continue resisting. When I inquired about his mental state, he responded that he felt a tremendous victory over the regime. He believed he had successfully overcome the regime's forces on two occasions.

When he arrived in Europe, his compatriots treated him as a hero, and from then on, he tirelessly worked within the resistance movement. When I asked him if he had suffered physical harm from the torture, he replied, '*I am grateful for bearing these scars on my body; they are a symbol of our victory over the regime.*'

My immersion in the political refugee community and discussion

To gain a deeper understanding, I immersed myself in the community of political refugees. I interacted with them in their environment and closely observed their lifestyle. My participants gave their time generously and welcomed my questions. They retained an excellent memory of past events and were able to recall each detail. Their life pattern remains very rich. It is beyond the scope of this project to describe every aspect of their lives, the commitment to liberate their homeland, and their psychological journey.

Over more than four decades, they have developed a unique culture and a language of resistance. Their way of life is notably distinct from that of mainstream society. I observed women's active leadership positions, well organised and with a natural discipline. There was a family relationship among tens of thousands of siblings. People were kind and supportive of each other. Honesty was embedded in their behaviour, with a readiness to make sacrifices. I was impressed with their adaptability to the difficulties they faced and the quality of their collective activity. I felt they were one body. Issues are resolved in favour of the community rather than for personal interest. They support each other's constant positive action. They are developing a language of responsibility and commitment; their hierarchy is built to a high level of trust and mutual respect. Their conversations are open; they are happy people, fulfilled in supporting each other.

I was particularly struck by their collective response to trauma. Their task on the battlefield deepens their worldview and philosophy of life. They told me the first conflict they faced was with their biological family after they dedicated their life to the cause. In *Existentialism is a Humanism*, Sartre tells the story of a pupil faced with the dilemma of caring for his mother or joining the French resistance. Sartre suggests that whatever choice the student makes, it is ultimately his responsibility as there is no pre-existing moral law to guide him. The emphasis is on the individual's freedom to choose and on the burden of responsibility that comes with it (Sartre, 2007). These people are able to prioritise joining the resistance movement over their biological families and to find their ideological family. Their culture of sacrifice is related to the highest level of spiritual achievement in Islam. I hold in my mind a comment one of them made: *'I don't want to die in my bed but to give my life on the battlefield.'*

Their language is full of the proud use of the word *'martyrs.'* I heard many of them say the martyrs remain alive within them, *'We continue our martyrs' wishes.' 'The blood of our martyrs guarantees our victory.'*

One of my challenges arose when I initially assumed that the individuals might disassociate themselves from their traumatic experiences. However, as I immersed myself more in their environment and way of life, this presumption gradually faded. I came to realise that their ultimate goal of a free Iran was central to their existence, motivating them to harness their traumatic experiences as catalysts for regime change. This transformation was not just individual but collective; they saw themselves not as individuals, but as soldiers fighting on the battlefield for their cause.

Their sacrifice of self for others provided the main texture of meaning to their lives. I was impressed by their kindness and consideration, their philosophical intelligence. Their empathic level and social awareness bore the fruit of interior discipline. Their cause is supported globally by over four thousand members of parliaments, seventy Nobel Prize winners, and one hundred and twenty-five ex-prime ministers and presidents. Despite repression, they are supported by many Iranians in exodus as well as within the country; they are also criticised by some groups of Iranians. Most of these are influenced by over seven hundred books and massive media programmes of propaganda the regime has published against them for over forty years.

With over a hundred thousand of their supporters executed over four decades, they kept their commitment unwavering and remained consistent to equality, individual rights and freedom, and the situation for women. Control over women's identities, sexuality, and labour has been central to reinforcing state power. The regime's portrayal of Islamised women as a symbol of Islam and de-Westernisation draws upon gender to define and redefine its own domestic and global objectives. Therefore, defending women's rights became a central project for those who wanted to bring democracy and equality to Iran (Assiter & Danesh, 2022).

Although I think of them as individuals, they moved from their personal space to join with others in fellowship. In their commitment and the choices they made, they exemplify 'self for others.' They crossed the boundaries which separate people and became 'with others and for others.' This became their life's purpose. They all believed that without helping other people, life would be meaningless.

I found that the four participants displayed a remarkable ability to cope with severe traumatic events. They attributed this resilience to their deep commitment to political causes and their active engagement in associated activities. Their experiences of trauma were directly linked to their involvement in political struggles. Essentially, their source of the existential threat wasn't loss, torture, or death threats; instead, it stemmed from feeling inadequate in fulfilling their responsibilities within their political endeavours. Trauma, a key focus of this discussion, is recognised as a complex and multifaceted issue. Understanding it requires a nuanced approach that considers various aspects including psychological, social, neurological, philosophical, economic, cultural, sociological, political, and spiritual dimensions. Traditional therapeutic methods may fall short of providing comprehensive and personalised solutions to address the diverse aspects of trauma. This chapter proposes an existential-phenomenological approach, which goes beyond conventional medical frameworks, to thoroughly examine the multifaceted nature of trauma in the context of political refuge.

Conclusion

This group of political refugees are individuals who are part of a resistance movement. They have directly challenged the authority of the incumbent government, and upon leaving their homeland, continue to overcome tangible threats to their lives. These refugees have made a conscious decision to depart their country based on sound judgement. By immersing in the culture and lifestyle of this group of political refugees, four main themes have been discerned: philosophy of life and belief system; community-oriented lifestyle; selflessness; and resilience in overcoming obstacles.

Following universal values, they believe that the fundamental aim of a political refugee is to engage in persistent opposition against the despotic ruler of their nation, exhibiting unwavering determination until their last breath. They demonstrate a remarkable level of endurance and resilience, finding contentment with meagre sustenance and refraining from voicing grievances. Their primary objective is to dismantle the oppressive regime enforced by governing authorities, particularly evident within the context of Iran. Their homeland holds profound significance, serving as both their place of origin and the central focus of their struggle. Possessing formidable mental fortitude, they are prepared to undertake traumatic challenges, demonstrating readiness to confront obstacles head-on. Metaphorically depicted as a potent force for change, political refugees display a readiness to confront any challenge, unimpeded by fear of mortality.

The chapter explores the impact of politics and power on therapy and the existential aspects of human existence. However, there is a lack of research on how political refugees experience psychological disorientation amidst political upheaval and how their trauma may connect to their altruistic actions for the greater good.

Trauma is a complex and multifaceted issue that needs a comprehensive understanding. This includes psychological, social, neurological, philosophical, economic, cultural, sociological, political, and spiritual dimensions. Traditional therapeutic methods have limitations in addressing the various aspects of trauma effectively. This chapter proposes an existential-phenomenological approach, going beyond the medical model, to better explore trauma's complexity, especially within the context of political refuge.

This group of political refugees exhibit resilience in overcoming trauma, perceiving themselves as frontline soldiers in the battle to liberate their homeland; this is their raison d'être. They have risen above the trauma they have endured. Their life experiences guide us to a landscape of human capabilities confronting existential crisis.

References

Ahearn, F. L. (Ed.). (2000). *Psychosocial Wellness of Refugees: Issues in Qualitative and Quantitative Research*. Berghahn Books.

Aidani, M. (2007). *Displaced narratives of Iranian migrants and refugees: Constructions of self and the struggle for representation* (Thesis). Faculty of Arts, Education and Human Development School of Psychology at the Victoria University.

Alayarian, A. (Ed.). (2007). *Resilience, Suffering and Creativity: The Work of the Refugee Therapy Centre*. Karnac Books. https://doi.org/10.4324/9780429479595

Bemak, F., Chung, R. C. Y., & Pedersen, P. (2003). *Counseling Refugees: A Psychosocial Approach to Innovative Multicultural Interventions*. Greenwood Publishing Group.

Bhugra, D., Craig, T., & Bhui, K. (Eds.). (2010). *Mental Health of Refugees and Asylum Seekers*. Oxford University Press. https://doi.org/10.1093/med/9780199557226.001.0001

Blackwell, D. (2005). *Counselling and Psychotherapy With Refugees*. Jessica Kingsley Publishers.

Burnett, A., & Thompson, K. (2005). Enhancing the psychological well-being of asylum seekers and refugees. In K. H. Barrett & W.H. George (Eds.), *Race, Culture, Psychology & Law* (pp. 205–224). Sage. https://doi.org/10.4135/9781452233536

Colin, L. (2011). *The Handbook of Transcultural Counselling and Psychotherapy*. Open University Press.

Dana, R. H. (2000). *Handbook of Cross-Cultural and Multicultural Personality Assessment*. Routledge. https://doi.org/10.4324/9781410602374

Danesh, A. 2019. *Exploring Iranian political refugees' experiences in Britain – Phoenix rises from the ashes – An existential-phenomenological study* (Thesis). Middlesex University/New School of Psychotherapy and Counselling (NSPC) Psychology.

Danesh, A., & Assiter, A. (2022). *Political Refugees, a New Perspective*. Rowman & Littlefield.

Elik, S. (2012). *Iran–Turkey Relations, 1979–2011: Conceptualising the Dynamics of Politics, Religion and Security in Middle-Power State*. Routledge. https://doi.org/10.4324/9780203803028

Espin, O. M. (1999). *Women Crossing Boundaries: A Psychology of Immigration and Transformations of Sexuality*. Routledge. https://doi.org/10.4324/9780203905241

Eyber, C., & Ager, A. (2002). Conselho: Psychological healing in displaced communities in Angola. *Lancet, 360*(9336), 871. https://doi.org/10.1016/S0140-6736(02)09961-0

Fiddian-Qasmiyeh, E., Loescher, G., & Long, K. (Eds.). (2014). *The Oxford Handbook of Refugee and Forced Migration Studies*. Oxford University Press. https://doi.org/10.1093/oxfordhb/9780199652433.001.0001

Frankl, V. E. (2004). *Man's Search for Meaning*. Ebury (Original work published 1946).

Frelick, B. (1988). *World Refugee Survey*. American Council for Nationalities Services.

Gregg, G. S. (2005). *The Middle East: A Cultural Psychology*. Oxford University Press. https://doi.org/10.1093/oso/9780195171990.001.0001

Herman, J. L. (1992). *Trauma and Recovery*. Basic Books.

Hinton, D., & Lewis-Fernández, R. (2011). The cross-cultural validity of posttraumatic stress disorder: Implications for DSM-5. *Depression and Anxiety, 28*(9), 783–801. https://doi.org/10.1002/da.20753

Hollifield, M., Warner, T., Lian, N., Krakow, B., Jenkins, J., Kesler, J., Stevenson, J., & Westermeyer, J. (2002). Measuring trauma and health status in refugees: A critical review. *The Journal of the American Medical Association, 288*, 611–621. https://psycnet.apa.org/doi/10.1001/jama.288.5.611

Jacobsen, B. (2006). The life crisis in an existential perspective: Can trauma and crisis be seen as an aid in personal development? *Existential Analysis, 17*(1), 39–54.

Joseph, S., & Linley, P. A. (2005). Positive adjustment to threatening events: An organismic valuing theory of growth through adversity. *Review of General Psychology, 9*, 262–280. doi:10.1037/1089-2680.9.3.262

Jost, J. T., & Sidanius, J. (2004). *Political Psychology: Key Readings*. Psychology Press. https://doi.org/10.4324/9780203505984

Langdridge, D. (2012). *Existential Counselling and Psychotherapy*. Sage.

Laungani, P. D. (2006). *Understanding Cross-Cultural Psychology: Eastern and Western Perspectives*. Sage.

Li, J. (2012). *Cultural Foundations of Learning: East and West*. Cambridge University Press.

Linesch, D. G. (Ed.). (2013). *Art Therapy With Families in Crisis: Overcoming Resistance Through Nonverbal Expression*. Routledge. https://doi.org/10.4324/9780203776827

Mandela, N. R. (2011). *Nelson Mandela by Himself: The Authorised Book of Quotations*. Pan Macmillan.

Montgomery, E. (1998). *Refugee Children From the Middle East*. Scandinavian University Press.

Morrice, L. (2011). *Being a Refugee: Learning and Identity: A Longitudinal Study of Refugees in the UK*. Trentham Books.

Overland, G., Guribye, E., & Lie, B. (2014). *Nordic Work With Traumatised Refugees: Do We Really Care*. Cambridge Scholars Publishing.

Papadopoulos, R. K. (Ed.). (2002). *Therapeutic Care for Refugees: No Place Like Home*. Carnac Books. https://doi.org/10.4324/9780429483875

Park, C. L., Cohen, L. H., & Murch, R. (1996). Assessment and prediction of stress-related growth. *Journal of Personality, 64*(1), 71–105. https://psycnet.apa.org/doi/10.1111/j.1467-6494.1996.tb00815.x

Pupavac, V. (2004). Psychosocial interventions and the demoralization of humanitarianism. *Journal of Biosocial Science, 36*(4), 491–504. https://doi.org/10.1017/S0021932004006613

Reyes, G., & Jacobs, G. A. (2006). *Handbook of International Disaster Psychology: Refugee Mental Health*. Greenwood Publishing Group.

Sadavoy, J. (1997). Survivors: A review of the late-life effects of prior psychological trauma. *American Journal of Geriatric Psychology, 5*(4), 287–301. https://doi.org /10.1097/00019442-199700540-00004

Samuels, A. (2015). *A New Therapy for Politics*. Karnac Books. https://doi.org/10 .4324/9780429471407

Sartre, J.-P. (2007). *Existentialism Is a Humanism*. Yale University Press. https://doi .org/10.2307/j.ctv15vwkgx

Splevins, K. A., et al. (2010). Vicarious posttraumatic growth among interpreters. *Qualitative Health Research, 20*(12), 1705–1716. https://doi.org/10.1177 /1049732310377457

Sue, D. (2015). *Counseling the Culturally Diverse: Theory and Practice*. Wiley.

Summerfield, D. (1999). A critique of seven assumptions behind psychological trauma programmes in war-affected areas. *Social Science & Medicine, 48*(10), 1449–1462.
https://doi.org/10.1016/S0277-9536(98)00450-X

Summerfield, D. (2008). How scientifically valid is the knowledge base of global mental health? *British Medical Journal, 446*, 992–994. https://doi.org/10.1136/ bmj.39513.441030.AD

Tedeschi, R. G., & Calhoun, L. G. (2004). Posttraumatic growth: Conceptual foundations and empirical evidence. *Psychological Inquiry, 15*(1), 1–18. http:// www.jstor.org/stable/20447194.

van der Veer, G. (1998). *Counselling and Therapy With Refugees and Victims of Trauma: Psychological Problems of Victims of War, Torture and Repression*. Wiley.

van Deurzen, E. (1997). *Everyday Mysteries: Existential Dimensions of Psychotherapy*. Routledge.

van Deurzen, E. (2012). *Existential Counselling & Psychotherapy in Practice* (3rd ed.). Sage.

Vera, E. (2012). *The Oxford Handbook of Prevention in Counseling Psychology*. Oxford University Press. https://doi.org/10.1093/oxfordhb/9780195396423.001 .0001

Wilson, J. P., & Drozdek, B. (Eds.). (2004). *Broken Spirits: The Treatment of Traumatized Asylum Seekers, Refugees and War and Torture Victims*. Routledge. https://doi.org/10.4324/9780203310540

Yalom, I. D. (1980). *Existential Psychotherapy*. Basic Books.

Chapter 10

The Impact of Active Military Service on Intimate Relationships: Trauma, Breakdown, and Breakthrough

Susan Iacovou

Introduction

In the spring of 1982, economic and political woes facing General Galtieri, the leader of the military junta in Argentina, and Margaret Thatcher, the Prime Minister of the UK, set the scene for the 10-week-long Falkland Islands conflict that would cost the lives of 655 Argentinian and 255 British servicemen along with three Falkland Islanders. This international conflict, taking place more than four decades ago, and over 8000 miles away from the United Kingdom, provides a context for the research described in this chapter.

Royal Navy servicemen returned from the Falklands War to a very different social, medical, and military environment than exists today. The concept of PTSD was a relatively new one – having been defined within the DSM-3 (American Psychological Association [APA], 2015) just two years earlier. The 'stiff upper lip' was still a key element of British cultural identity, and this was reflected in societal and military settings that remained uncomfortable with the open venting of feelings. The idea that human beings could be 'traumatised' by events in which they perceived their lives to be at risk was neither widely accepted nor understood in the medical profession, and certainly wasn't part of common cultural understanding.

Servicemen returning from the Falklands War, therefore, had no way to explain or make sense of the impact active service had upon their way of being in the world. They returned to a society that was largely oblivious to the psychological impact of combat. What's more, they returned to families and to partners who neither expected, nor knew how to respond to, the changes they saw in their sons/husbands/boyfriends.

The research described below explores if, and how, participants' ways of making sense of life, and their values, beliefs, and behaviours, are changed by their experiences of active service, and if, or how, these changes affect their relationships.

DOI: 10.4324/9781003493860-14

Literature review

This is necessarily a brief literature review containing the main headlines from the literature relevant to the research described in this chapter.

The Psychological Impact of War on Combatants

Over the years there have been a range of terms used to describe the psychological impact of war on combatants, such as 'Swiss disease' (Jones, 1995), the German 'heimweh' (homesickness), the Spanish 'estar roto' meaning 'to be broken' (Bentley, 1991), and the French 'vent du boulet' syndrome (Crocq & Crocq, 2000). As well as becoming part of common parlance, the phenomenon has always attracted attention from the medical profession. Eighteenth-century psychiatrist Pinel (1745–1826) coined the term 'cardiorespiratory neurosis' to describe the psychological symptoms he observed. During the American Civil War, physician Dr J. M. Da Costa (1871) described something that sounds very like what we now call PTSD, which he called 'irritable heart.' In 1914, right at the start of WWI, reports started to emerge of 'battle hypnosis' (Milian, 1915), something that, by the end of the war, would be described as 'shell shock' (Ganesh, 2015). And researchers studying psychiatric casualties in allied troops in WWII variously described the symptoms they observed as 'operational fatigue' (Grinker et al., 1946), 'traumatic war neurosis' (Kardiner & Spiegel, 1947), and 'combat exhaustion' (Swan, 1949).

From the early 1960s, a growing body of research emerged focusing on American veterans of the Vietnam War. It quickly became clear that delayed and chronic posttraumatic symptoms affected many veterans (Kulka et al., 1990), and political pressure to classify and treat the symptoms of the disorder led directly to the adoption of the current term 'Posttraumatic Stress Disorder' (PTSD) and its incorporation into the third edition of the *Diagnostic and Statistical Manual of Mental Disorders* (DSM-3) (APA, 2015).

The Psychological Impact of War on Veterans on the Falklands War

Following its incorporation in the DSM-3 (APA, 2015), there was a great deal of research into the phenomenon of PTSD in ex-servicemen from a wide range of wars including the Portuguese Colonial Wars (Ferrajão & Oliveira, 2015) and the Balkan Wars (Hasanović & Pajević, 2010). However, very little research exists into PTSD in veterans of the Falklands War.

Jones and Lovett (1987), in a small study of Welsh veterans of the war, found that acute psychiatric reactions to the war were rare and reported only three cases of what they called delayed reaction. Other authors have suggested, however, that the Falklands War was disproportionately traumatic (Quiroga & Seear, 2009). A study by O'Brien and Hughes (1991) included 64 Falklands War army veterans; half of the group reported at least some symptoms of PTSD, and 22% met the diagnostic criteria for PTSD. And Ørner et al. (1992) studied 53 Falklands War veterans and found that 32 of them met the diagnostic criteria for PTSD. While these studies involve small sample sizes, it is clear that the notion of the war being a 'psychiatric success' (Jones, 1995) is worthy of re-examination.

The Impact of Active Service on Intimate Relationships

Military life places unique demands on the intimate relationships of military personnel (Greenberg et al., 2011; Schumm et al., 2012). Much of the research to date focuses on the impact of relocation/separation on military relationships (McLeland et al., 2008; Ribeiro et al., 2023) or on the impact of military life on partners left at home (Ponder, 2021).

There is very little research that focuses on the impact of military life on relationships from the military person's perspective. Ruger et al. (2002), looking at marital duration in 3800 male veterans from WWII, the Korean War, and the Vietnam War, found that combat increased the rate of marriages ending by over 60%. A large-scale study by Hoge et al. (2006) collated survey responses from 25,000 soldiers who had experienced combat. Deployment to Iraq was associated with reduced marital satisfaction and increases in intentions to divorce and with Intimate Partner Violence (IPV). And a systematic review of 27 studies by Senior et al. (2023) in the US, UK, and Australia reported that every study found active service had a negative impact on the intimate relationships of military personnel.

Interestingly, research by Newby et al. (2005) on US army personnel sent to Bosnia indicated that some married personnel reported improvements and others reported deterioration in their marital relationship post-deployment. The 951 participants in this study were on a peace-keeping mission, e.g. they did not see combat. Despite this, Newby et al.'s (2005) research is an important reminder of the growing body of research that indicates that, in addition to negative consequences, some military personnel report positive outcomes from their experiences of deployment and war (Affect & Tennen, 1996; Tsai et al., 2015). This may offer support for Nietzsche's (1888/2012: 3) overused yet valid aphorism "what does not kill me, strengthens me," pointing us to the opportunities offered by adversity. The phenomenon Nietzsche described is today commonly termed post-traumatic growth (Tedeschi & Calhoun, 1996; Tedeschi et al., 2018). A posttraumatic growth model developed by Tedeschi and Calhoun (1996) forms the basis of treatment programmes that challenge the traditional medical model of trauma with its focus on symptom amelioration and are delivered instead by 'expert companions' (Tedeschi, 2023).

Tsai et al.'s (2015) study of 3157 US veterans looked at posttraumatic growth over a two-year period and found that it was prevalent – 50.1% of all veterans and 72% of veterans who screened positively for PTSD had at least moderate levels of posttraumatic growth. Perhaps it is not surprising that those who had experienced PTSD had the highest level of posttraumatic growth given the finding that PTSD, and in particular its shattering of worldviews, is what provides the opportunity for change and growth (Tedeschi & Moore, 2020).

One study that examined posttraumatic growth in military couples (Wick & Nelson Goff, 2014) found that those with high posttraumatic symptoms and low relationship satisfaction reported little or no posttraumatic growth, while those with low levels of posttraumatic symptoms and high levels of relationship satisfaction were able to recognise opportunities for growth in their traumatic experiences.

The Impact of PTSD on Intimate Relationships

Some research supports the hypothesis that any association between combat and relationship outcomes is mediated by PTSD or by symptoms of trauma exposure (Goff et al., 2007). For example, Renshaw et al. (2009) found that PTSD and not combat exposure was directly associated with marital satisfaction in their sample of National Guard soldiers returning from Iraq.

A body of research in this area suggests that combat veterans with PTSD, from a wide variety of wars, are particularly at risk for serious relationship issues (Cook et al., 2004; Waysman et al., 1993). Research by Riggs et al. (1998) looked at the relationships of 50 Vietnam veterans and their partners and found that 70% of veterans with PTSD and their partners reported clinically significant levels of relationship distress compared to 30% of veterans without PTSD and their partners. Studies involving large cross-sectional analyses of veterans returning from the wars in Iraq and Afghanistan have added to this research base, concluding that PTSD symptoms are associated with lower relationship satisfaction (Ponder, 2021; Wick & Nelson Goff, 2014). The emotional numbing symptoms associated with PTSD have been found to have the largest negative impact on relationship satisfaction (Campbell & Renshaw, 2018).

Comorbid Symptoms of Active Service and/or Trauma/PTSD

There are a number of comorbid effects or symptoms of Active Service and/or of trauma to acknowledge when seeking to understand the impact of such service on intimate relationships. For example, research has shown that alcohol misuse is more prevalent in post-deployment armed forces compared with the general population (Fear et al., 2010; Ramchand et al., 2011). And anger is widely recognised as an issue for military personnel who have experienced active service (Miller, 2019). The consequences of increased anger are also clear (Forbes et al., 2023) and found to be associated with impairments in mental health, physical health, and psychosocial functioning. The comorbidity of anger with PTSD has been identified in research both outside of the military setting (Olatunji et al., 2010) and within that setting (Forbes et al., 2023).

In the context of intimate relationships in particular, studies in the US have found a link between combat exposure and IPV amongst veterans of the Vietnam War (Beckham et al., 1998; Calvert & Hutchinson, 1990). And since then, a systematic review by Cowlishaw et al. (2022) exposed rates of 31.8% for recent IPV and 21% for victimisation behaviours in veteran personnel from a range of eras and conflicts.

A systematic review of domestic violence amongst military populations by Trevillion et al. (2015) found that 27.5% of military personnel with PTSD had perpetuated physical violence against a partner in the last year. The figure for psychological violence in the last year was a staggering 91%. These studies are of direct relevance to the question of the impact of active service on military relationships, as they suggest that PTSD in military personnel is associated with violent behaviour towards intimate partners.

A great deal of the research covered so far indicates that it is not combat itself, but rather PTSD or trauma-related symptoms, that impact on the relationships of military personnel. Therefore, this section concludes with a review of what the existential/phenomenological literature adds to our understanding of PTSD.

Existential/Phenomenological Conceptualisations of PTSD

Perhaps it is unsurprising, given the existential world's resistance to typologies, that there is only one explicit model of PTSD from an existential perspective. Harmand et al. (1993: 281) examined PTSD in Vietnam combat veterans. They describe the shock of war as "an event which, by its very nature, constitutes an exceptional form of reality (...) existence in its most severe form."

While there are no other explicit and defined existential models of trauma, the ways in which existential ideas and philosophies can be applied to the concept of PTSD are evident in some existential texts. For example, Oakley (2009) draws on Heidegger (1927/2010) when she describes PTSD as being confronted with wholly unfamiliar ways of being-in-the-world. Stolorow (2015) builds on Jacobsen's (2006) suggestion that trauma is best understood as an existential crisis shattering our previously held feelings of safety in the world and making us face up to our finitude. And Ioannou (2023) posits that trauma is a fundamental existential experience involving disrupted temporality, the irreversibility of time, a shattering loss of innocence, and loss of autonomy.

Very few research papers explore the use of existential concepts of PTSD in a military setting. A PhD dissertation by Grubbs (2013) evaluated the role of existential wellbeing in the occurrence of PTSD in nearly 350 US Air Force combat veterans and found that low levels of existential wellbeing significantly predicted PTSD. And Russian psychologist Magomed-Eminov (1997), researching Soviet veterans, drew on Frankl's (1978) logotherapy to define PTSD from an existential perspective as a loss of meaning.

A gap in the literature

Prior to the research described in this chapter, there was little that examined the impact of active service on the intimate relationships of servicemen and even less that examined the impact on ex-service personnel. In addition, there was almost no research carried out with veterans of the Falklands war and almost no existential-phenomenological counselling psychology research on the impact of active service on relationships or indeed on the impact of PTSD on relationships.

Methodology

Participants

All the participants came from a Royal Naval background (including the Royal Marines), had experience of active service during the Falklands War of 1982, and had at least one intimate relationship during or after their active service. The participants were aged between 19 and 39 when they served in the Falklands, and all but two of them (Tom and Arthur) were ship based throughout the conflict, with one being land based as a marine and the other being a medic and therefore being both ship and land based. Four of the participants were married at this point (one newly married, e.g. less than 6 months before the conflict started), one was engaged to be married, two had casual girlfriends, and two were single (see Table 10.1).

The relationship history of the participants at the time of interview was varied. Two participants (Tom and John) had been married only once and remained married. Two participants had been married and divorced once and had since remarried (James and Ron). Both were married to their second wives at the time of interview.

Table 10.1 Participant Demographics

Participant	Age now	Age joined Navy	Age during active service	Relationship status during active service
James	51	16	19	Casual girlfriend
George	53	16	21	Casual girlfriend
Tom	63	24	28	Married
Greg	51	16	19	Newly married
Paul	55	16	23	Married
Dennis	55	16	19	Single
Arthur	51	19	22	Engaged
Ron	71	18	39	Married
John	52	17	19	Single

Five of the participants – George, Greg, Paul, Dennis, and Arthur – had been married and divorced twice at time of interview. George and Paul were married for the third time, and Greg, Denis, and Arthur were in long-term relationships when they took part in the research.

Research method

Data was gathered using semi-structured interviews, and Interpretative Phenomenological Analysis (IPA) (Smith et al., 2009) was selected for data analysis. Following the steps required by IPA, an iterative and hermeneutic process produced 3 meta-themes and 10 themes as outlined in the analysis and findings below.

Analysis and findings

On joining the Navy, these participants embarked on a literal, temporal, and a psychological journey. It is perhaps unsurprising, therefore, that they described their experiences, and the impact of those experiences on their intimate relationships, in terms of their personal psychological journey. Three meta-themes and 10 themes of core relevance to the research question are highlighted in Table 10.2 and together tell the story of this journey over time – during active service, after active service, and now (e.g. at the point in time at which the research interview took place).

Figure 10.1 further illustrates this psychological journey. Most of the participants stopped at all/most of the destinations on this journey. The length of time spent by each of them at each spot varied; for many, the journey was frozen in time at particular spots for many years, even decades.

Table 10.2 Final Meta-Themes and Themes

Active Service	After Active Service	Now
EXISTENTIAL CONFRONTATIONS	**CHANGING**	**GROWTH AND RESILIENCE**
1 Existential confrontations	2 Changing self 3 Changing priorities 4 Overwhelming emotions 5 Alienation 6 Withdrawal and isolation 7 Going to a dark place 8. Breaking down	9 Sharing 10.Hope for the future

Exploring the psychological journey

Combat forced participants to confront the existential givens of death, freedom and limitations, meaninglessness, and absurdity (Theme 1). All of the participants described a confrontation with one or more of these 'ultimate concerns' (Yalom, 1980). Even 33 years after the events, the shock and disbelief were conveyed by the tone and body language of the participants along with their words.

> Greg: *It....yeah...it...it...it...they're there and then they're not there. And what's really upsetting about the way that people...obviously I know people die and people pass away...with modern warfare, it's so quick (mm) it...it...it's just bang...gone...*

These confrontations led them to question their existing view of the world and their place within it, leading to a life-opening opportunity (Jacobsen, 2006).

All the participants found that exposure to their existential situation changed them and the way they related to others (Theme 2).

> George: *The impact on my relationship, even though I started it in 82.... just devastating. I...I couldn....as if I couldn't cope with a close emotional bond with anybody, anymore.....But to go from being a loving boyfriend, fiancé, eh, to suddenly, changing to a person that I couldn't even love or respect myself, or even like, and to put that out on to another person, that's totally devastating and totally destroying to see that actually.*

Active service also changed participants' priorities and goals in life, particularly as far as intimate relationships were concerned (Theme 3) with a

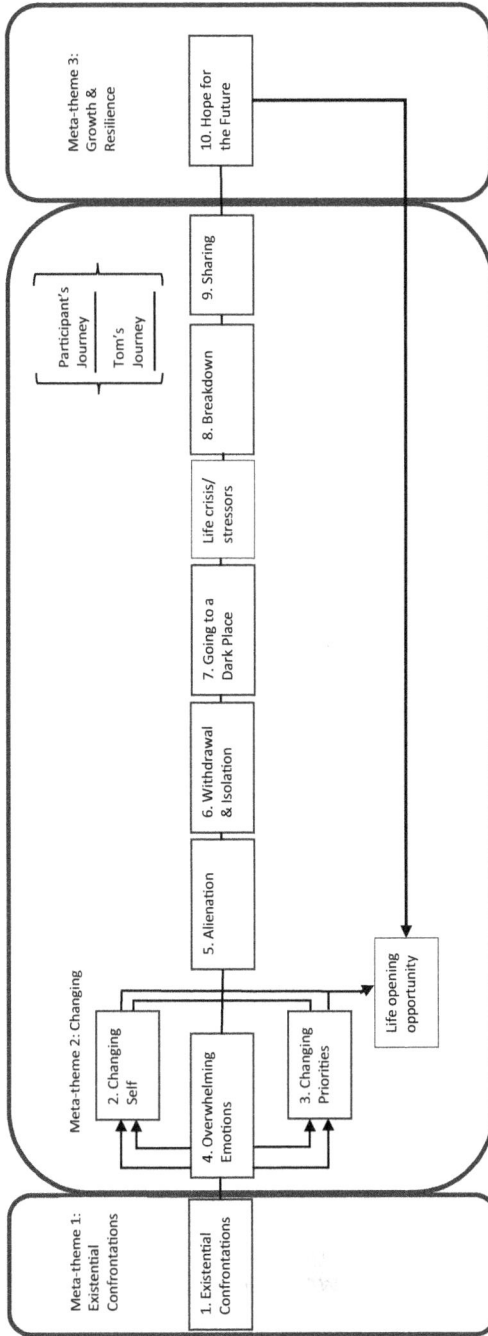

Figure 10.1 Destinations on a journey.

shift from freedom and adventure to relationship and children. Those who weren't in a relationship sought one out, many of them getting married quickly afterwards.

> James: *Em, it (active service) probably accelerated it quicker in terms of, having been close to death, wanting to get married, wanting a family and everything else. Eh, probably accelerated, eh, my thinking towards 'that's the next big thing I need to do' if you like, if there's a box in life I need to tick, I need to do this, and now, as soon as I can.*

Children then followed quickly for three of the participants. Those who were already married sought confirmation that they were cared for (in Greg's case) or looked forward to re-connecting with their wife (Ron), or to strengthening their relationship through prioritising the important things in life (Tom).

The existential crisis provoked by their experiences of combat, the resulting need to re-evaluate everything believed about the world and themselves, combined with their return from active service, provoked difficult and, for everyone except Tom, overwhelming emotions (Theme 4) that they felt ill-equipped to manage or understand. In response, most of the participants attempted to suppress, deny, or ignore these emotions.

For many of them, the predominant emotion was shame, emanating from a sense of failure and a conviction that they had let their colleagues down in some way. Perhaps it is unsurprising, therefore, given the research evidence of an intimate link between shame and anger (Elison et al., 2014; Hejdenburg & Andrews, 2011), that six of the participants in this research (James, Greg, George, Paul, Arthur, and John) experienced explosive and destructive anger and rage on their return from combat. It was variously described as something that would *'flash'* (Greg), *'smash'* (John), *'explode'* (George), *'erupt'* (James), and send them *'up the wall'* (Arthur) or *'storming out'* (Paul). This inevitably had a devastating effect on their relationships with their partners.

Convinced that no one would understand their experiences, and feeling different from those around them, they (with the exception of Tom and Dennis) experienced a sense of estrangement and alienation from friends, family, and partners (Theme 5). George describes feeling disassociated and absent when his girlfriend hugged him.

> George: *Then obviously my girlfriend got me in a hug but....I couldn't hug them back. I didn't feel it...not when I touched them, you know, I did put my arms....put my arms round them...but I didn't feel anything, as if I wasn't there.*

Feeling increasingly alienated and unable to manage or share the emotions provoked by their experiences, participants withdrew into themselves and retreated from their partners and the wider social world (Theme 6). They seemed to be reflecting on an alienation from their 'real selves,' a sense of 'otherness' or lack of recognition of who they were at that time that resulted in them making decisions about relationships, marriage, and children, when they were somehow not themselves or not in a fit state to make such life-changing choices.

Greg: *Em, I was different. Em, cause I'd done something, seen things, experienced things…that not many people around me had experienced.*

Participants responded to increasing feelings of alienation by withdrawing into themselves, retreating from their partners, and choosing to spend time alone and/or away from home. This withdrawal was described as a way of shutting themselves down, protecting themselves and their partners from pain.

Arthur: *I've shut people away. I don't like people getting close to me. I put a wall around me. I feel…safe. I feel….protected from people trying to get too close to me, so ultimately I know I'm not going to disappoint them, or hurt them, if something happens to me.*

After many years trying to hide the impact of active service, struggling to carry on their lives as normal, participants found themselves in a 'dark place' (Theme 7) dominated by re-experiencing the traumatic events in flashbacks and nightmares, excessive drinking, picking fights, and/or verbal or physical abuse of their partners. For many of the participants and their partners, these were times of desperation and deep despair.

George: *I…I just felt empty…I felt empty inside as if…and there was just blackness in there. I couldn't see the world like I had seen it before. I couldn't see the sunshine.*

Eventually, another trauma or series of stressful life events occurring between six and 33 years after active service took participants beyond the limits of their resilience and into breakdown (only Tom, Dennis, and John were exceptions).

George: *I was over at the local pub by the factory having a quiet drink…. and I just started crying. I just felt so drained, physically and emotionally and I started shaking.....I literally broke down, literally couldn't function anymore.*

Five of the participants were diagnosed with PTSD (APA, 2022):

Greg: *When I was diagnosed with PTSD in 2005/6 em, I started to have more issues with it. And I think that the third main relationship that broke down was because she just could not deal with that level of emotion, em, guilt, anger. Everything, for three or four years, from 2006 to when we broke up was all Falklands associated.*

Breakdown and/or diagnosis of PTSD created some difficulties for the participants, precipitating as it did initially further feelings of isolation, increased withdrawal, and further disruption of communication and connection between couples. However, for some participants the breaking down/diagnosis was a turning point in their relationships with their partners, offering an opportunity for posttraumatic growth (Tedeschi & Calhoun, 1995) and resilience (themes 9 and 10).

Sharing their thoughts and feelings with their partners seems to have been a life- and relationship-changing experience for most of the participants. As Greg vividly described, it was a coming out of sorts.

Greg: *I liken it to a gay man confessing his, em, his homosexuality. It was like, you know what? I went through the Falklands. This is who I am. This is what I did. This is what it meant to me.*

Tom's Story – The Roots of Resilience

One participant – Tom – reported a significantly different journey, and this is also illustrated in Figure 10.1. Like the others, his experiences of active service resulted in a sudden confrontation with existential givens, and this confrontation changed him and his priorities. However, he didn't experience symptoms of trauma. He reported positive changes in himself following his experience of active service, and his narrative offered evidence of resilience along with posttraumatic growth (Tsai et al., 2015).

Discussion

The findings of this study are discussed below, following the themes highlighted in the order in which they appeared in the psychological journey of the participants. Tom's psychological journey is again described separately.

Active Service Confronts Combatants with Existential Realities (Theme 1)

Even thirty-three years after the Falklands War, the shock and disbelief provoked by being "propelled into a confrontation with one's existential situation in the world" (Yalom, 1980: 67) was conveyed by the reports of the participants. While the DSM-5 (APA, 2022: 178) describes the circumstances necessary to create trauma, this current research suggests that in order for these circumstances to actually be traumatic, they must provoke in the individual a confrontation with existential givens. This theme provides support for the proposition that traumatic experiences disrupt or fracture our worldview (Spinelli, 2005), making us question all that we previously took for granted and confronting us with totally unfamiliar ways of being in the world (Heidegger, 1927/2010; Oakley, 2009). As Tedeschi et al. (2020: 22) state: "It's not so much the event itself that defines trauma, but how it changes one's core beliefs; those ways of thinking about how the world should work and what our lives are supposed to look."

Combat seems to have thrust the participants into the state of being-towards-death (Heidegger, 1927/2010) with its concomitant realisations that they were alone in the world, unable to hide or run away from death. This confrontation with death took then to a place where their worldviews and the meanings and values from which they were constructed appeared to no longer apply, echoing Oakley's (2009) and Greening's (1971) suggestions that trauma places us in a wholly unfamiliar place in the world and shatters our relationship with existence. The existential model sees such moments as 'life opening' opportunities (Jacobsen, 2006) and a chance to adopt a more authentic life. Clinical practice that helps individuals to understand what has occurred at a spiritual, personal, social, and physical level (van Deurzen, 2007), and offers opportunities to begin to make sense of the world in new ways, would perhaps have allowed these participants to take advantage of the "life opening" opportunity and to move towards posttraumatic growth (Tedeschi & Calhoun, 1995) earlier in their journey.

Active Service Changes People and Their Relationships (Themes 2 & 3)

All the participants in this study reported being changed in some way by their experience of active service. Yet they didn't always recognise these changes at the time. Recognition came many years later through therapeutic work or more general processing of their experiences or when their partners pointed out the changes to them (there are echoes here of Kierkegaard's (2005) assertion that life makes sense backwards but has to be lived forwards). Sartre (1943/1958) suggests that we can choose to be reflective or non-reflective. Arguably the participants in this study were act-ing in "bad faith" (Sartre, 1943/1958: 47) in choosing to be non-reflective. Heidegger (1927/2010) reminds us, however, that dwelling in the ontic, everyday world, is the natural state. Therapeutic exploration of their choice of focus might have encouraged them to explore the feelings of grief and the loss of something core to themselves and to recognise what was gained/ could be gained.

Active service also changed the participants' priorities in life as far as intimate relationships were concerned; a shift from freedom and adventure to relationship and children. Van Deurzen (2007) describes the existential dilemma of freedom versus connectedness, and we can understand the participants as having shifted on this spectrum from a point where free-dom was more valued, to a point where connectedness became the more important goal. This shift arguably took place as a result of their confronta-tion with life's finitude. As Yalom (1980: 165) states: "It is the awareness of death that promotes a shift in perspective and makes it possible for an individual to distinguish between core and accessory: to reinvest one and divest the other."

The confrontation with existential realities seems to have robbed par-ticipants of their sense that a life of travel and adventure in the Royal Navy would be meaningful and fulfilling. This supports Harmand et al.'s (1993) view that loss of meaning is central to the experience of trauma and Frankl's (1946/2004) theory that a sudden meaning vacuum created by an existential crisis will create an urgent desire on the part of the individual for the identification of new meaning.

All of the participants reported an increased sense of urgency to tick life's boxes (marriage and children being two of them) as a result of their experi-ence of active service. This provides support for what Paidoussis-Mitchell (2012: 37) describes as an existential principle around the confrontation of existential givens and its tendency to create in people "[t]he urgency for living well, authentically and meaningfully." Existential therapy could have helped participants to determine whether they were making authentic or inauthentic choices in these circumstances.

Overwhelming Emotions Change People and Their Relationships (Theme 4)

Most of the participants in this research attempted to suppress, deny, or ignore the overwhelming emotions their experiences evoked and to avoid the challenges these placed upon them to relate to themselves, the world, and their partners in different ways. For many of them, the predominant emotion was shame. This confirms research by Gonzalez et al. (2015) and Maguen et al. (2010) on the link between trauma and shame. Six of the participants in this research experienced anger and rage on their return from combat, and in the coming months and years this became a feature of their relationships, having a devastating effect upon them. This supports research that suggests anger and rage are commonly experienced in veterans of active service (Elbogen et al., 2010; Gonzalez et al., 2015). Unlike the medical model, which sees more 'extreme' emotions as symptomatic of a disorder (APA, 2022), in the existential view, emotions indicate how we are attuned to the world (Heidegger, 1927/2010) and the extent to which we are living in line with our values (van Deurzen, 2007). What my research adds is a possible explanatory framework of a. where these emotions come from (from existential confrontations and the fundamental changes they provoked in individuals) and b. why these emotions persist (due to an inability or unwillingness on the part of the Individuals to understand, share, and process these emotions). This has implications for clinical practice in that it underlines the importance of focusing on something more than the eradication of 'negative' emotions.

Alienation, Withdrawal, and Isolation and Their Impact on Relationships (Themes 5, 6 & 7)

Participants were alienated from their *'real selves,'* developing a sense of *'otherness.'* This sense of alienation from themselves (and increasingly from others) became a lasting theme within their lives, supporting Harmand et al.'s (1993) view that alienation is part of an existential model of PTSD. The research described here also places this alienation and withdrawal within a context (e.g. it illustrates that it is a response to a confrontation with existential givens and the overwhelming emotions they provoke).

The DSM-5 (APA, 2022: 162) describes "feelings of detachment or estrangement from others" as a symptom of PTSD, which is the result of an attempt to block or dissociate from difficult feelings. For the existential practitioner, however, alienation is merely a mode of existence, like any other mode, albeit one that is "achieved only by outrageous violence perpetrated by human beings on human beings" (Laing & Esterson, 1990: 78). Arguably the medical model provides an insufficient basis for understanding and treating posttraumatic stress, echoing van Deurzen-Smith's (1997: 14) criticism of therapeutic models that focus on the intra-psychic, defining human experience as self-sufficient, which she says increasingly isolates people within "an anthropocentric universe of their own making." A more optimistic view of alienation is proposed by Hegel (1807/1977) in which alienation is seen as something that an individual comes to recognise in themselves as a means for growth.

The findings of this research show that most of the participants responded to increasing feelings of alienation by withdrawing into themselves, retreating from the world and from their partners. This withdrawal was described by them as a way of shutting themselves down, protecting themselves and their partners from their overwhelming emotions. This supports previous research by Keeling (2014) that indicates that "bravado versus emotion" is a dilemma military couples have to negotiate following deployment.

This alienation and withdrawal had a devastating impact on the participants' intimate relationships. Six of the participants attributed marriage or relationship breakdowns to their alienation and withdrawal from their partners. This supports research that demonstrates that emotional numbing and withdrawal-related symptoms of PTSD are strongly related to relationship quality (Riggs et al., 1998).

Breaking Down and its Impact on Individuals and Relationships (Theme 8)

For many of the participants, active service ultimately led to a breaking down of their ability to function in their day-to-day lives. This breakdown was precipitated in each case by a new trauma or a series of stressful life events occurring six to thirty-six years after active service. Five of the participants were diagnosed with PTSD (APA, 2022), their experiences offering support for the link between combat and PTSD. This could also be taken as support for research speculating on the existence of delayed trauma (Horesh et al., 2011, 2015, newly defined in the DSM-5 [APA, 2022]) as occurring when an individual doesn't meet the full criteria for diagnosis until six months or longer after the event that precipitated the symptoms. However, the accounts of my participants seem to indicate that the symptoms of trauma existed for many years prior to their diagnosis with PTSD, offering more support for suggestions that delayed PTSD is not a phenomenon in itself but actually describes late diagnosis of an already existing disorder following the worsening of existing symptoms (Horesh et al., 2015).

The current research perhaps provides most support for a 'life change model' or 'vulnerability perspective' (Horesh et al., 2011) and the idea that life stressors finally exhaust the greatly depleted resources available to those suffering PTSD. This highlights the importance of timely assessment and intervention for military personnel at risk of developing PTSD not only on return from active service but also in the following years and decades.

Growth and Resilience Following Active Service and Its Impact on Individuals and Relationships (Themes 9 & 10)

The time of breakdown and/or diagnosis of PTSD created some difficulties for the participants, precipitating initially further feelings of isolation, increased withdrawal, and additional disruption of communication and connection between couples (confirming Allen et al.'s (2010) research in this area). However, the breakdown/diagnosis was for most participants a turning point in their relationships with their partners, offering an opportunity for growth and resilience.

It appears therefore that trauma is a socially embedded experience (Iacovou & Wiexel-Dixon, 2015) in that it is experienced in a social context, embedded in the cultural values in which the individual operates, and concerned with loss of meaning that the individual has created in a shared environment. As Bracken (2002: 148) states: "If trauma is about broken meanings, then it is a social phenomenon through and through." This has implications for clinical practice as intra-psychic models like CBT don't adequately address the social significance of trauma, nor do they equip the individual to explore the loss of meaning in the relationship space in which they operate.

Ultimately my research demonstrates that "delayed onset posttraumatic growth" (a term coined by the author of this chapter) can occur many years (in some cases decades) after the trauma is experienced. This growth seems to have been achieved through increased sharing with partners but also the way that support or treatment for PTSD enabled the participants to bring new meaning to their experiences, supporting the existential view of trauma as challenging individuals to find meaning (Adams, 2019; Frankl, 1978). Tedeschi et al. (2020: 9) state that "this is one of the paradoxes of posttraumatic growth, which is that from loss there can be gain." The posttraumatic growth (Tedaschi & Calhoun, 1996) participants described had a very positive effect on their ability to enter into and maintain more authentic relationships with others, supporting research on positive outcomes possible following traumatic experiences (Sledge et al., 1980; Tsai et al., 2015) (albeit outcomes that took some time to manifest themselves).

Tom's Experiences

As highlighted above, Tom's experiences were significantly different in many ways to those of his fellow participants. Like the other participants, his experiences of active service resulted in a sudden confrontation with existential givens, and this changed him and his priorities in some ways. However, unlike the other participants, the confrontation didn't result in the symptoms of trauma or the breakdown of a relationship. Tom reported positive changes in himself following his experience of active service (supporting research by Wick & Nelson Goff [2014], who found that couples with low levels of posttraumatic symptoms and high levels of relationship satisfaction can recognise opportunities for growth in experiences of trauma).

There are a number of demographic factors that may help explain why Tom's journey was different and that may have contributed to increased resilience compared to other participants: he was older when he joined the Navy (24 compared to average age of joining of 17); he was a Commissioned Officer (the rest were ratings); he had been happily married for 10 years at the point of active service (unlike most of the other participants); and he experienced more direct forms of combat on land (and arguably therefore had more agency) compared to the others who were for the most part on ships. And Tom did not experience significant symptoms of trauma, which may be the key reason why active service did not have a negative impact on his relationship. The fact that Tom still experienced posttraumatic growth perhaps contradicts Tedeschi and Calhoun's (1996) assertion that resilience does not lead to posttraumatic growth.

Conclusion

The existential perspective offers an additional, more complete, understanding of the impact of active service on ex-servicemen, and therefore on their relationships, than that offered by the medical model with its focus on PTSD as a disorder. It accepts that trauma is something that reveals the anxiety of existence, rather than creating it (Iacovou & Weixel-Dixon, 2015) and hence normalises much of what is experienced during posttraumatic stress. The findings from the current research add to the existential model by offering an alternative view of posttraumatic stress to that proposed by the medical model (see Figure 10.2).

Based on the new existential understanding of the trauma journey outlined in Figure 10.2, I offer some suggestions for working therapeutically with trauma below. It should not be considered definitive nor as an 'expert' opinion on the experience of posttraumatic stress. What can be stated with confidence is that an existential framework of understanding should recognise that:

- It is important to assist the client in creating a safe place for the therapy (Oakley, 2009) before undertaking any form of descriptively focused work. There is a need for them to reflect on the embodied nature of their experience and recognise/become confident of ways to manage their embodied responses to their experiences.
- The problems caused by trauma have their root in the existential vacuum (Frankl, 1978) provoked by a confrontation with existential givens which shatters or significantly disturbs the client's worldview.
- An existential vacuum is characterised by feelings of alienation and loss of meaning, which in turn create existential awareness (Yalom & Lieberman, 1991) and accompanying overwhelming emotions.

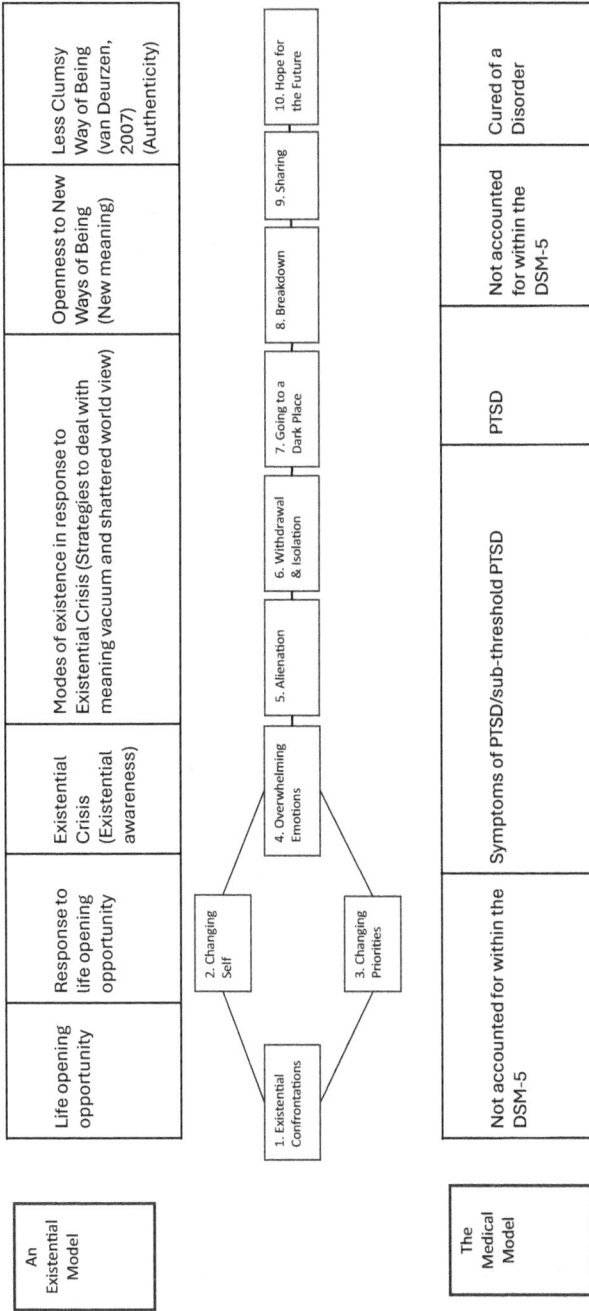

Figure 10.2 The medical model compared to an existential framework of PTSD.

- These emotions and attempts to deal with them through anger, violence, etc. represent frantic attempts to avoid the angst that arises from being confronted by existential givens and having the worldview destabilised or destroyed.
- These responses are ways of being in the world that can be explored therapeutically in terms of their impact on the individual and on their relationships, and the extent to which they help the individual identify a new life meaning upon which to base a new worldview.
- The aim is not to extinguish 'symptoms' but to hear what these symptoms have to tell the individual about their way of being in the world; to help them identify less clumsy ways to deal with the normal anxiety of existence.
- There is no experience that is inherently traumatic in and of itself (Bracken, 2002) it is our intentionality towards the world that imbues it with this meaning. This doesn't downplay or reduce the suffering experienced but rather reminds us that the meaning of anything is flexible and can be changed. The focus is upon allowing the individual to see the life-opening (Jacobsen, 2006) opportunities offered by the trauma – enabling them to recognise they can choose from a range of potential responses.
- The existential therapist's role in this process is not one of treatment provider or expert or medical professional, but rather of fellow traveller, encouraging the individual to describe their experiences and in doing so to hear themselves and be heard.
- Set in the present and not in the past, it is the relationship and the 'being with' qualities of the existential therapist (what Tedeschi & Calhoun (2016) describe as 'expert companionship') that provide the unique setting in which the client's lived reality can be expressed and examined.

References

Adams, M. (2019). *An Existential Approach to Human Development*. Palgrave Macmillan Education.

Affleck, G., & Tennen, H. (1996). Construing benefits from adversity: Adaptational significance and

dispositional underpinnings. *Personality, 634*(4), 899–922.

https://doi.org/10.1111/j.1467-6494.1996.tb00948.x

Allen, E., Rhoades, G., Stanley, S., & Markman, H. (2010). Hitting home: Relationships between recent deployment, posttraumatic stress symptoms, and marital functioning for army couples. *Journal of Family Psychology, 24*(3), 280–288. https://psycnet.apa.org/doi/10.1037/a0019405

American Psychological Association. (2015). *Diagnostic and Statistical Manual of Mental Disorders* (3rd ed.). Cengage Learning, Gale Virtual Reference Library.

American Psychological Association. (2022). *Diagnostic and Statistical Manual of Mental Disorders* (5th ed.). APA. https://doi.org/10.1176/appi.books .9780890425787

Beckham, J. C., Feldman, M. E., & Kirby, A. C. (1998). Atrocities exposure in Vietnam combat veterans with chronic posttraumatic stress disorder: Relationship to combat exposure, symptom severity, guilt, and interpersonal violence. *Journal of Traumatic Stress, 11*(4), 777–785. https://doi.org/10.1023/A:1024453618638

Bentley, S. (1991). *A Short History of PTSD: From Thermopylae to Hue Soldiers Have Always Had a Disturbing Reaction to War.* The VNA Veteran.

Bracken, P. (2002). *Trauma: Culture, Meaning and Philosophy.* Wiley.

Calvert, W. E., & Hutchinson, R. L. (1990). Vietnam veteran levels of combat: Related to later violence? *Journal of Trauma Stress, 3*(1), 103–113. https://doi .org/10.1007/BF00975138

Campbell, S. B., & Renshaw, K. D. (2018). Posttraumatic stress disorder and relationship functioning: A comprehensive review and organizational framework. *Clinical Psychology Review, 65,* 152–162. https://doi.org/10.1016 /j.cpr.2018.08.003

Cook, J. M., Riggs, D. S., Thompson, R., Coyne, J. C., & Sheikh, J. I. (2004). Posttraumatic stress disorder and current relationship functioning among World War II ex-prisoners of war. *Journal of Family Psychology, 18,* 36–45. https://psycnet.apa.org/doi/10.1037/0893-3200.18 .1.36

Cowlishaw, S., Freijah, I., Kartal, D., Sbisa, A., Mulligan, A., Notarianni, M. A., Couineau, A. L., Forbes, D., O'Donnell, M., Phelps, A., Iverson, K. M., Heber, A., O'Dwyer, C. O., Smith, P., & Hosseiny, F. (2022). Intimate Partner Violence (IPV) in military and veteran populations: A systematic review of population based surveys and population screening studies. *International Journal of Environmental Research and Public Health, 19*(14), 8853. https://doi.org/10 .3390/ijerph19148853

Crocq, M., & Crocq, L. (2000). From shell shock and war neurosis to posttraumatic stress disorder: A history of psychotraumatology. *Dialogues in Clinical Neuroscience, 2*(1), 47–55. https://doi.org/10.31887/DCNS.2000.2.1/macrocq

Elbogen, E. B., Wagner, H. R., Fuller, S. R., Calhoun, P. S., & Kinneer, P. M. (2010). Correlates of anger and hostility in Iraq and Afghanistan war veterans. *Am J Psychiatry, 167*(9), 1051–1058. https://doi.org/10.1176/appi.ajp.2010 .09050739

Elison, J., Garofalo, C., & Velotti, P. (2014). Shame and aggression: Theoretical considerations. *Aggression and Violent Behavior, 19*(4), 447–453. https:// psycnet.apa.org/doi/10.1016/j.avb.2014.05.002

Fear, N. T., Jones, M., Murphy, D., Hull, L., Iverson, A. C., Coker, B., Machell, L., Sundin, J., Woodhead, C., Jones, N., Greenberg, N., Dandeker, C., Rona, R. J., Hotopf, M., & Wessley, S. (2010). What are the consequences of deployment to Iraq and Afghanistan on the mental health of UK armed forces? *The Lancet, 375,* 1783–1797. https://doi.org/10.1016/S0140-6736(10)60672-1

Ferrajão, P., & Oliveira, R. (2015). The effects of combat exposure, abusive violence, and sense of coherence on PTSD and depression in Portuguese colonial war veterans. *Psychological Trauma: Theory, Research, Practice, and Policy, 8*(1), 1–8. https://psycnet.apa.org/doi/10.1037/tra0000043

Forbes, D., Adler, A. B., Pedlar, D., & Asmundson, G. J. G. (2023). Problematic anger in military and veteran populations with and without PTSD: The elephant in the room. *Journal of Anxiety Disorders, 96*, 102716. https://doi.org/10.1016/j.janxdis.2023.102716

Frankl, V. E. (1978). *The Unheard Cry for Meaning.* Simon & Schuster.

Frankl, V. E. (2004). *Man's Search for Meaning.* Ebury (Original work published 1946).

Ganesh, R., Sarkar, S. & Sagar, R. (2015). "Shell shock": An entity that predated combat-related posttraumatic stress disorder. *Journal of Mental Health and Human Behaviour, 20*(2), 85–87. https://doi.org/10.4103/0971-8990.174603

Goff, B., Crow, J., Reisbig, A., & Hamilton, S. (2007). The impact of individual trauma symptoms of deployed soldiers on relationship satisfaction. *Journal of Family Psychology, 3*, 344–353. https://psycnet.apa.org/doi/10.1037/0893-3200.21.3.344

Gonzalez, O. I., Novaco, R. W., Reger, M. A., & Gahm, G. A. (2015). Anger intensification with combat-related PTSD and depression comorbidity. *Psychological Trauma: Theory, Research, Practice, and Policy.* Advance online publication. http://dx.doi.org/10.1037/tra0000042

Greenberg, N., Jones, E., Jones, N., Fear, M. T., & Wessely, S. (2011). The injured mind in the UK armed forces. *Philos T R Soc B. 366*(1562), 261–267. https://doi.org/10.1098/rstb.2010.0210

Greening, T. (1971). *Existential-Humanistic Psychology.* Brookes/Cole.

Grinker, R. R., Willerman, B., Bradley, A. D., & Fastovsk, A. (1946). A study of psychological predisposition to the development of operational fatigue in officer flying personnel. *American Journal of Orthopsychiatry, 16*(2), 191–206. https://psycnet.apa.org/doi/10.1111/j.1939-0025.1946.tb05373.x

Grubbs, M. D. (2013). The role of existential well-being following combat in the development of posttraumatic stress disorder. *Dissertation Abstracts International, 73*(12). https://doi.org/10.1186/s40359-020-0388-7

Harmand, J., Ashlock, L., & Miller, T. (1993). Treating post-traumatic stress disorder among Vietnam combat veterans: An existential perspective. *Journal Of Contemporary Psychotherapy, 23*(4), 281–291. https://psycnet.apa.org/doi/10.1007/BF00946088

Hasanović, M., & Pajević, I. (2010). Religious moral beliefs as mental health protective factor of war veterans suffering from PTSD, depressiveness, anxiety, tobacco, and alcohol abuse in comorbidity. *Psychiatria Danubina, 22*(2), 203–210.

Hegel, G. W. F. (1977). *Phenomenology of Spirit* (trans. A. V. Miller). Clarendon Press (Original work published 1807).

Heidegger, M. (2010). *Being and Time* (trans. J. Stambaugh). State University of New York Press (Original work published 1927).

Hejdenberg, J., & Andrews, B. (2011). The relationship between shame and different types of anger: A theory-based investigation. *Personality and Individual Differences, 50*(8), 1278–1282. https://doi.org/10.1016/j.paid.2011.02.024

Hoge, C. W., Auchterlonie, J. L., & Milliken, C. S. (2006). Mental health problems, use of mental health services, and attrition from military service after returning from deployment to Iraq or Afghanistan. *JAMA, 295*(9), 1023–1032. https://doi .org/10.1001/jama.295.9.1023

Horesh, D., Solomon, Z., Keinan, G., & Ein-Dor, T. (2015). Delayed-onset PTSD Israeli combat veterans: Correlates, clinical picture, and controversy. In M. P. Safir, H. S. Wallach, & A. S. Rizzo (Eds.), *Future Directions in Post-Traumatic Stress Disorder: Prevention, Diagnosis, and Treatment* (pp. 97–129). Springer Science. https://psycnet.apa.org/doi/10.1007/978-1-4899-7522-5_5

Horesh, D., Solomon, Z., Zerach, G., & Ein-Dor, T. (2011). Delayed-onset PTSD among war veterans: The role of life events throughout the life cycle. *Social Psychiatry and Psychiatric Epidemiology, 46*(9), 860–870. https://doi.org/10 .1007/s00127-010-0255-6

Iacovou, S., & Weixel-Dixon, K. (2015). *Existential Therapy: 100 Key Points and Techniques.* Routledge. https://doi.org/10.4324/9781315709260

Ioannou, A. (2023). Existential theoretical foundations on trauma and implications for the therapeutic encounter. *Existential Analysis, 34*(1), 145–161.

https://www.thefreelibrary.com/Existential+Theoretical+Foundations+on+Trauma +and+Implications+for...-a0737512203

Jacobsen, B. (2006). The life crisis in an existential perspective. Can trauma and crisis be seen as an aid in personal development? *Existential Analysis, 17*(1), 39–54.

Jones, F. D. (1995). Psychiatric lessons of war. In F. D. Jones, L. R. Sparacino, V. L. Wilcox, J. M. Rothberg, & J. W. Stokes (Eds.), *Textbook of Military Medicine, Part 1 – War Psychiatry* (pp. 1–33). Office of the Surgeon General US Army.

Jones, G., & Lovett, J. (1987). Delayed psychiatric sequelae among Falklands war veterans. *The Journal of The Royal College of General Practitioners, 37*(294), 24–35.

Kardiner, A., & Spiegel, H. (1947). *War Stress and Neurotic Illness.* Paul. B. Hoeber.

Keeling, M. (2014). *UK military personnel and their romantic relationships: The impact of the recent conflicts in Iraq and Afghanistan* (Thesis). King's College London.

Kierkegaard, S. (2005). *Fear and Trembling.* Penguin (Original work published 1843).

Kulka, R. A., Schlenger, W. E., Fairbank, J. A., Hough, R. L., Jordan, B. K., Marmar, C. R., & Weiss, D. S. (1990). *Trauma and the Vietnam War Generation: Report of Findings From the National Vietnam Readjustment Study.* Bruner/Mazel. https://doi.org/10.4324/9781315803753

Laing, R., & Esterson, A. (1990). *Sanity, Madness and the Family.* Penguin.

Magomed-Eminov, M. S. (1997). Post-traumatic stress disorders as a loss of the meaning of life. In D. F. Halpern & A. Voĭskunskiĭ (Eds.), *States of Mind: American and Post-Soviet Perspectives on Contemporary Issues in Psychology* (pp. 238–252). Oxford University Press. https://doi.org/10.1093/oso/9780195103502 .003.0011

Maguen, S., Lucenko, B. A., Reger, M. A., Gahm, G. A., Litz, B. T., Seal, K. H., & Marmar, C. R. (2010). The impact of reported direct and indirect killing on mental health symptoms in Iraq war veterans. *Journal of Traumatic Stress, 23*(1), 86–90. https://doi.org/10.1002/jts.20434

McLeland, K. C., Sutton, G. W., & Schumm, W. R. (2008). Marital satisfaction before and after deployments associated with the global war on terror. *Psychological Reports, 103*, 836–844.

Milian, G. (1915). L'hypnose des Batailles. *Paris Med, 2.*

Miller, S. (2019). Anger and military veterans. *Columbia Social Work Review, 4*(1), 7–16. https://doi.org/10.7916/cswr.v4i1.1905

Newby, J. H., McCarroll, J. E., Ursano, R. J., Fan, Z., Shigemura, J., & Tucker-Harris, Y. (2005). Positive and negative consequences of military deployment. *Military Medicine, 170*(10), 815–819. https://psycnet.apa.org/doi/10.7205/MILMED.170.10.815

Nietzsche, F. (2012). *Twilight of the Idols.* CreateSpace Independent Publishing (Original work published 1888).

Oakley, S. (2009). Creating safety for the client: The London 7/7 bombings. In L. Barnett (Ed.), *When Death Enters the Therapeutic Space: Existential Perspectives in Psychotherapy and Counselling* (pp. 89–101). Routledge.

O'Brien, L., & Hughes, S. (1991). Symptoms of post-traumatic stress disorder in Falklands veterans five years after the conflict. *The British Journal of Psychiatry, 159*, 135–141. https://doi.org/10.1192/bjp.159.1.135

Olatunji, B., Ciesielski, B., & Tolin, D. (2010). Fear and loathing: A meta-analytic review of the specificity of anger in PTSD. *Behavior Therapy, 41*(1), 93–105. https://doi.org/10.1016/j.beth.2009.01.004

Ørner, R., Lynch, T., & Seed, P. (1994). Long-term traumatic stress reactions in British Falklands War veterans. *British Journal of Clinical Psychology, 33*(4), 457–459. https://doi.org/10.1111/j.2044-8260.1993.tb01079.x

Paidoussis-Mitchell, C. (2012). Traumatic bereavement: A phenomenological study. *Existential Analysis, 23*(1), 32–45.

Ponder, N. R. (2021). *Factors influencing the relationship satisfaction of military spouses* (PhD submission). Northcentral University ProQuest Dissertations Publishing.

Quiroga, D. F. G., & Seear, M. (2009). *Hors de Combat: The Falklands-Malvinas Conflict in Retrospect* (2nd ed.). Critical, Cultural and Communications Press.

Ramchand, R., Miles, J., Schell, T., Jaycox, L., Marshall, G.N., & Tanielian, T. (2011). Prevalence and correlates of drinking behaviors among previously deployed military and matched civilian populations. *Military Psychology, 23*(1), 6–21. https://doi.org/10.1080/08995605.2011.534407

Renshaw, K. D., Rodrigues, C. S., & Jones, D. H. (2009). Combat exposure psychological symptoms and marital satisfaction in National Guard soldiers who served in Operation Iraqi Freedom from 2005 to 2006. *Anxiety, Stress and Coping, 22*(1), 101–115. https://psycnet.apa.org/doi/10.1080/10615800802354000

Ribeiro, S., Renshaw, K. D., & Allen, E.S. (2023). Military-related relocation stress and psychological distress in military partners. *Journal of Family Psychology, 37*(1), 45–53. https://psycnet.apa.org/doi/10.1037/fam0001030

Riggs, D. S., Byrne, C. A., Weathers, F. W., & Litz, B. T. (1998). The quality of the intimate relationships of male Vietnam veterans: Problems associated with posttraumatic stress disorder. *Journal of Traumatic Stress, 11*(1), 87–101. https://doi.org/10.1023/A:1024409200155

Ruger, W., Wilson, S., & Waddoups, S. (2002). Warfare and welfare: Military service, combat, and marital dissolution. *Armed Forces & Society: An Interdisciplinary Journal, 29*(1), 85–107. http://www.jstor.org/stable/45346976

Sartre, J.-P. (1958). *Being and Nothingness* (trans. H. E. Barnes). Routledge (Original work published 1943).

Schumm, W. R., Roy, R. R. N., & Theodore, V. (2012). Separation and divorce. In B. A. Moore (Ed.), *Handbook of Counselling Military Couples* (pp. 157–181). Routledge.

Senior, E., Clarke, A., & Wilson-Menzfeld, G. (2023). The military spouse experience of living alongside their serving/veteran partner with a mental health issue: A systematic review and narrative synthesis. *PLoS One, 18*(5), 1–25. https://doi.org/10.1371/journal.pone.0285714

Sledge, W. H., Boydstun, J. A., & Rahe, A. J. (1980). Self-concept changes related to war captivity. *Archives of General Psychiatry, 37,* 430–443. https://psycnet.apa.org/doi/10.1001/archpsyc.1980.01780170072008

Smith, J. A., Flowers, P., & Larkin, M. (2009). *Interpretative Phenomenological Analysis: Theory Method and Research.* Sage.

Spinelli, E. (2005). *The Interpreted World: An Introduction to Phenomenological Psychology* (2nd ed.). Sage.

Stolorow, R. D. (2015). A phenomenological-contextual, existential, and ethical perspective on emotional trauma. *Psychoanalytic Review, 102*(1), 123–138. https://doi.org/10.1093/oxfordhb/9780198803157.013.85

Swan, H. (1949). *The Henry Swan Papers: Letters From Henry Swan to His First Wife, Mary Fletcher.* US National Library of Medicine.

Tedeschi, R. G. (2023). The post-traumatic growth approach to psychological trauma. *World Psychiatry, 22*(2), 328–329. https://doi.org/10.1002/wps.21093

Tedeschi, R. G., & Calhoun, L. G. (1996). The Posttraumatic Growth Inventory: Measuring the positive legacy of trauma. *Journal of Traumatic Stress, 9,* 455–471. https://psycnet.apa.org/doi/10.1002/jts.2490090305

Tedeschi, R. G., & Moore, B. A. (2016). *The Posttraumatic Growth Workbook: Coming Through Trauma Wiser, Stronger and More Resilient.* New Harbinger Publications.

Tedeschi, R. G., Moore, B. A., Falke, K., & Goldberg, J. (2020). *Transformed by Trauma: Stories of Posttraumatic Growth.* Boulder Crest.

Tedeschi, R. G., Shakespeare-Finch, J., Taku, K., & Calhoun, L. G. (2018). *Posttraumatic Growth: Theory, Research, and Applications.* Routledge. https://doi.org/10.4324/9781315527451

Trevillion, K., Williamson, E., Thandi, G., Borschmann, R., Oram, S., & Howard, L. M. (2015). A systematic review of mental disorders and perpetration of domestic violence among military populations. *Social Psychiatry and Psychiatric Epidemiology, 50*(9), 1329–1346. https://psycnet.apa.org/doi/10.1007/s00127-015-1084-4

Tsai, J., El-Gabalawy, R., Sledge, W. H., Southwick, S. M., & Pietrzak, R. H. (2015). *Post-Traumatic Growth Among Veterans in the USA: Results From the National*

Health and Resilience in Veterans Study. Cambridge University Press. https://doi
.org/10.1017/S0033291714001202

van Deurzen, E. (2007). *Existential Counselling and Psychotherapy in Practice*. Sage.

van Deurzen-Smith, E. (1997). *Everyday Mysteries: Existential Dimensions of Psychotherapy*. Routledge.

Waysman, M., Mikulincer, M., Solomon, Z., & Weisenberg, M. (1993). Secondary traumatization among wives of posttraumatic combat veterans: A family typology. *Journal of Family Psychology, 7*(1), 104–118. https://psycnet.apa.org/doi/10.1037/0893-3200.7.1.104

Wick, S., & Nelson Goff, B. S. (2014). A qualitative analysis of military couples with high and low trauma symptoms and relationship distress levels. *Journal of Couple & Relationship Therapy, 13*(1), 63–88. https://doi.org/10.1080/15332691.2014.865983

Yalom, I. D. (1980). *Existential Psychotherapy*. Basic Books.

Yalom, I. D., & Lieberman, M. A. (1991). Bereavement and heightened existential awareness. *Psychiatry, 54*(4), 334–345.

Chapter 11

Trauma: The Search for a Poisoned Chalice?

Niklas Serning

Introduction

> *Helicopters are terrifying when under threat – the noise, the too-small windows, the erratic movements side-to-side then up – and worst of all, rapidly down. We were given three minutes' warning to evacuate our outpost due to an incoming threat, the helicopter barely touched the ground as we jumped in, but as we tried to get altitude something went wrong. The pilot shouted something about the strong wind and lift, the engines were maxed out, lights flashed and we were being tossed about in the back. I will never forget that morning in Timor-Leste. But it was only that – terrifying. The idea that it would be traumatising never occurred to us.*

I was a humanitarian working in war zones before I retrained as a psychologist and subsequently officer in the British Army. At that time, my humanitarian colleagues and I did not use the term 'trauma' to describe the sometimes quite intense adverse events that befell us, such as that near miss in the helicopter, assaults, or the loss of colleagues by violent means. I therefore noted with curiosity and some surprise that the psychological literature and broader therapeutic discourse on humanitarians often focused on trauma.

Intrigued, I investigated the area for my doctoral dissertation (Serning, 2011) and found that none of my research participants – humanitarians recently returned from complex emergencies – saw themselves as traumatised. Adverse events were not seen as trauma, nor necessarily as having effects beyond the immediate agitation and subsequent sense making.

My objective with this chapter is to zoom in on what happens when a client begins – and ceases – to see an adverse event as a trauma. I will examine the phenomenology of applying a trauma label to an event or oneself. I will draw upon my doctoral research into humanitarians as well as case studies from my clinical private practice in order to do so.

DOI: 10.4324/9781003493860-15

Periadversarial growth in humanitarians

The first thing you do when you have decided to research something is to review the literature already created on the topic. Humanitarians and war were all about adverse events and trauma, with a smattering of posttraumatic growth (Barron, 1999; Downie, 2001; Ehrenreich, 2002; Eriksson et al., 2001; Jessen-Petersen, 2001; Larson, 2006; McFarlane, 2004; Reyes & Jacobs, 2006). There were some dissenting voices; for example, Thomas critiqued the broad brush with which traumatisation is liberally applied to suffering humanitarians, when more existential issues may be more useful to highlight. "The central discourse in most research on the mental health of humanitarian workers has been characterised by a preoccupation with risks, stress and trauma as it emphasises illness as opposed to health and well-being" (Thomas, 2008: 70). It seemed as if my old colleagues and I must have been outliers in our non-traumatised experiences, since the psychologists were pretty much agreed that warzones leave these fundamentally different imprints.

As I moved to the next stages of my research, interviewing humanitarians recently returned from complex emergencies, they sounded more like my old colleagues than what the psychologists described. There were accounts of hardship and fear for sure, and a good half of the participants mentioned persistent bodily discomforts that they linked to experiences in war zones, one of them for example mentioning *'an underlying level tension in my gut.'* There was a sense that these bodily symptoms were more automatic, more background experiences. They happened and gradually faded away – as one explained: *'whenever I hear certain noises, I assume it's a mortar, obviously only for about three seconds, and I think it will probably just take some time for that to go away,'* whilst the more emotional responses to the difficulties of coming back were in the foreground of the participants' experiences.

Of perhaps equal or greater importance was the worry of being traumatised or suffering from PTSD – illustrated by another participant: *'it's quite possible [ ] to be suffering from a mild form of post traumatic stress. [ ] there is a concern that there is an underlying long term effect that you can't quite put your finger on [ ] there's a big black hole about – was there any permanent effect?'* Note how the topics of traumatisation and PTSD, so prevalent in the media and aid organisations' support agendas, did not seem to pertain to the participants. If anything, it was the worry that one had 'got PTSD' rather than any traumatisation in itself that proved anxiety provoking. Looking at the above, we have a group of humanitarians that do experience distress whilst in extreme situations, but we never have any symptoms of PTSD, only the worry about catching it. One participant mentioned a colleague being a bit shaky, but nothing more than that: *'There was a member of my team who was getting a bit shaky and she was getting incredibly jumpy when there was explosions, and she was going through a bit of a rough patch.'* In summary, these events did not permanently stain the subsequent experiences of my participants.

The most difficult experiences were around reconnecting with the home that they had left behind. Having transformed during this intense time away, home did not feel like home anymore, and the mission country could not serve as a home either. The distress was existential, not physiological or traumatic. In their words: *'Not important that the counsellor knew about Afghanistan, since the issue wasn't Afghanistan, the issue was coming home. Even the issues that did originate in Afghanistan was more about missing the place rather than being traumatized by it.'*

In terms of posttraumatic growth, given that my participants didn't see themselves as traumatised in the first place, my first thought was that it wouldn't apply. However, a different label could be constructed where we replace the *post* with *peri* in order to make it in the now, and *traumatic* with *adversarial* to indicate that the event wasn't necessarily traumatically impacting but certainly adversarial and difficult. There was plenty of *peri-adversarial* growth – growth during adversity – as my participants faced their challenges. What would be deemed traumatising by many outsiders was actually described as exciting:

> *The first time it was a rocket siren and maybe the first few times I was scared and they all happened in my first week so it was good kind of initiation ahh but then after that there was, I mean yeah there was fear whenever there was a rocket siren I guess there was fear but generally you know my, when we were going down town for example you know on the helicopter. The first time I went in the helicopter I was scared but then gradually it just became excitement.*

The allure of trauma in clinical practice

More than a decade later, with part of my working week in clinical private practice, I notice two distinct versions of discourses around trauma. The first is represented by the clients that come to me having attached notions of trauma to themselves. These self-conceptions of trauma arise out of a breadth of situations, spanning those conventionally understood as traumatic as well as events that might be viewed by many as falling within the ordinary sphere of human experience. The second is the group of clients for whom trauma is the elusive Answer – the seekers that suffer and wish to find the reason for this suffering in a trauma long forgotten and hidden in their depths. For both categories, my challenge in therapeutic practice is opening up a space to examine and interrogate these ideas: for some clients, this has resulted in conflict. That conflict has sometimes developed into a productive and empowering period of growth, and it has sometimes failed to resolve.

Commencing with the first category, those that have experienced deep suffering and characterise this suffering as traumatisation, my first task is to truly listen, truly understand their experience. The event may be too charged to detail in initial sessions, and one tool is to see it as sealed in a box – whatever happened in that crashing helicopter is in that box – we may or may not open it, but we can discuss how you are here today, and what stories permeate your daily life. Inevitably, a client's lifeworld is far larger than the part relating to the adverse event, their personalities far wider and richer than simplistic products of a trauma. This is where existential therapy shines, in the mapping out of broad swathes of clients' lives – their meanings in life, their relations, their stories, their self-images – and also where the deepening effects of phenomenology can allow us to truly stare hard enough at a grain of sand to see the world.

Once we have situated them in a rich setting (or at least a rich understanding of a bleak setting), the focus on entrenched, stuck narratives begins. Traumatisation is most usually presented as an unassailable, concrete fact, and this is where I need to be respectful. If someone brings a firm conviction of their religion, politics, or the genesis of their suffering, it is not for me to deny it. But it is for me to offer the possibility to open up the conviction in order to transform it from a sedimented, inert, past choice and into a living choice in the now. If you are a committed atheist or Christian, and this causes you much suffering, take a long hard look at this tension. I need to respect the conviction as well as the person, and they are sometimes at odds – by opening up fixity, new ways forward can emerge. Are there less dogmatic ways to follow Jesus, are there more awe-inspiring ways to be an atheist? Is there any wriggle room in the traumatising effects of the trauma, is there any freedom or opportunity for a different choice in that millisecond where you get triggered?

This dance of truthfully and genuinely holding both scepticism and affirmation for the narrative that the client has created within their culture is one of the most difficult and satisfying parts of my job. Any disingenuousness is immediately picked up by the client – if I secretly think that they are underplaying or exaggerating their experience, they will know. At the same time, the narrative needs to be worked with. My answer is to work at the very edges of the client's narrative – the pregnant liminal zones where fixity blurs. My client may know that what happened was horrendous and has debilitated them forever, and I want to truly understand this core of their narrative, but once I understand it, I move to the edges and enquire into what parts of them aren't debilitated, and whether forever has to mean always. This is especially true when the trauma label has been applied by outside mores – when an event like an explosion, an assault, or a sexual event has taken place – and our culture insists that it be traumatising. Sometimes this extraneous narrative resonates and provides a sense of relief, but in other instances disagreement and refusal of the label can lead to judgement from others, as the victim is seen as being in denial or not 'sitting with their feelings.' Just like some people blame victims, others judge those that refuse to be victims.

I usually fail – but more often momentary stumbles rather than permanent crashes. Perhaps my queries in the liminal zone sound too much like the queries of those that deny my client's experience, perhaps my exploration of 'what works well' sounds like 'stop thinking about the bad stuff and move on.' On a good day, I catch this stumble and examine how this is for my client, how it is to be denied one's suffering. This can be beneficial in that it loosens the hold and resistance against anything that queries the trauma narrative – it ceases to be either affirmation or denial, it becomes affirmation and growth. I remember with great fondness and admiration clients that have travelled this journey from either self-imposed or culturally imposed paralysis in trauma narratives, how they first insisted on unequivocal affirmation and got it, how they were curious about slightly different narratives as an exception, and how they at the end grasped the free choice to fully own exactly who they are, including the fact that they have learnings derived from terrible experiences.

Moving on to the second case, those that look for the trauma that is the Answer, it is something that I have noticed increasingly over the past five years, possibly as a result of recovered memory ideas, hidden trauma narratives, and psychedelic therapies. A case study that Nina Lyon and I wrote in *Re-visioning Existential Therapy* (Serning & Lyon, 2020) may illustrate it:

Edward had tried everything – from the standard NHS treatments of cognitive behavioural therapy and counselling, to going further via eye movement desensitisation and reprocessing and psychodynamic therapies, and ending up in the domains of the psychospiritual and psychedelic. He tried hypnotherapy, emotional freedom techniques, rebirthing, trauma-focused body psychotherapy, and transpersonal therapy. He attended a series of ayahuasca ceremonies, which he hoped would bring him a breakthrough, and was disappointed to not find the relief that he had been expecting. He nonetheless felt that important unconscious transformations must have taken place, even if he was not yet consciously aware of them. His aim was to cut to the heart of his pain, find that nugget of trauma at the core of him that, once discovered and dealt with, would liberate him and allow him to live a good life. He was shy and timid, with low drive, and believed this to be a result of trauma due to early parental separation. This was how he had always been.

His was a genuinely impressive and moving account of hard work at finding a better way to live. However, I could not escape the feeling that he was looking for a singular trauma to explain his problems. As his account unravelled, I became increasingly convinced that this was mistaken. The nugget he was aiming for, whether it was an insecure core attachment, conditional love, or maladaptive core belief, didn't exist. Personality and social systems don't work like that: they are too complex and messy...

Maybe Edward could have changed into an extraverted, jovial, and happy man, but after twenty years of trying, I doubted it. Much to his disappointment, I tried to focus on how it would be to be as he was, what options he still had within the scope of his low drive and shyness. Did I give up on Edward? I'd rather say that I gave up on the imaginary Edward and worked with the real Edward that was sitting in my room. He never came back, and I will always hope that I was wrong, and that perhaps for him, there was this one thing that could be found, understood, and worked through in order to bring radical change. Failing that, and more likely in my view, I hope that he would learn to accept his situation and being, and learn to choose ways to enjoy life within these confines.

We want a coherent story and we want a good life without suffering, but rarely do we get either. The new trauma narratives, especially in conjunction with the latest hyperbolic claims of psychedelics, form a child's religion version of good and evil. This comic book depiction of the Baddie (The Trauma for Gabor Maté, Thanos in Marvel) and the Goodie (Ayahuasca for Maté, The Avengers for Marvel) makes for great entertainment, but real life needs more subtlety. I have yet to succeed in providing clients such as Edward definitive Answers, but occasionally I have made them curious about the more winding road less travelled, the messy reality of a million reasons that in some way lead to who you are, and the million choices that you can make to gradually adjust who you will be.

What do we mean by trauma and traumatisation?

As we delve deeper into the label of trauma, it may be pertinent to examine what trauma actually is. Given the subjective, popularised, and politicised nature of the social sciences, such an examination is complicated. Originally meaning 'wound' in Greek, it has gradually become reified as a categorically different wound, and I believe that the issue lies therein.

If we disregard the West and the last thirty years and survey the millennia of recorded history for psychic wounds and responses to them, there is little support for any categorical difference between trauma and regular suffering. Our own history and non-Western cultures seem to agree that suffering is the result of the event coupled with the person experiencing the event inside a culture. Being in a snake pit would be terrifying for me, intimidating for Crocodile Dundee, and delightful for a snake lover. The event (snakes or helicopters) is experienced through an individual in a culture, and the kind of and amount of suffering depend on the mindset of the individual as well as their surrounding culture.

We can see this in the radically different ways that people in different cultures indicate high levels of suffering – soldiers in the American Civil War experienced a sense of a weak heartbeat, Salvadorian women escaping civil war spoke of *calorias*, which was a sense of heat in the body, WW1 shell shock was largely physical tics and pains, whilst today's Western PTSD is characterised by dissociation and flashbacks (Watters, 2010). Do note that these experiences are fully real to the victim – they are not made up – but they are entirely culturally determined. Just like culture teaches us how to express most of our other emotions and needs, it teaches us how to express suffering. 'Trauma' is not a physiological biological linear brain process that can be remedied by codified and measured 'trauma therapies.' As therapists, we therefore need to understand the event, the experiencer, and the culture – this is hopefully what this book will achieve in terms of delving deeply into different kinds of difficult situations and having a phenomenological rather than reductive take on suffering.

Greek heroes and regular folk experienced niggles and catastrophes, and suffered accordingly in proportional amounts. Shakespeare's characters lament and gnash their teeth, but they don't dissociate or have flashbacks. The often brutal existence of regular folk in the Middle Ages and the routine torture and sexual violence of war created vast amounts of suffering, it even broke some people beyond recovery, but again the relationship between impact and effect seemed continuous.

We see this in non-Western cultures today as well, where catastrophes like tsunamis in Sri Lanka certainly cause suffering but not traumatisation. I had been working for the United Nations in Sri Lanka until merely a week before the tsunami in 2004, and my old colleagues recounted in consternation how a virtual army of Western counsellors descended upon the island, all intent on finding and curing trauma and labelling kids that would rather go back to school than do trauma therapy as being in 'denial.' A letter from the University of Colombo at the time firmly requested Western agencies to cease to treat suffering yet coping survivors as psychological casualties. According to this letter, seeing the effects of trauma as a physiological reaction in the brain rather than a cultural communication was not only incorrect, but deeply undermining of their resilience (University of Colombo, 2005). If Western ideas of trauma are so disabling and also so different from all other cultures in time and location, why do we even have these ideas?

I believe that it was the birth of psychotherapy in Europe a hundred years ago that also gave birth to a very uniquely Western take on suffering called trauma theory. Discussed by Freud (1896/1962) and Ferenczi (1933/1955) amongst others, extreme events were thought to be so unbearable that they became repressed, only to resurface as psychological symptoms. This hydraulic theory of the pressures of the mind is still only a theory with little backing in modern science, and most practitioners of therapy have now moved on from the complicated warrens of psychoanalytic thinking, but the separation between regular suffering and trauma remains. Trauma theory really took off with the work of Bessel van der Kolk in the Eighties, along with his intense lobbying for these ideas to be made official in the *Diagnostic and Statistical Manual of Mental Disorders*.

The therapeutic community has a tendency to take on the theory that resonates with it, not what has scientific backing, and it is the clients that suffer the effects. Even the most easily refuted theories and contentious authors are widely accepted. One example is polyvagal trauma theory (Porges, 2011), a neurobiological and evolutionary theory about trauma and its treatment that is fully refuted by basic neurobiology – the nervous system simply doesn't work like that (Grossman, 2016; Grossman & Taylor, 2007).

In terms of authors, Maté and van der Kolk are the main pillars in the area. Maté argues that pretty much everything stems from trauma (even cancer! [Maté, 2021]), and most can be healed with psychedelics – his simplistic and politicised theories are undermined by his over-reliance on early childhood attachment (attachment theory has largely been refuted by twin studies [Harris, 2010; Knopik et al., 2017; Serning, 2019]), whilst neglecting more parsimonious genetic impact. Van der Kolk (2015) was the original and main proponent of the separation of trauma from other suffering, responsible for decades of moral panics, recovered memory hoaxes, and pseudoscientific treatment forms (Carr, 2023).

Despite the lack of evidence (and sometimes solid evidence against these theories), the community takes them at their word without query or critique. Our schools and governing bodies would do well to mandate basic scientific grounding in their members. Such grounding should include the differentiation of correlation and cause – so that when Maté claims that racism increases asthma because of trauma (Maté, 2022), the reader should immediately start thinking about differential hypotheses – victims of racism are more likely to suffer from poverty, this is in turn linked to unhealthier homes, areas with increased pollution, less access to good health care, et cetera – the preferred hypothesis is not always the true one.

Training improvements should also stress the importance of drawing from a wide array of sources – the hippocampus seemed smaller in those diagnosed with PTSD from Vietnam, but this wasn't replicated in subsequent research (Jatzko et al., 2006). Finally, a solid grounding in statistics reduces the likelihood of being misled – Maté claims that there is a clear deterministic link between being a victim of abuse and injecting drugs (2012), yet only 3.4% of victims of repeated abuse inject drugs (Felitti, 1998).

But does it really matter what the therapists believe in terms of the aetiology of trauma? At the end of the day, therapy is about talking and understanding your client, something that can be done whether you believe that trauma is just another form of suffering, 'held in the body,' or indeed karmic effects of naughtiness in previous lives. A good therapist brackets their assumptions, and the only effect these theories would have is the administration of some breathing exercises or EMDR, both as harmless and useful as regular therapy. This is all true; however, what therapists think has an effect on how we manage our countries and people – for example, the US Army has spent half a billion dollars to combat PTSD with their Comprehensive Soldier Fitness programme, with no measurable effect whatsoever (Singal, 2021). Furthermore, the discourses that permeate therapy seep out into mainstream culture, furthering victimhood, defeatism, and objectification. It is to these issues we will now turn.

What happens when we apply labels of trauma?

Nassim Taleb famously distinguishes between fragile, robust, and antifragile (2012). Entities in the last category are characterised as becoming stronger when stressed, like a muscle that gets more powerful after receiving micro-tears in the gym, like the fire that wants the wind rather than the candle that gets snuffed out by it. Such antifragility is the story of all our lives – the stress of times tables and Chaucer made us count and read better, the stress on the football field made us run faster, the insistence to do better when we failed our friends made us better friends.

Western culture (Holland, 2019) is actually founded and thoroughly interwoven by a singular account of antifragile suffering. The greatest posttraumatic growth story ever told must be how Jesus' suffering on the cross led to a new covenant with God. This narrative served as the foundation for ideas about individualism, progress, and charity leading to the Enlightenment, the welfare state, and – yes – psychotherapy. Jesus' resolve falters as he bemoans his situation, yet he prevails and does in the end grow and transcend, becoming our culture's core example for how to grow from adversity. Granted, this is a difficult example to follow, and there have surely been occasions when the pressure got too high and we hit the wall, but this learning about ourselves and the world, coupled with recalling how others had endured that specific trial, and how we had endured other trials, hopefully got us to where we are today – stronger, wiser, and with increased freedom.

An individual convinced of their own resilience doesn't see themself as likely to be traumatised and is hence less inclined to interpret adverse experiences as traumatic, and is thus less psychologically vulnerable to them. By contrast, many of today's clients are enmeshed in narratives of trauma. These narratives have proliferated in online psychotherapeutic and quasi-therapeutic discourse and are characterised by a subjective concept creep in which any adverse experience is traumatic if it is individually deemed to be traumatic. As such, no trauma can be said to be more traumatic than any other trauma, indeed insisting that one is worse than another is claimed to be re-traumatising. Whilst this trope abounds, a seemingly opposite one manages to co-exist with it, one of competition in how bad one's situation is, a deeply distressing form of victim Olympics where occasional validation is quickly invalidated by someone else's worse experience. To paraphrase Orwell (1945), all traumas are equal, but some traumas are more equal than others.

Other characteristics of this conception of trauma are its anti-agentic quality and the particular moral universe it operates in, which is anticipated in part by Nietzsche's Genealogy of Morality (1887/1994). To be traumatised is to be largely helpless against one's own emotional responses, and to have the right to be taken care of by others in the world. Much of this care-taking of the traumatised is done by psychological professionals, who do so with genuine compassion and desire to help the wounded. However, the concept creep of the contemporary trauma narrative has recruited a sizeable new cohort of people into identifying with it, and in doing so sacrificing their own self-efficacy. The concept creep also creates opportunity for therapists believing themselves to be uniquely able to care for, heal, and hold the traumatised – often for generous remuneration.

What was it about the humanitarians I interviewed that enabled them to survive adverse events intact? It might be that they happened to share fortuitous neurological traits, but it might also be the case that they shared a worldview about the nature of their work that led them to process those events differently than they might have had they taken a more trauma-centric mindset. If narratives and social constructs can shape our perceptions and experiences in one direction or another, it seems desirable to examine which ones that are likely to be psychologically helpful in adverse conditions, since adverse conditions are an unfortunate and inescapable part of human experience. To identify into the trauma category is to place oneself in a class with little agency or freedom, undermining the possibility of growth when faced with these adversities. It is the essence of resentment, where we refuse the world as it is, where we insist on our rights whilst knowing that they can never be fulfilled – I am in pain, it is unfair, and I cannot do anything about it. By contrast, to paraphrase Scruton (2014), if we see the resentment of traumatisation as the curse that we put upon ourselves, then radical forgiveness of the world and its actors, and letting go of our right not to suffer, is the sacrifice that we make to absolve us of this curse.

My final point on the effects of labelling ourselves as traumatised relates to an understandable yet deeply problematic hybrid between full trauma victimisation and full ownership of what life has thrown at us. Posttraumatic growth should signify something positive arising from something negative, but looking closer at popular social media accounts, also occasionally mirrored in my practice, a different picture emerges. This is not Nassim Taleb's antifragile muscle becoming stronger through stress, this is the eternal tragedy of the heroic underdog. The focus is the trauma, the vulnerability, and the special care and dispensations requested by the victim, and the assertions that they have 'learnt so much' and 'become stronger' are foregrounded against an overarching backdrop of victimhood. Sadly, it seems that the 'growth' part is far too often there in order to make victimhood seem more heroic.

How do we reframe the trauma discourse in order to produce genuine, untainted growth? It is possible – but it takes solid commitment from both client and therapist to step past the poisoned narratives in this new culture of resentment. It was evident in my research, and I see it clearly with my colleagues in the Army, where many have experienced situations that would be generally described as traumatic. As a general rule, impact increases unit cohesion, sense of resilience, and willpower – even after the most gruelling of events (Jennings & McRandle, 2011). There are occasional individual descents into collapse, yet the aforementioned cohesion, resilience, and willpower allow the soldier or officer to 'crack on,' often with stronger and deeper resolve.

Ways forward

Given how the inscription of trauma seems to create a great risk of invalidating and disempowering us, how do we move forward in a more skilful way? Shall we jettison the term and simply talk about experiences of adversity and our reactions to it? This may seem radical, but the concept of trauma as a distinct form of suffering with categorically different effects is a very new one.

Moving away from the label, we could return to the consensus of other cultures and times where life happens and we do our best to learn from it. This book would then need to be revised as there would be no post-trauma to grow from. There would only be experience, some clusters of which are generally troubling for the individual, but all of which must be endured and learnt from with acceptance, resolve, and future focus. Our jobs in the caring professions would be to care and leap ahead to indicate antifragile ways of dealing with difficult experiences. Spurious theories would cease to tempt individuals to categorise their suffering as something different from suffering, requiring special treatment.

Maybe there really is such a thing as PTSD that happens in the most extreme of events. Maybe the amygdalae really can flood the hippocampus so that memories get encoded in the eternal present (Rothschild, 2000: 71). Were this the case, I don't know how we could have mentally endured hundreds of thousands of years as a species on the savannah, being hunted by hyenas, hunger, and each other, but maybe the shamans then were better than us therapists now. Or maybe the body keeps the score differently for humans in the modern West. I really don't know. But what I do know from my travels in clinical practice, war, and research, is that the trauma label is a double-edged sword to be used with extreme caution. If at all possible, see your suffering as something to endure, avoid, fight, resign yourself to, transform, or ignore. If this book can teach you to grow from it, we have done our job right. If it only validates your suffering and supports you in creating an identity around your suffering, we have failed.

There is no reason to query the intentions of most proponents of contemporary trauma culture as anything other than honourable. But what I have seen is that these good intentions have been a road to many of my clients' hell. Marx (1844) famously referred to religion as the opiate of the people – a soothing balm that allows relief yet thwarts the revolution. Perhaps we can see the current tendency towards the designation of much adversity as trauma as that. Comforting yet disabling – a poisoned chalice.

References

Barron, R. A. (1999). Psychological trauma and relief workers. In J. Leaning et al. (Eds.), *Humanitarian Crises: The Medical and Public Health Responses* (pp. 143–175). Harvard University Press. https://doi.org/10.1093/epirev/mxr026

Carr, D. (2023). Tell me why it hurts. *New York Intelligencer*. https://nymag.com/intelligencer/article/trauma-bessel-van-der-kolk-the-body-keeps-the-score-profile.html

Downie, S. (2001). Peacekeepers and peace-builders under stress. In Y. Danieli (Ed.), *Sharing the Front Line and the Back Hills: Peacekeepers, Humanitarian Aid Workers and the Media in the Midst of Crisis* (pp. 9–20). Baywood Publishing.

Ehrenreich, J. H. (2002). *Caring for Others, Caring for Yourself: A Guide for Humanitarian Aid, Health Care, and Human Rights Workers*. Center for Psychology and Society.

Eriksson, C. B., Vande Kemp, H., Gorsuch, R., Hoke, S., & Foy, D. W. (2001). Trauma exposure and PTSD symptoms in international relief and development personnel. *Journal of Traumatic Stress, 14*(1), 205–212. https://psycnet.apa.org/doi/10.1023/A:1007804119319

Felitti, V., Anda, R. F., Nordenberg, D., et al. (1998). Relationship of childhood abuse and household dysfunction to many of the leading causes of death in adults. *American Journal of Preventative Medicine, 14*(4), 245–258. https://psycnet.apa.org/doi/10.1016/S0749-3797(98)00017-8

Ferenczi, S. (1955). Confusion of tongues between adults and the child. In *Final Contributions* (pp. 156–167). Hogarth (Original work published 1933).

Freud, S. (1962). The etiology of hysteria. In J. Strachey (Ed.), *The Standard Edition of the Complete Psychological Works of Sigmund Freud* (Vol. III). Hogarth (Original work published 1896).

Grossman, P. (2016). *After 20 years of "polyvagal" hypotheses, is there any direct evidence for the first 3 premises that form the foundation of the polyvagal conjectures?* ResearchGate. https://www.researchgate.net/post/After-20-years-of-polyvagal-hypotheses-is-there-any-direct-evidence-for-the-first-3-premises-that-form-the-foundation-of-the-polyvagal-conjectures

Grossman, P., & Taylor, E. (2007). Toward understanding respiratory sinus arrhythmia: Relations to cardiac vagal tone, evolution and biobehavioral functions. *Biological Psychology, 74*(2), 263–285. https://doi.org/10.1016/j.biopsycho.2005.11.014

Harris, J. (2010) *No Two Alike: Human Nature and Human Individuality*. Norton.

Holland, T. (2019). *Dominion, the Making of the Western Mind*. Hachette.

Jatzko, A., Rothenhöfer, S., & Schmitt, A. (2006). Hippocampal volume in chronic posttraumatic stress disorder (PTSD): MRI study using two different evaluation methods. *Journal of Affective Disorders, 94*(13), 121–126. https://doi.org/10.1016/j.jad.2006.03.010

Jennings, B., & McRandle, J. (2011). *Attacking the Lion: A Study of Cohesion in Naval Special Warfare Operational Units*. Naval Postgraduate School.

Jessen-Petersen, S. (2001). Caring for staff in UNHCR. In Y. Danieli (Ed.), *Sharing the Front Line and the Back Hills: Peacekeepers, Humanitarian Aid Workers and the Media in the Midst of Crisis* (pp. 53–60). Baywood Publishing.

Knopik, V. S., Neiderhiser, J. M., DeFries, J. C., & Plomin, R. (2017). *Behavioral Genetics* (7th ed.). Worth. https://doi.org/10.1007/s10519-013-9598-6

Larson, L. C. (2006). *Prior Trauma, Health Behaviors, and Posttraumatic Stress Disorder in Humanitarian Aid Workers*. Fuller Theological Seminary, School of Psychology.

Marx, K. (1844). A contribution to the critique of Hegel's Philosophy of Right. In *Deutsch-Französische Jahrbücher, 7 & 10. Jahrbücher*.

Maté, G. (2012). Addiction: Childhood trauma, stress and the biology of addiction. *Journal of Restorative Medicine, 1*(1), 56–63.

Maté, G. (2021). *The Wisdom of Trauma*. Maurizio and Zaya Benazzo.

Maté, G. (2022). *For a healthier society, ditch the myth of normal*. Article by Travis Lupick. Science and Nonduality. https://scienceandnonduality.com/article/for-a-healthier-society-ditch-the-myth-of-normal/

McFarlane, C. A. (2004). Risks associated with the psychological adjustment of humanitarian aid workers. *The Australasian Journal of Disaster and Trauma Studies*. http://www.massey.ac.nz/~trauma/issues/2004-1/mcfarlane.htm

Nietzsche, F. (1994). *On the Genealogy of Morality* (trans. C. Diethe, ed. K. Ansell-Pearson). Cambridge University Press (Original work published 1887).

Orwell, G. (1945). *Animal Farm*. Secker and Warburg.

Porges, S. (2011). *The Polyvagal Theory: Neurophysiological Foundations of Emotions, Attachment, Communication, and Self-regulation*. Norton.

Reyes, G., & Jacobs, G. A. (Eds.). (2006). *Handbook of International Disaster Psychology*. Praeger.

Rothschild, B. (2000). *The Body Remembers, the Psychophysiology of Trauma and Trauma Treatment*. Norton.

Scruton, R. (2014). *How to Be a Conservative*. Bloomsbury.

Serning, N. (2011). *International aid workers' experience of support: An interpretative phenomenological analysis*. Middlesex University. https://repository.mdx.ac.uk/item/836y1

Serning, N. (2019). *Time to let go? The difficulties of simple conclusions from attachment theory*. Research Ed. https://researched.org.uk/2019/06/24/time-to-let-go-the-difficulties-of-simple-conclusions-from-attachment-theory/

Serning, N., & Lyon, N. (2020). The psychotherapeutic use of psychedelics. Reflections, critique and recommendations. In M. Bazzano (Ed.), *Re-visioning Existential Therapy* (pp. 263–270). Routledge.

Singal, J. (2021). *The Quick Fix: Why Fad Psychology Can't Cure Our Social Ills*. Farrar, Straus and Giroux.

Taleb, N. (2012). *Antifragile, Things That Gain From Disorder*. Penguin.

Thomas, R. (2008). *From Stress to Sense of Coherence: Psychological Experiences of Aid Workers in Complex Humanitarian Emergencies*. Oxford University.

University of Colombo. (2005, January 5). *Responding to the aftermath of the tsunami: Counselling with caution*. Press Release, University of Colombo.

van der Kolk, B. (2015). *The Body Keeps the Score: Brain, Mind, and Body in the Healing of Trauma*. Penguin.

Watters, E. (2010). *Crazy Like Us: The Globalization of the American Psyche*. Free Press.

Section 5

Trauma as it Emerges in the Therapeutic Encounter

Chapter 12

Applying a Hermeneutic Phenomenological Lens: A Literary Review Observes the Impact of Client Suicide on the Therapist

Mary Spring

Introduction

"A topic," notes McCaffrey et al. (2012: 221), "is a place of encounter, a place where things are going on, a place with its own life of exchanges and interconnections." What moved me then to conduct a systematic and critical observation of the current available literature in the particular domain of a therapist's response to the death by suicide of a client was reflective of what was going on inside me, of what I was meeting within and beyond myself in this place.

An existential lens supports the exploration of universal themes as uniquely lived and experienced by the person. To support a consideration of freedom, choice, meaning, aloneness, loss in its many different hues, the ambiguous and paradoxical shades of human nature and the endless 'givens' of one's life is to foster a contemplation of a lived and living and becoming life. Underpinning this philosophical perspective is my respect for the other person, a core belief that each person is a unique and somewhat invisible union of mind, body, heart, and soul, a regard for therapeutic process and its three living tenses of past, present, and future, and a conviction in the significance and richness of the therapeutic relationship that evolves between two people.

Reminded by Rilke (1989: 198), "So we live, forever taking leave," loss emanates from every therapeutic session. It weaves and nestles itself within the dissonant horizons of life stages, aging, physical decline, bereavement, and changes in work circumstances and relationships. The intimate encounter between the therapist and the client enters a particular realm when dying and death become the client's lived experience. As therapists, our own relationship with death and dying is stirred. We are prompted, if we choose, to engage with the finiteness of our very being, with "The abyss of nonbeing" (Tillich, 1952/2014: 30), what Yalom depicts as "The worm at the core of existence" (2008: 274).

DOI: 10.4324/9781003493860-17

Suicide, one of the four modes of death as recognised by the World Health Organization – natural, accidental, and homicidal being the other modes – has its etymological roots in two Latin words, *sui*, meaning 'of oneself' and *caedere*, 'to kill,' and is defined by the *Oxford Encyclopedic English Dictionary* (1991) as "the intentional killing of oneself." Given the frequency of suicide in society and in community, and the World Health Organization's 2021 publication *Suicide Worldwide in 2019: Global Health Estimates* estimating that 703,000 people die by suicide globally every year, it is fair to suggest that a therapist, in all likelihood, may find themselves in a profoundly unique situation and space if a client dies by suicide. Working from a fallacious assumption that we are professionally immune from vulnerability (C. L. Anderson, 2013) may provide a protection, of sorts, yet "as long as we consider death as something in the distant future, we remain estranged from our fundamental relatedness to death, our embodiment of death" (van Deurzen, 2010: 65). If we ever needed prompting, however, Heidegger unequivocally reminds us that death is "essentially and irreplaceably mine" (Heidegger, 1927/2010: 243).

Drawn to qualitative research, an exploration which, like therapy, enables the inherent "messiness of life" (Braun & Clarke, 2013: 20) to be potentially unearthed and understood, I consider that there are multiple versions of experience rather than one single version. Having completed a qualitative piece of research on this particular theme a number of years ago (Spring, 2020), I wished to return to this subject but now focus exclusively on a literary review and work from a philosophical hermeneutic paradigm which potentially would allow light to be thrown on the uniquely lived experience and lifeworld of the therapist when the therapeutic relationship is abruptly and irreversibly ended by a client's death by suicide.

"Reflexivity locates the researcher in the research project" (Holloway & Wheeler, 2002: 359). It is important then to acknowledge the personal dimensions, or what Gadamer terms "historically effected consciousness," which informed my interest in pursuing this literary review (Gadamer, 1960/2004: 391). Such horizons include a cousin dying by suicide and two students whom I taught making attempts at ending their lives. Thirdly, I live in a city on the west coast of Ireland where Atlantic beaches, headlands, slipways, and bridges claim numerous people to suicide.

There was another experience which may have coaxed me gently towards conducting this literature review. I am a tutor with a counsellor-psychotherapist training college in Ireland, and one Saturday in May of 2022, Covid restrictions necessitating the full day take place via Zoom, we broke for lunch. On our return I noticed that one learner was missing. Joe came back to his screen a half an hour or so later. In a state of deep shock, he shared with the class that his next-door neighbour had just been found dead in his bedroom. He had taken his own life. The rest of the afternoon's class proved to be a deeply sensitive experience. Joe, in these very early moments of grief and loss, talked about his young neighbour and about the mentoring-type connection he had had with him. And in the full class and over the next few hours, a dynamic, real-time conversation evolved amid a devastating reality. Defences down, learners checked into the trauma that was coursing through their own bodies and named what they felt. One person was forcefully reminded of a similar loss in her life. For others, it was the stark realisation that suicide could be part of the environment they were now training in. Different perspectives on suicide were aired. Old assumptions which stigmatise and pathologise suicide were passionately dismissed and new understandings grew. For me, I knew in my heart that big things had happened that day; tragedy had befallen a family, a community, and a class member, and a class had walked a particular path and had engaged meaningfully with mortality, with suicide, and with life. I was left with a strong sense that there need to be more conversations concerning death, dying, and suicide.

Methodology

A hermeneutic phenomenological approach to the review of literature underpinned this project. This philosophical and methodological standpoint considers and honours the essence of phenomenology. Van Manen succinctly identifies phenomenology as "the study of the primal, lived, pre-reflective, prepredicative meaning of an experience" (2017: 776). If practised well, he posits, it "enthrals us with insight into the enigma of life as we experience it" (779). Compatible, I considered, with my nature, my curiosity, lived experience, and philosophy of psychotherapy, phenomenology, as a form of inquiry, spoke strongly to me.

Descriptive and evocative rather than explanatory, phenomenology emphasises the subjective and unique encounter with everyday experience and, crucially, acknowledges that "how we ascribe meaning to an event, person or object is always filtered through an already existing experiential knowledge" (Eatough, 2012: 329). Hermeneutic consciousness in this very stance captures Heidegger's core tenet that we are beings who live in and through time (Heidegger, 1927/2010). Reminded by McLeod that "we cannot step outside culture and history" (McLeod, 2011: 30), hermeneutical interpretation is attentive to the socio-historical and cultural contexts of researcher and participants and the accompanying distance between the respective contexts. It emphasises that new understanding emerges, not from an eclipse of one world by the other, but from the delicate and constant dialogical co-existence or the "fusion of horizons" (Barrett et al., 2011: 189) which takes place between the reader's situated horizon and the situated horizon of the text.

Mirroring the hermeneutic circle's approach to the review of literature, my framework for this literary review involved two mutually intertwining circles. The outer movement encapsulated the search and acquisition circle; the inner circle encapsulated the ongoing search, analysis, and interpretation circle, this dialogue enabling the circles to travel and potentially sculpt new perspectives.

Time was given to sit in this place of "wondering engagement" (van Manen, 2017: 777). In a sometimes forward, sometimes backward cyclical movement between reading and dwelling with the texts, relevant publications which gave primacy to the 'emic' perspective continued to be prioritised. Rigorously upholding validity and reliability in a project that involved subjective experience, language, and understanding, texts were carefully reread and frequently read again, attention given to the rich descriptions of experience that lay plaited within the emerging patterns, clusters, and themes. Immersing myself in the individual accounts in what struck me as a near contemplative movement, and one that is at the very core of the underlying hermeneutic phenomenological approach, a deeper understanding of this project's purpose, its content, and the phenomenon began to slowly emerge.

Codes, compared by Braun and Clark to individual bricks and roof tiles of a house (2013: 207), were readily identified in the literature. Shock, grief, overwhelm, anxiety, guilt, isolation, the impact on professional practice and wellbeing, and the different support systems that were accessed stood out. Further crafting required that the aforementioned bricks and roof tiles, while remaining intact, would inform the three core phenomenologically based themes that eventually emerged. These three core themes would provide the scaffolding for the *Analysis and Findings*. The first theme, entitled *Hearing the News*, would pause to consider those fragile, early hours when a therapist heard of their client's death. The second theme, *Fear in its Different Colours*, would subsequently trace the therapist's encounter with different hues of fear, with attention given in particular to the experiences of distress, self-doubt, caution, and fear itself. In the third section of these findings, *Reconciliation with a New Truth*, the review would note the therapist's movement towards being reconciled with a raw and new reality.

A new stage in the project followed, one which mirrors the workings of the inner circle of the hermeneutic model. Here, in the accompanying intertwining of the two circles (the outer circle's search and acquisition continuing to be an ongoing process), the researcher reflected on the findings. I was mindful that this project was not a research project which involved therapists telling me their story of client suicide but a review of available literature on the impact of client suicide on the therapist as told to other researchers, and was, in effect, another step away from representing a participant's deeply personal experience of loss. The section entitled *Discussion* took the shape of an overview of three particular aspects that spoke strongly to me. These unfolding threads I discerned as *The Wounded Therapist*, *The Grieving Therapist*, and *The Changed Therapist*. This point of the project necessitated that I would, in a circular movement, vigilantly reread and once again, dwell with the individual accounts so that my *Discussion on Findings* would always be rooted in the documented accounts of people's lived experience and not in my memory of documented accounts of people's lived experience.

A *Conclusion* closed the review. It included a commentary on the learnings garnered from this literature review and considered its gaps and limitations. I left the hermeneutic circle.

Analysis and findings of the literature review: Three themes

Though qualitative papers, with their exploration of "the textured meanings and subjective interpretations of a fluid, uncertain world" (Finlay, 2011: 9), would be the principal focus of this search strategy and form the basis of the sections entitled *Analysis and Findings* and *Findings*, it was decided to observe, albeit briefly, quantitative pieces of research, my reasoning being that their content and data-based findings unequivocally confirmed the impact on the professional when a client dies by suicide.

From the late 1980s onwards, seminal work in America by Chemtob et al. (1988a, 1988b), Menninger (1991), Foster and McAdams (1999), and McAdams and Foster (2000) attest to the reality of client suicide and its affective impact on the professional. Chemtob et al. argue that client suicide should be acknowledged as an 'occupational hazard' not simply because of its frequency but also because of its impact on the therapist (1988a). Shock, loss, guilt, anger, anxiety, diminished self-esteem, self-doubt, fear of blame, fear of lawsuits, and the presence of intrusive and avoidant thoughts lasting for at least six months are observed in the data and depict the listening professional in crisis. These early papers confirm the disrupted identity in some professionals and record the therapist's adoption of a more cautious approach to client selection, the keeping of more conservative case notes, a greater alertness to suicidal cues, an increase in hospital referrals, and a heightened attention to legal matters (Grad & Michel, 2004; Hendin et al., 2000, 2004; McAdams & Foster, 2000). Finlayson and Simmonds' research (2018), consistent with the findings documented thirty years earlier by Chemtob et al. (1988a, 1988b) and McAdams and Foster (2000), among others, concludes that the suicide of a client is associated with increased intensity of emotional reaction and finds that the most intense feelings are shock, anger, guilt, distress, and sadness (Finlayson & Simmonds, 2018: 27–30). In the 1970s and 1980s, however, a viewpoint had begun to grow in mainstream psychological research which posited that a qualitative methodology of research lends itself towards a greater understanding of the lived experience (Eatough, 2012: 325). This perspective saw the emergence of a less data-focused and more phenomenon-based inquiry.

Theme 1: Hearing the News

If suicide is "an intensely private act," the very finality of this act evokes numerous emotional responses and lives on, in and among people (Grollman & Malikow, 1999: 3). This literature review observes a myriad of intensely distressing emotions that were felt by the therapist on hearing the news of a client's suicide. These personal accounts tell us of professional people who are immediately thrown into a particular space in time.

Though the narrative is brief in his account of losing a woman in a group he facilitated for people who had lost loved ones to suicide, Farberow (2005: 17) identifies the feelings of shock, disbelief, guilty, shame, and anger. In contrast, a sense of overwhelm is immediately heard in Neal's (2017) more graphic narrative account of hearing about her client's suicide. She was out for dinner one Sunday night when her phone rang. A police inspector identified himself and mentioned her client's name. "I knew," she writes, "what his next words would be. She was dead" (Neal, 2017: 174). Crowded there and then by the suddenness of its confirmation, her capacity to listen closed down. In the blur of disconnection, her imagination immediately took charge and ran riot. She plunged into a fantasy of the client standing at a railway station, a place whose sounds had often soothed her in the past, then taking her own life on the tracks:

> My mind was already busy sketching the scene: the man, in uniform, standing on a platform looking down at the activity below on the train lines as Aria's body was being photographed and taken away. (Neal, 2017: 174)

In fact, however, as the police officer subsequently informed Neal, the client had not died in the way she had imagined; she had died by inhaling a large dose of helium in an empty, temporary apartment. The overwhelm and internal chaos continued to be felt by Neal in the early days following her client's death. Fear, shame, disorganisation, isolation, and wanting to retreat from the world vigorously and distressingly jolted her "out of my everyday mode of existence" (Neal, 2017: 175).

Rycroft's (2012) account similarly captures a moment in time when the therapist 'knows' that something has happened even before she is told the news. Emma, an agitated sixteen-year-old client, had left in the middle of a family therapy session and had not returned. The police were immediately informed. The therapist then drove away from the centre with the client's mother in the car behind her. She continues:

I heard the repetitive clanging of the railway crossing boom gates. They were obviously stuck. When I saw the flashing lights of the ambulance my heart began to thump, I felt a cold sickness and I knew immediately something I hadn't previously even considered: that Emma had put herself in front of a passing train. (Rycroft, 2012: 84–85)

Margaret Clausen's depiction of her immediate experience as a therapist following the suicide of her client is another sensitive piece of qualitative literature (Clausen, 2015). In what is a thoughtful meditation on a particular type of loss, she witnesses being catapulted "into another environment which is foreign and therefore scary" (Clausen, 2015: 7). Early one morning she had checked her voice mail. Two messages, sent the previous evening, were from her client and from this client's psychiatrist respectively. The former informed the therapist that she would not be attending the following day's arranged session due to "a need to find new housing." The second message asked Clausen to phone the psychiatrist immediately she received the message. This she promptly did, and, as her heart pounded from her chest into her throat, she was told that her client had died by her own hand. The immediate affective response of the therapist was three-fold – she gasped, she cried, and she tried to conceal her upset. She felt groundless, impotent, and frustrated in the "loss of an incomplete, torn-apart relationship" (Clausen, 2015: 8).

Spring (2020) similarly illustrates the complex gamut of emotions that course through a therapist in the immediate aftermath of hearing the news of a client's suicide. One therapist recalled talking with a neighbour one morning about the recent death of an elderly neighbour known to both of them. In the midst of this conversation the neighbour said that: "Something worse has happened" (Spring, 2020). When then given the name of a person who had died by suicide overnight, the therapist was immediately stunned; she blurted out "she's my client" and felt a physical urge to throw up. In these raw, early moments, the therapist connected with the intense rage she now felt towards a locum doctor whom she had rung following her session two days earlier with the now deceased client. She had pointedly asked him to hospitalise her client. The locum had disagreed with her summation and her request.

Theme 2: Fear in its Different Colours

Fear is arguably one of the most paralysing of emotions. This part of the literature review illustrates four different shades of fear which permeated the therapists' fragmented lives following their client's death. Focusing on the lived phenomena of distress, self-doubt, caution, and uncompromising fear itself, this section will confirm that though the immediate emotional response to a client suicide may, on the surface, be considered as similar to the reactions of a bereft family and loved ones, additional feelings, as posited by Farberow (2005), may also be felt because of the unique professional caregiving role of the therapist.

Distress is sharply observed in Hendin et al.'s (2004) account of a practitioner who, for two years following his client's suicide, would jump up with anxiety when his telephone rang at night (Hendin et al., 2004: 1444). Sleep was disturbed for some therapists. In Hendin et al. (2000), another therapist writes:

> I was recurrently getting lost in a series of Kafkaesque corridors, stairways, or meandering trains, hopelessly late, woefully unprepared, or – in one dream – only partly clothed. (Hendin et al., 2024: 1444)

Tillman's account (2006) notes a therapist in the months following the client's death daydreaming about him; she imagined him dying alone in the woods and wondered what his body would have looked like when it was found. A school counsellor in Christianson and Everall's study echoes a similar reaction: "I was having a difficult time sleeping. I have incredible nightmares. To this day, at night time, it's like his face exploded and all I remember was blood and remnants" (Christianson & Everall, 2009: 162).

Another manifestation of fear quickly manifests itself in some therapists who feel an acute sense of professional **self-doubt**. Consistent with the findings in early quantitative research and pointing to the "shattered beliefs and assumptions around the efficacy of the therapeutic process" (Gutin, 2019a: 30), some therapists self-punitively consider leaving the profession, and some others discontinue work with suicidal clients (Hendin et al., 2000). One extract from Grad and Michel (2004) strikingly encapsulates a therapist's self-doubt. Here one witnesses a professional intruded upon, if not tortured, by intrusive rumination; thoughts are fuelled with doubt, self-criticism, guilt, failure, blame, and fear of collegial judgement:

> Questions started to eat me up, some of them rational and constructive, some totally irrational and difficult to comprehend:
>   What did I do wrong? What did I miss in the evaluation of her mental state? Why didn't I retreat from therapy before? Why did she do this to me? Was this a revenge of some sort? Is this because I am not a good enough therapist? Or maybe I am not a good person? Is this some sort of a punishment for something? I am probably no good for this vocation. Who will trust me now? Will I trust myself? (Grad & Michel, 2004: 76–77)

Caution is embedded in fear. Touching deeply on what Tillman (2006: 159) describes as "the core of narcissistic vulnerability," the literature points to self-agency being significantly eroded. A therapist's response to other clients changes, and a hypervigilant attitude towards depressive and suicidal cues is adopted (Hendin et al., 2000). One therapist reported that "when I have a client who is getting closer to thinking about suicide, my anxiety goes through the roof more than it did before, and I am clear suicide is not an option" (Tillman, 2006: 164).

"Often," write Tillman and Carter (2014: 66–67), "the suicide of a patient is fodder for gossip, speculation, blame, and the projection of fantasies about 'what went wrong' in a treatment, a presumed therapeutic error in assessment or treatment that may, or may not, have occurred or been a factor in the suicide." Into this milieu, **unvarnished fear** unleashes itself. Neal recalls that she "agonized over the possibility of another suicide" (Neal, 2017: 178). For some therapists, fear had another distressing edge, and that was the fear of "appearing fraudulent or inept in the eyes of our colleagues" and, more pointedly, being blamed by one's professional colleagues and peers (Fox & Cooper, 1998: 153). "I was convinced everyone blamed me and that the coroner's inquest would expose my incompetence," writes Neal (2017: 175). Tillman's account (2006) candidly portrays the disturbed connection between therapist and colleagues: one therapist, while attending the deceased client's memorial service, thought that several of her colleagues communicated a 'you fucked up' response to her. She subsequently felt that her trainees doubted her perspectives and that they were saying: "Why should we listen to you, look what happened to your patient" (Tillman, 2006: 165). Hendin et al. (2004: 1443) dramatically capture another near-threatening scene; here a hospital clinical director pointedly fixed his gaze on the therapist and said that the patient appeared "to have died the way she was treated, with a lot of people around her but no one effectively helping her." Four of the participants in Hendin et al.'s (2004) research were threatened with potential lawsuits. Two of the school counsellor participants in Christianson and Everall's research (2009) similarly feared litigation, one stating: "I phoned a lawyer (...) I was really afraid. And he [the lawyer] reassured me that I wasn't in trouble and that he would be there for me no matter what happened" (Christianson & Everall, 2009: 160). For another therapist in Grad and Michel's (2004) study, a different yet equally raw expression of fear was felt:

A few days after the suicide I developed a paranoid fear of her husband whom I had seen once with the patient. The thoughts that one day he would turn up and assault me or even kill me became more and more intrusive. I developed a fear of the dark (...) I never mentioned these fears to anyone, not even to my wife. I would have been ashamed to admit such irrational thoughts. (Grad & Michel, 2004: 78)

Theme 3: Reconciliation with a New Truth

Reconciliation flourishes, notes Massey (2009: 87), when attention is given to "mending the small ruptures that inevitably occur as two or more people navigate their way forward." Can, however, there be a reconciliation when one of the harshest realities has happened, when there has been an "unambiguous rejection of the therapeutic relationship we were attempting to create together" (C. L. Anderson, 2013: 127)?

The qualitative literature that underpins this review suggests that therapists move from a place in time where shame "isolates and evicts us from our relational home" (Clausen, 2015: 10) to another place in time – a place of profound posttraumatic growth. This transformative process enabled one therapist to say:

> What has happened has not been because of negligence or irresponsibility or ineptitude and that nothing we could say or do could change the outcome. Suicide cannot be predicted. One can try to do it all right and it may still turn out wrong. (Fox & Cooper, 1998: 153)

"Speaking about the unspeakable" (Fox & Cooper, 1998: 153) was the common pathway walked by numerous therapists in reconciling themselves with a new, unsettling truth. Silence would otherwise compound the isolating phenomenon (Neal, 2017: 177). Rycroft reflects:

> I wanted people not to dismiss my guilt but to help me examine the parameters of my responsibility, as well as what I might have done differently; to help me distinguish what was only apparent through hindsight. (Rycroft, 2012: 87)

Nurturing spaces were found and healing processes unfolded. In practising self-care, what Norcross and Guy Jr. (2007: 13) describe as "a human requisite, a clinical necessity, and an ethical imperative," some professionals returned to personal therapy (Hendin et al., 2000; Neal, 2017; Tillman, 2006) or attended their supervisor (Spring, 2020; Tillman, 2006). Here therapists confronted a second stigma, as highlighted by Gutin (2019a: 22), and this was the stigma surrounding a therapist's own emotional vulnerability. A myriad of emotions, thoughts, and fantasies were validated as therapists tried to make sense of their experience. A participant in Tillman's research reported that: "My supervisor met with me on Sunday and again on Monday. She was tremendous. I was devastated and my supervisor was a lifesaver for me during that time" (Tillman, 2006: 169). Another therapist was gently confronted by her supervisor and clinic director who pointed out that, in the month following the suicide of her eleven-year-old client, the therapist had put in a considerable amount of extra working hours. On reflection, she considered that this, unbeknown to herself, was an attempt to punish herself for "failing to prevent Annie's suicide" (G. O. Anderson, 2012: 28). For C. L. Anderson (2013), whose two deceased clients had died within a short period of time, one shooting himself, the second taking an overdose, supervision became a 'holding' environment. Here she was encouraged to name and understand 'the multiple intense emotions that I experienced' and became familiar with her 'seductive pull towards action.'

Some found support in talking and sharing their loss with a "special fraternity" (Tillman, 2006: 169) of colleagues who shared their own experience of losing a client to suicide. This was found to be more useful than empty reassurances "that the death was inevitable or even that the treatment had been a success" (Hendin et al., 2000: 2025). For some professionals in these different environments, ancient and not so ancient losses were rekindled and mourned (Spring, 2020: 52) and future losses pondered on. One therapist writes:

> I was reminded of my own children, whom I felt I could not bear to lose, even more so to suicide. (No one can bear to lose a child to suicide.) Annie's death reminded me of when my husband died suddenly of a heart attack when he was 43 and I was 34. Annie's death reminded me of when I was hospitalized for depression and an overdose when I was in my early twenties. I remembered feeling that I was in a narrow tunnel with only one option when I had overdosed. I have a faint memory of how very bad that felt, how bad it must have felt for Annie. Finally I had connected with her. (G. O. Anderson, 2012: 28–29)

Others met the deceased's parents, one therapist and mother engaging in phone conversations which enabled the shared construction of a narrative and an understanding around a son and a client's death (Fox & Cooper, 1998). Some therapists attended the funeral (Hendin et al., 2000). For another therapist who went to the church ceremony, "I chose to go. I needed to go to honour her (…) to honour us" (Spring, 2020: 52).

Clausen's anecdotal account captured the role played by ritual in supporting a therapist in her loss and grief. Giving her pain structure, scaffolding, and expression, she, along with a colleague, went to the place where her client had taken her own life, read a piece of personal reflection and poetry, and placed some flowers in the ground. Ritual was also brought into Clausen's therapy room. She writes:

> Keenly aware of how groundless I felt, I longed for grounding in the rituals of my sessions with Jill. I could not fathom scheduling another patient

in Jill's session times. I realized what I wanted was to keep my appointment with Jill. So I did just that: I kept my appointments with Jill for one year. Sometimes I went to a meditation space near my office for the appointment; sometimes I was in a natural setting. Other times, I spent it in my office. Wherever I chose to spend the sessions, I also was with Jill. Sometimes reading a book of poetry that evoked Jill, or intentionally recollecting parts of sessions. By the second week of appointments with Jill, I began writing during the time. I used poetry as a companion. Sometimes I wrote to Jill, sometimes extemporaneously to the Reader with a capital R. (Clausen, 2015: 9)

Not surprisingly, as part of the process of accepting a new harsh truth, the literature evidences change in the therapist's practice. Though this essay has already documented caution coming into the therapy room, there are also accounts which tell us that, with the passing of time, new possibilities in practice emerged and personal strengths came to the fore, practitioners integrating what they had experienced and allowing it to impact on their work in a constructive, dynamic, and transformative way: "I felt emboldened to talk frankly about life and death in a way that I had not done before" (Neal, 2017: 178). Another therapist noted that the experience made her "less afraid to cut through all the bullshit and able to say to the vulnerable client that I would be there as much as the client allows me to" (Spring, 2020: 52).

Therapists were observed from the literature to learn a new way of being in the world. Over time, they were seen to bear what is "uniquely solitary to bear" (Clausen, 2015: 7). Learning to live with the anxieties that will never go away" (Neal, 2017: 183) and learning to allow for "some inner turmoil" (Grad & Michel, 2004: 80), therapists were noted as moving through loss to a place of existential understanding where life begins to be realised as more noncertain and unpredictable than certain and predictable. Limitations of the work of therapy were understood at another level, as was the fragility of human nature. The fantasy that therapists can prevent a client ending their own lives was dismantled in the harshest of ways, the decision to end one's life slowly being recognised as another person's choice. "You are powerless essentially over the lives of people," spoke one therapist. "If you don't recognise that, you are trying to fix people and move them to a particular place" (Spring, 2020: 53).

Discussion

If psychotherapy is potentially a draining profession where "fatigue, stress and routine can dull our awareness, lull us into ethical sleep, put us on automatic when we need to wake up to what we are missing" (Pope &

Vasquez, 2007: 293), this literature review repeatedly chronicles the unexpected and jarring awakening when a therapist's client dies by suicide. Upholding the hypothesis that the trauma invokes many responses in the therapist, vigorous emotions are illustrated as assailing the professional listener. In the midst of such disturbance, new learning is seen to take place, new philosophical stances are adopted, new possibilities emerge, the practice of therapy alters, and discourse changes as therapists reconcile themselves with a new reality.

In this section of the literary review entitled *Discussion*, I will reflect on what was extrapolated from the findings. In a three-way divide, this discussion suggests that the therapist in truth becomes *The Wounded Therapist, The Grieving Therapist,* and *The Changed Therapist.*

The Wounded Therapist

The suicide of a client, suggests C. L. Anderson (2013), 'is a fundamentally destabilizing and overwhelming event.' The client's decision, brutal in its finality, deems that no other choices will be made in the future nor chances taken. What lies within this act is the devastating complexity of a now ruptured therapeutic relationship. One has been a listener; the other, cast as vulnerable, has been the person to be listened to and supported. Now, a new reality emerges, the client having moved "from one realm to another by force through death" (Hillman, 2016: 56). This review's findings suggest that the therapist is instantly wounded and left holding some of the client's suffering (James, 2012). Drawing on the most striking of metaphors, Neal evocatively compares her body to "an open wound" (Neal, 2017: 176). Pierced by what is at first an incomprehensible and unforeseen reality, the therapist's pre-reflected reactions explicitly mirror Heidegger's sense of "uncanniness, of *not-being-at-home*" (Heidegger, 1927/2010: 183). In the midst of this wounding, the narratives capture what is possibly, the most solitary, the most silent, and the most disenfranchising of professional experiences. Yet life, in the midst of this potentially immobilising and numbing trauma, is seen to continue asking of the therapist; children and school-related tasks need to be focused on (Christianson & Everall, 2009). Other client appointments are scheduled. The world does not stand still.

It is as if a second separation takes place, a therapist's estrangement from their old world somewhat mirroring the client's ultimate decision to separate from their world. But if the act of suicide is "towards a silence, a shelter from torment" (Heaton, 2009: 129), the research findings capture the tidal waves that storm the practitioner's psyche, the three living tenses of past, present, and future fighting to be heard and tended to. Fear, in its different colours and insidious in its presence, awakens and punctuates clinical practice. As previously recorded in early quantitative research, professional confidence and competence are seen to be immediately undermined. The illusion of the therapist's omnipotence – and that is all it is: an illusion – is shattered, as is the myth of potential positive influences on all other clients. Distressing questions beset the therapist in a culture where not only is suicide stigmatised but so too is the vulnerable listener. The fretful therapist wonders: "Was I really as skilled as I thought I was?" (Fox & Cooper, 1998: 152). Amid this intrusive rumination, a restless hypervigilance and caution, perhaps capturing the need to professionally self-preserve, come into practice. "An injury with profound and enduring consequences" (Tillman, 2006: 159), the therapist is witnessed as being deeply wounded.

The Grieving Therapist

As borne out in the literature, grieving is phenomenologically unique to each person – one's pathway of grief differing from another's. The universality may be in the experience of loss but not in the grieving, for grieving is informed by relationship. Death by suicide inevitably adds another disconcerting layer of complexity for the griever. Someone has died by their own hand and the therapist grieves the traumatic loss of someone whom they have known, someone whom they have been in relationship with, someone 'who despite our efforts actively chooses to turn away from us through death' (C. L. Anderson, 2013). It is too clichéd then to suggest that time will heal all wounds.

The observed literature focuses attention on the therapist's initial reactions to hearing of the client's sudden death and observes the subsequent impact on the therapist – insidious questions and unsettling emotions and physical sensations beginning to intrude and take root in the therapist. However, the literature also strongly illustrates the very real sense of relational loss that awakens in the bereft listener. Affirming the widely held perspective that "the therapeutic relationship is at the heart of therapy" (Barnett, 2009: 220), an ache is felt – an ache of absence. How paradoxical it is that a client is now so very present in their absence.

The findings suggest that therapists grieve in different ways. Attendance at parts of the funeral ceremony helps some, as does talking with the deceased's parents. For others, private ritual gives shape and personal expression to a therapist's loss, one practitioner keeping the appointment time for the next year and in that space sometimes writing either to or about her deceased client.

Human support systems prove to be critical for the bereaved therapists. Some therapists follow Malcolm's urging to the grieving Macduff to: "Give sorrow words: the grief that does not speak knits up the o-er wrought heart and bids it break" (*Macbeth*, Act 4, Sc. 3. 207–210). Personal therapy, supervision, and the support of empathic colleagues are seen to offer crucial support. Allowing for the expression of feelings and the telling of stories – two integral aspects of grieving – these supports are observed as giving balm to the intrusive thoughts and balance to the conflicting and complicated emotions.

The Changed Therapist

"If we really engage," suggests Casement (2020: 52), "with something previously unknown to us *we are changed by it.*" When a client dies by suicide, the therapist's sense of being-in-the-world is disturbed, and, as suggested in this review, the therapist is instantly changed. Engaging with a profound process, a narrative is ultimately constructed, one that allows for tragic circumstances and ultimate choices that have been made by others whom they have been in relationship with. In this most sensitive of movements, one that involves the feeling of instant shock and subsequently fear in its different colours, the therapist is seen to travel from "'what was or was not' to 'what is or is not'" (Spinelli, 2015: 85). An old assumptive worldview is deconstructed, if not demolished, and core beliefs are undermined. Lessons of life are slowly reframed. The ideal that suicide can be prevented is dismantled, and attitudes towards suicide, some internalised, stigmatised, and pathologised, are, by necessity, pondered on. Stung by two of the most profound of universal truths – one's vulnerability and temporality – the therapist is challenged to rebuild one's "ship of death" (Hillman, 2016: 51). Amidst a deeply felt sense that "something is always carried" (Spring, 2020: 53), a therapist is changed.

The findings of this review point to such traumatic experiences potentially and paradoxically being a catalyst for personal and professional growth (Gutin, 2019b: 18). The greatest professional fear has now been realised (Spring, 2020: 53). However, if fear becomes the dominant force in the therapist following a client suicide, then this grounding in the safe and cautious soil of the "they-self" (Heidegger, 1927/2010: 125) will erode the healing relational work of clinical practice. Such a traumatised stance is unsustainable in the therapy room. The alternative is to adopt a new way of being-in-the-world and a new way of being-with-others, an attitude which acknowledges thrownness, lived experience, fears, noncertainty, the unknown, and temporality, and which embraces risk-taking, courage, growth, and transformation.

A gap in the literature

Searching to find what Finlay describes as the "textual description of the essence of the phenomenon" (Finlay, 2011: 16), this literary review contributes to a knowledge and an understanding of the therapist's unique experience when a client dies by suicide. However, locating this literary review within extant literature proved to be a Sisyphean task, a relatively small body of qualitatively grounded literature only being available; only nine journal articles were sourced and they were complemented by an online narrative and chapters from two books. It's worth noting that the qualitative material sourced for this literature review stretched from 1998 to 2020. A shorter, more focused time period and more contemporary time-line might have lent other colourings to the findings. The available primary qualitative data for this literature review was informed by research conducted in six countries, four English-speaking nations – America, Canada, England, and Ireland – and two non-English-speaking countries – Slovenia and Switzerland. A broader demographic might have garnered more comparative findings. Alternatively, a focus on the literature from one country alone might also have offered more location-specific detail.

This literature review points to the need for further inquiry to take place. True to the hermeneutic tradition, which rejects a single authoritative reading, this project's reading and interpretation of findings is simply one person's situated reading and interpretation. If the horizon of another researcher had merged with the horizon of the studied texts, different themes in the *Findings* and an alternative *Discussion* would, in all likelihood, have been generated. Researchers are encouraged to be curious, wonder, and follow the questions that might come from engaging with this rich subject. Mining and shining a light on life situations invites us to become more familiar with the more vulnerable and trembling realms of our being and to understand at a deeper level the lives of the people who sit with us in our therapy rooms.

Conclusion

Living as we do in the shadows of death, a client's suicide is a profound situational, relational, and temporal fracture. The ultimate rupture takes place. In this space in time, a therapist is left bereft and thrown into a landscape that is unfamiliar. By processing this loss in ways and at a pace that is unique to each person, mystery unfolds in the harrowed heart and the therapist is left tender with loss, memory, absence, and learnings on life.

Located within relevant extant literature, this review confirms the reality of client suicide. It emerges in the telling of a therapist's uniquely lived experience, a hermeneutic phenomenological lens, underpinned by descriptive and sometimes taut detail, repeatedly allowing for the therapist to be heard. Wounding and loss, fear and disconnection, growth and courage are observed. And in each telling of the phenomenon, perhaps new horizons open and society's long stigmatisation of suicide is challenged.

Phenomenology, as a form of inquiry, necessitates "the attentive practice of thoughtfulness" (van Manen, 2016: 12). Conducting this project concerning the unique experience of the therapist when the client carries out "the most individual of acts" (Williams, 2014: 24) prompted me to listen in a reflective manner to the evidence as documented in the literature but, equally importantly, to listen to the manoeuvrings of my own heart. At times I dwelt with the lifeworlds of the therapists and was stilled by evocative images which captured the therapist's unique situation. In my journaling and personal therapy, and attentive to my own situated being and the acknowledged intersubjective connectedness and disconnectedness between me, the researcher, and the researched, I noted and acknowledged my fore-understandings, my internal assumptions, and biases. I returned to personal experiences of bereavement and suicide and felt the inner existential pull asking me to meaningfully consider impermanence, which nestles between the breathing of my first breath and the exhalation of my last breath. My own work as a psychotherapist slowed down. I began to listen more. Ultimately, I could not but linger and be moved by this review. I continue to be moved and a little bit changed. For that, I am deeply grateful.

References

Anderson, C. L. (2013). What we have to offer isn't enough. In K. Malawista & A. Adelman (Eds.), *The Therapist in Mourning: From the Faraway Nearby* (pp. 118–132). Columbia University Press.

Anderson, G. O. (2012). Who, what, when, where, how and mostly why? A therapist's grief over the suicide of a client. In K. M. Weiner (Ed.), *Therapeutic and Legal Issues for Therapists Who Have Survived a Client Suicide: Breaking the Silence* (pp. 25–35). Routledge. https://doi.org/10.1300/J015v28n01_03

Barnett, L. (2009). Conclusion: The therapeutic relationship, when death enters the therapeutic space. In L. Barnett (Ed.), *When Death Enters the Therapeutic Space: Existential Perspectives in Psychotherapy and Counselling* (pp. 219–223). Routledge.

Barrett, F. J., Powley, E. H., & Pearce, B. (2011). Hermeneutic philosophy and organizational theory. In H. Tsoukas & R. Chia (Eds.), *Philosophy and Organization Theory Research in the Sociology of Organizations* (pp. 181–213). Emerald. https://doi.org/10.1108/S0733-558X(2011)0000032009

Braun, V., & Clarke, V. (2013). *Successful Qualitative Research: A Practical Guide for Beginners*. Sage [Kindle version].

Casement, P. (2020). *Credo? Religion and Psychoanalysis*. Aeon Books.

Chemtob, C. M., Hamada, R. S., Bauer, G., Kinney, B., & Torigoe, R. Y. (1988a). Patients' suicide: Frequency and impact on psychiatrists. *The American Journal of Psychiatry, 145*(2), 224–228. https://doi.org/10.1176/ajp 145.2.224

Chemtob, C. M., Hamada, R. S., Bauer, G., Torigoe, R. Y., & Kinney, B. (1988b). Patient suicide: Frequency and impact on psychologists. *Professional Psychology: Research and Practice, 19*(4), 416–420. https://doi.org/10.1037/0735-7028.19 .4.416

Christianson, C. L., & Everall, R. D. (2009). Breaking the silence: School counsellors' experiences of client suicide. *British Journal of Guidance and Counselling, 37*(2), 157–168. https://doi.org/10.1080/03069880902728580

Clausen, M. (2015). *What Remains: The Aftermath of Patient Suicide.* http://www.psychotherapy.net/article/suicide

Eatough, V. (2012). Introduction to qualitative methods. In G. M. Breakwell, J. A. Smith, & D. B. Wright (Eds.), *Research Methods in Psychology* (4th ed., pp. 321–341). Sage.

Farberow, N. L. (2005). The mental health professional as suicide survivor. *Clinical Neuropsychiatry, 2*(1), 13–20.

Finlay, L. (2011). *Phenomenology for Therapists: Researching the Lived World* (1st ed.). Wiley.

Finlayson, M., & Simmonds, J. G. (2018). Impact of client suicide on psychologists in Australia. *Australian Psychologist, 53*(1), 23–32. https://doi.org/10.1111/ap .12240

Foster, V., & McAdams, C. R. (1999). The impact of client suicide in counselor training: Implications for counselor education and supervision. *Counselor Education and Supervision, 39*(1), 22–33. https://psycnet.apa.org/doi/10.1002/j .1556-6978.1999.tb01787.x

Fox, R., & Cooper, M. (1998). The effects of suicide on the private practitioner: A professional and personal perspective. *Clinical Social Work Journal, 26,* 143–157. https://doi.org/10.1023/A:1022866917611

Gadamer, H. G. (2004). *Truth and Method* (2nd ed.) (trans. J. Weinsheimer & D. G. Marshall). Continuum International (Original work published 1960).

Grad, O. T., & Michel, K. (2004). Therapists as client suicide survivors. *Women and Therapy, 28*(1), 71–81. https://doi.org/10.1300/J015v28n01_06

Grollman, E. A., & Malikow, M. (1999). *Living When a Young Friend Commits Suicide: Or Even Starts Talking About It.* Beacon Press.

Gutin, N. J. (2019a). Losing a patient to suicide: What we know. *Current Psychiatry, 18*(10), 15–32.

Gutin, N. J. (2019b). Losing a patient to suicide: Navigating the aftermath. *Current Psychiatry, 18*(11), 17–24.

Heaton, J. (2009). Reflections on suicide and despair. In L. Barnett (Ed.), *When Death Enters the Therapeutic Space: Existential Perspectives in Psychotherapy and Counselling* (pp. 119–131). Routledge.

Heidegger, M. (2010). *Being and Time* (trans. J. Stambaugh). State University of New York Press (Original work published 1927).

Hendin, H., Lipschitz, A., Maltsberger. J. T., Pollinger Haas, A., & Wynecoop, S. (2000). Therapists' reactions to patients' suicides. *American Journal of Psychiatry, 157,* 2022–2027. htttps://doi.org/10:1176/appi.ajp.157.12.2022

Hendin, H., Pollinger Haas, A. P., Maltsberger. J. T., Szanto, K., & Rabinowicz, H. (2004). Factors contributing to therapists' distress after the suicide of a patient.

The American Journal of Psychiatry, 161(8), 1442–1446. https://doi.org/10.1176/appi.ajp.161.8.1442

Hillman, J. (2016). Suicide and the Soul. Spring Publications.

Holloway, I., & Wheeler, S. (2002). *Qualitative Research in Nursing and Healthcare* (3rd ed.). Wiley-Blackwell [Kindle version].

James, D. M. (2012). Surpassing the quota: Multiple suicides in a psychotherapy practice. In K. M. Weiner (Ed.), *Therapeutic and Legal Issues for Therapists Who Have Survived a Client Suicide: Breaking the Silence* (pp. 9–24). Routledge. https://doi.org/10.1300/J015v28n01_02

Massey, S. D. (2009). Forgiveness and reconciliation: Essential to sustaining human development. In A. Kalayjian & R. F. Paloutzian (Eds.), *Forgiveness and Reconciliation: Psychological Pathways to Conflict Transformation and Peace Building* (pp. 83–96). Springer.
https://doi.org/10.1007/978-1-4419-0181-1_6

McAdams, C. R., & Foster, V. A. (2000). Client suicide: Its frequency and impact on counselors. *Journal of Mental Health Counseling, 22*(2), 107–121.

McCaffrey, G., Raffin-Bouchal, S., & Moulds, N. J. (2012). Hermeneutics as research approach: A reappraisal. *International Journal of Qualitative Methods, 11*(3), 214–229. https://doi.org/10.1177/160940691201100303

McLeod, J. (2011). *Qualitative Research in Counselling and Psychotherapy* (2nd ed.). Sage [Kindle version].

Menninger, W. W. (1991). Patient suicide and its impact on the psychotherapist. *Bulletin of the Menninger Clinic, 55*(2), 216–227.

Neal, S. B. (2017). The impact of a client's suicide. *Transactional Analysis Journal, 47*(3), 173–185. https://doi.org/10.1177/0362153717711701

Norcross, J. C., & Guy, J. D., Jr. (2007). *Leaving it at the Office: A Guide to Psychotherapist Self-Care.* The Guilford Press [Kindle version].

Oxford Encyclopedic English Dictionary. (1991). Suicide. In *Oxford Encyclopedic English Dictionary* (p. 1447). Oxford University Press.

Pope, K. S., & Vasquez, M. J. T. (2007). *Ethics in Psychotherapy and Counselling: A Practical Guide* (3rd ed.). John Wiley & Sons [Kindle version].

Rilke, R. (1989). The eight elegy. In S. Mitchell (Ed.), *The Selected Poetry of Rainer Maria Rilke* (p. 198). Vintage [Kindle version].

Rycroft, P. (2012). Touching the heart and soul of therapy: Surviving client suicide. In K. M. Weiner (Ed.), *Therapeutic and Legal Issues for Therapists Who Have Survived a Client Suicide: Breaking the Silence* (pp. 83–95). Routledge. https://doi.org/10.1300/J015v28n01_07

Shakespeare, W. (1977). *Macbeth.* New Penguin Shakespeare. Penguin.

Spinelli, E. (2015). *Practising Existential Psychotherapy: The Relational World* (2nd ed.). Sage [Kindle version].

Spring, M. (2020). Exploring the therapist's experience when a client dies by suicide. *Inside Out: The Irish Journal for Humanistic and Integrative Psychotherapy, 92,* 48–54. https://iahip.org/page-1076722

Tillich, P. (2014). *The Courage to Be* (3rd ed.). Yale University Press (Original work published 1952).

Tillman, J., & Carter, A. (2014). The trauma of patient suicide. In R. A. Deutsch (Ed.), *Traumatic Ruptures: Abandonment and Betrayal in the Analytic Relationship* (pp. 66–79). Routledge.

Tillman, J. G. (2006). When a patient commits suicide: An empirical study of psychoanalytic clinicians. *The International Journal of Psychoanalysis, 87*(1), 159–177. https://doi.org/10.1516/6UBB-E9DE-8UCW-UV3L

van Deurzen, E. (2010). *Everyday Mysteries: A Handbook of Existential Psychotherapy* (2nd ed.). Routledge. https://doi.org/10.4324/9780203864593

van Manen, M. (2016). *Researching Lived Experience: Human Science for an Action Sensitive Pedagogy* (2nd ed.). Routledge.

van Manen, M. (2017). But is it phenomenology? *Qualitative Health Research, 27*(6), 775–779. https://doi.org/10.1177/1049732317699570

Williams, M. (2014). *Cry of Pain: Understanding Suicide and the Suicidal Mind* (3rd ed.). Piatkus.

World Health Organization. (2021) *Suicide worldwide in 2019: Global health estimates*. WHO. https://apps.who.int/iris/handle/10665/341728

Yalom, I. D. (2008). *Staring at the Sun: Overcoming the Terror of Death*. Jossey-Bass [Kindle version].

Chapter 13

Carrying the Torch of Hope: An Investigation into the Experiences of Shared Interpersonal Trauma in the Therapeutic Relationship

Polina Lukanova

Introduction

Exposure to trauma is pervasive in societies worldwide (Magruder et al., 2017). Clients with trauma histories represent nearly 80% of clients at mental health clinics and require specialised knowledge on behalf of therapists (Jones & Cureton, 2014). With such a high prevalence rate, therapists in all settings will inevitably work with clients who are survivors of trauma. Trauma or traumatic experiences are broad terms encompassing a range of experiences that overwhelm the central nervous system and alter how memories are processed and recalled (van der Kolk, 2014).

Traumatic experiences have been differentiated in existing literature as either interpersonal (i.e. the direct result of actions by other people) or non-interpersonal (i.e. other life-threatening events, such as severe accidents) (Hughesdon et al., 2021). Interpersonal trauma has been found to have a variety of adverse effects on the personal and social functioning of the individual. It also tends to have one of the most significant adverse psychological consequences (Cunningham, 2003), affecting the person's beliefs about self, others, and the world (Biruski et al., 2014; ISTSS, 2018). It has also been associated with more severe posttraumatic stress disorder symptoms than non-interpersonal trauma exposure (Hughesdon et al., 2021). The reason for this is thought to be due to the intentionality of the act, in other words, having to come to terms with the idea of one person deliberately inflicting harm upon the other. It has also been proposed that human-induced trauma might be more difficult for clinicians to work with clinically than naturally caused trauma precisely because this type of work exposes the therapist to the 'potential boundlessness of human evil' (Danieli, 1994).

According to literature, the impact of trauma and traumatic events is not limited to the person who has suffered trauma, but can also indirectly affect the person exposed to trauma indirectly (American Psychological Association, 2013; Knight, 2013). Although all therapeutic work carries

DOI: 10.4324/9781003493860-18

the potential of an adverse impact on the therapist, trauma work has been found to have additional challenges associated with indirect exposure (Arvay, 2001; Bride et al., 2007).

The negative challenges accompanying indirect trauma[1] work have been conceptualised using a variety of terms, such as compassion fatigue[2] (CF), secondary traumatic stress[3] (STS), and vicarious trauma[4] (VT). As research stands at the moment, there seems to be more evidence for the secondary traumatic stress construct rather than a change in cognition, which is increasingly being thought of as a natural consequence of trauma work (Devilly et al., 2009; Diehm, 2007; Sabin-Farrell, 2000).

In addition, recent research has found that posttraumatic growth can occur while feeling some level of distressing emotions, which suggests that negative and positive impacts of trauma experiences are co-occurring and not mutually exclusive (Arnold et al., 2005; Ling et al., 2014; Linley et al., 2003). Posttraumatic growth refers to an ability to transform trauma and use adversity to one's advantage (Tedeschi & Calhoun, 2004) and can also occur due to indirect trauma exposure. Linley and colleagues (2003) have proposed that positive and negative implications from trauma work should be conceptualised as unique but assessed together, as focusing only on the negative aspects of the work does not give a balanced understanding of posttraumatic reactions. These findings call for a better understanding of the spectrum of indirect trauma exposure experiences and a more prominent recognition of the positive personal and professional outcomes as a result of engaging therapeutically with trauma clients.

The positive implications of trauma work are less known than the negative, and research in that direction is still limited (Brooks et al., 2016). Growth from adversity has been studied using a narrow sample of survivors such as cancer, transport accidents, and military combat participants (Barakat et al., 2006; Linley & Joseph, 2004), while excluding the potential range of intentional and non-intentional adversity which many people experience throughout their lifetime (Brooks et al., 2016). Some concepts that attempt to capture these positive aspects are compassion satisfaction[5] (CS), vicarious resilience[6] (VR), and vicarious posttraumatic growth[7] (VPTG).

The positive growth therapists describe concerning trauma work is centred around how they view humanity and spirituality. Therapists have reported admiring resilience in human beings and experiencing a form of spiritual broadening (Arnold et al., 2005; Splevins et al., 2010), growth concerning their professional identity, and enhanced professional capability as a result of realising that their work is valuable and that they can make a difference (Satkunanayagam et al., 2010; Shamai & Ron, 2009; Splevins et al., 2010).

A literature review

Both empathic engagement and history of trauma have been identified as factors contributing to both positive and negative implications of trauma work for therapists and provide valuable avenues for further research investigation. However, unlike empathic engagement, the role personal history of trauma plays has attracted many inconsistencies (Benatar, 2000; Cunningham, 2003; Dworking et al., 2016; Jenkins & Baird, 2002; VanDeusen & Way, 2006; Way et al., 2004). Studies regarding therapists' history of trauma and its relationship to the negative and positive impact on therapists are important due to the high prevalence of trauma in society, including in therapists (Jung, 1951; Magruder et al., 2017; Michalopoulos & Aparicio, 2012; VanDeusen & Way, 2006). Therefore, its role in posttraumatic reactions seems to be an essential point for examination (VanDeusen & Way, 2006).

A review of the literature which already exists on therapists with a history of trauma working therapeutically with traumatised clients highlighted an imbalance between quantitative (Adams & Riggs, 2008; Dworking et al., 2016; Jenkins & Baird, 2002; Makadia et al., 2017; VanDeusen & Way, 2006; Way et al., 2004) and qualitative studies on this topic, with only one qualitative study identified (Benatar, 2000). There also seems to be a shift in the literature from a preoccupation with the negative consequences to an interest in the positive impact of trauma work for therapists. This change in focus can be seen by the publication dates of the studies in this review, with more recent ones concentrating on the positive impacts of trauma work while the older ones have focused on adverse effects.

Overall, the studies which looked at the adverse effects of trauma work have found either STS symptoms or VT symptoms amongst therapists with a history of trauma, with only one study not finding support for secondary trauma symptomatology (Makadia et al., 2017). However, the quantitative studies elicit mixed results regarding whether a therapist's history of trauma is a contributing factor to the negative implications of trauma work.

On the other hand, the studies focused on examining the positive implications of trauma work on the therapist indicated that therapists with trauma histories tend to experience higher levels of compassion satisfaction than negative implications from trauma work (Brockhouse et al., 2011; Brooks et al., 2016; Jenkins et al., 2011; McKim & Smith-Adock, 2013; Somoray et al., 2017). However, similarly to those investigating the negative implications, whether a history of trauma in the therapist can be considered a significant predictor for positive growth is unclear.

Lastly, the results of this review show that studies on adverse effects of trauma work have mainly concentrated on sexual assault/child sexual abuse (CSA) and domestic violence (Benatar, 2000; Cunningham, 2003;

Dworkin et al., 2016; Jenkins & Baird, 2002; VanDeusen & Way, 2006; Way et al., 2004). However, by concentrating on sexual abuse traumas, other types of interpersonal traumas are neglected. This finding poses the question of whether researchers have neglected other interpersonal mal-treatment histories by concentrating solely on sexual abuse traumas and, therefore, is an important area of research investigation.

A gap in literature

As participants' voices are generally missing in quantitative research (Austin & Sutton, 2014), little is known about how participants experience the negative and positive implications of the work and what that experience is like. Understanding how participants experience the therapeutic work may provide valuable insights into the discrepancies in current research findings. As qualitative research relies on the collection of detailed infor-mation, it is thought to provide researchers with rich and deep insights into topics which cannot be sufficiently understood through quantitative meth-ods (Galdas, 2017; Merriam, 2015). This study's focus is on therapists with a history of interpersonal trauma[8] who work therapeutically with clients who also present with interpersonal trauma. A qualitative enquiry giving voice to this group of therapists may provide new insights into what role the therapist's history of trauma plays in the secondary trauma construct.

Methodology

As this research focuses on a complex and emotionally laden topic, Interpretative Phenomenological Analysis (IPA) was considered the best fit for this study. IPA's scope for in-depth exploration of first-hand accounts can provide valuable insight into how therapists with trauma histories experience the therapeutic work with traumatised clients. In addition, as an IPA researcher aims to uncover unique perspectives rather than verify or negate specific hypotheses (Smith et al., 2022; Smith & Osborn, 2015), the knowledge produced from this research will account for lived experience and how this experience has come into being.

I recognise that my role in this study was that of a co-constructor, help-ing the participant make sense of their lived experience of providing ther-apy to traumatised clients. Through listening to participants' accounts of the phenomenon, I played an active role in helping the participants make sense of their experiences and the meanings derived from these experi-ences. I aimed to capture the unfolding of each participant's idiosyncratic narrative and provide a rich and contextualised representation of the phe-nomenon under investigation through engaging in a dialogue between my way of being and the transcribed text of individual accounts (Eatough &

Smith, 2017, as cited in Willig & Stainton Rogers, 2017; Smith et al., 2009). To aid this process, I engaged in ongoing reflexive practice examining my feelings, reactions, and motives alongside the participants. As it is impossible to separate the phenomena from the participant's subjectivity, as well as for me to provide an objective understanding of their experiences, the knowledge produced by this research is a co-construction between participant accounts and my sense of their experiences (Smith et al., 2009).

Participants

All participants in this study were registered therapists. Rachael, Ruth, Cynthia, and Beth identify as person-centred therapists, while Anna, Susan, Rebecca, and David identify their practice as integrative. Their clinical experience ranged from 1 to 20 years post-qualification.

Analysis and findings

Navigating Challenges and Rewards in the Therapeutic Relationship

Difficulties with Managing Feelings of Fear and Overwhelm During Training

All participants described experiencing fear and overwhelm when working with trauma during their training. Participants attributed their challenges during training to not having a strong enough understanding of how trauma has impacted them and not having the theoretical knowledge and practical skills to feel confident in working with traumatised clients.

Anna described the difficulty she had in listening to horrific disclosures of trauma when working with a client who had suffered ritual abuse, and the impact this had on her:

> I was doing my garden and I was picking some dog poo up, because I have dogs, and I had a horrible, horrible – I was nearly vomiting. But I knew it wasn't my stuff. It was her stuff. Now that never happened to me as a child, but (…) Oh, it was really unpleasant. Really unpleasant.

Anna highlights the horror of her experience at the time. The repetition of words like *horrific* and *unpleasant* reflect the overwhelm she experienced as a result of hearing the client's traumatic lived experiences.

Susan also described an overwhelming experience during her training when working within a drug and alcohol unit. She attributed this to the severe problems and harrowing experiences that the clients had been through, as well as the feeling of powerlessness in terms of being able to make any changes. However, unlike Anna, who did not report any long-lasting negative implications, Susan described a cumulative negative impact:

> *I just mentally felt absolutely exhausted (…) and quite a lot of the trauma was also sort of in the transference, a lot of them were very, very, angry with the trauma they've had or angry with their parents, angry with the system or whatever (…) and that can really trigger my own trauma.*

Her words highlight the debilitating impact working with traumatised clients had on her during her training. The repetition of words such as *very* and *angry* convey the intensity of the client's distress and reflects the difficulty she had in managing it. Anna also highlights an added layer of difficulty in her experience resulting from her primary trauma being triggered in conjunction with managing the impact of her clients' harrowing stories.

Indeed, other participants attributed the fear and feeling of overwhelm they experienced to their traumatic material surfacing during client sessions. Rachael said:

> *I can still remember the feeling in the room (…) I felt like I have to be so careful and gentle with her (…) all through my training, a lot of the abuse stuff that had happened to me came up for me again. It was like, 'Oh, we're in this.' So, there was part of me that was in it. The wounded part of me was there too.*

She reflects on how working with trauma during her training had a significant impact, particularly highlighted by the ease with which she recalled the *intensity* of how it felt for her back then. In addition, she refers to her and the client as being *in this* together, which conveys a lack of clarity as to whether her perception of needing to be *gentle* with the client reflects the need of the client, her own need, or both.

Difficulties in Keeping 'Yourself Separate'

All participants stated, to varying degrees, the difficulty associated with keeping their subjective experiences separate from their clients in the therapeutic relationship. Unlike during their training, this difficulty seems to be accompanied by a sense of exhaustion and professional responsibility towards their clients. Anna described the exhaustion related to keeping herself separate from the client, saying it feels like *'multitasking all the time in sessions (…) if anything is triggered, it's like, "Ah. That was my stuff. Just pop that there," and we are back.'*

Anna conveys a sense of intensity and responsibility, which is elucidated by the repetition of the word *'really.'* The words *'and we are back'* reflect the difficulty of remaining present with the client's experience when her own is triggered. In addition, the words *'pop that there and we are back'* illustrates a need for a form of bracketing of her own experience in order for her to stay with the client's experience.

In contrast, for David, the difficulty of keeping things separate seemed to be exacerbated by having experienced the same type of trauma as his client. David described working with someone with whom he shared difficult life circumstances, as well as traumatic experiences, expressing the impact in the following way: *'this theme of unfairness really blindsided me (...) I need to detangle this for myself before I go back into the room and sit with this man.'*

David suggests that it's not necessarily the description of the client's traumatic experience that is difficult to stay with, but rather the feelings that the experience evokes in him. Referring to being blindsided in terms of the impact of the trigger can be seen as a reflection of the vulnerable state in which David found himself at that moment in time, as well as not having been aware of this theme being a possible trigger for him. The need to detangle and unpick highlights the difficulty David had in separating his personal experiences and feelings from those of the client and suggests that this is a time-consuming cognitive activity.

Cynthia, on the other hand, described the challenge of keeping herself separate as an embodied activity:

> So, outwardly I'm certainly able to be calm and supportive in that moment, it's the managing the internal feelings. It's not that suddenly something pops into my head (...) it's more that my body recognises it, it's more that... whoosh of feelings from your stomach.

The difficulty for Cynthia appears to centre around managing the embodied reminders of her traumatic material, which became triggered due to the similarities between her and the client's traumatic experience. There is a sense of the embodiment feeling resembling a form of flooding, reflected in the word *'whoosh.'*

Personal History of Trauma as an Asset

All participants alluded to the fact that experiencing trauma in their own lives aided them in their attunement to clients presenting with interpersonal trauma. Participants identified how examining the impact of trauma on their own lives has been key in their ability to provide understanding and empathy to their clients. The participants' comments conveyed a strong sense of personal understanding of the painful feelings that trauma can evoke. Anna described how healing and moving away from her trauma has informed her empathy for individual differences within the experience of trauma:

> When I have a client who comes to me with trauma, I seem to have a real deep empathy and insight into what they may be going through (...) I can really sit with them and really explore into a deeper level of a real impact because I am aware of how deeply it can impact.

Anna suggests that the impact of trauma is multi-layered, being at a depth that only those who have been through the experience can understand. In addition, there is a sense of an ability to engage and hold the complexity of drawing from her own experience to understand those of the client, while at the same time keeping in mind that their experiences are not the same. This mental separation seems to inform her understanding and empathy for the client without her clouding the client's experience with her own.

Rebecca referred to how understanding trauma's impact on her own life not only aids her in understanding the client but also informs her ability to maintain a mental separation:

> because I've got a very sort of disaffected family background, I think I'm very quick to see how family dynamics have impacted on the person and also to be able to hold the attachment to the family whilst also working with the distress and anger and hurt that they feel.

Rebecca conveys how her understanding of the impact of family dynamics on the individual is connected to her personal experience of having a disaffected family background. She conveys a strong sense of a need to be gentle with clients when they are faced with conflicting feelings due to her personal understanding of how challenging this can be.

David described how his trauma history is not only an asset to understanding the client but also how the client perceives it as an asset to being understood by the therapist:

> If you have been down to a very deep, dark place, I think there is an assumption that if you are sitting in front of a therapist, in order to understand that they may have been to a different dark place, but it's probably the same depth... it feels more than empathy. It feels more like I am able to reach over and hold your hand from the same place. Which is, I feel, is a little bit deeper.

David conveys a sense of trauma being a difficult experience to understand and that in order to understand, one must share in the experience. In addition, there is a sense of the depth of connection, providing the client with something he experiences as more than empathy, suggesting something unique about its nature; *'A bidirectional process: the positive implications from the therapeutic work with traumatised clients.'*

Seven participants referred to experiencing positive implications of the therapeutic work with traumatised clients and how these positive implications are experienced by both parties (the client and the therapist). Most participants attributed the positive feelings felt in the session to stem from establishing a connection with the client. Rachael described feeling a *'buzz'* from the therapeutic work, which she also attributed to the positive connection between herself and the client:

> *I think that relational depth that I experience with them, it's like a fundamental thing. It's such a positive thing that when I've come out, when I've finished my sessions, even if the sessions are heavy sessions, I feel positive.*

She conveys both the importance and the positive implication of establishing a connection with the client in the therapeutic relationship. There appears to be a reparative element to that connection, with this element being felt not only by the client, but also by the therapist in the form of feeling really positive and good after sessions. In addition, there is a sense of the connection with the client being something very powerful, which can turn a heavy session into something enjoyable.

Cynthia described how facilitating growth in her clients elicits positive feelings and added that it also helps her grow at the same time:

> *I've certainly found it very rewarding in working with clients who've experienced trauma and helping them to gain a better understanding to feel supported in their experience and to be able to move forward from there (...) and I think that that's also helped me to grow at the same time.*

Cynthia describes the reward as connected to facilitating the client's understanding and growth from their traumatic experience. There is a sense of the rewards Cynthia receives from working with trauma surpassing any challenges. She also described the therapeutic sessions as being mutually beneficial, facilitating the client's growth as well as her own.

Anna connected the positive feelings derived from the therapeutic encounter with traumatised clients to finding a sense of meaning in the work:

for me it's like turning trauma into triumph. It's like I have been able to heal and now I can sit with others, hopefully, through their journey and their process. And each time I do, I feel more healing.

There is a sense of victory over trauma in Anna's description of her ability to sit with others through their healing journey. There is also a sense of pride in her narrative, seemingly connected to the experience of feeling more healing each time, despite the adversity she has been through.

Getting to Know the Self: A Protective Quality

Valuing Self-Awareness in Ethical Practice

A common theme expressed by all participants was that of valuing self-awareness in their therapeutic work with traumatised clients. Participants perceived getting to know themselves as having a protective quality in their therapeutic work with traumatised clients. Susan highlighted how gaining self-awareness appeared to be valuable in managing the impact of the therapeutic work:

I'm more aware when something has an impact on me so (…) I'm more actively processing and journaling and thinking about checking in how I'm feeling (…) I see that as part of my job rather than, 'Oh, I'll get to it when I have the time' sort of thing.

She highlights the importance of self-awareness in terms of how this has led to a change of perspective in the way she views self-care and how she understands what it means to be a professional. In addition, there is a sense of the therapeutic work invading her life, with her seemingly being unable to separate herself from it. She seems to have undergone a change of perspective as she has developed her self-awareness, going from seeing her self-care as an optional adjunct to her work to seeing it as a vital part of her work and what it means to be a professional.

In a slightly different but similarly positive vein, Ruth described how self-awareness has aided her in her ability to look after herself:

once they've gone, I'm very much – yeah, I'm tired, I need time, I need space, I need to think about what they've done (…) I'm mindful about needing some space, needing some time, needing a walk or a bath or whatever, so that I can get over what they've spoken and get on with who I am and my life and what I need to do to look after myself.

Ruth's comments reflect a strong awareness of the situation and the need for time for herself after sessions. It seems the sessions with clients have the potential to deplete her energy, and she exhibits an awareness of needing time to replenish. There is also a sense of exhaustion, with the suggestion that her role as a therapist requires her to set herself aside and, therefore, a strong need to devote time to herself and what she needs after sessions. To this end, she conveys a need for a transitional activity, such as a walk, bath, etc., in transitioning from her role as a therapist to who she is in her personal life.

In contrast, Rebecca communicated a danger with regards to a lack of awareness in therapists with trauma histories, pointing out how awareness is key to ethical practice:

> I think if I been a therapist before I'd done a lot of therapy, it would have been really dangerous because I think it would have meant that I colluded or identified, tried to rescue maybe even became persecutory (...) I hadn't really realised how much my childhood had impacted me...

Rebecca conveys the notion that unresolved trauma in therapists can impinge on the therapeutic process and distort how the therapist perceives and responds to the client. The distortion she alludes to is highlighted by other participants when describing their experiences during training and the ongoing challenges they face due to their interpersonal traumatic history. She goes on to convey a sense of the self-awareness gained from personal therapy being a *'beam of light,'* helping her understand trauma's impact on her.

Presence Through the Body

Seven participants described the value of tuning into their body during their therapeutic work with traumatised clients, which they seem to suggest better enables them to access the present moment. Participants described achieving such presence through the body in different ways.

David described yoga as being a useful tool to aid in looking after himself after sessions with traumatised clients, saying:

> Before I do yoga, I feel really grumpy that I'm doing yoga. After I have done yoga, I feel like, 'Oh, yes. I am glad I did yoga' (...) you know so I think it's half a chore and half a self-care thing that is good to do.

He conveys an internal struggle between what he knows (cognitively), that yoga will make him feel better, and what he feels in his body, which is a resistance to doing it. It seems that for David, yoga is a means to an end, meaning he has to push himself to do it for its benefit rather than for enjoyment.

Susan also described the value of tuning in to her body as it allows her to process her feelings after sessions. However, in contrast to David, she described achieving this by keeping her body still in a meditative state:

> just sitting there, just being with how I'm feeling, is almost like empty-ing out some of this or letting the feelings surface. It's almost like I'll sit there and then suddenly, quietly, start crying, tears coming down or if I'm feeling really anxious and I'm really just quite down, and then it's this feeling of almost things are emptied out and just a calm kind of feeling at the end.

Susan conveys a sense that connecting with her body in stillness allows her to tap into feelings and emotions which are not accessible to her cog-nitively. Indeed, it seems she perceives her body as having the ability to transform negative feelings, such as anxiety, into positive feelings, such as calm. These differences the participants describe in how they tune into their bodies suggest therapists can achieve presence through the body in different ways, depending on preference.

Cynthia on the other hand highlighted the value in tuning into her body in order to remain grounded and present in sessions with clients:

> because when someone is (...) talking about a flashback or actually experiencing a flashback in the room, I think it can be easy to very strongly visualise that yourself, so almost you're kind of being drawn into that situation so it's (...) having a kind of checklist of the sort of things that you can do, 'Are my feet flat on the floor, are my hands on the arms of the chair,' and things like that, that I find that stops me from drifting away.

Cynthia's words suggest that connecting to her body acts as a protective quality, becoming a form of emergency brake which stops her from being pulled into the client's traumatic narrative. Although Cynthia recognises the value of connecting to her body in sessions with clients, she later added that she has a 'tendency to ignore [her] body saying, I'm tired, I'm stressed, I'm needing something,' highlighting an internal conflict and resistance similar to David's resistance in engaging with yoga practice.

Valuing a Trauma-Informed Supervisor

Five participants described the value of a trauma-informed supervisor in their therapeutic work with traumatised clients. David described valuing a trauma-informed supervisor in feeling understood and supported with his clinical work:

I suppose in supervision just an awareness of what trauma can look like so you know, a tolerance to hold a space for people whose behaviour may be very risky, but also to be aware that that doesn't necessarily mean a break in confidentiality (...) so to understand the thresholds are different I think is really important.

His words convey a sense of trauma being scary to work with if one lacks the necessary knowledge of trauma. The extract suggests that working with trauma differs from other presentations, requiring specialist knowledge to be understood. David also seems to highlight the potential for misunderstanding between him and a supervisor who is not trauma informed as they may not have the tolerance and thus consider the client's presentation risky.

Ruth also noted the value of a trauma-informed supervisor in feeling supported in her work with traumatised clients, as well as highlighted the difficulty she has in allowing herself to receive support, even if the supervisor is trauma informed:

I feel a little bit hesitant sometimes about revealing everything about myself or my practice or whatever, but I'm aware of that, and we have talked about that, through that (...) I think because the trauma is perpetrated by somebody more powerful, more knowing, and has a negative impact, it's quite easy to see a supervisor like that sometimes.

Her words convey both trust and mistrust in terms of her abilities, as well as towards the supervisor's intentions. There is a sense of her trusting the supervisor in her description of having spoken to her about how she feels in sessions with her, with them having talked through her worries. However, her comments reflect a perspective that reveals a tendency for her to see the supervisor in the same light as a perpetrator due to the supervisor's position of power, causing a perceived power imbalance. Despite saying that the issue of this power imbalance has been talked through, there is a sense of this issue being ongoing as she uses the present tense to describe her tendency to see the supervisor in a negative light.

'You're Affected All Your Life': The Permanent Imprint of Trauma

The Impact of Interpersonal Trauma on the Self

All the participants described the experience of interpersonal trauma as having a pervasive impact on their sense of self. For example, Rachael described this impact of trauma in the following way:

> *it kind of wiped me out as a person really, as an individual, I would say (...) It was a gang thing... they attacked me probably on four occasions over a number of years (...) so by the time they were finished with me I was nothing really. Nothing left in me.*

Rachael conveys the impact of interpersonal trauma on her life as equivalent to a natural disaster, wiping out her sense of self and leading her life in a different direction. There is a strong sense of vulnerability as a result of losing her sense of self, leading to a cumulative impact which she likens to a wildfire spreading and affecting all crevasses of her life. In addition, Rachael's comments convey a strong sense of pain and loss as she describes the impact of having endured years of abuse.

'It Doesn't Leave You': Facing Ongoing Challenge

Seven of eight participants described facing ongoing challenges stemming from their history of trauma, despite having engaged in personal development and understanding how these experiences have impacted them. They describe their primary trauma as being triggered and reverting back to an old way of being and seeing the world. Rachael described the heartbreak of being affected by trauma and described the ongoing challenges she faces as a vulnerability to stress:

> *I don't care about them. I think in that sense, it's processed as much as it's going to be, but I think I'm vulnerable to anxiety and depression at times. If I'm stressed, I'm vulnerable to go – do you know about windows of tolerance and all of that? I'm vulnerable to getting to my edges of that (...) If I go out at night and I see a gang of lads I'd be worried, even now. And that's when I was a teenager. I'm in my 60s now.*

She conveys a sense of injustice, loss, and grief at her life being forever affected by the deeds of another, with trauma processing portrayed as ongoing rather than as a goal to be achieved. There is a sense of fear when she describes her vulnerability to stress, which appears to be due to its unpredictability. In addition, the permanence of trauma's imprint is evident in her description of feeling worried even now in her 60s.

Discussion

The fear and overwhelm participants experienced during and after therapeutic sessions with traumatised clients during their training echo existing research findings which have found that novice therapists are more susceptible to secondary trauma (Adams & Riggs, 2008; Baird & Jenkins,

2003). The susceptibility of novice therapists to developing secondary trauma as a result of working therapeutically with traumatised clients can be understood through trauma's effect on the nervous system (van der Kolk, 2014). As trauma leads to nervous system dysregulation without knowing the impact trauma has had on them, the participants likely didn't know their triggers and how to deactivate their dysregulated state. This can also serve to explain why they described re-living their trauma in sessions with clients.

Susan's experience of hopelessness, anxiety, fatigue, and insomnia during her work with homelessness in a drug and alcohol service during training can be seen as conducive to compassion fatigue (Figley, 1995). Symptoms of compassion fatigue have been found to include feelings of anxiety, dissociation, isolation, physical ailments, and sleep disturbances (Figley, 1995, 2002). However, Susan also mentioned that her client's anger toward her was a trigger for her primary trauma,[9] reminding her of her 'raging' mother growing up. As Susan already had a primary trauma, the question arises as to whether the secondary traumatic symptoms she experienced were due to hearing her client's trauma or her client's trauma triggering her primary trauma. The concept of secondary traumatic stress (STS) does not consider whether the therapist has a primary trauma, which raises the question of whether the term STS can encompass this participant's experience.

Rachael and Beth, on the other hand, spoke of experiencing distress as a result of their primary trauma being triggered during therapeutic sessions with clients. Their accounts indicate that, unlike Anna, the distress they felt did not arise from hearing their clients' traumatic disclosures, but rather from what the traumatic disclosures triggered within their own experience. These findings pose the question of whether the negative implications these participants experienced were due to secondary trauma or primary trauma activation, as well as whether terminology such as compassion fatigue and STS are helpful in understanding the experiences of therapists with a history of trauma working therapeutically with traumatised clients.

Post-training, participants described their interactions with clients as both exhausting and positive, which relates to existing research findings indicating that positive and negative implications of the work are co-occurring and should be studied together (Ling et al., 2014; Linley et al., 2003).

The struggle in keeping their subjective experiences separate from those of the client appears to be a result of the shared experience of trauma between them. The therapists' negative personal experiences seem to enable them to identify with clients' problems and relate to them in an empathic manner. The concept of mirror neurons, which is thought to be the neurological basis for empathy (Gallese et al., 1996; Thagard, 2007), can further explain the participants' struggle to keep themselves separate. Neuroscience defines mirror neurons as brain cells which reflect the activity of another's brain cells and are thought to provide a direct internal experience of another person's actions or emotions (Rothschild, 2006). As mirror neurons have been found to play a role in the process of co-regulation, one can understand their experience with clients as them being pulled into mirroring their client's nervous system state. Thus, participants connecting to the body can be seen as a helpful self-regulation activity which helps their nervous system to remain in a calm state in sessions or alternatively aids them to move through states and reach a place of calm after sessions.

For example, Cynthia described utilising body awareness as a tool to stay present with her client in sessions, which seems to allow her to remain in a regulated nervous system state. Also, all participants mention using their body to ground themselves in the here-and-now as a self-care technique which seems to aid them in returning to a self-regulated state. These findings point to self-care techniques which focus on nervous system regulation to be essential for therapists with a history of trauma as it helps them maintain a self-regulated state, which in turn aids them in being present and engaged with clients. Without self-care techniques in place, their nervous system can become 'stuck' in one of the dysregulated nervous system states, which may make them more susceptible to triggers of their primary trauma and to experiencing the client's trauma vicariously through their nervous system.

The self-awareness gained from personal development appears to have assisted them in understanding the impact of trauma on their nervous system and equipped them with skills to manage dysregulation. Deb Dana (2018, 2020) suggests that safety in being with another comes before safety within the self and that when we feel safe with someone else, this allows us to understand how to self-regulate. Therefore, it seems that experiencing safety within their therapy has aided them in offering a sense of safety to their clients and engaging with them from a ventral vagal state.

The exhaustion participants referred to associated with keeping their subjective experiences separate from the client can be understood through the concept of concept of dual awareness, which is the ability to be aware of the outer world and inner world simultaneously (Rothschild, 2006). It can be seen as a protective skill mitigating the negative implications of trauma work. For this group of participants, the important factor contributing to the negative implications of the work seems to be whether they have insight and awareness into their history of trauma. This points to personal development being an essential aspect of therapeutic training for therapists with a history of trauma, which shows support to existing literature which has found personal therapy to be a contributing factor to the development of personal growth from working therapeutically with traumatised clients (Linley & Joseph, 2004).

The ongoing challenges that participants reported in their current practice seemed to be in relation to their primary trauma being triggered rather than secondary trauma from seeing clients. They described these challenges as triggers outside of their awareness, occurring in their personal life and in connection to client sessions. When triggered, participants described being pulled back into an old way of being and interacting with the world, which can be understood through Dana's (2020) notion of a 'home away from home.' She suggests that every person's default state is that of social engagement and that traumatic experiences pull us away from that regulated into either a sympathetic activation (fight and flight) or dorsal vagal (shutdown) state, which becomes our home away from home. Therefore, when presented with a trigger, the person is thought to go into their home away from home. Participants' experiences of facing ongoing challenges to their nervous system regulation and gaps in awareness suggest that healing from trauma can be seen as a continuous process rather than a destination to be reached.

Furthermore, understanding trauma also seems essential in facilitating a connection between the participants and their supervisor. Ruth described a perceived power imbalance in supervision and the tendency to see the supervisor as an authoritative figure. This could indicate the nervous system moving into a dysregulated state where the supervisor is perceived as a threat. If the therapist engages in supervision from a dysregulated nervous system state, this can impact their ability to reflect on their clinical work and receive the support they need from supervision. Existing literature has found supervision to be linked to experiencing positive growth from the therapeutic work with traumatised clients (Satkunanayagam et al., 2010). The experience of these participants suggests that for therapists with a history of trauma to be able to experience positive growth from supervision, the supervisor needs to understand trauma.

Finally, existing literature on positive growth in therapists with a history of trauma can aid in understanding the positivity participants experienced after therapeutic sessions with traumatised clients. Participants speaking fondly of the therapeutic work and feeling positively after sessions can also be understood through the concept of compassion satisfaction (Sacco et al., 2015), which is the pleasure and satisfying feelings derived from helping others. Susan and Anna described deriving a sense of meaning from the therapeutic work with traumatised clients, which relates to existing research which has found therapists experience growth concerning their professional identity as a result of perceiving their work as valuable and making a difference (Satkunanayagam et al., 2010; Shamai & Ron, 2009; Splevins et al., 2010). These findings also serve to potentially explain why a history of trauma for the therapist was also found to be a contributing factor to positive growth.

Whilst carrying out this research work, I noted two parallel processes between myself and the participants. These are explored below as it was deemed that they may provide valuable insight into the research process and my subjective experiences as a co-constructor of this research.

A struggle to keep separate has not only been identified as a theme in the participants' experiences of working with their clients but was also a running theme for me during this study's interviews, analysis, and write-up stage. I first noticed this during the interview stage, where I found my experience of trauma and therapeutic work with traumatised clients to resonate with what the participants spoke about in their practice. On further inspection of the interviews, I could see there were times during the interview when my subjectivity may have influenced my prompts. The familiarity I could see between myself and the participants caused the struggle to keep myself separate, which is also reflected in the participants' accounts of struggling to keep their subjectivity separate from that of clients who share similarities. Furthermore, part of how I worked through the analysis and discussion chapter was connected to how participants' accounts were talked about. I found myself struggling to break down the participant experiences into independent themes and discuss them separately from one another, as all seemed to interplay and link together.

Furthermore, during my first interview, I felt dissociated and unable to remain present. This feeling changed halfway through the interview, and the dissociated feeling shifted towards the end. I couldn't help but wonder whether I was picking up on something to do with that particular participant's experience or if my nervous system perceived the first interview as a threat leading to dissociation. In contrast, I found myself feeling positive after the interviews concluded. This once more seemed to be a parallel process between myself and the participants, as they seemed positive after the interview and reported enjoying the interview process. In particular, I recall speaking to one participant at the end of the interview who shared that she felt low at the beginning of the session and better at the end. This was interesting as I found myself having the same experience. I wonder whether this was a result of the connection and mutual understanding of a challenging topic that contributed to our positive mood at the end of the interview, which also happens to be the factors which participants identified to lead to positive feelings from sessions with traumatised clients. This experience also resonates with the findings on how the perceived similarity between therapist and client can facilitate safety and connection, which seems to have been the case in my experience with this client.

Conclusion

This study provides an in-depth knowledge on the experiences of therapists with a history of interpersonal trauma working therapeutically with traumatised clients. The findings suggest that whether a therapist's history of trauma can be considered a factor contributing to negative or positive implications of the work may depend on how much therapists have worked through their trauma in personal therapy, whether they feel sufficiently trained to work with trauma, and whether they prioritise self-care activities.

The findings of this research also raise an important question about what role the therapist's primary trauma plays in the secondary trauma construct. From the participants' accounts in this study, it was challenging to discern whether the negative implications they described resulted from primary trauma activation, secondary trauma, or a mixture of both. More research and exploration in this area would help discern whether terminology such as compassion fatigue, secondary traumatic stress, and vicarious trauma apply to participants with trauma histories or whether there is a need to conceptualise them separately.

As this is the first qualitative study of its kind, it has provided new insights into how therapists with a history of trauma experience therapeutic work with traumatised clients. The findings suggest that therapists and training institutions would benefit from paying particular attention to factors such as personal therapy, self-care techniques, and trauma training when working therapeutically with trauma. These participants' accounts suggest that when these factors are considered, the therapist's trauma history can become an aid in understanding the client as well as a source of hope for healing.

Notes

1 This term will be used to refer to the therapist's exposure to a client's trauma experience through the process of their therapeutic engagement with clients (Ling et al., 2014).

2 CF has been described as the empathic strain and general exhaustion resulting from dealing with people in distress over time and is mainly a term used in research with nurses and doctors (Figley, 1995)

3 STS refers to trauma symptoms, such as intrusions, avoidance, and arousal (Figley, 1995), similar to posttraumatic stress disorder triggered by secondary trauma exposure (Ling et al., 2014).

4 VT refers to the cumulative effect of empathic engagement with clients affected by trauma, affecting the individual's experience of the self, other, and the world in a negative way (McCann & Pearlman, 1990; Pearlman & Mac Ian, 1995).

5 CS refers to the sum of all the positive feelings a person derives from helping others (Sacco et al., 2015).

6 VR is a term describing the positive impact on and personal growth of therapists resulting from exposure to clients' resilience (Engstrom et al., 2008).
7 VPTG refers to the positive growth one can experience as a result of indirect
  trauma exposure (Arnold et al., 2005).
8 Interpersonal trauma encompasses experiences such as sexual assault/CSA
  and domestic violence, as well as other forms of maltreatment, such as
  physical abuse, emotional abuse, and emotional neglect (Mauritz et al.,
  2013).
9 *Primary trauma refers to the first-hand experience of trauma in the therapist.

References

Adams, S. A., & Riggs, S. A. (2008). An exploratory study of vicarious trauma
among therapist trainees. *Training and Education in Professional Psychology,*
2(1), 26–34. http://doi.org/10.1037/19313918.2.1.26

American Psychological Association. (2013). *Diagnostic and Statistical Manual*
of Mental Disorders –DSM-5 (5th ed.). https://doi.org/10.1176/appi.books
.9780890425787

Arnold, D., Calhoun, L. G., Tedeschi, R., & Cann, A. (2005). Vicarious posttraumatic
growth in psychotherapy. *Journal of Humanistic Psychology, 45*(2), 239–263.
https://doi.org/10.1177/0022167805274729

Arvay, M. J. (2001). Secondary traumatic stress among trauma counsellors: What
does the research say? *International Journal for the Advancement of Counselling,*
23, 283–293. https://doi.org/10.1023/A:1014496419410

Austin, Z., & Sutton, J. (2014). Qualitative research: getting started. *The Canadian*
Journal of Hospital Pharmacy, 67(6), 436–440. https://doi.org/10.4212/cjhp
.v67i6.1406

Baird, S., & Jenkins, S. R. (2003). Vicarious traumatisation, secondary traumatic
stress, and burnout in sexual assault and domestic violence agency staff.
Violence & Victims, 18(1), 71–86.

Barakat, L. P., Alderfer, M. A., & Kazak, A. E. (2006). Posttraumatic growth in
adolescent survivors of cancer and their mothers and fathers. *Journal of Paediatric*
Psychology, 31, 413–419. http://dx.doi.org/10.1093/jpepsy/ jsj058

Benatar, M. (2000). A qualitative study of the effect of a history of childhood sexual
abuse on therapists who treat survivors of sexual abuse. *Journal of Trauma &*
Dissociation, 1(3), 9. http://dx.doi.org/10.1300/J229v01n03_02

Biruski, D. C., Ajdukovic, D., & Stanic, A. L. (2014). When the world collapses:
Changed worldview and social reconstruction in a traumatized community.
European Journal of Psychotraumatology, 11(5), Article 24098. http://doi.org/
doi: 10.3402/ejpt.v5.24098

Bride, B. E., Radey, M., & Figley, C. R. (2007). Measuring compassion fatigue.
Clinical Social Work Journal, 35, 155–163. http://doi.org/10.1007/s10615-007
-0091-7

Brockhouse, R., Msetfi, R. M., Cohen, K., & Joseph, S. (2011). Vicarious exposure to
trauma and growth in therapists: The moderating effects of sense of coherence,
organizational support, and empathy. *Journal of Traumatic Stress, 24*(6), 735–
742. http://doi.org/10.1002/jts.20704

Brooks, M., Lowe, M., Graham-Kevan, N., & Robinson, S. (2016). Posttraumatic growth in students, crime survivors and trauma workers exposed to adversity. *Personality and Individual Differences, 98*, 199–207. http://doi.org/10.1016/j.paid.2016.04.051

Cunningham, M. (2003). Impact of trauma work on social work clinicians: Empirical findings. *Social Work Journal, 48*(4), 451–459. http://doi.org/10.1093/SW/48.4.451

Dana, D. (2018). *The Polyvagal Theory in Therapy: Engaging the Rhythm of Regulation*. Norton.

Dana, D. (2020). *Befriending Your Nervous System: Looking Through the Lens of Polyvagal Theory* [Audiobook]. Sounds True. https://resources.soundstrue.com/podcast/deb-dana-befriending-your-nervous-system/

Danieli, Y. (1994). Countertransference, trauma, and training. In J. P. Wilson & J. D. Lindy (Eds.), *Countertransference in the Treatment of PTS* (pp. 368–388). Guilford Press.

Devilly, G. J., Wright, R., & Varker, T. (2009). Vicarious trauma, secondary, traumatic stress or simply burnout? Effect of trauma therapy on mental health professionals. *Australian and New Zealand Journal of Psychiatry, 43*, 373–385. http://doi.org/10.1080/00048670902721079

Diehm, R. M. (2007). *Factors influencing the impact of secondary exposure to trauma* (Unpublished doctoral thesis). Deakin University, Australia.

Dworkin, E. R., Sorell, N. R., & Allen, N. E. (2016). Individual-and setting-level correlates of secondary traumatic stress in rape crisis centre staff. *Journal of Interpersonal Violence, 31*(4), 743–752. http://doi.org/10.1177/0886260514556111

Eatough, V., & Smith, J. A. (2017). Interpretative phenomenological analysis. In C. Willig & C. Stainton Rogers (Eds.), *The Sage Handbook of Qualitative Research in Psychology* (pp. 193–209). Sage.

Engstrom, D., Hernandez, P., & Gangsei, D. (2008). Vicarious resilience: A qualitative investigation into its description. *Traumatology, 14*, 13–21. http://doi.org/10.1177/1534765608319323

Figley, C. R. (1995). Compassion fatigue: Toward a new understanding of the costs of caring. In B. H. Stamm (Ed.), *Secondary Traumatic Stress: Self-Care Issues for Clinicians, Researchers, and Educators* (pp. 3–28). Sidran.

Figley, C. (2002). Compassion fatigue: Psychotherapists' chronic lack of self-care. *Psychotherapy in Practice, 58*(11), 1433–1441.

Galdas, P. (2017). Revisiting bias in qualitative research: Reflections on Its relationship with funding and Impact. *International Journal of Qualitative Methods, 16*(1). https://doi.org/10.1177/1609406917748992

Gallese, V., Fadiga, L., Fogassi, L., & Rizzolatti, G. (1996). Action recognition in the premotor cortex. *Brain: A Journal of Neurology, 119*(2), 593–609. https://doi.org/10.1093/brain/119.2.593

Hughesdon, K. A., Ford, J. D., Briggs, E. C., Seng, J. S., Miller, A. L., & Stoddard, S. A. (2021). Interpersonal trauma exposure and interpersonal problems in adolescent posttraumatic stress disorder. *Journal of Traumatic Stress, 34*(4), 733–743. https://doi.org/10.1002/jts.22687

ISTSS. (2018) *Childhood trauma*. ISTSS. https://istss.org/public-resources/trauma-basics/what-is-childhood-trauma

Jenkins, S. R., & Baird, S. (2002). Secondary traumatic stress and vicarious trauma: A validational study. *Journal of Traumatic Stress, 15*(5), 423–432. http://doi.org/1020193526843

Jenkins, S. R., Mitchell, J. L., Baird, S., Whitfield, S. R., & Meyer, H. L. (2011). The counselor's trauma as counseling motivation: Vulnerability or stress inoculation? *Journal of Interpersonal Violence, 26*(12), 2392–2412. https://doi.org/10.1177/0886260510383020

Jones, L. K., & Cureton, J. L. (2014). Trauma redefined in the DSM-5: Rationale and implications for counseling practice. *The Professional Counselor, 4*(3), 257–271.

Jung, C. (1951). *Fundamental Questions of Psychotherapy*. Princeton University Press

Knight, C. (2013). Indirect trauma: Implications for self-care, supervision, the organization, and the academic institution. *The Clinical Supervisor, 32*(2), 224–243. http://doi.org/10.1080/07325223.2013.850139

Ling, J., Hunter, S. V., & Maple, M. (2014). Navigating the challenges of trauma counselling: How counsellors thrive and sustain their engagement. *Australian Social Work, 67*(2), 297–310. http://doi.org/10.1080/0312407X.2013.837188

Linley, P. A., & Joseph, S. (2004). Positive change following trauma and adversity: A review. *Journal of Traumatic Stress, 17*, 11–21. http://doi.org/10.1023/B:JOTS.0000014671.27856.e

Linley, P. A., Joseph, S., Cooper, R., Harris, S., & Meyer, C. (2003). Positive and negative changes following vicarious exposure to the September 11 terrorist attacks. *Journal of Traumatic Stress, 16*, 481–485. https://psycnet.apa.org/doi/10.1023/A:1025710528209

Magruder, K. M., McLaughlin, K. A., & Elmore Borbon, D. L. (2017). Trauma is a public health issue. *European Journal of Psychotraumatology, 8*(1), 1375338. http://doi.org/10.1080/20008198.2017.1375338

Makadia, R., Sabin-Farrell, R., & Turpin, G. (2017). Indirect exposure to client trauma and the impact on trainee clinical psychologists: Secondary traumatic stress or vicarious traumatization? *Clinical Psychology & Psychotherapy, 24*(5), 1059–1068. http://doi.org/10.1002/cpp.2068

Mauritz, M. W., Goossens, P. J. J., Draijer, N., & van Achterberg, T. (2013). Prevalence of interpersonal trauma exposure and trauma-related disorders in severe mental illness. *European Journal of Psychotraumatology, 4*(1). https://doi.org/10.3402/ejpt.v4i0.19985

McCann, I. L., & Pearlman, L. A. J. (1990). Vicarious traumatization: A framework for understanding the psychological effects of working with victims. *Journal of Trauma Stress, 3*(1), 131–149. https://doi.org/10.1007/BF00975140

McKim, L., & Smith-Adcock, S. (2014). Trauma counsellors' quality of life. *International Journal for the Advancement of Counselling, 36*(1), 58–69. https://doi.org/10.1007/s10447-013-9190-z

Merriam, S. B. (2015). *Qualitative Research: A Guide to Design and Implementation* (4th ed.). Jossey-Bass.

Michalopoulos, L. M., & Aparicio, E. (2012). Vicarious trauma in social workers: The role of trauma history, social support, and years of experience. *Journal of Aggression, Maltreatment, and Trauma, 21*, 646–664. http://doi.org/10.1080/10926771.2012.689422

Pearlman, L., & Mac Ian, P. S. (1995). Vicarious traumatization: An empirical study of the effects of trauma work on trauma therapists. *Professional Psychology: Research and Practice, 26*, 558–565. http://doi.org/10.1037/0735-7028.26.6.558

Rothschild, B. (2006). *Help for the Helper: The Psychophysiology of Compassion Fatigue and Vicarious Trauma*. Norton.

Sabin-Farrell, R. D. (2000). *The impact on UK mental health workers of working with traumatised clients* (Unpublished doctoral thesis). University of Sheffield.

Sacco, T. L., Ciurzynski, S. M., Harvey, M. E., & Ingersoll, G. L. (2015). Compassion satisfaction and compassion fatigue among critical care nurses. *Critical Care Nurse, 35*, 32–42. http://doi.org/10.4037/ccn2015392

Satkunanayagam, K., Tunariu, A., & Tribe, R. (2010). A qualitative exploration of mental health professionals' experience of working with survivors of trauma in Sri Lanka. International. *Journal of Culture and Mental Health, 3*(1), 43–51. http://dx.doi.org/10.1080/17542861003593336

Shamai, M., & Ron, P. (2009). Helping direct and indirect victims of national terror: Experiences of Israeli social workers. *Qualitative Health Research, 19*(1), 42–54. http://dx.doi.org/10.1177/1049732308327350

Smith, J. A., Flowers, P., & Larkin, M. (2009). *Interpretive Phenomenological Analysis: Theory, Method, and Research*. Sage.

Smith, J. A., Flowers, P., & Larkin, M. (2022). *Interpretative Phenomenological Analysis: Theory, Method and Research* (2nd ed.). Sage.

Smith, J. A., & Osborn, M. (2015). Interpretative phenomenological analysis is a useful methodology for research on the lived experience of pain. *British Journal of Pain, 9*(1), 41–42. https://doi.org/10.1177/2049463714541642

Somoray, K., Shakespeare-Finch, J., & Armstrong, D. (2017). The impact of personality and workplace belongingness on mental health workers' professional quality of life. *Australian Psychologist, 52*(1), 52–60.

Splevins, K. A., Cohen, K., Joseph, S., Murray, C., & Bowley, J. (2010). Vicarious posttraumatic growth among interpreters. *Qualitative Health Research, 20*(12), 1705–1716. https://doi.org/10.1177/1049732310377457

Tedeschi, R. G., & Calhoun, L. G. (2004). Posttraumatic growth: Conceptual foundations and empirical evidence. *Psychological Inquiry, 15*(1), 1–18. http://www.jstor.org/stable/20447194

Thagard, P. (2007). I feel your pain: Mirror neurons, empathy, and moral motivation. *Journal of Cognitive Science, 8,* 109–136.

van der Kolk, B. A. (2014). *The Body Keeps the Score: Brain, Mind, and Body in the Healing of Trauma*. Viking.

VanDeusen, K. M., & Way, I. (2006). Vicarious trauma: An exploratory study of the impact of providing sexual abuse treatment on clinicians' trust and intimacy. *Journal of Child Sexual Abuse, 15*(1), 69–85. http://doi.org/10.1300/J070v15n01_04

Way, I., VanDeusen, K. M., Martin, G., Applegate, B., & Jandle, D. (2004). Vicarious trauma: A comparison of clinicians who treat survivors of sexual abuse and sexual offenders. *Journal of Interpersonal Violence, 19*(1), 49–71. http://doi.org /10.1177/0886260503259050

Willig, C., & Stainton Rogers, W. (2017). *The SAGE Handbook of Qualitative Research in Psychology*. Sage. http://doi.org/10.4135/9781526405555

Chapter 14

Vicarious Trauma and Growth in Mental Health Workers

Simon Wharne

Introduction

Burnout has been a concern in caring professions for many years. It is addressed in an extensive field of literature, in which it is also described as compassion fatigue and vicarious trauma (Bartoskova, 2015). More recently, the phenomenon of vicarious growth has also been explored (Barrington & Shakespeare-Finch, 2013; Manning-Jones et al., 2015; Tedeschi et al., 2018; Tsirimokou et al., 2022). In this chapter, I provide a brief and selective literature review. I then set out a summary of the findings from a study I conducted using a phenomenological research approach. The chapter also extends the reflexive element of that study.

There are points of reflection that I would like to highlight. For example, I thought originally that I chose this topic because it was relevant to my employed role. I worked in community mental health services in a setting where we had problems recruiting and retaining workers. Many of my colleagues would be off work at times with stress-related illnesses. Many would move on to work in less challenging roles. I wondered about the colleagues who stayed with the difficult work. What enabled them to do that, and what kind of resilience did they possess? It was during the research process that I realised that my motivation was driven much more by my own experience of vicarious trauma and growth.

I recall that while I was conducting the research, I attended a conference, hearing presentations on vicarious trauma. During that day I joined in a workshop, exploring the question of how we can support workers who are at risk of experiencing this form of trauma. I found myself in a group with senior paramedics, police officers, and fire service managers. As we worked through an exercise, it became clear to us that we had all attended the conference for similar reasons. We were trying to address our own vicarious traumas, while also seeking ways to support our colleagues. This was a transformative moment for me, as I saw my own way of being reflected in others. We were working in different professions, but

DOI: 10.4324/9781003493860-19

encountering the same dilemmas, holding the same concerns. This was a moment of connection, after which I no longer felt so alone.

I have often worked with clients who are marginalised in society. Clients who are living difficult lives, frequently distressed by their enduring mental health problems. For several years I managed a service in which it was a battle, every day, to keep our service users housed, in social networks, occupied, and moving towards more sustainable and meaningful lives. Many turned to the use of drugs and alcohol, to crime, and many were caught up in abusive relationships. There were deaths by misadventure and suicide, with drawn-out internal enquiries. At the same time, we faced constant demands for audits and reports, related to imposed targets. For example, we were commissioned to provide a seven-day service, but I could not keep enough staff. At times I covered weekends, carrying on without a break.

I recall that it was a stressful job in terms of work demands, but I was keen and committed, so that did not trouble me so much. It was more the loss and waste of young lives that pulled at my emotions and occupied my thoughts. I was frustrated that we could not do more to help those who were suffering. Thinking back, I recall that in my own life, I could have become one of those distressed young people. There were difficult periods for me, but opportunities came along. In the process of reviewing my life, I began to experience a sense of gratitude. At one time, I might have been resentful and jealous when others were succeeding and I struggled, but I came to understand that I was one of the fortunate people. As I read material for my literature review, I learnt that this gratitude was an aspect of posttraumatic growth. This growth inspires a desire to be closer to others, to help others who are struggling (Benatar, 2000; Harrison & Westwood, 2009; Satkunanayagam et al., 2010; Steed & Downing, 1998; Tedeschi et al., 2018).

A literature review

Working in the caring professions can create a potential for both vicarious traumatisation and for vicarious posttraumatic growth. Most of the findings reviewed in this literature review are specific to psychological therapies, while others are general across caring professions. The review is strategic and limited. Literature could have been included where researchers ask questions about personality style, suicidality, or systemic processes in institutional settings. Some of this was reviewed in the original study (Wharne, 2019). Here, however, we will focus in on the question of what it is like to experience vicarious posttraumatic growth.

It is found that practitioners feel sadness, anger, fear, frustration, helplessness, powerlessness, despair, and shock, along with somatic phenomena, such as numbness, nausea, and tiredness (Bartoskova, 2015; Cohen & Collens, 2013; Iliffe & Steed, 2000; Manning-Jones et al., 2015; Pistorius et al., 2008). Somatic responses can cause insomnia or irritability, and general disruption in life, where workers feel detached but find that it is difficult to 'switch off' (Splevins et al., 2010; Steed & Downing, 1998). In their work roles, practitioners struggle to comprehend and make sense of the trauma of others. There are realities which newly qualified professionals might not have encountered before in their lives (Cohen & Collens, 2013), although it is found that novice practitioners are less likely to experience vicarious trauma (Ben-Porat, 2015). It is also observed that vicarious trauma increases then decreases, in a U-shaped curve, where seasoned and experienced practitioners recover their sense of resilience (Wang & Park-Taylor, 2021).

When a practitioner has experienced significant traumas in their own life, this raises questions of whether they will be more vulnerable to vicarious trauma, or more prepared and able to avoid it. Many practitioners report that they had suffered mental health problems before they became qualified professionals (Straussner et al., 2018). Research is inconclusive, with some finding that practitioners who report personal experiences of trauma have more negative vicarious responses (Pearlman & Mac Ian, 1995), and some finding no differences between the two groups (Ben-Porat, 2015; Benatar, 2000). It seems that practitioners must work to come to terms with the experiences of their clients, a kind of 'serving humanity' (Michalchuk & Martin, 2019). This work can also be understood as a form of 'emotional labour' (Kirwan & O'Driscoll, 2023), and perhaps practitioners who have lived experience of trauma have already done some of that work.

It is found that practitioners will often take a proactive stance in response in their work. Practitioners will resist the negativity which can be induced by distressing accounts of harm and abuse. They might, for example, change their ways of living, seeking balance and engaging in physical exercise and healthy eating, resting, and meditating (Bober & Regehr, 2006; Hernandez-Wolfe, 2018; Steed & Downing, 1998). Some engage in political activism as they try to combat cynicism and channel their anger (Iliffe & Steed, 2000). Many report that it is important to separate work and personal life, and many make use of psychological therapy themselves (Pistorius et al., 2008). An experience of spiritual development is described in some studies (Arnold et al., 2005; Hernandez-Wolfe, 2018).

An active stance is thought to be important in the use of relational strategies (Colman et al., 2018). This supports the finding that the use of empathy and positive coping strategies are aids in the development of growth (Ogińska-Bulik & Michalska, 2022). It is found that growth is more likely to develop in practitioners when they establish a deeper empathetic connection with their clients (Brockhouse et al., 2011). A sense of coherence, the availability of social support, empathy, and the bond within the working alliance are identified as factors which influence vicarious trauma and growth (Linley & Joseph, 2007; Linley et al., 2005). These experiences can be thought of as a part of the practitioner's professional development, a process of establishing their identity (Kang & Yang, 2022).

Empathy seems to be important, and in existential thinking it is understood as a multi-layered phenomenon (Stein, 1921/1989). There is a sensing in at a bodily level, by which we are alerted to what might be happening for the other person. This will cause us to anticipate what it would be like for us to experience the difficulties which they endure. If an empathetic connection remains at this level, it is likely to induce an accumulating form of vicarious trauma. However, a deeper empathetic connection can be established in the mutual acceptance that the trauma has happened for the client, in their world. The experience asks something of them. This separation is thought to be important in preventing vicarious trauma (Badger et al., 2008).

Practitioners can find themselves witnessing the client's transformation, as that client turns to face uncomfortable truths. It is primarily the client who must make sense of what has happened for them. Empathy at this deeper level has moved through interpersonal communications and identifications, to be resolved with a recognition of separateness and difference (Stein, 1921/1989). The practitioner, meanwhile, is now more aware that distressing events can happen in life. They are also required, therefore, to develop their own personal response to this knowledge.

Practitioners can fall into a cynical stance with a bleak outlook (Benatar, 2000). When professionals who are parents become aware of the extent and the effects of child abuse, for example, they become over-protective of their own children (Pistorius et al., 2008). Also, with their awareness of unacknowledged harms and distress in society, practitioners express the view that friends and family would not be able to understand (Splevins et al., 2010). A form of stigma can be attached to the practitioner, due to the nature of their work (Verhaeghe & Bracke, 2012). Practitioners are then at risk of isolation. They are often proactive, educating and supporting each other, promoting an inclusive and non-authoritarian working environment (Harrison & Westwood, 2009). They can experience positive responses, such as living life more fully, treating others differently, and becoming more emotionally expressive in their relationships (Deaton et al., 2021).

A tolerance for ambiguity can be a factor that mitigates against the development of vicarious trauma (Dagan et al., 2015). Engaging with distressed clients can be transformative; with a new awareness of hidden trauma, practitioners reconsider what is important for them in life. It will have been a surprise to some practitioners that their clients cope and grow in diffi-cult circumstances (Splevins et al., 2010). Practitioners report that they feel they have gained wisdom, insight, and an increased sense of self-worth (Benatar, 2000; Hernandez-Wolfe, 2018; Pistorius et al., 2008; Splevins et al., 2010). An educational process is suggested, in which 'threshold concepts' are grasped (Kirwan & O'Driscoll, 2023). A sense of empower-ment and self-validation are also reported, and practitioners feel that they are more compassionate and accepting towards others, feeling a sense of humility (Benatar, 2000; Ben-Porat & Itzhaky, 2009; Hernandez-Wolfe, 2018). A process can take place in which practitioners question what they are doing with their lives (Goldbatt et al., 2009; Hernandez-Wolfe, 2018), and they engage in a form of existential meaning making (Benatar, 2000; Harrison & Westwood, 2009; Hernandez-Wolfe, 2018; Satkunanayagam et al., 2010; Steed & Downing, 1998).

A gap in the literature

Most of the literature reviewed above is survey based and quantitative. These studies observe growth at a single point in time, and a gap is found in a need for longitudinal studies (Tsirimokou et al., 2022). It is also implied that growth will only come about for practitioners if that growth is happen-ing first for their clients (Edelkott et al., 2016; Engstrom et al., 2008), but this is not consistently demonstrated across studies. Also, understandings at a deeper level can often be gained through qualitative studies.

Methodology

In the research that I present here, I addressed resilience in mental health staff, specifically in relation to their concern that clients might die. The study was approved by the ethics board of the New School of Psychotherapy and Counselling, a sub-committee of the ethics board of Middlesex University, London. I recruited participants who worked in community mental health services in the UK. I conducted semi-structured interviews using a con-versational style. Participants were enabled, thereby, to provide detailed descriptions of their concerns and experiences. I transcribed the recordings of these interviews and wrote them up in narrative form. I engaged in a succession of readings, annotations, and analyses, following principles set out by Max van Manen (van Manen, 1990).

Participants

Adam and Ben are Social Workers employed in Community Mental Health Services. Carys is a Senior Counsellor in a Primary Mental Health Service.

Dave is a Peer Worker in Secondary Mental Health Services. Ellen and Gina are Counsellors, employed in Primary Care Counselling Services, and Fiona is a Team Leader for a community mental health team and a Registered Mental Health Nurse.

Analysis and findings: Three themes

1. **Not-disengaging in an emotional process:** An experience of being with, but separate, detached, but empathetic and consistent. A need to manage relationships, moving from meditative to active, while facing dilemmas due to an encounter with death within an institutional system.

The participants in this study describe how they feel present with others. This draws them into emotional dynamics, while at the same time they are working to hold themselves as separate. This is achieved through an empathetic connection with the emotionality of the other, while at the same time remaining calm and consistent in their own emotional state. They describe how they manage relationships, moving between listening, meditative, and active positions, as they face dilemmas within the institutional setting in which they work. In those institutions, the phenomenon of death will bring them up against conflicting duties.

In an encounter with a suicidal client, Ellen uses double-negatives to express the combined active and passive position in which she finds herself: *'I suppose not-disengaging myself but knowing that it is their choice and they're autonomous.'* In her ambiguous position, Ellen is choosing to let herself be pulled into an emotional encounter with her client, while separating herself and acknowledging the client's autonomy. Carys describes a similar experience, being concerned that she will not be able to deal with the situation. She is feeling that: *'It's all going to be too much, I don't even really want to know about... so, it's a kind of push me pull you, situation.'* Both Ellen and Carys seem to be reluctantly stepping into an emotive and dynamic interaction with clients who talk of taking their lives. This will heighten their awareness that people cannot be controlled, and some people do take the action of ending their own lives.

It appears that participants are often doing a lot of work to maintain a calm appearance and to respond to situations in a consistent manner. Fiona manages staff in a service where there is an ever-present risk of clients dying. She explains that in providing support to her staff members, *'I would probably suppress a lot of how I am feeling.'* Gina will also control her emotional responses, working with a client who is at risk *'in the way that I took her threat of suicide, in caring but not showing fear or worry.'* Both are acting as responsible professionals who have a duty to manage situations. To achieve this, they must read emotional dynamics. Carys will be supervising trainees, and she explains that *'I feel like I have to be alert the whole time.'* She observes that trainees have not learnt to hold the complex position of being empathetic, calm, and consistent, in the face of emotive conversations about possible risks. They are not yet pulled into the kind of emotional regulation and hypervigilance that senior practitioners maintain.

Participants describe how they move from a passive listening position to taking an active stance. Carys explains: *'So it felt, um, so first of all I had the panic, and then I had um, the distress, thinking; "Gosh this is only a young man, what a waste of a life," um and, then I realised that I had to take control of the situation.'* Carys connects emotionally with the intensity of the risk. She recalls feeling that what is happening for this suicidal young man could happen for one of her children. Then, she achieves a separation: *'I calmed down and then I just focused on the young man... I realised it was his life and his distress, and I, I started to, you know, look after him as best I could.'* In that looking after, Carys moves to an active stance. Ben describes similar shifts, and he refers to the concept of emotional intelligence. An active intervention for Ben is *'to be able to sort of read your emotions, being able to, you know, try and say the right thing at the right time.'* Participants are not repressing emotions but reading and managing them, responding strategically.

Ben explains that there are policies and procedures in his work setting, which he is required to follow. He observes that: *'Too many things pulling you in different directions does take its toll.'* Adam also picks up on this, saying: *'Sometimes our views and our values can kind of go against the grain of what our employer's expectations are or what we should be doing.'* Ben observes that: *'You want to support someone to make their choices, but then also, you have to weigh that up against the risk of um, dying.'* Carys explains that, when institutional systems are set up to manage workflow, they can become a tick-box process in which there is no human interest or connection. She is concerned about this in relation to her suicidal client, and she asked herself: *'Can I trust a Risk Assessment Team to actually get him assessed this evening?'* She decided to rearrange her work schedule to liaise and ensure that this happened.

2. **Growth through enduring difficulties:** An experience of different kinds of resilience, while feeling deconstructed, powerless, raw, and surrendering to being out of control. A need to go through transitions which involve reflection and letting go. Finding personal meaning.

Participants face challenging situations in their employed role. They become emotionally aware while engaging with a client who is at risk, while also navigating complex institutional systems. They reveal a significant degree of tolerance and resilience in this work. Many describe formative experiences through which these personal qualities were forged. Dave refers to his own prior experiences of suicidality. He explains that these impulses were a response to severe posttraumatic stress, which came about for him following his active military service. He describes how he was at first denying his difficulties, and he explains: 'Resilience is accepting that you've got a problem.' Carys also mentions her own traumatic experiences, saying: 'Part of recovery is accepting where you are right now.' It is this ability to be present with the more distressing aspects of existence, with troubling realities, which enables these participants to endure through their unpredictable and demanding work tasks.

In her therapeutic work, Carys reflects on the difficulty that many people have in being present with the truths of their existence: 'People resist understanding, they really don't want to look at it, it's almost like they've built a whole life on looking the other way and the last thing they want is to suddenly see what is there for them.' Other participants recognise this commonplace denial. Dave says: 'We all think we know ourselves, um, and I thought I knew myself really well until I got ill, and then I realised I wasn't indestructible.' It is not then that participants are hardened to difficult realities, it is more that they can tolerate a sense of human vulnerability, staying with an awareness of challenging existential truths. They can maintain their balance when the possibility of death is brought sharply into focus.

Participants explain that past traumas had shaped the way that they approach their lives. Adam says: 'I remember, well, at school being bullied for about ten years, constantly, and obviously at the time I hated that, it was awful, you know verbal and physical bullying is awful for anyone, but that kind of, changed and moulded me as an adult.' Adam spoke about the understanding that he gained of what it is like to be a member of a minority group in a discriminatory society. Carys describes an austere and brutal childhood but recalls the supportive sense of facing things together in a family network. Ellen also mentions the resilience in her family. Gina talks about her traumatic experiences, saying: 'This trauma and this really bad thing that happened, really made me kind of strong.' Again, this strength is not a denial or a hardened invincibility, but a connection with the realities of suffering, austerity, and trauma.

Gina feels able to hear the distress of clients in her therapeutic work, while retaining that calm and consistent stance. She says that when a client presents as suicidal, 'It didn't seed me any fear, or anything, it was just good about, being more, present and raw, kind of, even more caring.' Similarly, Ben describes his difficult experience, saying: 'that actually gives me a bit of empathy that I can think actually that I do sort of understand *how powerless this person may feel or how difficult it is for this person to actually move on.'* For many participants, this learnt ability to tolerate austerity, brutality, and powerlessness seems to be an important foundational experience.

Carys describes how she came to understand that it is not always possible to take control in challenging situations: *'It is a false, um, sense of control when you think you are in control [laughs], um and it only works so far, then actually, the anxiety increases because you are trying to control something.'* She explains that it is better to go with events and to work with what comes up: *'You're not in control, so why pretend, might as well surrender yourself um, to the situation and see what happens and then, deal with things as they happen.'* This would be an essential skill in working with clients who are at risk. Ben also picks up on this: *'To then feel, sort of like you have no power, might actually give you a good grounding to think well actually this is, you know, maybe this is how people are experiencing.'* He explains that it is more skilful to work with an awareness of personal powerlessness.

In the work that they describe, participants are not impervious to the distress of their clients. Carys explains that: *'It took me two or three days, to recover, from the young man's experiences, or the experience of being with a young man who was in such distress and how that affected me.'* This reveals the depth of engagement and the extent of the emotional work that is done to be with people in their distress. Resilience is not an avoidance of human distress, but a healthy ability to encounter it and to recover. Gina describes similar experiences: *'I could really, kind of get stuck and, um, get stuck with the emotion and with the thoughts of how can someone, like, have been through all of this.'* She describes the slow process of recovery: *'I slowly made my peace with that in the sense that, um, in the sense that I let it go, yeah, I learnt how to let go of clients after they leave the room, or at least intend to let go of them, sometimes it's impossible.'* Perhaps, with experience, practitioners are less affected, or recover sooner, but it seems that to be affected emotionally is a part of their work.

3. **Being human under the scrutiny of authority:** Experiencing the shock of sudden death, then answering to authorities and remaining balanced. A need to be human, while professional and accountable. Reaching out to others who have suffered.

Despite their heightened awareness, sudden deaths still come as a shock for participants, and it is often the uncertainty of these events that troubles them. Fiona describes a situation in which a young woman that she helped had fallen from a balcony and died. It was not known whether she had intended to take her life or not: *'It wasn't fully clear that this was an intended outcome, um, for me that was very difficult.'* She explains that she found the attitude of her managers unhelpful, when *'feeling that things were being discounted and minimised.'* She explains that her concerns are still unresolved: *'As I drive past, it's on your mind, still sort of affected by it, and I think still just the sadness of wasted life and um, could things have been different?'* Carys also reflects on the challenges of uncertainty, the random nature of risk in suicidality. She observes how a client at risk will present unexpectedly in the routine of her week, and in her supervision of trainees.

Gina describes mixed feelings in response to a client who took their own life: *'It was a mix of a shock and deep sadness, um, and it did really, well, half of it was, I really cared for her.'* The proximity of death can be profoundly disturbing, as Gina explains: *'Realising that death is really close, and then especially in this moment it was so close I felt, like my heart just opened and I felt love and sadness at the same time for my family, and for the people that I care for.'* It seems then, that the transformative impact of a sudden death is felt in the moment. There is an immediate response in which participants shift in their views and attitudes.

Gina describes a change in her outlook: *'It just felt like, shit, this can happen any time, just so vulnerable and so, like in touch with what's really important, in this life and what's not.'* This is an awareness that cuts deeply into participants, so that they can experience a kind of hypervigilance, always anticipating and trying to be prepared for another sudden death. Ben explains that in his work he is constantly trying to balance risks. He observes that if practitioners take steps to control a situation, suicidal people can feel that they have lost their autonomy: *'If you then take everything away from someone then they don't, they don't have a stake in it.'* While at the same time, there are professional standards and legal requirements: *'You have to balance that with the, you know, the risks and autonomy and all of our frameworks, and legislation.'* Participants find that it is an arduous task to constantly maintain a balanced and useful response to risk. Adam says: *'I'm just trying to, not be reactive, but try and look at it, put it into context and perspective, um you know sometimes I do, get frustrated.'* This is another example of that complex combination of passive and active positions. Adam explains how difficult this can be: *'You've left feeling angry, upset and frustrated and worn out.'* This balanced approach is a hard discipline to maintain.

An empathetic connection demands a constant and careful checking in, to ensure that passive and active stances are adopted in a mutually engaged manner. It is also a necessary discipline to remain attuned to the powerlessness and meaninglessness that we can experience when encountering harsh realities. Mostly we want to set these truths aside, but when participants engage in an empathetic manner with those who are currently suffering, they must maintain an awareness of these things. Carys says: '*I recognise that feeling of meaninglessness as well, it's not like it doesn't touch me sometimes.*' In a similar observation, Ben says: '*Maybe experiencing a bit of powerlessness every now and then is a good way to maybe build resilience.*' Perhaps it is helpful for participants to be reminded of their own struggles.

In the connectivity that participants achieve through empathetic engagement with their clients, a kind of sharing can be experienced. Carys explains: '*It puts me in a place of um, shared humanity, that we're all in this together, um, that somehow just in sharing that, it's quite strengthening.*' Participants are perhaps less alone in the trauma and austerity that they have endured. Carys expresses the view that sharing experiences is strengthening for the practitioner and the client: '*real sort of mutuality of feeling something, about human, being human.*' This can be a problem in institutional contexts where practitioners must maintain a rational and impartial stance in their work. Ben observes that: '*If something touches me emotionally, I'm going to feel more, likely to work more, which maybe is wrong in a way but, that's how humans work isn't it?*' Emotional connection is a part of the role, but Ben explains that he has been criticised for being over-involved and trying to 'rescue' people. Adam, however, explains that: '*You need to come across as a human, and you need to have a human, human element to the work.*' This can be difficult for participants to manage.

Practitioners face conflicting demands. Ben explains how practitioners '*need to show empathy and, you know, be able to connect to someone on a human level, as well as, you know, your professional level.*' Some participants describe tensions with supervisors and managers. These are brought about when the participant has an emotional connection with a client who has died or is at risk of dying. More senior practitioners in the organisation hold rigidly to professional and institutional processes, leaving the practitioner with feelings such as anger, frustration, and a sense of isolation. Since she has experienced the death of her clients, Fiona explains that: '*It certainly made me, more, um, thoughtful and careful about other clinicians who are going though similar experiences.*' She explains that she did not feel supported by senior managers when she struggled, and she is now motivated to support and care for fellow practitioners.

When participants support each other in their awareness of the potential for death, they share understandings. Dave challenges the commonly held belief that: '*Because you're a nurse or a doctor you're tough, you can cope with anything.*' By moving away from this macho stance, participants are aligning with subversive and fringe positions. Adam describes how he enjoys working with clients who do not fit in with society: *'They can be marginalised by society, you know, I like working with people who are, if you like, on the edges of society.'* It seems likely that this marginalisation is associated with experiences of trauma. When that is, people are aware of traumatic realities which most people do not want to think about. Ben is aware of these realities, saying: *'Sometimes people do die and that is a fact of life.'* Most people do not maintain an acute awareness of this fact, but this is an intrusive and present truth for participants in this study.

Dave explains that it was only when he recognised that he had problems, that he felt more connected with others: *'Oh my God; I am just like everyone else.'* This is that sense of interconnection with others in the experience of struggling with the harsh realities of trauma. Dave explains: *'The more I got involved in helping others, I realised that's where I needed to be, but also I found that I was getting better.'* This engagement in mutual support seems to be a key feature that enables participants to overcome their own traumatic experiences and to be there for others.

It might be assumed that an intrusive awareness of the possibility of death is a problem, a 'symptom' of posttraumatic stress disorder for example. However, Carys observes:

> *A lot of life is done on automatic pilot, and we have a sort of façade, and everybody is pretending that everything's OK, um, and that can be a little bit samey and probably meaningless, whereas, when, when some of those moments with clients, and you really feel, that sort of, what human beings feel, together.*

Gina describes a similar experience: *'I find it challenging and humbling most of all, because I always leave the sessions feeling more grateful and more humble and less self-centred.'* There is, again, an intersubjective connection for participants, when they feel empathy for clients who experience traumas, reminding them of the fragility and mortality of the human condition.

Discussion

The findings set out above are aligned with much of the results reported in the literature review, particularly in the desire that participants feel to be closer to others, to help others who are struggling (Benatar, 2000; Harrison & Westwood, 2009; Satkunanayagam et al., 2010; Steed & Downing, 1998). These findings suggest that vicarious growth is an aspect of a life-long coming to terms with traumatic experience. I wonder if the choice that participants make, to work in the caring professions, is related to their difficult early life experiences, such as austerity, powerlessness, bullying, and trauma. Participants can, however, maintain a distinction between their own experiences and those of their clients. They recognise that the trauma is something that is happening in the client's world, a separation which is thought to be protective (Badger et al., 2008). It seems likely that clients will feel that the practitioner is drawn in, engaged, and that they understand, while the practitioner retains a sense of balance and agency.

The ambiguity participants describe, when they are being both passive and active, is addressed in the work of Simone de Beauvoir (1949/1997) and Maurice Merleau-Ponty (1945/1962). De Beauvoir develops ambiguity into a form of ethics, and Merleau-Ponty explores the embodied nature of this intersubjectivity. He observes the ambiguity of touch. When flesh is in contact with flesh, it is not always clear whether we are touching or being touched. This can inform our understanding of the combined passive and active position that participants take up.

As I consider these findings again, I realise that the phenomenon of posttraumatic growth arose spontaneously in the research study. It was not the case that I adopted assumptions and modelling and then sought evidence to support them. What strikes me now is that ambiguous switching between isolation and belonging, and between active and passive positions. This happens in therapeutic encounters, and in interactions with colleagues. Participants are skilled at retaining their emotional coherence in the liminal spaces of difficult transitions. In the original analysis, I was more concerned by the potential for conflict between participants and their senior colleagues. I see now that the participants' relationships with clients and colleagues are similar, where they are working to maintain a coherent and emotionally engaged stance.

As observed in the literature review, posttraumatic growth creates a desire to be closer to others and to help those who suffer. Participants in this study experience that desire. It seems, however, that they can only achieve a precarious sense of belonging. Many explain how they value the sense of connection they gain, in an experience of being grounded in the truth of the human condition. Some describe how they support other staff, when the institutional system does not allow much space for human emotionality. Sometimes, however, practitioners can feel that they are alone in making a human emotional connection with their clients, unsupported by senior colleagues. Without the participants' strength and determination, it seems that their clients would otherwise meet only with an impersonal and bureaucratic system.

Participants observe that they get something from their encounters with clients. They are exposed to trauma vicariously, an experience which reconnects them with troubling realities. Following influential themes in existential philosophy, we might propose that this heightened awareness of human mortality, fragility, and transience is useful. It helps, perhaps to orientate participants to the true nature of what it means to be human. It connects them with others who are also encountering this reality. When they maintain their awareness and connection with others, participants feel less alone. They can manage their emotional responses through a complex form of advanced empathy. This empathy involves a flow of emotional connection, while also maintaining a separation. Participants are aware that, while traumatic experiences are happening for the client, they are not currently happening for them. Maintaining that ambiguous separation and connection seems to draw the practitioner into a position of strength, enabling a proactive stance and leading to an effective intervention.

Conclusion

The accounts that these participants give are inspiring. They connect us with a sense of what it means to be human, in all its vulnerability, mortality, and suffering. The stance that participants take enables them to experience these realities as strengthening. In health care services that are often underfunded, where there is a shortage of qualified and experienced staff, employees will still find positive ways to connect with others and thrive. Unfortunately, institutional bureaucratic responses are often risk adverse, constituting a form of emotional disconnection and denial. Despite that avoidance, participants in this study are making human connections, surviving, and thriving.

Having moved on in my career, I do not now go to work every day with a concern that a client might have died. I no longer fear that an inquiry will bring about the closure of the services that I manage. I find that I am experiencing a degree of survivor guilt, but I also feel grateful that I had the opportunity to grow and learn in a challenging work role. In conducting this research, I am strongly motivated by a desire to explore and to understand what was happening. I know that it is challenging to work in mental health care, that senior colleagues are not always supportive. I am concerned that there are settings in which sustainable responses to the risk of death, and to actual incidences of death, are not achieved. There is a potential perhaps for bullying and oppressive behaviours. I am concerned that practitioners will feel compelled to repeatedly write up lengthy risk assessments, anticipating the scrutiny of a risk-adverse culture, while only engaging with their client at a superficial level and failing to find meaning in the encounter.

What messages should you take from the findings reported here? I hope that you can appreciate how important it is to maintain an empathetic stance towards clients who are in distress. When they are feeling so distressed, that is, that risking their own life seems to be a viable option. I suspect that they are questioning the purpose and meaning of life, while many, it seems, are living lives that have exposed them to unendurable traumas. I hope that you can appreciate the determination, skill, and endurance of mental health professionals who turn up to work every day. They do not know if, on that day, they will be pulled again into a challenging emotional encounter with the reality of death. If you are in a position to direct more funding and resources into mental health care, please do organise that. These practitioners need adequate training, support, and supervision to maintain the positive stance that they take.

References

Arnold, D., Calhoun, L. G., Tedeschi, R., & Cann, A. (2005). Vicarious posttraumatic growth in psychotherapy. *Journal of Humanistic Psychology, 45*(2), 239–263. https://doi.org/10.1177/0022167805274729

Badger, K., Royse, D., & Craig, C. D. (2008). Hospital social workers and indirect trauma exposure: An exploratory study of contributing factors. *Health and Social Work, 33*, 63–71. https://doi.org/10.1093/hsw/33.1.63

Barrington, A. J., & Shakespeare-Finch, J. (2013). Working with refugee survivors of torture and trauma: An opportunity for vicarious post-traumatic growth, *Counselling Psychology Quarterly, 26*(1), 89–105. https://psycnet.apa.org/doi /10.1080/09515070.2012.727553

Bartoskova, L. (2015). Research into post-traumatic growth in therapists: A critical literature review. *Counselling Psychology Review, 30*(3), 57–67. https://doi.org /10.53841/bpscpr.2015.30.3.57

Ben-Porat, A. (2015). Vicarious post-traumatic growth: Domestic violence therapists versus social services department therapists in Israel. *Journal of Family Violence, 30*, 923–933. https://doi.org/10.1007/s10896-015-9714-x

Ben-Porat, A., & Itzhaky, H. (2009). Implications of treating family violence for the therapist: Secondary traumatization, vicarious traumatization, and growth. *Journal of Family Violence, 24*(7), 507–515. https://doi.org/10.1007/s10896-009 -9249-0

Benatar, M. (2000). A qualitative study of the effect of a history of childhood sexual abuse on therapists who treat survivors of sexual abuse. *Journal of Trauma & Dissociation, 1*, 9–28. https://psycnet.apa.org/doi/10.1300/J229v01n03_02

Bober, T., & Regehr, C. (2006). Strategies for reducing secondary or vicarious trauma: Do they work? *Brief Treatment and Crisis Intervention, 6*(1), 1–9. http:// doi.org/10.1093/brief-treatment/mhj001

Brockhouse, R., Msetfi, R., Cohen, K., & Joseph, S. (2011). Vicarious exposure to trauma and growth in therapists: The moderating effects of sense of coherence, organisational support and empathy. *Journal of Traumatic Stress, 24*(6), 735– 742. https://psycnet.apa.org/doi/10.1002/jts.20704

Cohen, K., & Collens, P. (2013). The impact of trauma work – A meta-synthesis on vicarious trauma and vicarious growth. *Psychological Trauma: Theory,*

Research, Practice, and Policy, 5(6), 570–580. https://psycnet.apa.org/doi/10.1037/a0030388

Colman, A. M., Chouliara, Z., & Currie, K. (2018). Working in the field of complex psychological trauma: A framework for personal and professional growth, training, and supervision. *Journal of Interpersonal Violence, 36*(5–6), 2791–2815. https://doi.org/10.1177/0886260518759062

Dagan, K., Itzhaky, H., & Ben-Porat, A. (2015). Therapists working with trauma victims: The contribution of personal, environmental, and professional-organizational resources to secondary traumatization. *Journal of Trauma & Dissociation, 16*(5), 592–606. https://doi.org/10.1080/15299732.2015.1037038

Deaton, J. D., Wymer, B., & Carlson, R. G. (2021). Supervision strategies to facilitate vicarious post traumatic growth among trauma counselors. *Journal of Counselor Preparation and Supervision, 14*(4). https://digitalcommons.sacredheart.edu/jcps/vol14/iss4/12

de Beauvoir, S. (1997). *The Second Sex* (trans. H. M. Parshley). Vintage (Original work published 1949).

Edelkott, N., Engstrom, D. W., Hernandez-Wolfe, P., & Gangsei, D. (2016). Vicarious resilience: Complexities and variations. *American Journal of Orthopsychiatry, 86*(6), 713–724. http://doi.org/10.1037/ort0000180

Engstrom, D., Hernandez, P., & Gangsei, D. (2008). Vicarious resilience: A qualitative investigation into its description. *Traumatology, 14*(3), 13–21. https://doi.org/10.1177/1534765608319323

Goldblatt, H., Buchbinder, E., Eisikovits, Z., & Arizon-Mesinger, I. (2009). Between the professional and the private: The meaning of working with intimate partner violence in Social Workers' private lives. *Violence Against Women, 15*(3), 362–384. https://doi.org/10.1177/1077801208330436

Harrison, R. L., & Westwood, M. J. (2009). Preventing vicarious traumatization of mental health therapists: Identifying protective practices. *Psychotherapy: Theory, Research, Practice, Training, 46*(2), 203–219. http://doi.org/10.1037/a0016081

Hernandez-Wolfe, P. (2018). Vicarious resilience: A comprehensive review. *Revista de Estudios Sociales, 66*, 9–17. https://doi.org/10.7440/res66.2018.02

Iliffe, G., & Steed, L. G. (2000). Exploring the counselor's experience of working with perpetrators and survivors of domestic violence. *Journal of Interpersonal Violence, 15*, 393–412. https://doi.org/10.1177/088626000015004004

Kang, J. H., & Yang, S. (2022). A therapist's vicarious posttraumatic growth and transformation of self. *Journal of Humanistic Psychology, 62*(1), 151–164. https://doi.org/10.1177/0022167819889490

Kirwan, G., & O'Driscoll, B. (2023). Applying Threshold Concept Theory in Social Work management education: The pedagogy of emotional labour in Social Work practice. In M. Arnold (Eds.), *Handbook of Applied Teaching and Learning in Social Work Management Education* (pp. 23–37). Springer. https://doi.org/10.1007/978-3-031-18038-5_2

Linley, P. A., & Joseph, S. (2007). Therapy work and therapists' positive and negative well-being. *Journal of Social and Clinical Psychology, 26*(3), 385–403. https://psycnet.apa.org/doi/10.1521/jscp.2007.26.3.385

Linley, P. A., Joseph, S., & Loumidis, K. (2005). Trauma work, sense of coherence, and positive and negative changes in therapists. *Psychotherapy and Psychosomatics, 74*(3), 185–188. https://doi.org/10.1159/000084004

Manning-Jones, S., de Terte, I., & Stephens, C. (2015). Vicarious posttraumatic growth: A systematic literature review. *International Journal of Wellbeing, 5*(2), 125–139. https://doi.org/10.5502/ijw.v5i2.8

Merleau-Ponty, M. (1962). *Phenomenology of perception* (trans. C. Smith). Routledge (Original work published 1945).

Michalchuk, S., & Martin, S. L. (2019). Vicarious resilience and growth in psychologists who work with trauma survivors: An interpretive phenomenological analysis. *Professional Psychology: Research and Practice, 50*(3), 145–154. https://doi.org/10.1037/pro0000212

Ogińska-Bulik, N., & Michalska, P. (2022). The role of empathy and cognitive trauma processing in the occurrence of professional posttraumatic growth among women working with victims of violence. *International Journal of Occupational Medicine and Environmental Health, 35*(6), 679–692. https://doi .org/doi: 10.13075/ijomeh.1896.01945

Pearlman, L. A., & Mac Ian, P. S. (1995). Vicarious traumatization: An empirical study of the effects of trauma work on trauma therapists. *Professional Psychology: Research and Practice, 26*(6), 558–565. https://doi.org/10.1037/0735-7028.26 .6.558

Pistorius, K. D., Feinauer, L. L., Harper, J. M., Stahmann, R. F., & Miller, R. B. (2008). Working with sexually abused children. *The American Journal of Family Therapy, 36*, 181–195. https://doi.org/10.1080/ 01926180701291204

Satkunanayagam, K., Tunariu, A., & Tribe R. (2010). A qualitative exploration of mental health professionals' experience of working with survivors of trauma in Sri Lanka. *International Journal of Culture and Mental Health, 3*(1), 43–51. https://psycnet.apa.org/doi/10.1080/17542861003593336

Splevins, K., Cohen, K., Joseph, S., Murray, C., & Bowley, J. (2010). Vicarious posttraumatic growth among interpreters. *Journal of Qualitative Health Research, 20*, 1705–1716. https://doi.org/10.1177/1049732310377457

Steed, L. G., & Downing, R. (1998). A phenomenological study of vicarious traumatization amongst psychologists and professional counsellors working in the field of sexual abuse/assault. *The Australasian Journal of Disaster and Trauma Studies, 2*(2).

Stein, E. (1989). *On the Problem of Empathy* (trans. W. Stein). ICS Publications (Original work published 1921).

Straussner, S. L. A., Senreich, E., & Steen, J. T. (2018). Wounded healers: A multistate study of licensed social workers' behavioral health problems. *Social Work, 63*, 125–133. https://doi.org/10.1093/sw/swy012

Tedeschi, R. G., Shakespeare-Finch, J., Taku, K., & Calhoun, L. G. (2018). *Posttraumatic Growth: Theory, Research, and Applications.* Routledge. https:// doi.org/10.4324/9781315527451

Tsirimokou, A., Kloess, J. A., & Dhinse, S. K. (2022). Vicarious post-traumatic growth in professionals exposed to traumatogenic material: A systematic literature review. *Trauma, Violence, & Abuse, 0*(0). https://doi.org/10.1177/15248380221082079

van Manen, M. (1990). *Researching Lived Experience: Human Science for an Action Sensitive Pedagogy.* The Althouse Press.

Verhaeghe, M., & Bracke, P. (2012). Associative stigma among mental health professionals: Implications for professional and service user well-being. *Journal of Health and Social Behaviour, 53*(1), 17–32. https://doi.org/10.1177/0022146512439453

Wang, X., & Park-Taylor, J. (2021). Therapists' experiences of counseling foreign-national sex-trafficking survivors in the U.S. and the impact of COVID-19. *Traumatology, 27*(4), 419–431. https://doi.org/10.1037/trm0000349

Wharne, S. (2019). *How do mental health practitioners understand and experience resilience?* (PhD thesis). Middlesex University.

Section 6

Making Sense of Our Work with Trauma

Chapter 15

Trauma and Existence: Existential-Humanistic Understandings of Trauma, with Existential-Analytic and Phenomenological Implications for Practice

Marc Boaz

Trauma and existence

The phenomenological accounts contained in this book describe the ways in which traumatising experiences can directly confront us with our existence (following Boaz, 2022a: 132–136). Our traumatic confrontations are not merely intellectual, conceptual, or cognitive reflections on the nature of human existence. These confrontations are intensely embodied encounters that have lasting visceral, sensorial, emotional, relational, and spiritual impacts on our experience of temporality, spatiality, our self, others, and our understanding of the world around us. In trauma we encounter the intertwining of:

(a) our life, body, and perceptual fields with those of others (*intercorporeality*),
(b) our embodied affectivities with those of others, which continuously modify our emotional and bodily resonances (*interaffectivity*), and
(c) our ontological closeness between human and non-human beings (*interanimality*) (see Boaz, 2022a: 138–142).

We further can experience fragmentations and distortions in our experiences of space-time and our agentic potential, including modes of *existing-out-of-time-and-space* or dissociation (see Boaz, 2022a: 142–150).

Traumatic experiences can give rise to unfathomable pain, tormenting distress, incomprehensible horror, torturous terror, and a deep sense of existential loneliness and isolation (following Herman, 1992/2022; Freyd, 1996). Paradoxically, traumatic existential confrontations can also give rise to new meanings and purposes, and expose us to hitherto unknown potentialities and possibilities in our lives, and in our relation to ourselves, others, and the world around us (following Tedeschi et al., 2017). The paradoxical synthesis of trauma as both devastating to, and emancipating

DOI: 10.4324/9781003493860-21

us from, our lifeworlds is a terrifying realisation for some of us, and a liberatory prospect for others.

Calhoun and Tedeschi (2006: 6, see also Tedeschi & Calhoun, 1995) suggest that it is in the existential and spiritual domains that the most significant posttraumatic growth is experienced. In their revised inventory of posttraumatic growth (Tedeschi et al., 2017: 13–14), they add to the items on spirituality, new existential ones focusing on the extents to which people report having:

(a) a greater clarity about life's meaning,
(b) being better able to face questions of life and death,
(c) more connectedness with all of existence, and
(d) a greater sense of harmony following experiences of trauma.

Existential psychologies and psychotherapies have a complicated relationship with the concept of trauma, and growth related to experiences of it, not least because there has been a historical tendency to subsume interpersonal trauma into broader ideas about human suffering. Before delving into existential approaches to trauma below, I would ask the reader to consider some of the core issues related to contemporary existentialisms of trauma.

Firstly, van Deurzen and Adams (2016: 224) describe the existential distinction between the ontic and ontological as being simply "on the one hand, the essential, necessary and universally valid conditions of human existence – the ontological – and on the other hand, the concrete, changing and practical aspects of existence – the ontic." Within existential formulations of trauma there are frequently problematic differentiations between the 'fear' of so-called 'ontic' trauma (i.e. in the visceral physicality of rape), and the anxiety resulting from a special sensitivity to 'ontological' trauma or crisis (i.e. the terrifying realisation of our finitude) (see Holzhey-Kunz, 2016; Jacobsen, 2006).

Secondly, many existential writers (including some in this collection) rely on an unhelpful interchangeability between the meanings of terms: 'trauma' as experience, event, response, pathology, or an explanatory device. This conceptual confusion is replicated in:

(a) the bizarre use of new neurobiological Cartesian dualisms (i.e. trauma is primarily stored and processed in the body), and
(b) the dominance of locationist myths about affective operations of the brain and traumatic states, even within existentialist works (see Boaz, 2022a: 71–80, building on Feldman Barrett, 2017a, 2017b, 2021; Mudrik & Maoz, 2015).

Finally, the ambivalence and ambiguity around trauma-specific work can be seen in the relative absence of it in many contemporary existential trainings. Where it does appear in existential education and practice, many rely on other orientations to lead or guide their approach (i.e. psychoanalytic, eye movement desensitisation and reprocessing, or trauma-focused cognitive behavioural therapy), which creates ontological as well as epistemological contradictions and confusions for training and practising psychotherapists.

Elsewhere I have undertaken a more substantive description of classic, contemporary, and existential approaches to psychotraumatology (see Boaz, 2022a). In this chapter, I build upon my previous work by delving into a more descriptive analysis of existential-humanistic formulations of interpersonal trauma (as potentially shattering lifeworlds). In doing so, I add new additional existential-analytic and phenomenological observations. Given the limited space, I will focus more substantively on the re-illusionment and disillusionment of lifeworlds, and so readers may want to consult my other writings (Boaz, 2022a) for more substantive explorations of the embodied, temporal-spatial, and relational features of interpersonal trauma. Finally, I turn to consider the implications for existential psychotherapies, introducing new methodological approaches I have been developing through recent research and practice.

In this chapter I will primarily focus on interpersonal traumas. By 'interpersonal' I mean the direct relationships, (inter)actions, and encounters between two or more people which are experienced as traumatic (consciously or non-consciously) by at least one of the people involved. The use of 'direct' here denotes an actual contact or connection between these persons, whether or not they are 'known' to each other. This definition would include acts, actions, and relations that we describe as neglect of a child or adult; child, peer, and domestic abuse (including emotional, psychological, physical, sexual forms, controlling, humiliating and coercive behaviour, grooming, gang membership); physical or sexual violence (including rape, assault, attacks, people trafficking); torture and inhuman and degrading treatment (including some culturally specific practices such as female genital mutilation).

Confrontations with existence

Existential writers have frequently characterised traumatic experiences as confronting and disclosing the foundations of our existence (following Frankl, 1946/2004), or our 'existential givens' (following Yalom, 1980). I have similarly defined traumatic experiencing as "confrontations with reality" (Boaz, 2022a: 132–136). In this chapter I will more simply *define trauma as a confrontation with existence*. By this I mean that:

(a) our ontic experiences of interpersonal trauma are always simultane-
     ously ontological experiences – they are *onto-ontic entanglements*
     (contra to Holzhey-Kunz, 2016; Jacobsen, 2006),
(b) our experiences of trauma are the actualities of confrontations with
     existence, and
(c) traumatic confrontation(s) reveal(s) specific phenomenological details
     about what happens when we are confronted by our own existence.

Above, I use the term *onto-ontic entanglement* to refer to the philosophical
proposition that there can never been a meaningful differentiation between
ontic and ontological experience, as one is always entangled within the
other.

Having defined trauma here as a direct confrontation with our existence, we can consider what is confronted, and the existential movements
we make in relation to these confrontations.[1] Whilst there is somewhat an
agreement that it is our existence itself that is being confronted, there is not
a consensus on the element of our existence being confronted. I suggest
that what is being confronted is:

(a) our worlds as we know them, and
(b) the specific ways we exist in our worlds.[2]

I call our world as we know it, and the specific ways we exist in our world,
our *mode(s) of existence* (Boaz, 2022a).

Other existential-phenomenologists have used terms including lifeworlds, worldviews, world-designs, and world-constructs (cf. Binswanger,
1946/1958, 1963, 1984–1985/1986). In my conceptualisation, existential
mode(s) are the multiple and specific ways we exist in our worlds, which
incorporate (but cannot be reduced to) our worldviews, world-constructs,
lived experiences, embodiments, emotions, meanings, relationships, and
enactments (see also Boaz et al., 2024, for a similar descriptive application). As existential movements, traumatic experiencing can be disruptions
to (Krippner et al., 2012), shocks to (Janet, 1901; Längle, 2007), or shat-
terings of (Janoff-Bulman, 1992) our modes of existence, lifeworld, world-
construct, or worldview.

The shattering of worldviews

Krippner et al. (2012: 11) suggest that the traumatic disruption of a person's worldview occurs both in our personal life narrative and, existentially, in what we understand the world to be, and our place within it. The
authors go further in proposing that an experience can only be considered

existentially traumatic when it *both* confronts *and* shatters the existing personal myths we have about the nature of reality and human existence. Our personal myths (or ontological beliefs) are the stories, rules, ideas, or ways of living that we use to understand and maintain our worldview (31). Other theorists have varyingly termed these myths the metaphors (Lakoff & Johnson, 1980/2003) or scripts (Steiner, 1990) that we live by. For Krippner and colleagues, the traumatic shattering of our worldviews and personal myths is incredibly distressing, but can also give rise to profound psychospiritual and existential realisations, including directly facing any reality-denial and reality-augmentation of contextual environments (2012: 117; see also Boaz, 2022a: 177—183; Lantz & Meshelemiah, 2002).

Similarly, Hoffman et al. (2013: 2, 6) describe trauma as having the potential to existentially shatter our fundamental systems of meaning and relating (building on Greening, 1990). They suggest that this existential shattering can profoundly disrupt how we experience ourselves and the world around us. It is seen as a destruction and annihilation of our 'entire worldview' and so we have no way of returning back to '"normal"' nor 'integrating' the experiences into former ways of existing (Hoffman et al., 2013: 3). For Hoffman and colleagues, the defining features of an existential shattering are:

(a) the event is sudden, irreversible, and unexpected,
(b) it caused a severe disruption to the person's meaning and relating (self and world-construct),
(c) it forced a confrontation with one or more of the givens of existence,
(d) it leaves the person feeling groundless, and
(e) it results in a sense of disillusionment with a formerly held or cherished belief or system of meaning (4–5).

For me, Hoffman and colleagues' features of an existential shattering offer an important and astute insight into just one of the possible responses to a confrontation of existence through trauma. However, I contend below that these need not be features of a 'shattering' per se.

Both Krippner (2012) and Hoffman (2013), with their respective colleagues, propose an ontological separation between those experiences that are ontically traumatic and those traumatic experiences that are existentially (ontologically) shattering. These sentiments echo the separation of ontic and ontological dimensions of trauma differentiated elsewhere in existential psychology (Jacobsen, 2006: 65–66) and Daseinsanalysis (Holzhey-Kunz, 2016). Let us consider for a moment why the distinction between ontic and ontological forms of trauma is problematic (see Boaz, 2022a: 9–11, 106–108 for a fuller critique).

Hoffman and colleagues (2013: 4) write of hypothetical cases of two women – one who experienced their rape as an existential shattering, and one as an ontic traumatisation without an existential shattering. Below is an extract of this description:

> A woman is raped violently in her home. Although she was severely traumatized, the incident did not provoke her to engage with the deeper questions of existence and, after therapy, she was able to resume her life as she had lived before the rape. *The rape was not a shattering experience for this woman, as the trauma did not force her to confront the givens of existence.* However, another woman who experiences the same scenario will be radically changed by the rape as she confronts her life, the choices she had made and not made as well as her way of being in the world. As a result, she may struggle with issues of despair and meaninglessness; however, if she is able to successfully confront these challenges she may over time make career changes, have more fulfilling relationships, and feel more engaged with life. (Hoffman et al., 2013: 2, 6: my emphasis)

This abstract description of the two rapes is somewhat unsettling – though it reflects a number of similar case examples used throughout existential texts. It is assumed that two women can experience rape as 'the same scenario.' Whilst labelled as 'rape' as a generalised term, the lived interpersonal enactments of a rape are always unique to the specific features of the sexual violence as it occurs between two people and their own subjective experiences of the violence and violation. Those of us who have experienced rape know that whilst there is comfort and liberation in the commonality of survivors' experiences, the differences of circumstances, meaning, and responses can be deeply stark. Rape is never 'the same scenario,' but always a unique encounter sharing features of interpersonal violence we socially code as rape. Moreover, rape is never merely a so-called ontic experience. As I have written above, interpersonal traumas are always onto-ontic entanglements. As such, rape is always ontologically violent – be it through stranger violence, intimate partner violence, gang exploitation, crimes of war, etc. Contra to Jacobsen (2006), Hoffman and colleagues (2013: 4), and Holzhey-Kunz (2016), *interpersonal trauma always involves a confrontation with existence*, and we should be psychotherapeutically attuned to the particular ways people respond to this confrontation.[3] The form the existential confrontation takes is always unique, given the visceral and interpersonal nature of the encounters, as are those different foundations existence that are confronted.

It is important to note the features of human existence that are omitted from the short imagined vignette of the two rapes. The example lacks any consideration or appreciation of existential ideas of contingency, situatedness, and contextuality. And so we might ask ourselves who can afford the time, space, or resources to more immediately or explicitly experience rape as an existential shattering. In my personal and clinical experience, many more of us are immediately concerned with surviving the circumstances of our life (which may contain further complexity and/or adversity), and at least temporarily incorporate the rape(s) as something either 'severely traumatising' or normalise it as something difficult and part of our life experiences. This does not mean that existential questioning or shattering is not present nor foundational in the way we exist in our worlds. Rather, it means we cannot, at the time, risk asking ourselves or facing more existential questions. The existential project of finding meaning through survivorism, survivalism, or even partial-denial (see Boaz, 2022a: 157–160) is more urgent or necessary to sustain our existence (see also Herman, 1992/2022, for similar sentiments).

Within the re-illusionment of traumatic experiencing (that is, the incorporation of a confrontation with existence within a pre-existing worldview or mode), we must also understand that focusing on forms of survival is attending to existential questions and protecting against (in many ways) a more substantive shattering of our worldviews. For some of us, this becomes a purposeful and meaningful way of existing because of our dependency on others or the precarity of our contextual positions. We might think beyond rape to those of us who have been a child dependent on a violent or volatile parent, those who are financially abused by their controlling partners, those who are ritually and sexually humiliated whilst on zero-hour and insecure contracts, those aspiring athletes who are sexually assaulted by sports coaches, those who endure frequent coercion and emotional abuse and live in institutional environments (hospitals, boarding, residential schools, care homes), etc.

Finally, contextuality relates to the meaning we have of our experiences of interpersonal violence. It was only within recent history that rape within marriage was deemed an illegal and criminal act in the United Kingdom (R v R [1991] UKHL 12; R v R [1991] 3 WLR 767; Sexual Offences Act 2003), and it remains permissible in many societies around the world. As such, without a framework to understand rape (in this case within marriage), many people will face reality-augmentation and socio-cultural denial of their experiences, rending them merely unwanted, unpleasant, or regretted sexual acts, and/or an accepted expression of connubial rights and normative sexual politics and relations.

Shattered foundations and the contextuality of betrayal

Continuing with the contextuality of ideas of existential shattering, let us turn to a more popularised theory in the existential-humanistic canon, and critiques and expansions offered by the field of betrayal trauma theory. Janoff-Bulman (1992) suggests that experiences of trauma shatter our fundamental assumptions about the world, which underpin our worldview (see Vos, 2018: 83 for a similar sentiment). She identifies our three core assumptions as:

(a) the world is benevolent,
(b) the world is meaningful, and
(c) we have self-worth (Janoff-Bulman, 1992: 3–17).

Embracing these fundamental assumptions enables us to generalise that we are safe and secure in the world, we can trust others, and that in some way we are invulnerable to the dangers and threats that the world poses (18–21). The fundamental assumptions are generalisable expectations we have of the world formed over time since childhood. However, these assumptions are also illusionary as they do not represent the reality of the world, and the very real possibilities of exposure to danger, threat, and death. While maintaining these illusions might be useful in navigating our worlds, they are maladaptive if we do not reality-test them to situate ourselves in the context in which we find ourselves (21–24). In simultaneously maintaining and reality-testing our illusions, we are able to understand our limitations and those of our context.

Most of us do not examine our fundamental assumptions and the nature of our life experiences, meaning that small reality-tests suffice in situating our lived assumptions within the context of our lives. In contrast, experiences of interpersonal trauma fundamentally shatter these assumptions (Janoff-Bulman, 1992: 51). Janoff-Bulman suggests that an event or situation is traumatic if it is appraised by the person as *shattering the illusion* of their fundamental assumptions. More specifically, she proposes that an event or situation being "out of the ordinary" or being "directly experienced as threats to survival and self-preservation" is what makes the experience(s) traumatic (53–58). Personal experience of the event or situation is powerfully disconfirming of the fundamental assumptions, as the evidential data is grounded in the reality of the person's lived experience (54). Furthermore, the threat to survival and self-preservation discloses the fragility of our human existence, and the possibility of our death and annihilation (56– 61). This existential confrontation, for Janoff-Bulman, is a core part of what makes an event traumatic in the shattering of our fundamental assumptions.

For me, the work of Gómez (2023) and Freyd (1996) challenges the universality of Janoff-Bulman's propositions. Their research provides important insights into the ways in which the forms and degrees of social betrayals of interpersonal trust in trauma might affect our ability to remember, make sense of, and/or incorporate our experiences. Their research demonstrates that many of the trauma-related phenomena observed (i.e. dissociation and amnesic memory) in those of us who have experienced interpersonal traumas emerge from a need or motivation to maintain (for survival or interdependency) important familial, cultural, and social relationships – even when they directly remain to cause us harm, injury, and violence or continue to do so. Their work on institutional trauma (see also[4] Smith & Freyd, 2014) and cultural betrayal trauma (Gómez, 2023) also reveals that many of us will not have begun with the protective fundamental assumptions Janoff-Bulman describes and presumes.

Drawing on descriptions of complex and developmental traumas (Boaz, 2022a; Herman, 1992; 1992/2022; van der Kolk, 2005), it can be understood how those of us who experience interpersonal trauma from birth, or have lived it repeatedly throughout our childhoods and adolescences, may form illusionary assumptions of parental, cultural, or systemic benevolence, meaning, and self-worthiness as a way of protecting ourselves from the harsh reality of our interpersonal relationships. This may be driven by the incomprehensibility of the threats or violence we experience, and/or our need to maintain social connections through our dependency on family, friends, and cultural or trusted relationships in our lives. These protective illusions of relational benevolence do not equate to a reality of interpersonal safety, even though it might provide some protection from other contextual traumas (including structural racism and gender-based violence in wider society). We might think here of the ways in which people retain relationships with an abusive parent as a partial protection from racist or religious violence in the local community, or where gang exploitation feels paradoxically safer as it offers forms of protection from wider violence in the community.[5]

We might also develop more adverse foundational assumptions including:

(a) the world is cruel or harsh,
(b) the world is meaningless,
(c) we will be left powerless, hopeless, and/or helpless in the world,
(d) we all have self-disgust or self-hate,
(e) we must betray ourselves to survive.

These adverse fundamental assumptions might be reified and compounded by contextual inequities and traumatisations. Socio-cultural betrayals might include racism or intra-cultural betrayal and abuse (Gómez, 2022, 2023), or familial or institutional betrayals including incest or the denial of systematic abuse by religious, judicial, or educational institutions (building on Freyd, 1996; Freyd & Birrell, 2013; see also Smith et al., 2014). The adverse assumptions may be present in the formulation of a worldview by a child experiencing interpersonal violence, or arise through multiple and cumulative disillusionments of pre-existing benevolent illusionary assumptions. As Frankl (1946/1986: 43–44, 65–68) and Vos (2018: 65–68) suggest, we can still discover courage to find meaning and even joy (see also Lukas, 1986: 106–119) in the face of these adverse fundamental assumptions based on our experiences of suffering and adversity in the world. And so, paradoxically these adverse foundational assumptions can too be meaningful, and provide the ground for discovering purpose in response to them.

Further, both illusioned and disillusioned foundational assumptions become normalised by us because they constitute the basis of our social and relational worlds, and so become synthesised into our modes of existing in the world. Building on Gómez and Freyd further, I would propose that in cases of complex interpersonal traumas, exposure to other non-traumatising environments and peoples may paradoxically make visible alterities in our fundamental assumptions (be they benevolent or adverse, illusioned or disillusioned). The exposure to alterities in foundational assumptions might become moments of confrontation with reality as it:

(a) demonstrates the possibility of different fundamental assumptions about the world (alterity of experience),
(b) re-contextualises our experiences and relationships as being traumatic,
(c) exposes us to structural, contextual, and situational inequalities between different worldviews, normativities, and modes of existing,
(d) gives rise to an unbearable pain related to the injustices in our worlds (and the injustices we have faced),
(e) confronts us directly with our throwness into a context, situation, and set of relationships not of our choosing nor making, and
(f) makes apparent our own lived contingencies and limitations as agentic beings.

Finally, it is important to note that for some of us, decontextualising our experiences is a powerful way of rendering the traumatic confrontation with existence tolerable and understandable. For some of us, seeing the context for what it is (neglectful, abusive, violence, coercive, etc.) would be both intolerable and may open up the possibility of further contextual victimisation. Decontextualisation need not lead to a denial of the reality of a traumatic situation; rather, it may become the basis for recreating experienced dynamics in other contexts in order to pre-reflexively make sense of what has been confronted of our existence. Decontextualising our experience in this way gives us a way of indirectly making sense of our worldviews in safe, tolerable, and more creative ways. Whilst using this mode of survival can open up the growthful possibility of liberating others who may be our kin (see Boaz, 2022a: 159–160 on modal activism; 2022b; Boaz et al., 2024), it too risks a problematic displacing of conflict and harm into new relationships and environments.

Trauma as existential de-anchoring

For me, the existential-analytic stance of Längle offers a useful extension to the notion of the shattering of worldviews used in existential-humanistic traditions. He writes that experiences of trauma lead to changes in both our structural (existential) *anchoring* of the experience, and our ability to process the experience *as part of our existence* (Längle, 2007: 111). Changes in our anchoring in existence and processing of experience(s) as part of our existence fundamentally disrupt our *comprehension of existence*. For me, our lived comprehension of existence is a more powerful way of describing what is challenged when we confront our existence within interpersonal trauma. Our comprehension of existence includes our embodied sense of:

(a) what the world is, and its limitations and conditions (leading to shock),
(b) our own life and life force (leading to pain),
(c) our identity and relationship to others (leading to feelings of loss), and
(d) the demands and horizons of our life situation – leading to a contextual incomprehensibility (Längle, 2007, 111, 114; 2008).

Comprehension of existence here does not mean we understand all of our existence, but rather that there is a form or sense of coherence in our lived understanding of existence, and our search for the meaning of life.

Rather than shattering of a *worldview*, Längle suggests that trauma results in a *de-anchoring of our existence rendering our existing ways of understanding ourselves, the world, and others incomprehensible.* For me this is an alternative formulation of Hoffman and colleagues' (2013) last two features of existential shattering (groundlessness and disillusionment). Drawing heavily on the work of Freyd (1994, 1996), Längle (2007: 114) proposes that the deepest impact of trauma can be a shock to (*Erschütterung*), or a shattering of, our basic trust in something greater, which can hold us and absorb our human experience of the traumatic situation(s). This bears some resemblance to Janoff-Bulman's (1992) notion of a fundamental assumption of benevolence.

The quality and texture of Längle's conceptualisation is important as it implies a deeply felt and experiential focus in both in our de-anchoring and incomprehensibility of existence. The embodied, sensorial, and visceral nature of interpersonal trauma centres around our anchorage in existence. Merleau-Ponty notes that we have "our anchorage in the world" through our body – it is our "general means of having a world" (1945/2012: 147). This anchorage is intertwined in complex ways with the generative influence of our embodied acts on the world around us, and those of others (147; see also 84; 1964/1968: 48–49 and 142 on reversibility). Threats and violations of our bodily integrity are always impressions made on our embodiment, and our anchorage in the world, and in existence. This is what I meant when I asserted earlier that interpersonal trauma is always ontologically violent. My preference here for Längle's term *de-anchoring* emerges out of the more direct attention it places on a lived, moving, and embodied relationship with existence (see Boaz, 2022a for more on existential movements). De-anchoring is always existentially growthful as we are in a primordial state of becoming and emergence, although not all forms of growth are healthy per se – e.g. hypertrophied spirituality could lead to atrophied relational depth.

For Längle, the experience of trauma acts as a disillusioning betrayal of our personal existential foundations required for us to find meaning, motivation, and action in the world. In the face of de-anchoring we may become fixative in our position to hold our comprehension of existence together, i.e. by becoming hostile, holding suspicious attitudes towards the world, or withdrawing socially (Längle, 2007: 111–114). We may also experience negative forms of disillusionment in our personal capacity to process our existence[6] (111, 113–114). This might include a loss of personal feelings of agency and meaning-making. Through my own clinical work I have witnessed how a lack of agency and feelings of powerlessness and meaninglessness can exacerbate traumatisation and lead to further victimisation. A sense of lack of agency can leave us feeling dependent on, and entrapped in, coercive or controlling relationships. Meaninglessness can give way to a fatalistic attitude, underpinned by painful feelings of dehumanisation and self-worthlessness.

Building on Längle (2007: 110–111), I suggest (Boaz, 2022a: 165) that both the prospect of, and an actual experience of, our de-anchoring gives rise to an acute existential horror.[7] Our existential horror relates to our incomprehensibility of both the reality of our situation, and simultaneously our foundations in our existence. For Längle, existential horror is an expression of shock (*Erschütterung*) or harrowing (*Erschütternden*) wonderment arising from the incomprehensibility of the depths of existence, and our lack of trust and understanding in the face of this incomprehensibility (2007: 110).

Alongside the existential horror of our incomprehensibility of existence is our existential terror. I describe existential terror as an actual, and perceived anticipation of, repeated traumatic experiencing the next time we encounter the person(s), or others in the world. Existential terror arises from (and to the extent to which we have incorporated) the traumatic experiencing in our body schema (Merleau-Ponty, 2001/2010: 44) and mode(s) of existence. Existential terror is intensified if we have had multiple or enduring experiences of interpersonal trauma, and if we remain in contact with the traumatising person/people, or if the threat of the person/people terrorising us remains.

Whilst de-anchoring and incomprehensibility can be existentially terrifying and horrifying, they also are encounters of awe and wonderment at a pre-reflexive dimension of consciousness. We might here think of an undefined shape emerging out of a forest at night. The existential horror emerges out from the darkness of the forest and the undefinable shape moves towards us. We are compelled to look in a horrific awe at its existence and the horrific wonderment of its movement towards us. We too feel existential terror arise in us as we feel ourselves move towards the horrific shape – an existential wonderment that we are in some way related to the horrific shape, and that we may wander towards it. Our existential horror and terror have an entanglement and reversibility that remind us too of our capacity to be in awe and wonderment about our situation and existence.

I have chosen to write the description above in this way not as an abstraction of more visceral sexual violence, but rather because in my clinical practice I have found that existential horror and terror are also experiences of liminality (see Boaz, 2022a: 178–170; Boaz et al., 2024) and so are (at least initially) described in allegoric and metaphorical terms, and tempo-spatially through our pre-reflexive consciousness. For a more visceral example, we might consider the phenomenological accounts people give of having deep realisations and thoughts about the nature of human inter-dependency within the midst of an experience of sexual violence. Whilst described clinically as dissociative, such realisations are working with the existential horror and terror of the incomprehensibility of the traumatic encounter, and are ways of questioning our existence and making meaning out of the confrontation.

As Freyd (1996) notes further:

Sometimes we are so overwhelmed by the horror of our world that we are blind to its wonder; sometimes we are fortunate enough to be so overwhelmed by the wonder of the world that we are blind to its horror. When fragmented by betrayal blindness [the denial of betrayal trauma] we sometimes see neither the horror nor the wonder. But whether we see them or not, both elements exist. (Freyd, 1996: 194)

Finally, the phenomenon of de-anchoring and incomprehensibility discloses that interpersonal trauma is a crossing of thresholds (*limen*), a further existential confrontation with the liminality of our existence. As our dissociative experiences, states, and sensations (*existing-out-of-time-and-space*) demonstrate, we are primordially liminal beings – that is, existing between worlds of experiencing. *Existing-out-of-time-and-space* are traumatic liminal modes because they are ways of existing outside of, and between, different modes of existing and worlds of experiencing. Whilst some of us live more liminal lives (following Boaz et al., 2024), others of us will encounter our liminality through traumatic experiences. In this sense, interpersonal trauma is a crossing of existential thresholds, and it is the experience of liminality that is crucial in the uncanny realisation of the limitations and constrictions in our ways of living, and the possibility of new modes of experiencing (for more discussion on modes of liminality see Boaz, 2022a 168–173; 2022b).

On (re)(dis)illusionment

According to Janoff-Bulman (1992: 118–132), we need to discover ways of re-finding benevolence, meaning, and self-worth in the world in order to incorporate traumatic experiences into our worldview. She writes that this allows the person to "arrive at a new, nonthreatening assumptive world, one that acknowledges and integrates their negative [traumatic] experiences and prior illusions" (117). Shattered assumptions can be rebuilt and integrated into new illusions through:

(a) suffering for a purpose (133–135),
(b) learning lessons about oneself and life, or reconsidering what is important to us (136–138),
(c) attitudes we take towards others, including seeing our suffering as a form of altruism (138– 139), and
(d) finding choice "even in the face of uncontrollable, unavoidable and negative outcomes" (140).

While we may not be free from the reality of the traumatic experience, we can agentically choose the ways we integrate this into our sense of self, others, and the world we live in. As such, for Janoff-Bulman (1992: 175; 1989; Janoff-Bulman & Berg, 1998/2013), both illusionment and disillusionment offer a creative potential for the person to find new ways of existing in relation to the reality of the world, and new meanings within it.

In rebuilding our shattered assumptions through the discovery of choice, Janoff-Bulman (1992) proposes that existentially choice can be realised through our 'interpretations and reinterpretations, appraisals and reappraisals, evaluations and revaluations made of the traumatic experience and one's pain and suffering.' Drawing on Freyd (1996) and Gómez (2023), those of us facing more complex traumas may need to go further, and reconstruct our worldviews more substantively, in order to incorporate all that has been confronted about the adverse foundations of our existence. This would involve either incorporating, or more radically transforming, existing adverse foundational assumptions into new worldviews, which allow for a sense of meaning, purpose, and agentic power. At the same time there is a need to acknowledge the situated potential for greater agency, rather than assuming there will always be an opportunity for radical and unlimited freedom.

The authors above have written of illusionment and disillusionment, and this is my starting point for understanding what happens when we are confronted with our existence through interpersonal trauma. Jaspers (1954/2003) suggests that we cannot 'evade or change' a boundary situation; rather, we must acknowledge and confront it (1954/2003, 1948, 1956, 1971/1995). Traumatic experiences would be an example of Jaspers' boundary situation (Grenzsituation), in that the acts themselves disrupt the lived worldview of the person and bring them into a stark confrontation with the realities of human relating.

For me, the notion of a limit, border, frontier, or boundary within the experienced traumatic situation is crucial. Phenomenologically, interpersonal trauma is described as threats to and incursions into people's boundaries. Whether they be of bodily integrity or understandings of human relationships, the traumatic form of human relating takes us beyond the limit of what is expected, known, understood, meaningful, safe, and so on. As such, we could understand a feature of 'traumatic' experiencing as being the movement beyond a known mode of existing and relating. Building on this further, Jaspers (1948, 1956, 1971/1995) provides us with a description of the phenomenon of illusionment and disillusionment (Enttäuschung).

When we are confronted by the reality of a situation, we can experience disillusionment with the reality we have known, and a sobering up to the reality that lies before us (see Boaz, 2022a, chapters 5–8 for further detailed illustration; Bush [Boaz], 2018). The confrontation with the reality of our existence results in Ernüchterung – that is, a sobering up to the reality of our situation and our existence. Sobering up here means seeing the reality of our situation as it is – that is, understanding our existence as it is in the present, with all the limitations, possibilities, resonances, dissonances, constrictions, and freedoms we have. Sometimes the excruciating sobering up to reality is more intensely painful than the experience of disillusionment, as it contributes to a sense of primal annihilation and discontinuity of existence (building on Winnicott, 1974, 1965/2018a, 1967/2018,

1965/2018b). For some of us, this sobering up to the reality of our existence is so painful that we are compelled to anaesthetise ourselves of the psychic pain or banish it from our conscious memory, creating an amnesic void in place of our harrowing pain.[8] For me, it is the entangled experience of both *Enttäuschung* and *Ernüchterung* that enables the person to find altered or new modes of existing in the moment – initially as adaptations to the confrontation – and over time – through the (re)(dis)covery and expansion of new modes of experience.

Traumatic confrontations with existence leave us *existing-at-the-edge* of our known worlds and modes of existence (see Boaz et al., 2024, for further phenomenological detail and descriptions). In the *existing-at-the-edge* position we encounter the possibility of re-illusionment and disillusionment (Boaz, 2022a: 134). We may turn to incorporate our newly confronted existence into our own re-illusionment about the world, and (re)cover our relations within it. Contrastingly, we may also turn towards our disillusionment with the world by sobering up through (dis)covering new modes of existing. These turns are shaped by our context, and the worlds we inhabit (echoing Janoff-Bulman, 1992: 147–161).

I suggest that by taking up new disillusioned or re-illusioned modes of existence, we are aware (even in a pre-reflexive way) that these new modes arise from, and endure in relation to, our traumatic confrontations with our existence. Further, disillusioned or re-illusioned modes of existence are a taking up of possible responses to survive and make meaning out of the experiences we have had. Thus, the taking up of new disillusioned or re-illusioned modes of existence enables us to retain the potentiality of our agentic being, and open up our future.

(Re) and (dis) are modal tensions in the re-covering/dis-covering of existence through a traumatic confrontation.[9] Between re-illusionment and disillusionment, there are more liminal modal movements. These I have referred to as (re)(dis)illusionment and (re)(dis)covery. (Re)(dis)covery is the modal experimentation within and between known and unknown horizons of human experiencing, to generatively elaborate modes of existing. (Re)(dis)covery is a form of synthesis ((re)(dis)illusionment), which enables us to honour both the modes that enabled us to survive our traumatic experiences and situations (re-illusionment), and the emergent modes we generate to find new ways of existing and relating to others (disillusionment).

The terms re-illusionment, disillusionment, and (re)(dis)illusionment do not do justice to the excoriating pain of our lived experience and realisations in confronting our potential de-anchoring of existence and the ensuing incomprehensibility. Realisations are not cognitive, but felt and lived as embodied and sensorial experiences. More viscerally, re-illusionment, disillusionment, and (re)(dis)illusionment are somatically encountered in the immensity of oscillating states of *existing-out-of-time-and-space* (dissociation), through the freezing and shaking of the body, the grinding of teeth, the cramping of muscle, and the nauseating ambiguity and viscosity of bodily fluids. These somatic encounters are not merely stress responses to adverse stimuli, they are existential torment, questioning, and even horrific wonderment. The existential (or so-called ontological) emerges here not on the horizon beyond the so-called ontic, but as part of a lived entanglement within it.

Finally, our existential anchorage is the means by which we orientate ourselves in our existence and our worlds – and therefore in relation to specific traumatic experiences and relationships (see Boaz, 2022a: 172–173). When we re-orientate ourselves in existence, we are (re)turning to modes that resonated before the traumatic confrontation and therefore experience re-illusionment. In contrast, when we are disorientated, we generatively create new horizons of experiencing and modes of existing, which incorporate what we have confronted of our existence, and thus is a form of disillusionment. We might also experience a (dys)orientation, which embraces or re-makes pathologising ideas and identifications about our traumatic confrontations with existence.[10]

Existential guilt, regret, and shame

Our disillusioned or re-illusioned modes of existing represent an awakening of our primordial impulse to philosophise, and to find the kind of person we want to become. Frankl (1946/2004) describes this as the destruction of our illusions, and the possibility of finding curiosity, courage, and hope in the future, which gives rise to new meaning in our lives. Within our primordial impulse to philosophise and find new meaning and modes of existing, we may encounter existential regret, shame, and guilt (see Boaz, 2022a: 154–157 for a more detailed phenomenological account). Briefly, by existential guilt I mean the experiential gap between the modes of existing we are living in, and the ones we want to be moving in. Existential guilt can give rise to an existential regret where we experience a concern over the time-space we have spent living in specific re-illusioned or disillusioned modes. Through existential guilt and regret we may be faced with our existential shame, which is a sense of worthlessness and valuelessness relating to the modes we are in or have lived in.

Our existential shame can transform into existential forms of humiliation and embitterment. When the existential shame is directed towards ourselves, it becomes existential humiliation characterised by rumination, suspicion, and lack of faith in the possibility of modal movement or change. We experience this existential humiliation as becoming the ground or surface for other people's experiences. When the existential shame is directed towards others, it transforms into an existential embitterment where we have a seeming hatred of the modal movements and expressions of others.

Existential shame can therefore also lead to a secondary shock and disillusionment when we encounter other people who exhibit similar modes that we have inhabited in the past. This can lead to an intolerance for others who reflect back to us our shame of modes of survival, and can be exacerbated through feelings of repulsion and self-disgust. Paradoxically, for some of us this may be transformed into a more positive potential for understanding and compassion for the ways we have survived, and made sense of, our experiences in the past. As such, what we have encountered of existence, and its sedimented forms of existential guilt, regret, shame, and humiliation (and any emerging existential growth), remain spectral within the re-illusioned and disillusioned modes of existence we live in (see Boaz, 2022a: 183–185 for a more substantive discussion on trauma and spectrality).

Constrictive and expansive horizons

De-anchoring and incomprehensibility of existence impact our horizons of experiencing. Schneider and May (1995: 141) write that our "human consciousness is characterised by a constrictive-expansive continuum," of which we are only conscious of at a physiological, environmental, cognitive level, and "pre- or sub-conscious" at a psychosexual, interpersonal, and experiential level (141). For Schneider and May, it is our dread of becoming positioned at one (or both) of the polarities of constrictive/expansive (freedom/limitation) horizons that gives rise to "dysfunction, extremism, or polarisation" (141). Dysfunctions, extremism, and polarisation here refer to the ways we go about managing, mitigating, or making sense of (at conscious and pre-/sub-conscious levels) our existential dread. In my own work I describe the specific *ways we live* our constricted and/or expanded horizons and use the terms *modal constriction* and *modal expansion* (see Boaz, 2022a: 190–192). De-anchoring and the incomprehensibility of existence in trauma can leave us disorientated in our relationship with our horizons of experiencing.

Whilst I do not concur with Schneider and May's (1995: 141–144) formulation of "acute," "chronic," or "implicit" traumas, I do agree that what is confronted of our existence is fragmented and refracted through an existential constrictive–expansive dynamic. Traumatised constrictive/expansive horizons are filled with agonising conscious and pre-conscious dreads that crowd out our felt sense of possibilities, and continue the interpersonal terrors we have faced (following Herman, 1992/2022). These terrors can be exacerbated by trauma-related phenomena including flashbacks, traumatic memories, and somatisations (features of *existing-out-of-time-and-space*).

At the extremities, we find those of us who experience hyper-expansions including depersonalisation (a form of *existing-out-of-time-and-space*) and hyper-constrictions, where we might avoid all but necessary social and relational contact (building on Schneider & May, 1995).

The context of the traumatic relationship(s) or encounter(s) will also shape our attempts to re-anchor ourselves within the constrictive–expansive dynamic, and make our existence meaningful and comprehensible. For example, when contexts move to protect perpetrator(s), we might constrict our horizons to a contra-modal position against the institution, taking up a stance against them, and focusing all our existence on retribution and justice. In contexts that deny the reality of the violence we have faced, we may take up more abstracted modalities where we suspect that we or others may be a figment of our imagination or question what is real (as in depersonalisation/derealisation).

My own phenomenological investigations suggest that Schneider and May (1995: 145) are correct in their principle that "the *confrontation with* or integration of constrictive/expansive polarities promotes healing, vitality, and health" (145, original emphasis). Somewhat in line in Schneider and May's ideas on experiential liberation, I suggest that we need not pathologise our fragmentations and refractions, but rather understand them to be the creative and growthful endeavours we use to preserve our primordial wisdom. This wisdom is the pre-reflexive sensing that we can actively find new modes and modal expressions within, between, and beyond our known modes of existence. The psychotherapeutic task is not to correct modal constrictions or expansions, but rather to support people to (re)(dis)cover new modal movements and horizons of experiencing, by which they can relate to themselves, others, and those around them in new ways.

Descriptive summary

By way of summary of the discussion above, we can phenomenologically describe:[11]

(i) Interpersonal trauma is invariably a confrontation with existence – although we can acknowledge the features or foundations of the existence that confronts us will vary according to the specificity and uniqueness of our own lives, experiences, and the contexts in which we live.

(ii) Traumatic confrontations with existence are a form of existential de-anchoring, and expose us to the incomprehensibility of our existence, our worldviews, and the modes we have been existing in.[12]

(iii) In the face of a traumatic confrontation with reality, existential de-anchoring, and incomprehensibility, we make existential movements

- including re-illusionment, disillusionment, and (re)(dis) illusionment
  - to (re)/(dis)cover our existential anchorage and establish a comprehensibility in existence.
(iv) Our existential movements in the face of traumatic confrontations
  can give rise to feelings of existential horror and terror, and experiences of existential guilt, regret, shame, humiliation, and embitterment – we may also encounter intense experiences of liminality and
  spectrality.
(v) Our contexts (personal, familial, cultural, social, structural, systemic,
  ecological, etc.) shape our possibilities for modal movement, and can
  constrict or expand our horizons of experiencing and relating. Contexts
  are more constrictive the greater the extent to which they bring in reality-augmentation and reality-denial.
(vi) Our existential movements are the embodiments of our confrontations
  with existence and attempts to re-anchor our existence and bring a
  sense of coherence and meaning (comprehensibility) to our existence
  and experiences.

For some of us, we fragment and/or refract what we have confronted of
existence across different experiential and perceptive axes and horizons
of existence – these might include refractions in our time-arcs (constricted
or expensive experiences of personal time), lived-time (i.e. desynchronisa-
tion, where we feel we are in a state of being 'too late' or of being 'too
early' in relation to the social processes of our time), syntony (our reso-
nance in the world), embodiment (i.e. modes of existing-out-of-time-and-
space), agentic potential (locating our ability to exercise power, choice,
responsibility, and action across the axes of past-future, dream-waking,
fantasy-reality worlds).

Implications for practice

In the section below I turn to consider the implications of the above discussion about psychotherapeutic practice. Elsewhere I have discussed my
own existential model for working with interpersonal trauma (Boaz, 2022a:
193–204), to create more liberatory horizons (Boaz, 2022b), and work with
experiences of liminality (*existing-between-worlds*) (see Boaz et al., 2024).
Whilst not intended as a phasic psychotherapy model, the four features of
the model can be described as:

(a) establishing and expanding horizonal communication – by which I
  mean explicitly attending to, and naming, what we are encountering
  in the therapeutic relationship,

(b) inquiring into traumatic confrontations with existence – using phe-nomenological inquiry to understand worlds of experiencing and what was confronted of existence within the trauma(s),

(c) examining past and present modes of existing – including ways of sur-viving and any arising existential guilt, regret, shame, or humiliation, and

(d) expanding and experimenting with new modal movements and modes of existing – encouraging more expansive horizons and ways of existing.

Since generating the earlier model, I have been working to clarify and dis-til the methodological components. Whilst these are ongoing theoretical, clinical, and applied endeavours, I include below an overview of emerg-ing ways of practising that attend to what Calhoun and Tedeschi (2006) might describe as psychotherapy-supported posttraumatic growth. Given the limited space available in this chapter, I will introduce a small selection of approaches I draw upon in order to provide the reader with a general understanding of some of the ways in which I am working at present. The aim is to present new ideas and material below, so readers may want to consult earlier work (Boaz, 2022a) for further implications for practice.

Mapping personal and collective ontographies

Through descriptive phenomenological inquiry and interpretative herme-neutic dialogue, I work with people[13] to map out their personal ontogra-phies. Lynch (2019: 154) describes ontography as "Investigations that aim to describe the contingent and organisationally embedded work of social agents to propose, inscribe, or dispute particular ontological matters." I build on this[14] socio-philosophical description by applying it more exis-tentially to mean *inquiring into the deeply personal ways in which we live (and have lived) our world-making and world-sustaining ideas and prac-tices.* Our personal ontographies are shaped by, and embedded within, *collective ontographies.* Collective ontographies contain contextual, ances-tral heritages, collective and kinship normativities, and familial narratives, propositions, myths, actions, rules, and expectations.

The aim of the ontographic mapping is to understand the "existential structures of the world[s] the [person] lives in" (Stanghellini, 2022: 76), their modes of existing within these worlds, and begin to identify:

(a) what of existence was confronted by the person in traumatic experiencing,

(b) the ways in which the person has re-illusioned, disillusioned, and (re) (dis)illusioned themselves in relation to these confrontations,

(c) the ways in which contextual and systemic factors have influenced and impacted the person's re-illusionments, disillusionments, and (re)(dis)illusionments,

(d) how de-anchoring and the incomprehensibility of existence have been incorporated by the person across different domains of existence/lifeworlds,

(e) clarify existential questions and dilemmas arising from people's confrontations, re-illusionments, disillusionments, and (re)(dis) illusionments,

(f) how *a–e* have resulted in specific constrictive/expansive dynamics across the different dynamics of existence/lifeworlds, and

(g) how *a–f* have manifested as the person's lived modes of existing, their meaning-making and become sedimented in existential life projects, and

(h) identify the ways in which existential terror, horror, guilt, regret, shame, and humiliation may be incorporated into the person's modes of existing.

Mapping of personal and collective ontographies can be aided through the use of contemporary existential and phenomenological frameworks for describing domains of existence or lifeworlds. To name but a few here that I have used in my own practice: van Deurzen's (2010: 129–168; 2014) physical (*umwelt*), social (*mitwelt*), personal (*eigenwelt*), and spiritual (*überwelt*) worlds; Wilson and Appel's (2013) *Whare Tapa Wha* of the *tinana* (physical), *taha whanau* (social), *taha hinengaro* (thinking-feeling), *taha wairua* (eco-spiritual) domains; van Manen's (2014) dimensions of relationality (lived self-other), corporeality (lived body), spatiality (lived space), temporality (lived time), and materiality (lived things); Stanghellini's (2022; see also Messas et al., 2018) domains of lived time, lived space, lived body, intersubjectivity, and selfhood; and my own four dimensions of personal, intersubjective, contextual, and dispersed existence (Boaz, 2022a: 175). More recently I have also been co-developing frameworks focusing on liminality and ways of mapping our *existing-at-the-edge* and *movement-between-worlds* onto our ontographies (see Boaz et al., 2024). All of these frameworks have different strengths and limitations in mapping personal and collective ontographies, and so I tend to move between, and synthesise, these approaches for a more comprehensive phenomenological and dimensional understanding.

Ontographies are not reductive maps of causation, origins, or explanations – they are a generative meaning-making process of growth, by which the person comes to understand themselves, and at the same time make commitments and choices that transform their lives. The therapeutic value of ontography resides in the descriptive and hermeneutic interpretations that give rise to possibilities for:

(a) existential anchoring,
(b) a sense of comprehensibility, and
(c) beginning to give coherence to personal and collective ontographies.

Through phenomenological inquiry and therapeutic dialogue, we identify and clarify lived existential questions the person has about what they confronted of existence in trauma(s), and open up the (re)(dis)covery of meaning and purpose in their lives. Growth is cultivated as the person begins to locate themselves as the focus of exploration, and to understand their agentic position as the experiential agent within their lives. A common intervention I use is to draw the person's attention to the fact that they are the person who is moving across their different worlds of experiencing and modes of existence. For some people this is a profound realisation, whereas for others, the emerging awareness is that the process of ontography is an experiential and relational rather than intellectual or conceptual exercise, and through it, traumatic confrontations with existence can be held and worked through.

The therapeutic process allows the person to stay with uncertainties, unsureties, ambiguities, unknowns, contradictions, and nuances in personal and collective ontographies. Importantly, the process allows for a non-linear and non-chronological unfolding of meaning-making. Here the importance of phenomenological horizontalisation can be seen. The person's first disclosure of trauma can be a way of testing the psychotherapist's response and ability to hold the more complex and enduring experiences across their ontographies. Alternatively, the significance of the traumatic confrontations with existence may not have been realised due to the person's re-illusionment, and as such the descriptive features of the trauma may be refracted or fragmented across an ontography, rather than disclosed as a specific encounter(s). Disclosed traumatic encounters and situations themselves should be held with care, understanding, and in-dwelling, but not verticalised as the reductive origin or narrative/explanatory pinnacle of a person's ontography. Finally, in my clinical experience the domains of existence in which the person's confrontations with existence have been refracted and fragmented come to the fore in the therapeutic relationship. Therefore, the person will bring to the therapeutic relationship (both reflexively and pre-reflexively) those existential questions and domains that feel both intolerable, and that they yearn to explore and experiment with in the present.

Existential questions can appear within the therapeutic relationship in the form of reflexive and pre-reflexive thoughts, attitudes, and words, or they can be articulated through our repertoire of sounds, movements, relational actions, personal and spiritual rituals, passions, and resonances in art and music. Clarified fundamental existential questions arising from traumatic confrontations can also fragment and refract through the dimensions of our existence. By way of illustration see the example of *existing-out-of-time-and-space* in Figure 15.1.

Cultivating reflexivity and encountering pre-reflexive experience

In existential psychology and psychotherapy, we embrace a liberatory and agentic stance (Boaz, 2022a, 2022b; Boaz et al., 2024). This means that we aim to cultivate people's reflexive consciousness. By reflexive consciousness, I follow other phenomenologists in using the etymological root to mean *consciousness 'bending back' upon itself*. The reflexive mode of consciousness is an intentional consciousness where our own lived-experience is the focus of curiosity, awareness, unknowing, and exploration. Encountering our reflexive consciousness within traumatic confrontations with existence can become simultaneously surprising, awe-inspiring, liberatory, and joyous, and/or become a frightening, painful, and/or overwhelming influx of reflexive awareness of the reality of our lives, and our situatedness in existence. Traumatic confrontations with existence have the potential to both throw our consciousness back on itself (sometimes violently) and disperse our consciousness, so that the existential confrontation remains incorporated into our pre-reflexive consciousness.[15]

By the pre-reflexive mode of consciousness, I mean the obscured, confusing, partially or fully unformulated, unrepresented, and unsymbolised forms and shapes of our experiences (building on Stern, 1983, 2003). In my description, pre-reflexive consciousness is also intentional as a movement of existence; however, our pre-reflexive intentionality is dispersed through traumatic confrontations due to our de-anchoring and incomprehensibility of our existence (contra Sartre, 1936/1957). For Giorgi (1983: 142–143), phenomenological reflexivity is "taking up again what we have experienced, lived through or acted upon [pre-reflexively]." Continuing, he explains that:

> The objects of [reflexion] are the [pre-reflexive] experiences or structures. Thus, [reflexion] elaborates what is given in [pre-reflexive] experience. It tries to clarify what was actually lived through by making as explicit as possible hidden assumptions and implicit perspectives of the

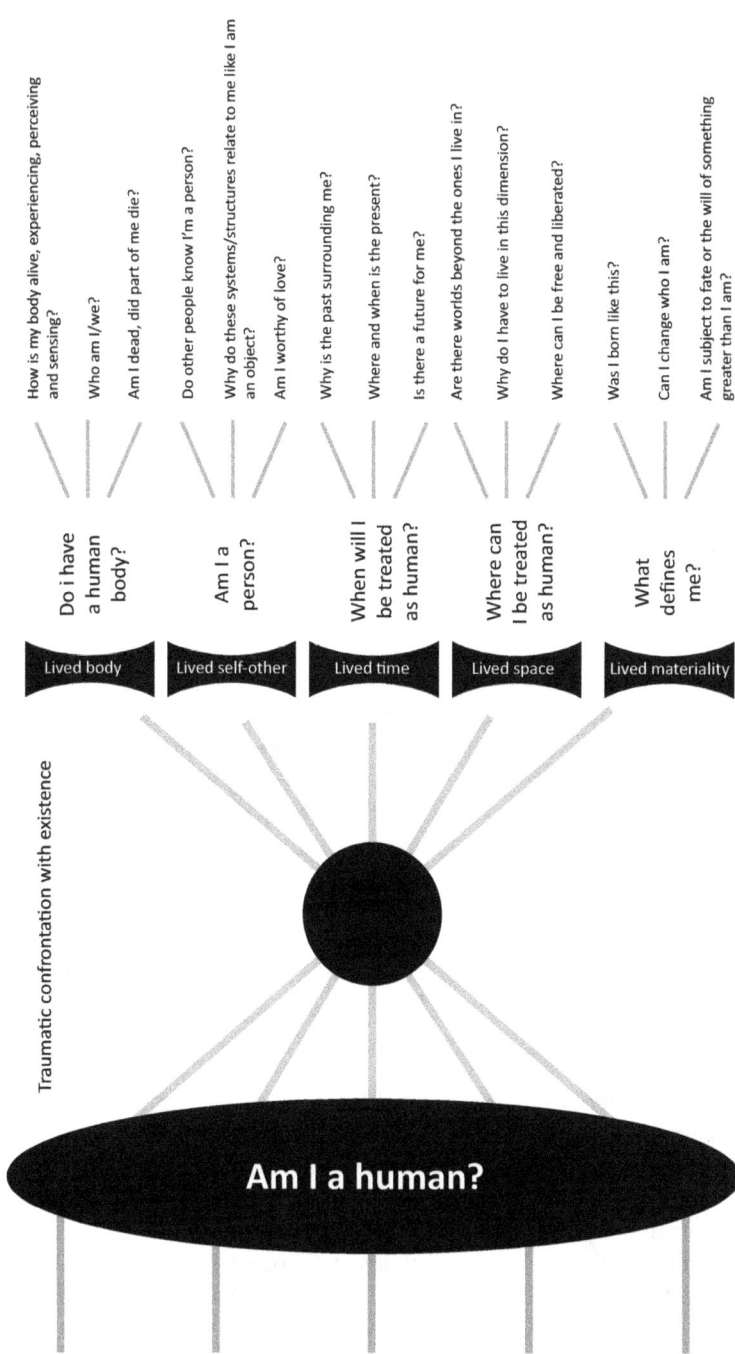

Figure 15.1 The refraction of existential questions arising from one person's traumatic confrontation with existence, involving an experience of dehumanisation and resulting in dissociative states (derealisation and depersonalisation). This illustration uses van Manen's (2014) dimensions of existence.

experiential acts and the proximate horizons of the experienced objects that are always experienced contextually. (Giorgi, 1983: 143)

Our reflexive mode of consciousness enables us to turn to consider the ways we have personally shaped, and been shaped by, our experiences, and how the enactments and experiences of others have impressed upon us as relational beings. Further, we can begin to explore underlying ideas and assumptions we have about ourselves, others, and the world around us. These ideas and assumptions disclose the norms, values, and ideals of the contexts in which we live and have lived (for more detail see Boaz, 2022b).

In addition to clarifying what we have lived through, how we have lived, and the contextuality of our living, the reflexive mode of consciousness enables us to also understand what of existence was encountered and confronted pre-reflexively in our traumas. This gives a new meaning to the contextuality mentioned by Giorgi, as it incorporates existential dimensions of our human experiencing. An *existential reflexivity* might be delineated more specifically as focusing on consciousness bending back on itself to:

(a) unearth and clarify existential questions and dilemmas arising from confrontations with existence,
(b) be curious about the ways we incorporate these existential questions and dilemmas (both reflexively and non-reflexively) into our modes of existing,
(c) identify the ways we may have re-illusioned, disillusioned, and (re) (dis)illusioned ourselves through our confrontations with existence,
(d) contextualise (a)–(c) within the societies, cultures, systems, and structures we have lived,
(e) search for, and experiment with actions, meanings, and purposes in relation to (a), (b), (c), and (d), and any corresponding problematic constrictions and expansions in horizons of experiencing, and
(f) more reflexively elaborate new modes of existing.

Cultivating our existential reflexivity enables us to see the ontological positions we have taken up throughout our ontographies, and the ways these have been lived as our modes of existing. Ontological positions have their own foundational conceptualisations and assumptions about (for example) what constitutes personhood, the self (or non-self), models of human agency, relationships and responsibilities with others, our environment, spirituality, and the worlds around us. Understanding our ontological positions within our ontographies cultivates a sense of comprehensibility and coherence in our existence. As such, existential reflexivity offers us an experiential realisation of re-anchorage in existence, as a reflexive and agentic person. It is vital here to re-emphasise that our existential reflexivity is an experiential and lived endeavour, rather than a conceptual one. We feel into and experience our ontological positions, and they are lived by us as our modes of existing. Thus, existential reflexivity is our embodied experience of emergence – and demonstrates the existential philosophical proposition that we emerge in the present in a state of constant becoming. As such, our reflexive mode of consciousness becomes both liberatory and generative, allowing for self-transcendence, growth, futurity, and new forms of meaningful suffering (building on Frankl, 1988; Minkowski, 1933/1970; Schneider & May, 1995).

Working with a person's pre-reflexive mode of consciousness can add additional complexity to the therapeutic encounter and relationship. When what we encounter of existence is too painful, terrifying, horrifying, or destabilising, the experience of the confrontation is embraced by our pre-reflexive consciousness and pre-reflexively incorporated into our modes of existing. Therapeutically, we can see how people pre-reflexively surround themselves with the same existential dilemmas or questions, in order to make sense of and experiment with new modes of existing. When they are ready to re-experience the existential confrontation reflexively, they report becoming surrounded by an existential dilemma, theme, or question across all of their domains of existing. This may also include enactments in the therapeutic relationship itself. The immensity of the experience of being surrounded by the same existential question can act as an impetus for directly facing the traumatic confrontation of existence (following Wang's 2011 and 2016 formulation of Zhi Mian). As Calhoun and Tedeschi (2006: 7) note, it is "the satisfactory response to the major existential questions and to the questions about how to live one's life in the fullest way possible, [which] may be more important than the reduction of psychological discomfort." In my personal and clinical experience, directly facing the pre-reflexive traumatic confrontation of existence can be encouraged through the use of creative imagination, metaphor, poetry, illustration, movement, and even abstract descriptions, all of which give our pre-reflexive experience an increasing reflexive clarity and comprehensibility.

Encountering our daimonics

In this final implication for practice, I draw on May's (1969/2007) notion of the *daimonic* in human existence,[16] although in many ways I am also re-characterising it.[17] According to May, the daimonic is an "archetypal function of human experience – an existential reality," which is defined as *"any natural function which has the power to take over the whole person"* (123, original emphasis). Readers might understand the 'power to take over the whole person' in:

(a) the energetic force or seemingly altered state of the traumatising person(s), and
(b) the force of our own hate, rage, or spite towards others when we are reminded of the traumatisation or traumatising enactments.

Let us first take (a) the altered state of the traumatising person. May eloquently describes how a diminishing sense of relational contact, relatedness, and apathy, could give rise to violence. He writes:

> When one cannot affect or even genuinely touch another person, violence flares up as a daimonic necessity for contact, a mad drive forcing touch in the most direct way possible. This is one aspect of the well-known relationship between sexual feelings and crimes of violence. To inflict pain and torture at least proves that one can affect somebody... if I cannot affect or touch anybody, I can at least shock you into some feeling, force you into some passion through wounds and pain; I shall at least make sure we both feel something, and I shall force you to see me and know that I also am here!... To be actively hated is almost as good as to be actively liked; it breaks down the utterly unbearable situation of anonymity and aloneness. (May, 1969/2007: 31)

For further illustration, let us consider (b) the force of our own hate, rage, or spite towards others when we are reminded of our traumatisation or traumatising enactments. In sessions,[18] a person describes to me how a smaller, quieter friend's hands feel incomprehensibly big and strong as they grip their neck and push them to a wall during an unexpected sexual attack. The same person recounts being in a coffee shop, when a dismissive barista who, after getting their order wrong, raises their eyebrows and laughs sheepishly, reminds the person of the friend's response when they subsequently saw them. The person responds to the barrister by throwing the coffee across the shop; they reported this feeling *'beyond my control'* and as an *'intense rage.'*

The daimonic can be both a destruction and constructive force, and in most cases will be both. The above is an example of destructive daimonics. The person in later sessions provides us with a description of constructive daimonics. They tell me that they see their former friend in the street. Whilst experiencing a strong somatic response, they feel a purpose energy propelling them towards the dance class they are going to. When they arrive, they feel more emotionally connected to the rehearsal and discover new nuances in the choreography that enable them to express the narrative of the dance more fully. In both the destructive *beyondness* of control and constructive propelling towards emotional *connectedness*, the person experiences the dialectic of the diamonic. May (1969/2007: 123) suggests that "all life is a flux between these two aspects of the daimonic."

In the context of traumatic confrontations with existence, the daimonic can arise as a destructive force in wanting to destroy:

(a) ourselves,
(b) those who have traumatised us,
(c) those who did not protect us or failed to support us,
(d) those cultures, systems, and structures that enabled or permitted the violence, or failed to support us in the wake of trauma, and
(e) the traumatising societies and worlds we live in.

Annihilatory existential movements are therapeutically understandable and comprehensible, and the want to destroy our selves, or worlds, or be destroyed, in many ways mirrors the reality of our own de-anchoring and incomprehensibility of existence. It is critical that as existential psychotherapists we are able to approach people's destructive daimonics as existential tensions and questions, rather than seeking to pathologise them or render them understandable through ideas of risk to self or other (see also Boaz, 2022a: 65–70).

There is a deep discomfort for many of us in recognising our destructive daimonics. The notion that we may have a destructive daimonic, for some, compounds our de-anchoring and the incomprehensibility of our existence. For some of us, the awareness and/or experiencing (even pre-reflexively) of our destructive daimonics can lead to overly identifying with those who have committed violence and harm against us. The paradox for those of us who have experienced interpersonal violence is that turning or leaning further into it with predominantly destructive daimonics transforms our modes of survival into modes of violence. As King (1967/2010: 64–65) pertinently notes: "the ultimate weakness of violence is that it is a descending spiral, begetting the very thing it seeks to destroy (...) violence merely increases hate. So it goes. Returning violence for violence multiplies violence, adding deeper darkness to a night already devoid of stars."

And so, as existentialists we know that in encountering traumatic enactments, we too have the human capacity and potential for hate, rage, disgust, envy, persecution, violence, and perpetration against others (on an individual and collective basis). To understand destructiveness as a human daimonic is to painfully recognise that we are more than merely victims subject to the whims of others, but rather we have had an existential confrontation: all humans have the capacity for destruction. There is no us and them when it comes to daimonic destructiveness; what divides us is ethical and reflexive. There is a tyranny in self-ignorance, self-deception, and disavowing ourselves of our own capacity for destructiveness. As Baldwin (1955/2017: 178) poignantly reminds us: "people who shut their eyes to reality simply invite their own destruction, and anyone who insists on remaining in a state of innocence long after that innocence is dead turns [themselves] into a monster."

Our destructive daimonics are dialectically related to our constructive diamonics. It is only by turning to reflexively engage with, and explore, our destructive daimonics that we can comprehend the ways in which we can experiment with and create new ways of becoming in the present (what I would term *modal elaboration*). Constructive daimonics are expressed in our impulsion to philosophise, our (re)(dis)covery of new modes of existing and new horizons of experiencing, and actions we take to transform the world around us for the better (see Boaz, 2022a: 189–204, 157–159 on survivalism and survivorism).

Therapeutically, we must encourage the person to increasingly hold the existential tension that there is a dynamic relationship between destruction and construction (growth). In my own practice, exploring crises in the therapeutic relationship can be a powerful way of naming and working through destructive daimonics, and more reflexively exploring what existential questions may be being asked about the person's ethics, values, responsibility, and choices in how they are in the world. Further, it allows for meaningful explorations of structural and systemic factors that have perpetuated violence, and a validation of the want to destroy and/or transform them. In holding an experiential space between annihilation/destruction and generation/creation, the person is more free to (re)(dis)cover their existential anchoring and anchoring in existence.

I have begun to describe existentially and therapeutically the flux or dynamic between destructive and constructive daimonics as forms of modal change – that is, the movement between different modes of our existence. As I have written elsewhere, "modal change is not a singular movement from one mode of existing to another. In the temporal-spatiality of disillusionment and re-illusionment there is an interpenetration and intertwining of existing and emergent modes" (Boaz, 2022a: 146, and see 146, 148, 160, 191 and 195 for more description). Many of the people I work with describe self-annihilation or self-destruction – a want or wish to not exist or cease to exist. This may be expressed as suicidality, or more pervasively as wanting the ways in which they have been surviving to end. That is, the modes of existing they have elaborated in their confrontation with existence through disillusionment/re-illusionment to come to an end.

In *modal change*, and even *modal death*, we encounter something coming to an end. We may conclude that it is ourselves that need to end, and yet through phenomenological exploration what frequently emerges is that it is specific modes of existing that people yearn to bring to an end. As excruciating as modal change and modal death is, it also is experientially the intertwining of old and new modes of existing and so is existentially an experience of emergence and becoming. Emergence from modal death contains the possibility of new constructive incorporations of our traumatic confrontations with existence, and thus new modes of existing and new horizons of experiencing. As psychotherapists we can encourage the person to identify and explore existential questions and dilemmas emerging from modal death and change, and cultivate the ground for the person experimenting with new modes of existence.

Finally, May (1969/2007: 129) suggests that encountering our daimonics is a "profound blow to our narcissism." This must be a guidepost for trauma psychotherapists. As psychotherapists we must have delved deeply into our own daimonics to identify and understand the ways in which they manifest in our modes of existing and our practice. Only in this way can we ensure our therapeutic work is sensitive to the potential ways our presence can transform rituals of humiliation into rituals of healing, and experiences of dehumanisation into humanisation (or potentially vice versa).

Conclusion

In this chapter I have attempted to consider the existential-humanistic understandings of interpersonal trauma, and use existential-analytic and phenomenological approaches to suggest implications for practice. In doing so, I have proposed that interpersonal trauma is always a confrontation with existence, and these confrontations result in forms of existential de-anchoring, and expose us to the incomprehensibility of our existence, our worldviews, and the modes we have been existing in. I suggest that our existential movements of re-illusionment, disillusionment, and (re)(dis) illusionment can disclose the ways in which we have incorporated the traumatic confrontation into our modes of existing. Further, I have sought to describe how our traumatic confrontation with existence is contextually situated, and how personal, familial, cultural, social, structural, and systemic ontographies shape our possibilities for modal movement. Further, I have described the resulting constriction or expansion of our horizons of experiencing and relating to ourselves and the world around us.

Calhoun and Tedeschi (2006), and writers in this collection, suggest that posttraumatic growth can emerge spontaneously from a traumatic encounter itself. I have included here a consideration of working with personal and collective ontographies, existential reflexivity, and pre-reflexive experience, and our daimonics to provide psychotherapeutic support for people's growth. By identifying, clarifying, and answering existential questions and dilemmas the person has, we can enable them to directly face their confrontation with existence, and experiment with new modes of existing in their lives. My hope is that alongside the important contributions in this collection, the emerging ideas and approaches I have included above provide stimulus for further research, critique, and exploration in the field of a nascent existential psychotraumatology.

Notes

1 I use here the term *existential movements*, as my philosophical premise is that all existence is movement, and I have come to understand that the ways in which movement as a temporal-spatial axes allows for richer phenomenological descriptions of our experiences (for further discussion see Boaz, 2022a).

2 For a discussion on the plurality of worlds see Boaz et al. (2024).

3 Given previous misreadings of this critique, I want to clarify that I am not dismissing here the important contributions these authors have made to existential theory and practice. My criticism centres on the specific philosophical (and thus clinical) proposition that only some traumatic encounters confront us with existential givens.

4 See also Ahmed (2021) for a more phenomenological account of institutional betrayal in relation to raising concerns and complaints within academia.

5 See Allen (2013) and Luyten and Fonagy (2019) for an alternative formulation focused on the betrayal of trust and resulting impacts on theories of mentalisation and losses of epistemic trust.

6 I have illustrated these alterations in the conditions for existence across embodiment, time-space, movement-between-worlds, and in terms of relationality in my recent work (see Boaz, 2022a).

7 For a more extensive discussion of existential horror and terror, see Boaz (2022a: 165–167).

8 See also Miller (1981/1984) and Freyd (1996) on systemic pressure to forget painful traumatic memories.

9 The use of brackets '( )' has a philosophical meaning; as (re), (dis) and (re)(dis) all are different existential movements (turns) in relation to a covering/covered up (illusion/illusionment of) reality or existence.

10 For further illustration see Boaz et al. (2024: 6–7) on the "the (un)becoming invalid position/paradox," which arises from our from (re)(dis)orientations.

11 See for an earlier phenomenological description Boaz (2022a: 132, 134–135) on which this builds and refines.

12 For those of us who have multiple and cumulative experiences of interpersonal trauma across our childhood, existential de-anchorage and incomprehensibility of existence become a foundational and nascent orientation in how we experience ourselves, others, and the world around us. This discloses further the existential relevance of natality within trauma, rather than primarily death (see Arendt, 1958/1998: 90; Stone, 2019).

13 I use the terms 'person' and 'people' below to humanise those of us who enter counselling, psychotherapy, psychology, or psychiatry; other colleagues might prefer 'client' or 'patient.'

14 Those readers familiar with narrative, auto-pathobiographical, autobiographical, and auto-ethnographical methods may see some resemblance to ontography, and ontography may include elements of these approaches; however, the focus is more explicitly on ontographic constructions, and the ways in which these have been, and are, lived by the person.

15 I use here the terms 'reflexive' and 'pre-reflexive consciousness' as somewhat of a theoretical simplification to avoid the need for a deeper exploration and discussion on opposing views and ideas within existentialism and phenomenology over what constitutes our human consciousness – reflexive and pre-reflexive, and conscious, sub-conscious and unconscious.

16 Here I give a brief overview of daimonics as a dynamic and dialectical force in human existence; however, there is insufficient space to elaborate on the ways in which it relates to our pre-reflexively consciousness or existential unconscious.

17 I am somewhat hesitant to use May's writings here as his work lapses into what may be read as the somewhat racist, misogynistic, classist, heterosexist, disablist, and overly Christianised forms of moralism of his times. These components have for me always problematised May's more astute existential observations. In the context of the daimonic, it seems that in his own writings he was unable to see the destruction and violence he was perpetuating by including this prejudicial moralising. I have mentioned the dilemma elsewhere (Bush [Boaz], 2020) in relation to May and more substantively Heidegger too, and know that many of my colleagues included in this collection, and in the field, continue to work hard to challenge the prejudicial basis of some of the founding existential practitioners.

18 Specific details have been changed to retain the person's confidentiality and anonymity.

References

Ahmed, S. (2021). *Complaint!* Duke University Press.

Allen, J. G. (2013). *Mentalizing in the Development and Treatment of Attachment Trauma*. Routledge. https://doi.org/10.4324/9780429477263

Arendt, H. (1998). *The Human Condition* (2nd ed.). University of Chicago Press (Original work published 1958).

Baldwin, J. (2017). *Notes of a Native Son*. Penguin Books (Original work published 1955).

Binswanger, L. (1958). The existential analysis school of thought. In R. May, E. Angel, & H. F. Ellenberger (Eds. and trans.), *Existence: A New Dimension in Psychiatry and Psychology* (pp. 191–213). Basic Books (Original work published 1946).

Binswanger, L. (1963). *Being in the World: Selected Papers of Ludwig Binswanger* (trans. J. Needleman). Basic Books.

Binswanger, L. (1986). Dream and existence (trans. J. Needleman). In K. Hoeller (Ed.), *Dream and Existence* (pp. 79–106). *Review of Existential Psychology and Psychiatry 19*(1) (Original work published 1984–1985).

Boaz, M. (2022a). *An Existential Approach to Interpersonal Trauma: Modes of Existing and Confrontations with Reality*. Routledge. https://doi.org/10.4324/9781003181675

Boaz, M (2022b). Specialisation from an Existential Perspective: The value of liminality and existing-between-worlds. *Existential Analysis, 33*(1), 28–41.

Boaz, M., Barker, M. J., van Deurzen-Smith, D., Millman, R., & Spandler, H. (2024). *Features of NeuroQueer Existential-Phenomenology.* Report of the Renewing Phenomenological Psychopathology small grant from the University of Birmingham and Wellcome Trust. Existential Academy/New School of Psychotherapy & Counselling.

Bush [Boaz], M. (2018). On the phenomenon of Enttäuschung: A rejoinder to Roy Schafer's psychoanalytic formulation of "disappointment" and "disappointedness." *Existential Analysis, 29*(2), 189–197.

Bush [Boaz], M. (2020, April). Haunted by Heidegger. *Hermeneutic Circular,* 6–8.

Calhoun, L. G., & Tedeschi, R. G. (2006). The foundations of posttraumatic growth: An expanded framework. In L. G. Calhoun & R. G. Tedeschi (Eds.), *Handbook of Posttraumatic Growth: Research & Practice* (pp. 3–23). Lawrence Erlbaum Associates Publishers.

Feldman Barrett, L. (2017a). *How Emotions are Made: The Secret Life of the Brain.* Macmillan.

Feldman Barrett, L. (2017b). The theory of constructed emotion: An active inference account of interoception and categorization. *Social Cognitive & Affective Neuroscience, 12*(1), 1–23. https://doi.org/10.1093/scan/nsx060

Feldman Barrett, L. (2021). *Seven and a Half Lessons About the Brain.* Picador.

Frankl, V. E. (1986). *The Doctor and the Soul: From Psychotherapy to Logotherapy* (3rd ed., revised and expanded, trans. R. Winston & C. Winston). Vintage Books (Original work published 1946).

Frankl, V. E. (1988). *The Will to Meaning: Foundations and Applications of Logotherapy.* Plume.

Frankl, V. E. (2004). *Man's Search for Meaning.* Ebury (Original work published 1946).

Freyd, J. (1996). *Betrayal Trauma: The Logic of Forgetting Childhood Abuse.* Harvard University Press.

Freyd, J., & Birrell, P. (2013). *Blind to Betrayal: Why We Fool Ourselves, We Aren't Being Fooled.* John Wiley & Sons.

Freyd, J. J. (1994). Betrayal trauma: Traumatic amnesia as an adaptive response to childhood abuse. *Ethics & Behavior, 4*(4), 307–329. https://doi.org/10.1207/s15327019eb0404_1

Giorgi, A. (1983). Concerning the possibility of phenomenological psychological research. *Journal of Phenomenological Psychology, 14*(2), 129–169.

Gómez, J. M. (2022). When solidarity hurts: (Intra)cultural trust, cultural betrayal sexual trauma, and PTSD in culturally diverse minoritized youth transitioning to adulthood. *Transcultural Psychiatry, 59*(3), 292–301. https://doi.org/10.1177/13634615211062970

Gómez, J. M. (2023). *The Cultural Betrayal of Black Women and Girls: A Black Feminist Approach to Healing from Sexual Abuse.* American Psychological Association. https://psycnet.apa.org/doi/10.1037/0000362-000

Greening, T. (1990). PTSD from the perspective of existential-humanistic psychology. *Journal of Traumatic Stress, 3*(2), 323–326.

Herman, J. L. (1992). Complex PTSD: A syndrome in survivors of prolonged and repeated trauma. *Journal of Traumatic Stress, 5*(3), 377–391.

Herman, J. L. (2022). *Trauma and Recovery: The Aftermath of Violence – From Domestic Abuse to Political Terror.* Basic Books (Original work published 1992).

Hoffman, L., Cleare-Hoffman, H. & Vallejos, L. (2013). *Existential Issues in Trauma: Implications for Assessment and Treatment* (paper delivered at 121 Annual Convention of the American Psychological Association, July/August, 2013). Honolulu.

Holzhey-Kunz, A. (2016). Why the distinction between ontic and ontological trauma matters for existential therapists. *Existential Analysis, 27*(1), 16–27.

Jacobsen, B. (2006). The life crisis in an existential perspective: Can trauma and crisis be seen as an aid in personal development? *Existential Analysis, 17*(1), 39–53.

Janet, P. (1901). *The Mental State of Hystericals: A Study of Mental Stigmata and Mental Accidents.* (trans. C. Rollin Corson). G. P. Putnam's & Sons.

Janoff-Bulman, R. (1989). The benefits of illusions, the threat of disillusionment and the limits of inaccuracy. *Journal of Social and Clinical Psychology, 8*(2), 158–176. https://psycnet.apa.org/doi/10.1521/jscp.1989.8.2.158

Janoff-Bulman, R. (1992). *Shattered Assumptions: Towards a New Psychology of Trauma.* Free Press.

Janoff-Bulman, R., & Berg, M. (2013). Disillusionment and the creation of value: From traumatic losses to existential gains. In J. H. Harvey (Ed.), *Perspectives on Loss: A Sourcebook* (pp. 35–47). Routledge (Original work published 1998).

Jaspers, K. (1948). *Philosophie.* Springer-Verlag.

Jaspers, K. (1956). *Philosophie.* Springer-Verlag.

Jaspers, K. (1995). *Philosophy of Existence* (trans. R. F. Grabay). University of Pennsylvania Press (Original work published 1971).

Jaspers, K. (2003). *Way to Wisdom: An Introduction to Philosophy* (2nd ed.). Yale University Press (original work published 1954).

King, M. L., Jr. (2010). *Where Do We Go From Here? Chaos or Community.* Beacon Press (Original work published 1967).

Krippner, S., Pitchford, D. B., & Davies, J. (2012). *Post-Traumatic Stress Disorder* (Biographies of Disease). Greenwood.

Lakoff, G., & Johnson, M. (2003). *Metaphors We Live By.* University of Chicago Press (Original work published 1980).

Längle, A. (2007). Trauma und Existenz. *Psychotherapie Forum, 15*, 109–116. https://doi.org/10.1007/s00729-007-0200-7

Längle, A. (2008). Haltungen und praktische Vorgangsweisen in existenzanalytischer Paartherapie und Beratung. *Existenzanalyse, 25*(2), 12–23. https://laengle.info/downloads/Paartherapie%20EA%202008-2.pdf

Lantz, J., & Gyamerah [Meshelemiah], J. (2002). Existential family trauma therapy. *Contemporary Family Therapy, 24*(2), 243–255. https://psycnet.apa.org/doi/10.1023/A:1015341307140

Lukas, E. S. (1986). *Meaning in Suffering: Comfort in Crisis Through Logotherapy* (trans. J. B. Fabry). Institute of Logotherapy Press.

Luyten, P., & Fonagy, P. (2019). Mentalizing and trauma. In A. W. Bateman & P. Fonagy (Eds.), *Handbook of Mentalizing in Mental Health Practice* (2nd ed., pp. 79–102). American Psychiatric Association.

Lynch, M. (2019). Ontography as the study of locally organized ontologies. *Zeitschrift für Medien und Kulturforschung, 10*(1), 147–160. https://doi.org/10.25969/mediarep/18719

May, R. (2007). *Love and Will*. W. W. Norton & Co. (Original work published 1969).

Merleau-Ponty, M. (1968). *The Visible and the Invisible* (A. Lingis, Trans., C. Lefort, Ed.). Northwestern University Press (Original work published 1964).

Merleau-Ponty, M. (2012). *Phenomenology of Perception* (trans. D. A. Landes). Routledge (Original work published 1945).

Merleau-Ponty, M. (2010). *Child Psychology and Pedagogy: The Sorbonne Lectures 1949–1952*. (Trans. T. Welsh). Northwestern University Press (Original work published 2001).

Messas, G., Tamelini, M., Mancini, M., & Stanghellini, G. (2018). New perspectives in phenomenological psychopathology: Its use in psychiatric treatment. *Frontiers in Psychiatry, 9*, 466. https://doi.org/10.3389/fpsyt.2018.00466

Miller, A. (1984). *Thou shalt not be aware: Society's Betrayal of the Child* (trans. H. & H. Hannum). Farrar, Straus & Giroux (Original work published 1981). https://doi.org/10.1176/ps.36.4.412

Minkowski, E. (1970). *Lived Time: Phenomenological and Psychopathological Studies* (trans. N. Mitzel). Northwestern University Press (original work published 1933).

Mudrik, L., & Maoz, U. (2015). "Me & my brain": Exposing neuroscience's closet dualism. *Journal of Cognitive Neuroscience, 27*(2), 211–221. https://doi.org/10.1162/jocn_a_00723

R v R [1991] UKHL 12. http://www.bailii.org/uk/cases/UKHL/1991/12.html

R v R [1991] 3 WLR 767.

Sartre, J.-P. (1957). *The Transcendence of the Ego: An Existentialist Theory of Consciousness* (trans. F. Williams & R. Kirkpatrick). The Noonday Press (Original work published 1936).

Schneider, K. J., & May, R. (1995). *The Psychology of Existence: An Integrative, Clinical Perspective*. McGraw-Hill.

Sexual Offences Act [2003]. www.legislation.gov.uk/ukpga/2003/42/contents

Smith, C., & Freyd, J. (2014). Institutional betrayal. *American Psychologist, 69*(6), 575–587. https://doi.org/10.1037/a0037564

Smith, C. P., Gómez, J. M., & Freyd, J. J. (2014). The psychology of judicial betrayal. *Roger Williams University Law Review, 19*(2), 451–475. https://doi.org/10.1037/a0037564

Stanghellini, G. (2022). Understanding other persons: Guide for the perplexed. In M. Biondi, A. Picardi, M. Pallagrosi, & L. Fonzi (Eds.), *The Clinician in the Psychiatric Diagnostic Process* (pp. 71–80). Springer Nature. https://psycnet.apa.org/doi/10.1007/978-3-030-90431-9_5

Steiner, C. M. (1990). *Scripts People Live: Transactional Analysis of Life Scripts* (2nd ed.). Grove Press.

Stern, D. B. (1983). Unformulated experience: From familiar chaos to creative disorder. *Contemporary Psychoanalysis, 19*(1), 71–99. https://psycnet.apa.org/doi/10.1080/00107530.1983.10746593

Stern, D. B. (2003). *Unformulated Experience: From Dissociation to Imagination in Psychoanalysis*. The Analytic Press. https://doi.org/10.4324/9780203767375

Stone, A. (2019). *Being Born: Birth and Philosophy*. Oxford University Press. https://doi.org/10.1093/oso/9780198845782.001.0001

Tedeschi, R. G., & Calhoun, L. G. (1995). *Trauma and Transformation: Growing in the Aftermath of Suffering*. Sage. https://psycnet.apa.org/doi/10.4135/9781483326931

Tedeschi, R. G., Cann, A., Taku, K., Senol-Durak, E., & Calhoun, L. G. (2017). The Posttraumatic Growth Inventory: A revision integrating existential and spiritual change. *Journal of Traumatic Stress, 30*(1), 11–18. https://doi.org/10.1002/jts.22155

van der Kolk, B. (2005). Developmental trauma disorder: Toward a rational diagnosis for children with complex trauma histories. *Psychiatric Annals, 35*(5), 401–408. https://psycnet.apa.org/doi/10.3928/00485713-20050501-06

van Deurzen, E. (2010). *Everyday Mysteries: A Handbook of Existential Psychotherapy* (2nd ed.). Routledge. https://doi.org/10.4324/9780203864593

van Deurzen, E. (2014). Structural Existential Analysis (SEA): A phenomenological research method for counselling psychology. *Counselling Psychology Review, 29*(2), 70–83. https://doi.org/10.1007/s10879-014-9282-z

van Deurzen, E., & Adams, M. (2016). *Skills in Existential Counselling & Psychotherapy* (2nd ed.). Sage.

van Manen, M. (2014). *Phenomenology of Practice: Meaning-Giving Methods in Phenomenological Research and Writing*. Routledge. https://doi.org/10.4324/9781315422657

Vos, J. (2018). *Meaning in Life: An Evidence-Based Handbook for Practitioners*. Palgrave Macmillan.

Wang, X. (2011). Zhi Mian and existential psychology. *The Humanistic Psychologist, 39*(3), 240–246. https://doi.org/10.1080/08873267.2011.592465

Wang, X. (2016). Zhi Mian: Approaching healing/therapy through facing reality: A Chinese approach to existential thinking and practice (lecture from World Congress for Existential Therapy 2015). *Existential Analysis, 27*(1), 4–15.

Wilson, P. M., & Appel, S. W. (2013). Existential counselling and psychotherapy and Māori clients. *Asia Pacific Journal of Counselling and Psychotherapy, 4*(2), 137–146. https://doi.org/10.1080/21507686.2013.822400

Winnicott, D. W. (1974). Fear of breakdown. *International Review of Psycho-Analysis, 1*(1–2), 103–107.

Winnicott, D. W. (2018). The concept of clinical regression compared with that of defence organisation. In C. Winnicott, R. Shepherd, & M. Davis (Eds.), *Psycho-Analytic Explorations* (pp. 193–199). Routledge (Original work published 1967).

Winnicott, D. W. (2018a). The concept of trauma in relation to the development of the individual within the family. In C. Winnicott, R. Shepherd, & M. Davis (Eds.), *Psycho-Analytic Explorations* (pp. 130–148). Routledge (Original work published 1965).

Winnicott, D. W. (2018b). The Psychology of Madness: A contribution from psychoanalysis (a paper prepared for the British Psycho-Analytical Society, October 1965). In C. Winnicott, R. Shepard, & M. Davis (Eds.), *Psycho-Analytic Explorations* (pp. 119–129). London: Routledge (Original work published 1965).
Yalom, I. D. (1980). *Existential Psychotherapy*. Basic Books.

Index

For Product Safety Concerns and Information please contact our EU
representative GPSR@taylorandfrancis.com
Taylor & Francis Verlag GmbH, Kaufingerstraße 24, 80331 München, Germany

www.ingramcontent.com/pod-product-compliance
Lightning Source LLC
Chambersburg PA
CBHW050333270326
41926CB00016B/3431